ASIAN STUDIES ASSOCIATION OF AUSTRALIA

Women in Asia Series

Editor: Louise Edwards (University of New South Wales)

Editorial Board:

Hyaeweol Choi (University of Iowa)
Melissa Crouch (University of New South Wales)
Michele Ford (The University of Sydney)
Trude Jacobsen (Northern Illinois University)
Tanya Jakimow (University of New South Wales)
Lenore Lyons (Independent scholar)
Vera Mackie (University of Wollongong)
Anne McLaren (The University of Melbourne)
Mina Roces (University of New South Wales)
Dina Siddiqi (New York University)
Andrea Whittaker (The University of Queensland)

Founding Editors: Susan Blackburn and Lenore Manderson

50. Comfort Women and Post-Occupation Corporate Japan
by Caroline Norma 2018

51. Women's Empowerment in Indonesia: A Poor Community in Jakarta
by Sri Wiyanti Eddyono 2018

52. Hong Kong Rural Women under Chinese Rule: Gender Politics, Reunification and Globalization in Post-colonial Hong Kong
by Isabella NG 2019

53. Gender, Violence and Power in Indonesia: Across Time and Space
Edited by Katharine McGregor, Ana Dragojlovic and Hannah Loney 2020

54. Islam, Women's Sexuality and Patriarchy in Indonesia: Silent Desire
Irma Riyani

A full list of titles in this series is available at: www.routledge.com/ASAAWomen-in-Asia-Series/book-series/SE0594

Islam, Women's Sexuality and Patriarchy in Indonesia

This book explores the intimate marital relationships of Indonesian Muslim married women. As well as describing and analysing their sexual relationships, the book also investigates how Islam influences discourses of sexuality in Indonesia, and in particular how Islamic teachings affect Muslim married women's perceptions and behaviour in their sexual relationships with their husbands. Based on extensive original research, the book reveals that Muslim women perceive marriage as a social, cultural, and religious obligation that they need to fulfil; that they realise that finding an ideal marriage partner is complicated, with some having the opportunity for a long courtship and others barely knowing their partner prior to marriage; and that there is a strong tendency, with some exceptions, for women to consider a sexual relationship in marriage as their duty and their husband's right. Religious and cultural discourses justify and support this view and consider refusal a sin (*dosa*) or taboo (*pamali*). Both discourses emphasise obedience towards husbands in marriage.

Irma Riyani is a Lecturer in Theology at the State Islamic University Sunan Gunung Djati, Bandung, Indonesia

Islam, Women's Sexuality and Patriarchy in Indonesia
Silent Desire

Irma Riyani

LONDON AND NEW YORK

First published 2021
by Routledge
2 Park Square, Milton Park, Abingdon, Oxon OX14 4RN

and by Routledge
52 Vanderbilt Avenue, New York, NY 10017

Routledge is an imprint of the Taylor & Francis Group, an informa business

© 2021 Irma Riyani

The right of Irma Riyani to be identified as author of this work has been asserted by her in accordance with Sections 77 and 78 of the Copyright, Designs and Patents Act 1988.

All rights reserved. No part of this book may be reprinted or reproduced or utilised in any form or by any electronic, mechanical, or other means, now known or hereafter invented, including photocopying and recording, or in any information storage or retrieval system, without permission in writing from the publishers.

Trademark notice: Product or corporate names may be trademarks or registered trademarks, and are used only for identification and explanation without intent to infringe.

British Library Cataloguing-in-Publication Data
A catalogue record for this book is available from the British Library

Library of Congress Cataloging-in-Publication Data
A catalog record has been requested for this book

ISBN: 978-0-367-48751-5 (hbk)
ISBN: 978-1-003-04272-3 (ebk)

Typeset in Times NR MT Pro
by KnowledgeWorks Global Ltd.

To my Mom for her endless support and prayers

Contents

List of illustrations viii
Acknowledgements ix
Series Editor's Foreword xi

Introduction: the intertwining of religion, feminism, and sexuality 1

1 Marriage and sexuality: the Indonesian context and Islamic perspectives 27

2 Situating sexuality in fieldwork 71

3 Women's perceptions and expectations of marriage and sexual relations 80

4 Prelude to marriage: finding the right *Jodoh* (soul mate) for life 103

5 Marital adjustment and household management 121

6 Women's experiences of marital sexual relationships: sex as a duty 139

7 Women's experiences of marital sexual relationships: sex as a right 173

8 Women, Islamic texts, and knowledge construction 186

Conclusion 217

Glossary 226
Abbreviations and acronyms 236
Index 238

Illustrations

Figures

1.1	My husband's Indonesian marriage book (*buku nikah*)	34
1.2	My own (wife's) Indonesian marriage book (*buku nikah*)	34
1.3	*Shighat Taklik Talak*	47
3.1	Islamic Marriage and Sex Manual, Book 1	88
3.2	Islamic Marriage and Sex Manual, Book 2	89
3.3	*Uqud al-Lujayn*	90
3.4	*Qurratul 'Uyun*	91
3.5	*Al-Liqa baina al-Zawjayni*	92
8.1	Road conditions outside the *pesantren* al-Thani on Thursdays	193
8.2	Road conditions outside the *pesantren* al-Thani on days other than Thursday	194

Table

8.1	Various Islamic disciplines	189

Maps

1.	Map of Java	5
2.	Map of West Java	6

Acknowledgements

I would like to express my deepest gratitude for the completion of this book to my former supervisor, Prof. Lyn Parker. She provided extensive support, guidance, and kindness during my years of study at the University of Western Australia, Perth as well as during the process of the publication of this book. She has enriched my research experience and broadened my intellectual insight. I am also indebted to Asst/Prof. Laura Dales who has provided valuable comments and encouragement and contributed to the positive outcome of my work. I would like to thank the reviewers for their constructive feedback and I wish to thank Routledge and in particular Prof. Louise Edwards as the series editor for giving me the opportunity to publish my work. I gratefully acknowledge Dr. Carolyn Brewer for her invaluable editing of the manuscript.

This book would not have been possible without the financial support of the Directorate General for Islamic Higher Education of Indonesia (DIKTIS). This project was enabled under a program in which I participated called the Research Fellowship and Sabbatical Leave Luar Negeri (RFLN-SL). It was provided by DIKTIS and awarded in 2019 to 25 of the best research projects. I am especially indebted to Prof. Dr. M. Arskal Salim, M.Ag, Director of Islamic Higher Education of Indonesia, Dr. Suwendi, M.Ag, Head Division of Research and Community Development, and Dr. Mahrus, M.Ag, Head of Research Department at DIKTIS.

I am particularly grateful for the friendship of my Indonesian colleagues who shared my PhD journey at the University of Western Australia: Mba Ike, Mas Hari, Mba Danau, the late Mba Cessy, Mba Endah, Mba Ezmi, Mas Mimin, Mas Yuyun, and many others whom I cannot name individually. I also thank my colleagues in the Asian Studies Department for the critical discussions we engaged in and the suggestions we were able to provide on each other's work: Mee, Brooke, Kieran, Andrew, Wen, Emma, Moshe, and Kelsie.

I also thank the State Islamic University Sunan Gunung Djati Bandung for allowing me to pursue my academic endeavours abroad. I also acknowledge the support of my colleagues at Ushuluddin Faculty, UIN Sunan Gunung Djati Bandung, especially 'the cantikers' for being my second family.

A special thanks to my husband, Asep Muhamad Iqbal, for the wonderfully supportive role he played in the family, as always. This book would not have been possible without his extreme support and love. I also thank my sons, Nabiel Kemal Pramana and Nathan Kafi Pranaya, for their understanding and patience.

Finally, I would like to express my sincere thanks to my wider family—on both sides—who were always there for me. To my mother-in-law, Didoh Hidayatulmilah, for support and understanding. To my sisters Teh Yanti Nuriah, Teh Nina Nurmila (for inspiration), Teh Nunung Nurdianah and Lilis Rahmi, and brother (Iing Irfan Nugraha), and especially my mother (E. Turinah), to whom I dedicate this book, for her endless prayers, day and night, which gave strength to my life. Unfortunately, my father (O. Gholib. R) is no longer with us to see my achievement, but I am sure he would be proud. May he always be surrounded with God's love.

The case study on women's sexual agency in Chapter 7 first appeared in *Women's Studies International Forum,* 69 (2018). Parts of the discussion on divorce in Chapter 5 first appeared in *Indonesia and the Malay World,* 44 (128) (2015).

Irma Riyani
Redhouse-Rasamala, Bandung
April 2020

Series Editor's Foreword

The contributions of women to the social, political and economic transformations occurring in the Asian region are legion. Women have served as leaders of nations, communities, workplaces, activist groups and families. Asian women have joined with others to participate in fomenting change at micro and macro levels. They have been both agents and targets of national and international interventions in social policy. In the performance of these myriad roles women have forged new and modern gendered identities that are recognisably global and local. Their experiences are rich, diverse and instructive. The books in this series testify to the central role women play in creating the new Asia and re-creating Asian womanhood. Moreover, these books reveal the resilience and inventiveness of women around the Asian region in the face of entrenched and evolving patriarchal social norms.

Scholars publishing in this series demonstrate a commitment to promoting the productive conversation between Gender Studies and Asian Studies. The need to understand the diversity of experiences of femininity and womanhood around the world increases inexorably as globalisation proceeds apace. Lessons from the experiences of Asian women present us with fresh opportunities for building new possibilities for women's progress the world over.

The Asian Studies Association of Australia (ASAA) sponsors this publication series as part of its on-going commitment to promoting knowledge about women in Asia. In particular, the ASAA Women's Forum provides the intellectual vigour and enthusiasm that maintains the Women in Asia Series (WIAS). The aim of the series, since its inception in 1990, is to promote knowledge about women in Asia to both academic and general audiences. To this end, WIAS books draw on a wide range of disciplines including anthropology, sociology, political science, cultural studies, media studies, literature, and history. The series prides itself on being an outlet for cutting edge research conducted by recent PhD graduates and postdoctoral fellows from throughout the region.

The Series could not function without the generous professional advice provided by many anonymous readers. Moreover, the wise counsel provided by Peter Sowden at Routledge is invaluable. WIAS, its authors and the ASAA are very grateful to these people for their expert work.

Louise Edwards (UNSW Australia)
Series Editor

Introduction
The intertwining of religion, feminism, and sexuality

> There is no simple and straightforward way to liberate women and sexuality from religion, nor is it straightforwardly obvious that religion cannot play a role in this liberation.
>
> (Alcoff and Caputo 2011, 9.)

Feminism and sexuality are two topics that are often viewed as controversial and sensitive in the study of Islam. Feminism is controversial both in theory and application in Islam, and sexuality is strictly regulated and controlled in many Muslim societies. In Indonesian society, the discussion of sexuality is seen not only as sensitive (related to personal and private practice) and dangerous (related to moral anxiety), but also as curious (tempting and seductive). As sexuality in Indonesia is taboo, researching sexuality in the country provides a significant challenge. In this book, I attempt to entwine sexuality, feminism, and religion in exploring women's sexuality in Indonesian society.

I examine the relationship between Islamic teachings on sexuality and married Muslim women's perceptions of these teachings. I also examine the relationship between these perceptions and women's stated behaviour in their marital sexual relationships. I argue that religious teachings significantly influence married Muslim women's perceptions and behaviours in their marital relationships. Unfortunately, the teachings that have most influence are those that suggest sex in marriage is women's duty instead of their right. There are other Islamic teachings that suggest that marital sexual relationships be based on mutual sharing and fulfilment. However, the latter are less well known than the former. It is important to recall those primary Islamic texts that teach that ideal marital sexual relationships evoke the sexual rights of women in marriage. Therefore, I also aim to analyse the political interests behind the construction and dissemination of Islamic texts regarding marriage and sexuality in Indonesia.

The study of women has been a prominent topic in Islamic religious discourse since the late-nineteenth century. Many scholars have studied Islamic texts in search of teachings about various aspects of women's positions in Islam, such as the original creation of woman, women's inheritance, polygyny, marriage, and divorce. Many of these texts are believed to be the basis of women's oppression. However, the study of women's sexuality has received little attention. Of the limited work that is available, the foremost resources on Islam and sexuality are Basim Musallam (1983), Fatna Sabbah (1984), Abdelwahab Bouhdiba (1985), Riffat Hassan (1990), and Kecia Ali (2006). They provide theoretical perspectives derived from the Qur'an, Hadith (the Prophet's sayings) and *fiqh* (Islamic jurisprudence).

The study of the role of Islam in shaping sexuality is still concentrated in Middle Eastern societies and has been addressed by Fatima Mernissi (1987), Sahla Haeri (1989), Pinar Ilkkaracan (2002), and Abdessamad Dialmy (2010). Ilkkaracan (2002) notes that women's sexual subjugation in Egypt and Maghreb is not the result of Islamic precepts on sexuality as such, but is a mixture of political, economic, and social inequality that has developed across the ages. In Egypt and Maghreb, Islamic teaching is frequently used to benefit male sexuality and repress female sexuality.

In Indonesia, which is not an Islamic state but has a Muslim majority, Islamic texts have been used to justify male dominance over females in issues such as polygyny and marital violence. However, unlike in Egypt or Iran, where some Muslim women struggle against the clergy, the *hijab* (Islamic veil), and gender segregation (Ahmadi 2006; Moghadam 2002), Indonesian Muslim women are typically more relaxed on issues of veiling and gender segregation.

When Islam spread through what is now Indonesia, it adapted to diverse ethnic, cultural, and social realities. The process of Islamisation in Indonesia took place with an enculturation of Islamic teachings and local customs. Thus, religious beliefs and practices are shaped by the cultural context and vice versa. The intersection between cultural norms and religious teachings to a certain extent also 'influenced the conceptualization of gender differences' (Robinson 2009, 12).

The majority of Indonesian Muslims can be categorised as moderate, and many belong to mainstream organisations such as Nahdlatul Ulama (NU) and Muhammadiyah (Azra and Hudson 2008; Sukma and Joewono 2007). These two mainstream organisations support modernity, democracy, human rights, and gender equality. There are also small groups of radical Muslim organisations such as the Islamic Defenders Front (FPI), Hizbut Tahrir (The Party of Liberation), and Majelis Mujahidin Indonesia (Mujahidin Council of Indonesia)—these last two have been banned in Indonesia—but they have limited influence in Indonesia as a whole (Azra and Hudson 2008; Muhtadi 2009).

During the New Order regime (1968–98), gender ideology promoted woman's primary role as wife and mother (Robinson 2009; Suryakusuma 1996). In the post-1998 reform era, there have been greater opportunities to change Indonesia's gender ideology; significant contributions have been made with a female president, the establishment of a 30 percent gender quota for all political parties' candidates, and the enactment of a law against domestic violence in 2004 (UU PKDRT no. 23/2004). The Reform era also opened up the discussion of sexuality—the results of which can now be seen in Indonesian magazines and newspapers, and on radio and television (Handajani 2005; Holzner and Oetomo 2004; Munti 2005). However, there are still double standards in regard to sexuality, as can be seen in the Pornography Law of 2008 and local regulations requiring school girls and female civil servants to wear the *jilbab* (Islamic headscarf) (Noerdin 2002; Wichelen 2010). The contemporary Islamic revival is socially conservative; giving religious authority to a normative gender ideology that locates women in the home and makes them responsible for the household.[1]

While Islam plays a significant role in shaping sexuality, studies of this role, in particular in shaping women's sexuality, are rare. Several scholars have undertaken research on other aspects of sexuality in Indonesia. Lily Munir (2002) has written on power relations in marital sexuality, Nurul Idrus (2003) on the cultural practices of gender, sexuality, and marriage in Bugis society, Yasir Alimi (2004) on deconstructing sexuality discourse, Linda Rae Bennett (2005) on single women's sexuality and reproductive rights, Dédé Oetomo (1996) and Tom Boellstorff (2005) on *banci* (transgender) and Muslim gays, Ratna Munti (2005) on sexuality and globalisation, Lyn Parker (2008) on adolescent sexuality, Nina Nurmila (2009) on women in polygamous marriages, Evelyn Blackwood (2007) on lesbianism, and Sharyn Davies (2010) on various representations of gender and sexuality. However, these studies do not specifically investigate the processes involved in how Islam influences discourses of sexuality in Indonesia and, in particular, how Islamic teachings influence married Muslim women's perception of, and behaviour in, their marital sexual relationships.

Certain Islamic teachings on sexuality that are circulated in Indonesia are more dominant than other teachings. For example, the Hadith concerning the obligation of women to satisfy men's sexual needs in marriage is better known than the Hadith on the duty of men to fulfil women's sexual needs, and even takes precedence over the Qur'anic verse that discusses the mutual satisfaction of the couple. For example, the Hadith compiled in Shahih al-Bukhari (1997, vol. 7, Hadith no. 5193, 90) and narrated by Abu Huraira includes the following passage: 'The Prophet said, "If a man invites his wife to sleep with him and she refuses to come to him, then the angels send their curses on her till morning."' This passage is more popular than the Qur'anic verse on the mutual relationship of wife and husband that states: 'Permitted to you, on the night of the fasts, is the approach to your wives. They are your garment and ye are their garments' (Q. 2: 187). In this study, I will seek to uncover why some teachings are favoured over others, and also to determine the political interests of Muslim authorities regarding the dissemination of Islamic teachings on sexuality in Indonesia. In this context, political interest is defined as the power relations involved in religious knowledge production (Foucault 1990) and how knowledge and ideas are distributed in society, by whom and for what purpose. In this book, I will explore the power strategies that operate in this production of knowledge and the dissemination of religious discourse on sexuality.

The objective of this book is to investigate how Islamic teachings on sexuality affect the perceptions and behaviour of married Muslim women in Indonesia in their sexual relationships with their husbands.

Significance of the research

Research on sexuality is still limited in Indonesia, especially on heterosexual relationships. In this study I will make a contribution to the body of knowledge on the religious construction of female sexuality in Indonesia, with a particular emphasis on married women's sexuality. My research will also contribute new knowledge about women's understandings of their sexuality and their sexual practices. Valerie Hull (1982, 118) pointed out that '[t]here is very little research [in Indonesia] on the sexual life of married couples.' Besides, as Parker (2008, 19) mentions, there appears to be more research on 'alternative sexualities' than there is on 'hegemonic heterosexuality.' This study will contribute to the study of the sexual life of the married couple; a research area that has attracted little attention from scholars of contemporary Indonesia. More broadly, this study will enhance our understanding of gender relations in Indonesia, and in particular of the religious dimensions of gender ideology and gender systems.

In addition, my work will also contribute to an understanding of the role of Islam in shaping Indonesian culture, and the role of Indonesian culture in shaping the practice of Islam. This has been overlooked in previous studies, especially relating to gender and sexuality (Robinson 2001). Robert Hefner (1997) and Sonja van Wichelen (2010) note that most studies that focus on Islam are conducted in the Middle East. The Indonesian cultural context makes a difference; for example, it is widely acknowledged that Muslim women in Indonesian society are much more active in public life than Muslim women in most Middle Eastern societies. The reverse is also true. Islam in Indonesia has played an important role in shaping not only the culture but also the nation, and this role has been neglected as a topic of scholarly enquiry.

In developing countries, according to Evelyne Accad (2000), research on sexuality is overlooked compared to other issues such as hunger, poverty, and unemployment. In the Indonesian context, where the economic situation is quite stable, I believe it is important to address how women experience everyday life in relation to their marital sexuality. The majority of women I interviewed considered marital sexual relations to be their duty rather than their right. I argue that they arrived at this understanding through influences from social, legal, and religious 'scripts' (Simon and Gagnon 1984) during the socialisation process. In this book, I will emphasise the religious teachings that significantly influence the perceptions and

Introduction 5

behaviour of married Muslim women in their marital and sexual relationships with their husbands.

The Islamic resurgence in contemporary Indonesia has increased both the piety and the public expression of piety among Indonesian Muslims. Many Muslims are motivated by religious teachings in many aspects of life. However, as Hefner notes (2010, 1033), much of the scholarly analysis of this resurgence is concentrated on the macro-level (the state, global capitalism, and secular modernity) and less on the micro- and meso-levels of the 'self, family, and everyday life.' Therefore, it is important to observe this new phenomenon in women's daily interactions with their husbands.

The study setting

This study is set in West Java (Map. 1). This region of Indonesia is experiencing rapid population growth as a result of increased employment and education opportunities. After independence, large numbers of people moved from rural areas to the cities in West Java to find employment (Hugo 1981). Hundreds of factories were built in these areas and manufacturing activities in the Tangerang, Bekasi, and Sukabumi areas have increased to such an extent that they are now seen as an expansion of the industrial districts of Jakarta (Map. 2). The factories in West Java employ both local and migrant workers and, since 1961, increasing numbers of these workers are female who have moved from the agricultural sector (Sajogyo and Wahyuni 1994). Thus the industrial development of West Java has had a significant impact on the status of women and gender relations in the family.

Map 1 Map of Java

Source: Google Maps, Map data @2020 Google, available at: https://www.google.co.id/maps/@-7.5840659,110.2551072,7z (accessed 17 February 2020). Used in accordance with Google Maps Attribution Guidelines.

6 Introduction

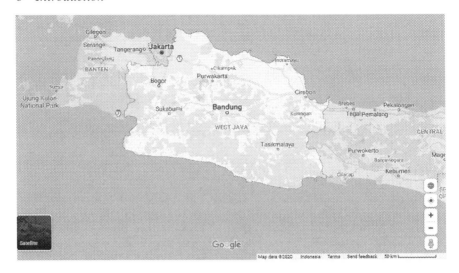

Map 2 Map of West Java

Source: Google Maps, Map data @2020 Google, available at: https://www.google.com/maps/@-6.8665407,106.4835641,8z (accessed 17 February 2020). Used in accordance with Google Maps Attribution Guidelines.

West Java is inhabited by more than 43 million people (Badan Pusat Statistik Jawa Barat 2020). West Javanese people are usually called *urang sunda* (Sundanese) as this is the dominant ethnic group in this region (Suryadinata, Arifin, and Ananta 2003). The Sundanese have a different language, culture, and history to the Javanese in Central and East Java. West Javanese people speak Sundanese. Traditionally, Sundanese did not distinguish between speech levels (*undak-usuk basa*). However, with the influence of Javanese feudalism and Dutch colonialism, speech levels which differentiate between refined language (*basa lemes*) and coarse language (*basa kasar*) have become part of Sundanese society.

Like the Javanese, the Sundanese family system is bilateral. This means that both mothers' and fathers' lines are acknowledged equally. However, the household head of the family is male, whether that is the husband or the father. This is in accordance with the state gender ideology (Sariyun 2006). Historically, women have had a high status and are respected in Sundanese society. This is represented by the role of Sunan Ambu as the highest female deity in the celestial world (*kahyangan*) and Nyi Pohaci Sanghiang Sri as the agrarian goddess who provides rice paddies (Tohari 2013). Scholars believe that following the occupation of Sunda by the Javanese kingdom of Mataram in 1575 there was a shift in Sundanese culture from an egalitarian to a feudal society (Adimihardja 1980; Ekadjati 1995; Kahmad 2006).

There have been a number of studies of women in West Java. Researchers have focused on women labouring in factories (Hancock 2001; Mather 1985;

Warouw 2004, 2008), home industrial employment (Grijns 1987; Grijns et al. 1994; Silvey 2004), maternal and infant mortality (Iskandar et al. 1996; Shefner-Rogers 2004; Utomo 1996), family planning (Newland 2001), domestic violence (Binahayati 2011), the implementation of Islamic *sharia* and its effect on women's wellbeing (Noerdin 2002; Turmudi 2004; Dalmeri 2012), Sundanese Islam and the role of *ulama* (Islamic scholars) and *tarekat* (Sufi order) (Horikoshi 1976; Millie 2008; Newland 2000). Few studies, however, have examined gender relations, especially in marriage and sexuality, in this region.

In this study, I aim to expand understandings of gender issues in the West Java region. The study site is in the eastern part of the city of Bandung. The site is serviced by an interprovincial main road connecting Central and East Java. The road is very busy and often congested with traffic. The East Bandung population is concentrated along this main road, and the population density is high. Rental properties and housing complexes are common because they are needed to meet the high housing demands of the population. The cost of accommodation ranges from moderate to very high. There are also many factories and four higher education institutions (state owned and private; secular and Islamic) along the main road.

In East Bandung, the population is predominantly Sundanese who speak Sundanese. However, the community is heterogeneous and there are many migrants from various districts including West and Central Java who come to Bandung to find jobs in the factories and to study. Their occupations vary and include factory labourers, petty traders, construction workers, academics, and government officials. As the locals compete with migrants for jobs and the migrants are often more educated and wealthier than the local population, this can cause tension.

Research methods

I employ a qualitative methodology. In qualitative research, the study encompasses not only 'understanding, describing, explaining, unravelling, illuminating, chronicling, and documenting [the] social life' of others, but also the interaction of the self with the participants and the research context (Leavy 2014, 1). Thus, this method accommodates and encourages the active engagement of the researcher with the entire process of the research. The qualitative methodology used in this research involves two main components: fieldwork and textual study. For fieldwork, I use two data collection methods—in-depth interviews and Focus Group Discussions (FGD). In-depth and open-ended interviews are used to uncover 'people's views of reality' (Reinharz 1992, 18) during fieldwork. Through interviews, the researcher has an opportunity to acquire 'people's ideas, thoughts, and memories' (ibid., 19), allowing research participants to express things in their own words, and to elaborate on those topics that are of most interest to them. During fieldwork, I was influenced by feminist ethnography,

8 *Introduction*

which builds close connections with the participants in a less hierarchical and exploitative manner (Oakley 1981). This is particularly important in the process of researching a sensitive topic like sexuality.

The participants

Field research was conducted in Bandung, the capital city of West Java, from May to July 2012. I selected Bandung for two reasons. There is a very limited amount of socio-cultural research that has been undertaken in this area, particularly on sexuality, and because it is my home town. Western scholars have mainly conducted research in Java (Central and East Java), Sumatra (Padang and Aceh), Bali, Lombok, and Sulawesi as mentioned in Chapter 1, but have ignored West Java.

I interviewed 42 primary participants, mainly married Muslim women and a number of their husbands. It was necessary to interview the husbands in order to understand both sides of the story in the marital relationship. The participants were selected from different educational and economic backgrounds in order that data would come from a range of different experiences and understandings. The participants' educational backgrounds vary, from women who had never finished primary school to women who had a doctorate degree. The cohort included: never finished primary school (3), finished primary school (6), junior secondary school (2), and senior high school (17). Fifteen of the 16 women who had completed senior high school continued their study at university: diploma (2), undergraduate degree (4), master's degree (4), and doctorate (4). Some women were newly married and some had long-term marriages; some had children and some did not. Five of the 42 women were divorced, four were widowed, and one was separated from her husband. The participants' ages were between 18 and 59 years, and their occupations included housewives (7), housekeeper (1), petty traders (6), teachers (20), and lecturers (8).

Interviews were also carried out with officials from the KUA (Office of Religious Affairs), who provide pre-marital information sessions for prospective couples, and also with religious leaders. The latter were mostly leaders of Islamic boarding schools (*kyai*), who are regarded as having the authority to choose and interpret the religious texts on sexuality that are to be taught to their students.

Along with interviews, group discussions can be a valuable instrument for encouraging participants to exchange views and share experiences on the topic being researched. FGDs enable researchers to observe and participate in dynamic interactions between members of the group, and to identify how people perceive issues and justify their opinions to their peers (Berg 2007; Stewart, Shamdasani, and Rook 2007).

Three FGDs were conducted during fieldwork. Ethical considerations of sexuality research in Indonesia suggest that it is inappropriate to conduct mixed-sex FGDs (Hilber et al. 2010). In my case, a mixed-sex FGD on sexuality was possible but on the condition that the participants were close friends and already familiar with one another's marital stories. In this FGD, the discussion among participants was lively and engaged. In other group discussions, the women at first were too shy to start the discussion and had to be encouraged to speak. In my opinion, this silence was due to the lingering taboo on the discussion of sexuality in Indonesian society, such that many women were hesitant to speak openly. However, when one of them was brave enough to speak out, the other members would contribute (*menimpali*) and we were able to have an active discussion. Speaking in a humorous way is another strategy used to decrease awkwardness when a woman has to refer to a 'sexual organ' or 'sexual word/phrase' or when describing sexual intimacies, and this made the discussion more interesting.

Information about the research was given to all the participants and informed consent was obtained. All participants' names are pseudonyms for reasons of confidentiality. Interviews and FGDs were carried out either in Sundanese or the Indonesian language. All interviews and discussions were audio recorded. Most of the participants were recruited through my work friends' connections at my home university. Some of them were students and colleagues, and the others were women I met while observing *majlis ta'lim*. During fieldwork, I met the primary participants twice: first to inform them about the research and to ask whether any of them would participate and second to interview those who agreed to take part. A total of 74 participants were recruited for this study, 42 of whom were primary participants.

The contestation of Islamic feminism and hermeneutics

The textual aspect of my study operated within the framework of Islamic feminism and hermeneutics. Feminism and religion are both contested terms in both fields. Some feminists have accused religion of contributing to inequality between men and women through its teachings; while religious studies has long been dominated by male scholars with an 'androcentric presupposition' who have ignored gender and feminist theory in their analysis (Gross 1996; King 1995, 2).

In non-Western, developing, and Islamic countries and societies, there is a heightened resistance to use of the term 'feminism.' Not only is the term associated with the West but it is also linked to a colonial ideology (Donaldson and Pui-lan 2002; Jayawardena 1986). Feminists in developing countries often criticise the assumption of Western feminists that feminist theory is universally applicable—that is, they analyse the lack of cross-cultural analysis, and argue that Western feminism fails to consider specific socio-economic and cultural contexts (Mohanty 1991). Islamic feminists, like Sa'dyiia Shaikh (2003) and Amina Wadud (2008), make similar criticisms.

In many Muslim countries, as Deniz Kandiyoti (1991, 7) notes, any attempt to associate with feminism leads to accusations of 'betrayal' of one's own cultural authenticity. In Indonesia, many Indonesians consider 'feminism' a 'non-indigenous' concept and irrelevant to Indonesian values (Sadli 2002). Nevertheless, although the term feminism is rejected, 'this does not mean that a feminist consciousness and agenda are absent' in Islamic countries (Karam 1998, 6). Muslim women's movements began questioning inequality between men and women in many Muslim countries in the 1990s. These movements gained inspiration from the adoption of the Convention on the Elimination of all forms of Discrimination against Women (CEDAW) internationally, including among Muslim countries,[2] and the expansion of the international women's movement (Mir-Hosseini 2011). Several women's movements adopted the term feminism with the aim of liberating women from various oppressions they experienced in everyday life. In this way, Islamic feminism has become an integral part of the global contemporary Islamic movement in many Muslim countries (Mahmood 2001).

The use of the phrase 'Islamic feminism' is undoubtedly controversial in the Islamic context. There are disagreements not only about the concept but also about its applicability. There has been heated discussion of this topic in Iran (Ahmadi 2006; Moghadam 2002) and Egypt (Badran 1989, 1995; Karam 1998). There has also been heated discussion of the differences between secular and Islamic feminisms (Badran 2005). Several Muslim scholars, including Haideh Moghissi (1999) and Valentine Moghadam (2002), have criticised the phrase 'Islamic feminism' as they believe feminism is incompatible with Islam. Other Muslim scholars suggest that in the Islamic context great care should be taken in using this term. Nayereh Tohidi (2007) advises use of 'Muslim feminist' rather than 'Islamic feminist': the former term seems to be less troubling as it refers to personal identity ('a Muslim who is feminist') rather than the religion as a whole. The word Islam in 'Islamic feminism' is also problematic: which Islam is represented in this phrase? Thus, Raja Rhouni suggests using 'islamic feminism' with a small 'I,' which she borrowed from Mohammed Arkoun, to indicate the diverse practice of Islam in contemporary times and throughout history (Rhouni 2008).

Ziba Mir-Hosseini (2011) argues that although there has been heated debate surrounding the term, Islamic feminism can be used without hesitation. She further indicates that 'Islamic' in this phrase means 'finding inspiration and even legitimacy in Islamic history and textual sources' (ibid., 68). She challenges those who argue that it is impossible to be a feminist and at the same time have a strong faith.

Margot Badran argues that although the term 'feminism' originated in the West it is not western. She states that 'feminisms are produced in particular places and are articulated in local terms' (2002a, 1). Islamic feminism in this study follows Badran's definition:

> a feminist discourse and practice articulated within an Islamic paradigm, … [it] derives its understanding and mandate from the Qur'an, seeks rights and justice for women, and for men, in the totality of their existence. (2002a, 1.)

Badran's work on Islamic feminism has made a valuable contribution to the discussion. She has consistently developed and articulated the history, definition, and goals of Islamic feminism (particularly in Egypt), and how they are distinct from those of Western feminism (1989, 1995, 2002a, 2002b, 2005, 2011). Although she differentiates between secular and Islamic feminism (2005), she recognises that there has been a mutual relationship between the two in their goal to achieve equality and justice for women. Similarly, Mir-Hosseini (2011, 76) 'calls for a reconciliation and transcendence of the distinction' between secular and Islamic feminism to achieve the same goal.

Other work on Islamic feminism has been published by Miriam Cooke (2001, 2002). Cooke's work is useful because of her concept of 'multiple critiques.' A 'multiple critique' refers to women who 'criticize the various individuals, institutions, and systems that limit and oppress them while making sure that they are not caught in their own rhetoric' (2002, 151). Like Badran, Cooke (2002) emphasises that feminism does not belong to only one culture; it belongs wherever it seeks gender justice. Cooke (2001) suggests that feminism is not only an ideology but also a tool for analysing the ideas and forces that lead to unjust gender relations in society.

In this study, I will use the term 'Islamic feminisms' for two reasons. First, Muslim scholars who fight for gender equality in Muslim societies derive their concepts from, and base their beliefs in, Islamic teachings, so the term 'Islamic' is appropriate. Second, there is no need to avoid using the word feminism in conjunction with the word Islamic because feminism does not necessarily refer to an ideology but to an activity that highlights gender equality. However, in application, it is important to use it with care and sensitivity. For example, in implementing the idea of feminism it is necessary to adapt to the local cultural scene to be accepted. Many scholars in this field still avoid being labelled feminist in order to minimise prejudice. Zainah Anwar (2009), one of the founding members of Sisters in Islam (SIS) of Malaysia, identifies herself as a Muslim feminist because she says there is human agency in understanding God's message by using the word Muslim rather than Islamic. In Indonesia, several women activists also identified as Muslim feminists rather than Islamic feminists (Doorn-Harder 2006; Qibtiyah 2012).

Some scholars self-identify as feminist (e.g. Hassan (2001) calls herself a feminist theologian), while others are still reluctant to call themselves feminist. Wadud (2006) refuses to call herself a feminist, even though she admits that she is doing feminist work and uses feminist methodology. She emphasises '*pro-faith* and *pro-feminist*' perspectives that are based on the Qur'an as a transcendent and ultimate reality (Wadud 2008, 436). Badran (1995) classifies these Muslim women as feminists not because of their self-identification but because of their ideas, agendas, and actions. Thus, they can be called what Parker (2007) identifies as 'faith-based feminist[s],' as they operate within the Islamic perspective.

There is a growing body of literature on the theory and methodology of Islamic feminism as well as a growing number of scholars who are devoted to developing this formulation in the Middle East, particularly in Egypt and Iran. Indonesian Islam, and in particular Indonesian Islamic feminism, is often overlooked in the Islamic world, despite Indonesia having the most populous Muslim population in the world (Hefner 1997; Offenhauer 2005; Parker 2007). In Indonesia, the discussion of feminism is perhaps not as vigorous as in the Middle East, but there is no doubt that an Indonesian feminism has evolved.

While the word feminism is an imported Western term, Indonesian feminism should not be regarded as being similar to Western feminism (Robinson 2009). The term feminism in the Indonesian context denotes a non-indigenous concept and is often considered irrelevant to Indonesia (Sadli 2002). It is often considered to be part of a Western conspiracy and even associated with Zionism, as an attempt to destroy Islam. More moderate opponents consider it contrary to Islamic teachings and local culture (Muttaqin 2008). Particular objections emerge on issues like preferred sexual orientation and abortion. There are differences in terms of the history, concepts, and struggles of feminism. Susan Blackburn (2004) also notices that a different understanding of the word feminism in Indonesia has a connection with Indonesian nationalism, Islam, and the New Order ideology, although the latter is currently receding. Nevertheless, Saparinah Sadli (2002) hesitates to call the process of seeking equality between men and women Indonesian feminism as she argues that an Indonesian theory of feminism has not yet been well established. Indonesian feminism has its own significance, since early Indonesian history was 'built on the empowering aspects of indigenous models of femininity: the acknowledged important role of women in household economies and cultural traditions that did not prevent women from assuming public office' (Robinson 2009, 65).

Two categories of feminism exist in Indonesia, namely secular and Islamic feminism. The secular feminists, mostly from the middle-upper class, opened up the road to the adoption of feminism in Indonesia upon their return from study abroad in the 1980s (Nurmila 2011, 36; Robinson 2009). The secular feminists, although they are Muslim, do not base their feminist activities in Islamic sources (Nurmila 2011). Nor are they familiar with Islamic teachings, as they were educated in secular educational institutions rather than Islamic ones (Nurmila 2011). That said, Islamic feminists derive support for their actions from Islamic sources (Qur'an and Hadith) (Doorn-Harder 2006). They are familiar with Islamic teachings as most of them have been educated in a *pesantren* (Islamic boarding schools) or a State Institute for Islamic Studies (IAIN) (Feillard and Doorn-Harder 2013; Nurmila 2011).

Islamic feminism in Indonesia is indebted to work by Islamic feminists in the Middle East and North America, particularly Mernissi, Hassan, and Wadud. Intensive discussions concerning women, gender and Islam began in the 1990s (Doorn-Harder 2006; Nurmila 2011; Robinson 2006; Syamsiyatun 2008). Kathryn Robinson (2006, 2009) mentions that in the

1990s many Indonesian Islamic scholars began to refer to the works of the international Islamic feminists mentioned above to support their cause. However, Nurmila (2011, 54) points out that Indonesian Islamic feminists are not simply replicating those works 'but instead synthesizing their works and producing something new.' A note should be made here that not all issues discussed by international Muslim feminists are relevant to the Indonesian context. Issues such as honour killings discussed by Hassan are not experienced by Indonesian Muslims. Issues hotly debated among Islamic feminists in Indonesia are related to polygyny and the implementation of *sharia*-based law, which in most cases is discriminating for women (Feillard and Doorn-Harder 2013).

Pieternella van Doorn-Harder (2006) states that Islamic feminism, in Indonesia, has formed its own unique brand of Islamic feminism. This feminism differs from that in other Muslim countries in the Middle East as well as its neighbour, Malaysia. Indonesian Islamic feminists contribute greatly to what Nur Hidayah (2012, 191) describes as 'Indonesianising Islamic feminism' in order to suit the needs of Indonesian Muslim women, and 'feminising Indonesian Islam' using religious texts to challenge patriarchal interpretations. Feminism in the Indonesian context is defined by Doorn-Harder (2006, 37) as an effort 'to improve the condition of women and men of all classes, strive for equality between sexes and classes, and engage in Islamic discourse with the goal of empowering women, men and the suppressed.'

Islamic feminists have extended hermeneutical approaches in their understanding of Islamic sources to provide a comprehensive understanding that supports gender equality and to counter a literalist understanding of Islamic texts that marginalises women's position in Islam.

In this book, I employ a hermeneutical approach to reading Islamic texts. In particular, especially in Chapter 8, I use a feminist hermeneutical approach offered by Islamic scholars. An Islamic feminist hermeneutical approach proposes that the Qur'an is compatible with modernity and supports gender equality. The Islamic feminists' hermeneutical approach emphasises the need to reread and reinterpret the Qur'an and to challenge patriarchal interpretations of the Qur'an within an egalitarian and antipatriarchal epistemology (Barlas 2002, 2006; Wadud 1999, 2006). Among those who apply the hermeneutic model to their work in analysing Islamic texts are Azizah al-Hibri (1982), Hassan (1994), Wadud (1999), and Asma Barlas (2002).

Their hermeneutical approach involves the following: *first*, linguistic and grammatical analyses of the Qur'anic text; *second*, application of the concept of the unity of the Qur'an, suggesting that the verses in the Qur'an are related to each other and should not be read separately; *third*, application of moral and ethical criteria (Hassan 1994; Wadud 1999). Their main concerns are rereading and reinterpreting the Qur'an, and emphasising not only its textual meaning but also its socio-historical context. They challenge the patriarchal interpretation of the Qur'an and reinterpret it within an egalitarian and anti-patriarchal epistemology (Al-Hibri 1982; Barlas 2002, 2006).

Wadud's method of reading the Qur'an is called the hermeneutics of *tawhid*. She explains further:

> I propose a hermeneutics of *tawhid* to emphasize how the unity of the Qur'an permeates all its parts. Rather than simply applying meanings to one verse at a time, with occasional references to various verses elsewhere, a framework may be developed that includes a systematic rationale for making correlations and sufficiently exemplifies the full impact of Qur'anic coherence.
>
> (Wadud 1999, xii)

The concept of *tawhid,* as conceived by Wadud, is different from how most Muslims understand it. Most Muslims understand *tawhid* not as the unity of the Qur'an but as the theological concept of God as the one and only God (monotheism). The concept of the unity of the Qur'an is called *wahdah mawdlu'iyyah li al-Qur'an*. Later, in her article 'Engaging *Tawhid* in Islam and Feminisms' (2008, 436), she clarified her '*tawhidic* paradigm' as the expansion of Islamic monotheism which means 'God is one, God is unique, God is united and God unites all things.' Inherent in this meaning, she explains, is 'the basis for non-discrimination and a challenge to patriarchy in Islamic worldviews' (ibid., 437).

Conservative interpretations tend to sustain hegemonic knowledge construction in the name of shaping the tradition and the methodology that sustains a patriarchal reading of the texts. Wadud (2006, 206) emphasises that her method is to try to challenge 'the inherent sexist biases of the historicity of words.' She said that the Qur'an was revealed in the specific socio-historical context of patriarchal Arabia of the 7th century. This socio-historical context affects meaning construction through cultural and linguistic constructions.

Barlas (2002) is another scholar who employs hermeneutics in Qur'anic interpretation. Like Wadud, she begins her hermeneutical reading of the Qur'an by discussing the idea of *tawhid* (the Oneness of God) as the basis for an anti-patriarchal reading. Barlas starts her method by exposing God's self-disclosure, which consists of three principles: 'divine unity, justness and incomparability.' By divine unity (*tawhid*), she demonstrates the 'indivisibility of God's Sovereignty to challenge the theory which assumes maleness as an extension of God's rule' (ibid., 13). By justness, she reveals the term *zulm* (doing harm to others by transgressing their rights) in the Qur'an, which clarifies that God never does any *zulm* to anybody. From analysing this term she suggests that divine justice is 'respect for the rights of the human as a moral agent' (ibid., 14). And God's 'incomparability' means that anthropomorphic terms cannot be applied to God; this rejects the attribution of God as male, as represented in the

Arabic-gendered language used in the Qur'an, because, as she argues, 'God is beyond sex/gender' (ibid., 21). Barlas challenges the patriarchal reading of the Qur'an and exposes the egalitarian voices of the Qur'anic text, which she claims, 'have been submerged or lost because of the patriarchal nature of its exegesis and the gendered nature of human language' (ibid., 22).

When reading the text to derive its intrinsic meaning, Barlas suggests to also *read behind the text* to reconstruct the historical context surrounding the revelation or the text production and to *read in front of the text* to re-contextualise the text in the present context. By applying this method, Barlas arrived at the conclusion that the Qur'an is an egalitarian text that established the principle of the equality of the sexes (2002, 21, 25).

In Indonesia, the discourse of the hermeneutical approach to the Qur'an has attracted favourable attention from modern scholars like Nurcholish Madjid (1996), Nassaruddin Umar (1999), Taufik Amal and Samsu Panggabean (2005), and several Islamic feminists such as Lies Marcoes-Natsir (Sciortino, Marcoes-Natsir, and Mas'udi 1996), and Musdah Mulia (2005).

Madjid's work on Qur'anic interpretation was influenced by Fazlur Rahman, his supervisor at the University of Chicago (Johns and Saeed 2004). Like Rahman, Madjid (1996, 2005) argues that it is important to examine the historical context of the revelation in order to bring to the discussion the universal and normative message of Islam and apply it to contemporary realities.

Umar (1999) analyses the Qur'an by giving attention to semantics, semiotics, hermeneutics, and knowledge of *asbab al-nuzul* (the specific context following the revelation). He has criticised various forms of gender bias in Qur'anic interpretations including the gender bias of: male interpreters, the Arabic language, Arabic grammar, and also *fiqh* (Islamic jurisprudence).

Marcoes-Natsier is a leading Islamic feminist in Indonesia and, through the non-government organisation the Society for *Pesantren* and Community Development (P3M), she has promoted the critical study of religious texts: the Qur'an, the Hadith and classical texts. Principally, P3M focuses on interpreting the Qur'an in relation to reproductive rights. The organisation aims to promote the equality of women and men based on Qur'anic verses and, as a precondition for respect for reproductive right, rejects women's subordination to men (Sciortino et al. 1996).

However, I must acknowledge that few Muslims in Indonesia accept this hermeneutical approach to the Qur'an. There are many who reject it, particularly conservative and radical Islamic writers such as A. Husaini (2008) and Fauzan al-Anshari (2008). They argue that hermeneutic analysis originated in the West and is used in Biblical interpretation, and therefore it is not a suitable tool with which to analyse the Qur'an. They say that as the words in the Qur'an are divine and sacred applying this approach could be sacrilegious. They attack scholars who apply this method, not only in

Indonesia but elsewhere, and accuse scholars like Abu Zayd, Rahman, and Arkoun of blasphemy.

Employing both a feminist framework and a hermeneutic approach for this research is important as these perspectives use critical examination to open the discourse to discussions of equity and social justice. The feminist perspective enables us to highlight women's experiences and to consider their experiences as knowledge (Harding 1987). It also allows us to analyse the power relations that influence the social organisation of sexuality that privileges male sexuality and ignores female sexuality. A hermeneutical approach interrogates the domination of knowledge production and distribution by certain authoritative religious powers and enhances opportunities for other voices to contribute to knowledge production.

Chapter overview

As well as the introduction and conclusion, this book contains eight interrelated chapters. The chapters address women's life histories through their experiences of marriage and sexual relationships.

Chapter 1

'Marriage and Sexuality: The Indonesian Context and Islamic Perspectives' reviews ethnographic research on marriage and sexuality in the Indonesian context and from Islamic perspectives. Much of the available research on the Islamic influence on sexuality has been undertaken in Middle Eastern countries. To my knowledge, this book is one of the few studies focusing on marital sexual relations that include religion in the Indonesian context.

Chapter 2

'Situating Sexuality in Fieldwork' details the researcher's experiences in conducting fieldwork on sexuality. I discuss how I benefited from employing self-reflexivity where I positioned myself in this research as both researcher and participant.

Chapter 3

'Women's Perceptions and Expectations of Marriage and Sexual Relations' presents the results of my research in the field, exploring women's perceptions and expectations of marriage and sexual relations. This chapter also presents women's acquired knowledge on marriage and sexuality from various sources such as Islamic books on marriage, sex manuals, *kitab* (classical Islamic textbooks), *pengajian* (religious gatherings), and peer conversations. These sources inform women about ideal marital and sexual relationships.

Chapter 4

'Prelude to Marriage: Finding the Right *Jodoh* (Soul-Mate) for Life' discusses women's experiences as they prepare for marriage, including their mate preference, engagement and the marriage proposal. I also describe the role of the KUA and its program of pre-marital information sessions (SUSCATIN). This chapter also shows that there are various ways for women to find a mate, from arranged marriage to self-choice involving a romantic relationship.

Chapter 5

'Marital Adjustment and Household Management' analyses the adjustment process that many of the female participants in this study described experiencing in the first years of marriage. I argue that there are five areas of difference between marriage partners that may need negotiation, namely, family origin and upbringing, personal character, ethnic background, age, and class. This chapter also covers household arrangements and the division of labour between the spouses, and its effect on marital conflict.

Chapter 6

'Women's Experiences of Marital Sexual Relationships: Sex as a Duty' contains the main argument of the book. It elaborates on women's experiences of marital sexual relations with their husbands. In this chapter, I argue that the lack of knowledge concerning sexual relations in marriage affects women's initiation into sex on the 'first night' (*malam pertama*), usually the wedding night. The data presented in this chapter shaped my main argument: that many women perceive sex in marriage as their duty and their husbands' right. Some of the women also experience sexual violence from their husbands. In this chapter, I also provide a discussion on women's experiences of sex and reproduction and the etiquette of sexual relations in Islam.

Chapter 7

'Women's Experiences of Marital Sexual Relationships: Sex as a Right' presents the voices of a few women participants in this study who occasionally negotiate with their husbands about their preferences during sex. These women are able to express their desires in many aspects of sex, for example, initiation of sex, sexual communication, sexual stimulation, positions adopted, and the frequency of sex. Where women mobilise strategies to experience pleasurable sex, there is evidence of the exercise of agency. The strategies also enable women to avoid sex, that is, they draw on Islamic texts that enable them to not-act.

Chapter 8

'Women, Islamic Texts, and Knowledge Construction' focuses on how Islamic teachings affect women's perceptions and behaviours in their marital sexual relations. Further, this chapter delves into how women encounter texts that encourage women to be obedient towards their husbands in sexual relations and that privilege men's desire. Two sites were noted by my female participants as having authority in disseminating religious teaching, namely, *pesantren* (Islamic boarding schools) and *majlis ta'lim* (religious study gatherings). In this chapter, I provide alternative texts that counter the dominant texts that suggest sex is the women's duty. Critical reading of the texts, using a hermeneutical approach, is also provided. I introduce an NGO that promotes women's reproductive rights in Islam in rural Eastern Bandung.

Conclusion

The 'Conclusion' synthesises earlier chapters. In the first part, I restate the main research questions and findings of this project. My argument is supported by data provided in the consecutive and interrelated chapters that I presented in this book. The general argument that I make is that despite the changing patterns in economic and social aspects of marriage in Indonesia, marital sexual relations still emphasise a normative gender ideology that suggests that sex in marriage is the wife's duty and the husband's right. Although I acknowledge the diversity of practices across Indonesia, I argue that this norm is widely accepted.

Notes

1. Normative in this book means based on dominant and accepted norms in Indonesian society.
2. CEDAW was adopted on 18 December 1979 by the United Nations General Assembly. Indonesia ratified CEDAW on 13 September 1984. As at 6 September 2015, the convention had been ratified by 189 countries.

References

Accad, Evelyne. (2000). 'Sexuality and sexual politics: Conflicts and contradictions for contemporary women in the Middle East.' In Pinar Ilkkaracan (ed.), *Women and Sexuality in Muslim Societies*, 37–50. Turkey: Women for Women's Human Rights (WWHR).

Adimihardja, Kusnaka (1980). *Beberapa catatan tentang masyarakat Sunda di Jawa Barat* (Several notes on a Sundanese community in West Java). Bandung: Universitas Padjajaran.

Ahmadi, Fereshteh. (2006). 'Islamic Feminism in Iran: Feminism in a new Islamic context.' *Journal of Feminist Studies in Religion*, 22(2), 33–53, DOI: 10.2979/FSR.2006.22.2.33.

Al-Anshari, Fauzan. (2008). 'Setahap demi setahap pesantren diintervensi' (Step by step pesantren are being penetrated). *Republika Online*, 16 December, originally retrieved from: https://republika.co.id/search/setahap%20demi%20setahap%20 pesantren%20diintervensi (20 January 2012).
Al-Bukhari, Muhammed Ibn Ismaiel. (1997). *The Translation of the Meanings of Shahih al-Bukhari: Arabic–English, vol. 7,* trans. Muhammed Muhsin Khan. Riyadh, Saudi Arabia: Darussalam, available from: https://archive.org/stream/TheTranslationOf TheMeaningsOfSahihAl-Bukhari-Arabic-English9Volumes/Sahih%20Al-Bukhari-Arabic_English_Volume-7-Ahadith-5063-5969#page/n9/mode/2up (accessed 15 January 2020).
Alcoff, Linda and John D. Caputo (eds.). (2011). *Feminism, Sexuality and the Return of Religion.* Bloomington, IN: Indiana University Press.
Al-Hibri, Azizah. (1982). 'A study of Islamic herstory: Or how did we ever get into this mess?' In al-Hibri (ed.), *Women and Islam,* 207–19. Oxford: Pergamon Press, DOI: 10.1016/0277-5395(82)90028-0.
Ali, Kecia. (2006). *Sexual Ethics and Islam: Feminist Reflections on Qur'an, Hadith, and Jurisprudence.* Oxford: One World.
Alimi, Yasir. (2004). *Dekonstruksi seksualitas postkolonial: Dari wacana bangsa hingga wacana agama* (Decontruction of postcolonial sexuality: From nation discourse to religious discourse). Yogyakarta: Lembaga Kajian Islam dan Sosial – Institute for Islamic and Social Studies Foundation (LKiS).
Amal, Taufik Adnan and Samsu Rizal Panggabean. (2005). 'A contextual approach to the Qur'an.' In Abdullah Saeed (ed.), *Approaches to the Qur'an in Contemporary Indonesia,* 107–33. Oxford: Oxford University Press.
Anwar, Zainah. (2009). 'Introduction.' In Anwar (ed.), *Wanted: Equality and Justice in the Muslim Family,* 23–63. Selangor: Musawah and Sister in Islam.
Azra, Azyumardi and Wayne Hudson. (2008). 'Political modernity and Indonesian Islam: A manifesto.' In Azra and Hudson (eds), *Islam beyond Conflict: Indonesian Islam and Western Political Theory,* 5–7. Ashgate: Aldershot.
Badan Pusat Statistik Jawa Barat (West Java Census Bureau Centre), available at https://jabar.bps.go.id/dynamictable/2020/06/03/606/jumlah-penduduk-menurut-kelompok-umur-di-provinsi-jawa-barat-2010-2020.html Updated publication on 03 June 2020. (Accessed 26 July 2020).
Badran, Margot. (1989). 'The origins of feminism in Egypt.' In Arina Angerman and Geerte Binnema (eds), *Current Issues in Women's History,* 153–70. London: Routledge.
Badran, Margot. (1995). *Feminists, Islam, and Nation: Gender and the Making of Modern Egypt.* Princeton, NJ: Princeton University Press.
Badran, Margot. (2002a). 'Islamic feminism: What's in a name?' *Cairo: Al-Ahram Weekly Online,* 17–23 January 2002 Issue No. 569. Available at: https://web.archive.org/web/20150320074746/http://weekly.ahram.org.eg/2002/569/cu1.htm (accessed 26 July 2020)
Badran, Margot. (2002b). 'Feminism and the Qur'an.' In J. D. McAuliffe (ed.), *Encyclopaedia of the Qur'an, vol. 2, E–I,* 199–203. Leiden: E. J. Brill.
Badran, Margot. (2005). 'Between secular and Islamic feminism: Reflections on the Middle East and beyond.' *Journal of Middle East Women's Studies,* 1(1), 6–28, DOI: 10.1215/15525864-2005-1002.
Badran, Margot. (2011). 'From Islamic feminism to a Muslim holistic feminism.' *IDS Bulletin,* 42(1), 78–87, DOI: 10.1111/j.1759-5436.2011.00203.x.

Barlas, Asma. (2002). *'Believing Women' in Islam: Unreading Patriarchal Interpretations of the Qur'an*. Austin: University of Texas Press.

Barlas, Asma. (2006). 'Qur'anic hermeneutics and sexual politics.' *Cordozo Review*, 28(1), 143–51, available from: https://pdfs.semanticscholar.org/d190/0b0b9f0-650fbb030c47721e87c4725f66736.pdf (accessed 8 January 2020).

Bennett, Linda Rae. (2005). *Women, Islam and Modernity: Single Women, Sexuality and Reproductive Health in Contemporary Indonesia*. London: Routledge Curzon.

Berg, Bruce Lawrence. (2007). *Qualitative Research Methods for the Social Sciences*. Boston: Pearson/Allyn and Bacon.

Binahayati, Rusyidi. (2011). 'Perceptions and attitudes towards violence against wives in West Java, Indonesia.' PhD dissertation, State University of New York, Albany.

Blackburn, Susan (2004). *Women and the State in Modern Indonesia*. Cambridge: Cambridge University Press.

Blackwood, Evelyn. (2007). 'Transnational sexualities in one place: Indonesian readings.' In Saskia E. Wieringa, Evelyn Blackwood, and Abha Bhaiya (eds.), *Women's Sexualities and Masculinities in a Globalizing Asia*, 181–99. New York: Palgrave Macmillan, DOI: 10.1057/9780230604124_10.

Boellstorff, Tom. (2005). *The Gay Archipelago: Sexuality and Nation in Indonesia*. Princeton, NJ: Princeton University Press.

Bouhdiba, Abdelwahab. (1985). *Sexuality in Islam*. London: Routledge, DOI: 10.4324/9780203706916.

Cooke, Miriam. (2001). *Women Claim Islam: Creating Islamic Feminism through Literature*. New York: Routledge.

Cooke, Miriam. (2002). 'Multiple critique: Islamic feminist rhetorical strategies.' In Laura E. Donaldson and Kwok Pui-lan (eds). *Postcolonialism, Feminism and Religious Discourse*, 142–60. New York: Routledge.

Dalmeri. (2012). 'Prospek Demokrasi: Dilema antara Penerapan Syariat Islam dan Penegakan Hak Asasi Manusia di Indonesia (Democration Prospect: The Dillema of Syari'ah Islam Implementation and Pulfilling Human Rights).' *Salam: Jurnal Studi Masyarakat Islam*, 15(2), 228–239, Available from http://ejournal.umm.ac.id/index.php/salam/article/view/1632/1769 (Accessed 27 July 2020).

Davies, Sharyn Graham. (2010). *Gender Diversity in Indonesia: Sexuality, Islam and Queer Selves*. London: Routledge, DOI: 10.4324/9780203860953.

Dialmy, Abdessamad. (2010). 'Sexuality and Islam.' *Journal of Contraception and Reproductive Health Care*, 15, 160–68, DOI: 10.3109/13625181003793339.

Donaldson, Laura E. and Kwok Pui-lan. (2002). *Postcolonialism, Feminism and Religious Discourse*. New York: Routledge.

Doorn-Harder, Pieternella van. (2006). *Women Shaping Islam: Reading the Qur'an in Indonesia*. Urbana: University of Illinois Press.

Ekadjati, Edi Suhardi. (1995). *Kebudayaan sunda: Suatu pendekatan sejarah* (Sundanese culture: An historical approach). Jakarta: Pustaka Jaya.

Esterik, Penny van (ed.). (1982). *Women of Southeast Asia*. Illinois: Centre for Southeast Asian Studies, Northern Illinois University.

Feillard, Andrée and Pieternella van Doorn-Harder. (2013). 'A new generation of feminists within traditional Islam: An Indonesian exception.' In Jajat Burhanuddin and Kees van Dijk (eds.), *Islam in Indonesia: Contrasting Images and Interpretations*, 139–59. Amsterdam: Amsterdam University Press, DOI: 10.2307/j.ctt46mwqt.12.

Foucault, Michel. (1990). *The History of Sexuality, vol. I: An Introduction*. London: Penguin.
Grijns, Mies. (1987). 'Tea-pickers in West Java as mothers and workers: Female work and women's jobs.' In Elsbeth Locher-Scholten and Anke Niehof (eds.), *Indonesian Women in Focus*, 104–19. Leiden: KITLV Press.
Grijns, Mies, Inez Smyth, Anita van Velzen, Sugiah Machfud, and Pudjiwati Sajogyo (eds). (1994). *Different Women, Different Work: Gender and Industrialization in Indonesia*. Aldershot: Avenbury.
Gross, Rita M. (1996). *Feminism and Religion: An Introduction*. Boston: Beacon Press.
Haeri, Sahla. (1989). *Law of Desire: Temporary Marriage in Shi'i Iran*. Syracuse: Syracuse University Press, USA.
Hancock, Peter. (2001). 'Gender empowerment issues from West Java.' In Susan Blackburn (ed.), *Love, Sex and Power: Women in Southeast Asia*, 75–88. Clayton, Vic.: Monash Asia Institute.
Handajani, Suzie. (2005). 'Globalizing local girls: The representation of adolescents in Indonesian teen magazines.' MA thesis, The University of Western Australia, Perth.
Harding, Sandra. (1987). *Feminism and Methodology*. Indiana: Indiana University Press.
Hassan, Riffat. (1990). 'An Islamic perspective.' In Jeanne Becher (ed.), *Women, Religion and Sexuality: Studies on the Impact of Religious Teaching on Women*, 93–128. Geneva: World Council of Churches.
Hassan, Riffat. (1994). 'Women's interpretation of Islam.' In H. Thijssen and J. Saffe (eds.), *Women and Islam in Muslim Societies: Poverty and Development – Analysis and Policy*, 113–21. The Hague: Netherlands Institute of International Relations.
Hassan, Riffat. (2001). 'Challenging the stereotypes of fundamentalism: An Islamic feminist perspective.' *The Muslim World*, 91(1–2), 55–70, DOI: 10.1111/j.1478-1913.2001.tb03707.x.
Hefner, Robert W. (1997). 'Islam in an era of nation-states: Politics and religious renewal in Muslim Southeast Asia.' In Robert W. Hefner and Patricia Horvatich (eds.), *Islam in an Era of Nation-States: Politics and Religious Renewal in Muslim Southeast Asia*, 3–40. Honolulu, HI: University of Hawai'i Press.
Hefner, Robert W. (2010). 'Religious resurgence in contemporary Asia: Southeast Asian perspectives on capitalism, the state, and the new piety.' *The Journal of Asian Studies*, 69(4), 1031–47, DOI: 10.1017/S0021911810002901.
Hefner, Robert W. and Patricia Horvatich (eds). (1997). *Islam in an Era of Nation-States: Politics and Religious Renewal in Muslim Southeast Asia*. Honolulu, HI: University of Hawai'i Press.
Hidayah, Nur. (2012). '"Feminising" Islam in contemporary Indonesia: The role of progressive Muslim women's organisations.' PhD thesis, University of Melbourne.
Hilber, Adriane Martin, Terence H. Hull, Eleanor Preston-Whyte, Brigitte Bagnol, Jenni Smit, Chintana Wacharasin, and Ninuk Widyantoro. (2010). 'A cross cultural study of vaginal practices and sexuality: Implications for sexual health.' *Social Science and Medicine*, 70(3), 392–400, DOI: 10.1016/j.socscimed.2009.10.023.
Holzner, Brigitte M. and Dédé Oetomo. (2004). 'Youth, sexuality and sex education messages in Indonesia: Issues of desire and control.' *Reproductive Health Matters*, 12(23), 40–49, DOI: 10.1016/S0968-8080(04)23122-6.
Horikoshi, Hiroko. (1976). 'A traditional leader in a time of hange: The 'kijaji' and 'ulama' in West Java.' PhD thesis, University of Illinois, Urbana, Champaign.

Hugo, Graeme J. (1981). *Population Mobility in West Java*. Yogyakarta: Gadjah Mada University Press.

Hull, Valerie J. (1982). 'Women in Java's rural middle class: Progress or regress?' In Penny van Esterik (ed.), *Women of Southeast Asia*, 100–23. Illinois: Centre for Southeast Asian Studies, Northern Illinois University.

Husaini, A. (2008). 'Harus disikapi secara ilmiah' (Should be dealt with scientifically). Republika Online, 15 December, available from: https://www.republika.co.id/berita/dunia-islam/islam-nusantara/08/12/15/20282-adian-husaini-harus-disikapi-secara-ilmiah- (accessed 2 September 2011).

Idrus, Nurul Ilmi. (2003). '"To take each other": Bugis practices of gender, sexuality and marriage.' PhD thesis, The Australia National University, Canberra.

Ilkkaracan, Pinar. (2000). 'Introduction.' In Pinar Ilkkaracan (ed.), *Women and Sexuality in Muslim Societies*, 1–15. Istanbul: Women for Women's Human Rights.

Ilkkaracan, Pinar. (2002). 'Women, sexuality, and social change in the Middle East and Maghreb.' *Social Research*, 69(3), 753–79.

Iskandar, Meiwita B., Budi Utomo, Terence Hull, Nick G. Dharmaputra, and Yuswardi Azwar (1996). *Unraveling the Mysteries of Maternal Death in West Java: Reexamining the Witnesses*. Depok: Center for Health Research, Research Institute, University of Indonesia.

Jayawardena, Kumari. (1986) *Feminism and Nationalism in the Third World*. London: Zed Books.

Johns, Anthony H. and Abdullah Saeed. (2004). 'Nurcholish Madjid and the interpretation of the Qur'an: Religious pluralism and tolerance.' In Sahu Taji-Farouki (ed.), *Modern Muslim Intellectuals and the Qur'an*, 67–96. Oxford: Oxford University Press.

Kahmad, Dadang. (2006). 'Agama Islam dan budaya Sunda' (Islamic religion and Sundanese culture). In Ajip Rosidi, H. Edi S. Ekadjati, and A. Chaedar Alwasilah (eds.), *Konferensi International budaya Sunda* (International conference of Sundanese culture), vol. I. Bandung: Yayasan Kebudayaan Rancage.

Kandiyoti, Deniz. (1991). 'Introduction.' In Deniz Kandiyoti (ed.), *Women, Islam and the State*, 1–21. London: Macmillan Press, DOI: 10.1007/978-1-349-21178-4_1.

Karam, Azza M. (1998). *Women, Islamism and the State: Contemporary Feminisms in Egypt*. London: Macmillan Press.

King, Ursula. (1995). 'Introduction: Gender and the study of religion.' In Ursula King (ed.), *Religion and Gender*, 1–38. Oxford: Blackwell.

Leavy, Patricia. (2014). 'Introduction.' In Patricia Leavy (ed.), *The Oxford Handbook of Qualitative Research*, 1–13. Oxford: Oxford University Press, DOI: 10.1093/oxfordhb/9780199811755.013.033.

Madjid, Nurcholish. (1996). 'In search of Islamic roots for modern pluralism: The Indonesian experiences.' In Mark R. Woodward (ed.), *Toward a New Paradigm: Recent Developments in Indonesia Islamic Thought*, 89–116. Arizona: Arizona State University.

Madjid, Nurcholish. (2005). 'Interpreting the Qur'anic principle of religious pluralism.' In Abdullah Saeed (ed.), *Approaches to the Qur'an in Contemporary Indonesia*, 209–25. Oxford: Oxford University Press.

Mahmood, Saba. (2001). 'Feminist theory, embodiment and the docile agent: Some reflections on the Egyptian Islamic revival.' *Cultural Anthropology*, 16(2), 202–36, DOI: 10.1525/can.2001.16.2.202.

Mather, Celia. (1985). '"Rather than make trouble, it is better just to leave": Behind the lack of industrial strikes in the Tangerang region of West Java.' In Haleh Ashfar (ed.), *Women Work and Ideology in the Third World*, 153–80. London: Tavistock Publication.
Mernissi, Fatima. (1987). *Beyond the Veil: Male-Female Dynamics in Muslim Society* (rev. ed.). Bloomington, IN: Indiana University Press.
Millie, Julian. (2008). 'Non-specialists in the *pesantren*: The social construction of Islamic knowledge.' *Review of Indonesian and Malaysian Affairs*, 42(1), 107–24.
Mir-Hosseini, Ziba. (2011) 'Beyond "Islam" vs "feminism".' *IDS Bulletin*, 42(1), 67–77, DOI: 10.1111/j.1759-5436.2011.00202.x.
Moghadam, Valentine M. (2002). 'Islamic feminism and its discontents: Toward a revolution of the debate.' *Signs*, 27(4), 1135–71, DOI: 10.1086/339639.
Moghissi, Haideh. (1999). *Feminism and Islamic Fundamentalism: The Limits of Postmodern Analysis*. London: Zed Books.
Mohanty, Chandra Talpade. (1991). 'Under western eyes: Feminist scholarship and colonial discourses.' In Chandra Talpade Mohanty, Ann Russo, and Lourdes Torres (eds.), *Third World Women and the Politics of Feminism*, 51–80. Bloomington, IN: Indiana University Press.
Muhtadi, Burhanuddin. (2009). 'The quest for Hizbut Tahrir in Indonesia.' *Asian Journal of Social Science*, 37, 623–45, DOI: 10.1163/156853109X460219.
Mulia, Musdah. (2005). *Muslimah reformis: Perempuan pembaru keagamaan* (Reformist Muslim women: A religious revivalist). Bandung: Mizan.
Munir, Lily Zakiyah. (2002). '"He is your garment and you are his ...": Religious precepts, interpretation, and power relations in marital sexuality among Javanese Muslim women.' *SOJOURN: Journal of Social Issues in Southeast Asia*, 17(2), 191–220, DOI: 10.1355/SJ17-2C.
Munti, Ratna Batara. (2005). *Demokrasi keintiman: Seksualitas di era global* (Democracy of intimacy: Sexuality in the global era). Yogyakarta: LKiS.
Musallam, Basim. (1983). *Sex and Society in Islam: Birth Control Before the Nineteenth Century*. Cambridge: Cambridge University Press.
Muttaqin, Farid. (2008) 'Progressive Muslim feminists in Indonesia from pioneering to the next agendas.' MA thesis, Ohio University.
Newland, Lynda. (2000). 'Under the banner of Islam: Mobilising religious identities in West Java.' *The Australian Journal of Anthropology*, 11(2), 199–222, DOI: 10.1111/j.1835-9310.2000.tb00056.x.
Newland, Lynda. (2001). 'The deployment of the prosperous Family: Family planning in West Java.' *NWSA Journal*, 13(3), 22–48, DOI: 10.2979/NWS.2001.13.3.22.
Noerdin, Edriana. (2002). 'Customary institutions, *syariah* law and the marginalisation of Indonesian women.' In Kathryn Robinson and Sharon Bessell (eds.), *Women in Indonesia: Gender, Equity and Development*, 179–86. Singapore: Institute of Southeast Asian Studies, DOI: 10.1355/9789812305152-021.
Nurmila, Nina. (2009). *Women, Islam and Everyday Life: Renegotiating Polygamy in Indonesia*. London: Routledge.
Nurmila, Nina. (2011). 'The influence of global Muslim feminism on Indonesian Muslim feminist discourse.' *Al-Jami'ah*, 49(1), 33–64, DOI: 10.14421/ajis.2011.491.33-64.
Oakley, Ann. (1981). 'Interviewing women: A contradiction in terms.' In Helen Roberts (ed.), *Doing Feminist Research*, 30–61. London: Routledge and Kegan Paul.
Oetomo, Dédé. (1996). 'Gender and sexual orientation in Indonesia.' In Laurie J. Sears (ed.), *Fantasizing the Feminine in Indonesia*, 259–69. Durham: Duke University Press, DOI: 10.1215/9780822396710-012.

Offenhauer, Priscilla. (2005). *Women in Islamic Societies: A Selected Review of Social Scientific Literature*. Washington, DC: Federal Research Division Library of Congress, available from: http://www.loc.gov/rr/frd/pdf-files/Women_Islamic_Societies.pdf (accessed 11 November 2014).

Parker, Lyn. (2007). 'Of faith and feminism: Imagining discursive feminist space for Muslim.' *Outskirts: Feminism along the Edge*, 17, available from: http://www.outskirts.arts.uwa.edu.au/volumes/volume-17/parker (accessed 24 November 2011).

Parker, Lyn. (2008). 'Theorising adolescent sexualities in Indonesia – Where "something different happens".' *Intersections: Gender and Sexuality in Asia and the Pacific*, 18(Oct.), available from: http://intersections.anu.edu.au/issue18/parker.htm (accessed 27 April 2011).

Qibtiyah, Alimatul. (2012). 'Feminist identity and the conceptualisation of gender issues in Islam: Muslim gender studies elites in Yogyakarta, Indonesia.' PhD thesis, University of Western Sydney.

Reinharz, Shulamit. (1992). *Feminist Methods in Social Research*. New York: Oxford University Press.

Rhouni, Raja. (2008). 'Rethinking "Islamic feminist hermeneutics": The case of Fatima Mernissi.' In Anita Kinsilehto (ed.), *Islamic Feminism: Current Perspectives*, 103–15. Tampere Peace Research Institute. Occasional paper, no. 96.

Robinson, Kathryn. (2001). 'Gender, Islam and culture in Indonesia.' In Susan Blackburn (ed.), *Love, Sex and Power: Women in Southeast Asia*, 17–30. Clayton, Vic.: Monash Asia Institute.

Robinson, Kathryn. (2006). Islamic influences on Indonesian feminism. *Social Analysis*, 50(1), 171–77, DOI: 10.3167/015597706780886012.

Robinson, Kathryn. (2009). *Gender, Islam and Democracy in Indonesia*. London: Routledge, DOI: 10.4324/9780203891759.

Sabbah, Fatna A. (1984). *Woman in the Muslim Unconscious*. New York: Pergamon Press.

Sadli, Saparinah. (2002). 'Feminism in Indonesia in an international context.' In Kathryn Robinson and Sharon Bessell (eds.), *Women in Indonesia: Gender, Equity and Development*, 80–91. Pasir Panjang: Institute of Southeast Asian Studies, DOI: 10.1355/9789812305152-014.

Sajogyo, Pudjiwati and Ekawati Sri Wahyuni. (1994). 'An introduction to the economy and people of West Java.' In Mies Grijns, Inez Smyth, Anita van Velzen, Sugiah Machfud, and Pudjiwati Sajogyo (eds.), *Different Women, Different Work: Gender and Industrialization in Indonesia*, 29–46. Aldershot: Avenbury.

Sariyun, Yugo. (2006). 'Kehidupan keluarga masyarakat Sunda' (Family life in Sundanese society). In A. Rosidi, E. S. Ekadjati, and A. C. Alwasilah (eds.). *Konferensi International Budaya Sunda* (International conference on Sundanese culture), 40–49, Bandung: Yayasan Kebudayaan Rancage.

Sciortino, Rosalia, Lies Marcoes-Natsir, and Masdar F. Mas'udi. (1996). 'Learning from Islam: Advocacy of reproductive rights in Indonesian pesantren.' *Reproductive Health Matters*, 4(8), 86–96, DOI: 10.1016/S0968-8080(96)90305-5.

Shaikh, Sa'dyiia. (2003). 'Transforming feminism: Islam, women and gender justice.' In Omid Safi (ed.), *Progressive Muslims on Justice, Gender and Pluralism*, 147–62. Oxford: Oneworld.

Shefner-Rogers, Corinne L. (2004). 'Pregnancy knowledge, attitudes and practices in Indonesia: Does husband's social support make a difference?' PhD thesis, Johns Hopkins University, Baltimore, MD.

Silvey, Rachel. (2004). 'Gender, socio-spatial networks, and rural migrants in West Java.' In R. Leinbach, (ed.), *The Indonesian Rural Economy: Mobility, Work and Enterprise*, 134–51. Singapore: Institute of Southeast Asian Studies, DOI: 10.1355/9789812305275-012.
Simon, William and John H. Gagnon. (1984). 'Sexual scripts.' *Society*, 22, 53–60, DOI: 10.1007/BF02701260.
Stewart, David W., Prem N. Shamdasani, and Dennis W. Rook. (2007). *Focus Groups: Theory and Practice*. Thousand Oaks: SAGE Publication, DOI: 10.4135/9781412991841.
Sukma, Rizal and Clara Joewono (eds.). (2007). *Islamic Thought and Movements in Contemporary Indonesia*. CSIS (Centre for Strategic and International Studies). Yogyakarta: Kanisius.
Suryadinata, Leo, Evi Nurvidya Arifin, and Aris Ananta. (2003). *Indonesia's Population: Ethnicity and Religion in a Changing Political Landscape*. Indonesian Population Series, 1. Pasir Panjang: Institute of Southeast Asian Studies, DOI: 10.1355/9789812305268.
Suryakusuma, Julia I. (1996). 'The state and sexuality in New Order Indonesia.' In Laurie. J. Sears (ed.), *Fantasizing the Feminine in Indonesia*, 92–119. Durham: Duke University Press.
Syamsiyatun, Siti. (2008). 'Women negotiating feminism and Islamism in Indonesia: Experiences of Nasyiatul Aisyiah 1985–2005.' In Susan Blackburn, Bianca Smith, and Siti Syamsiyatun (eds.), *Indonesian Islam in a New Era: How Women Negotiate their Muslim Identities*, 14–65. Clayton: Monash Asia Institute.
Tohari, Heri Mohamad (2013). 'Feminisme Sunda kuno: Studi interpretasi kritis akulturasi nilai-nilai kesetaraan gender Sunda-Islam dalam carita pantun Sri Sadana' (Classical Sundanese feminism: Critical interpretation of gender equality values in Sunda-Islam in the Sri Sadana poem). *Jurnal Etika dan Pekerti* (Journal of Ethics and Character), 1(2), 13–26.
Tohidi, Nayereh. (2007). 'Muslim feminism and Islamic reformation: The case of Iran.' In Rosemary Radford Ruether (ed.), *Feminist Theologies: Legacy and Prospect*, 93–116. Minneapolis, MN: Fortress Press.
Turmudi, Endang. (2004). 'Diskursus penerapan syariat Islam: Studi kasus di Tasikmalaya' (The discourse of Islamic shari'a implementation: Case study in Tasikmalaya). In Kutut Suwondo, Nico L. Kana, and Pradjarta Dirdjosanjoto (eds.), *Partisipasi dan demokrasi: Dinamika politik local di Indonesia* (Participation and democracy: The dynamic of local politic in Indonesia), 109–13. Salatiga: Pustaka Percik.
Umar, Nasaruddin. (1999). *Argumen kesetaraan jender: Perspektif Al-Qur'an* (The argument of gender equality: Qur'anic perspective). Jakarta: Paramadina.
Utomo, Budi (1996). 'Health and social dimensions of infant feeding in Indramayu, West Java.' PhD thesis, The Australian National University, Canberra.
Wadud, Amina. (1999). *Qur'an and Woman: Rereading the Sacred Text from a Woman's Perspective*. Oxford: Oxford University Press.
Wadud, Amina. (2006). *Inside the Gender Jihad: Women Reform in Islam*. Oxford: Oneworld.
Wadud, Amina. (2008). 'Engaging *tawhid* in Islam and feminism.' *International Feminist Journal of Politics*, 10(4), 435–38, DOI: 10.1080/14616740802393858.
Warouw, Johannes Nicolaas. (2004). 'Assuming modernity: Migrant industrial workers in Tangerang, Indonesia.' PhD thesis, The Australia National University, Canberra.

Warouw, Johannes Nicolaas. (2008). 'Industrial workers in transition: Women's experiences of factory work in Tangerang.' In Michele Ford and Lyn Parker (eds), *Women and Work in Indonesia*, 104–19. London: Routledge.

Wichelen, Sonja van. (2010). *Religion, Politics and Gender in Indonesia: Disputing the Muslim Body*. New York: Routledge, DOI: 10.4324/9780203850657.

Legislation and conventions

Convention on the Elimination of all forms of Discrimination against Women (CEDAW), 1979, available from: https://www.un.org/womenwatch/daw/cedaw/cedaw.htm (accessed 18 February 2020).

Indonesia, Law on Pornography (Law no. 44/2008), Undang-Undang Republik Indonesia, Nomor 44 Tahun 2008, Tentang Pornografi (UU tentang Pornografi), adopted 30 October 2008, available from: http://www.dpr.go.id/dokjdih/document/uu/UU_2008_44.pdf (accessed 26 February 2020).

Indonesia, Law on the Elimination of Domestic Violence (Law no. 23/2004), Undang-Undang tentang Penghapusan Kekerasan dalam Rumah Tangga (UU PKDRT), adopted 22 September 2004, available from: https://www.ilo.org/dyn/natlex/natlex4.detail?p_lang=en&p_isn=91238&p_country=IDN&p_count=611 (accessed 26 February 2020).

1 Marriage and sexuality
The Indonesian context and Islamic perspectives

Research on gender issues in contemporary Indonesia has increased significantly in recent years. A large and growing body of literature has emerged addressing gender relations in Indonesia (Ford and Parker 2008b; Robinson 2001). The Reform era—since 1998—has offered good opportunities for various discussions in Indonesia that include gender equality. Nevertheless, other challenges have also emerged related to fundamentalist movements opposing gender equality. Gender relations are an important element in the study of women in Indonesian society, and they play a key role in marriage and sexuality where responsibilities are divided according to gender roles. Sexuality is a site from which women are mainly excluded. Women's sexuality (in or outside of marriage) is highly controlled by men, society, and the state (Berninghausen and Kerstan 1992; Mather 1985; Wolf 1992).

In this chapter, I review the existing literature addressing marriage and sexuality in the Indonesian context and from Islamic perspectives. The discussion is divided into two sections. The first section explores ethnographic research on marriage and sexuality in the Indonesian context, and the second the academic literature on marriage and sexuality in Islam. These reviews are important because they show how gender plays a significant role in marriage and sexuality in Indonesia, as well as in Islam. I aim to clearly map the research already conducted by other scholars related to marriage and sexuality, to position my own research within it and to identify how my research contributes to existing knowledge. This book addresses gender relations in marriage with specific attention to married women's experiences of their sexual relations, particularly in West Java, which is comparatively neglected in the literature.

The Indonesian context

Ethnographic research on marriage: gender contested

Much of the ethnographic research related to marriage has been concentrated in Java (Berninghausen and Kerstan 1992; Brenner 1998; Geertz 1961; Jay 1969; Koentjaraningrat 1985; Sullivan 1994; Wolf 1992). While other research has been done in Sulawesi (Blackburn 2001; Idrus 2003) and Lombok (Bennett, Andajani-Sutjahjo, and Idrus 2011; Platt 2017), very little has been conducted in West Java. Some of these authors have supported the notion that women have high status and authority in the family (e.g. Blackwood 1995b; Geertz 1961; Hull 1982; Jay 1969). Others challenge this idea by asserting that women still experience subordination in every aspect of their lives, especially within family life (Brenner 1998; Sullivan 1994; Wolf 1992).

Marriage in Indonesia is almost universal and represents an important phase of life. Marriage establishes a new household and marks the achievement of adult economic and social status. It is the only institution where a man and a woman can legally engage in sexual relations. The expectation of marriage is even greater for women than for men. This is because women are expected to guard their sexual purity and sanctity before being married, with virginity considered important for women but not men.

Marriage also signifies the recognition of gendered roles for women in society and in the nation. In Indonesia, the gender roles attached to women, as promoted by the state during the New Order regime, were that women's responsibility was to stay at home and be good wives and mothers, manage the household, and take care of the children. Men's duty was in the public sphere as provider and protector of the family (Blackwood 1995b; Robinson 2009; Suryakusuma 1996). Although the regime has long ended, its gender ideology remains intact. The state gender ideology influences the gender relations of everyday life and has become a stereotype that governs the allocation of roles between males and females in Indonesian society. Kathryn Robinson (2009) argues that this state gender ideology has failed to consider diverse gender practices throughout Indonesia. The government has reduced the roles of men and women to the public and private spheres, respectively.

Hilda Geertz's work (1961) shows that women in Javanese society have a relatively strong position. Javanese women are employed in various occupations in and around the community. Women also control the household economy and make major decisions for the family concerning household expenses, children, and family rituals (Koentjaraningrat 1985). By contrast, Norma Sullivan (1994) argues that women in Indonesia still experience subordination in the family. She compared the relationship between wife and husband to that of manager and master. The wife (manager) will spend all household expenses in accordance with the husband's (master's) will and instructions. Similarly, Suzanne Brenner (1998) stated that even though women have authority over the household economy, because they are the ones who perform the business, this does not directly gain them high status. In Solo, the site where Brenner did her research, dealing with money is associated with low status. High status, which can only be claimed by men, is acknowledged through self-control and spiritual potency (Brenner 1998; on men's self-control see Adamson 2007).

Furthermore, married women are assessed for their ability to satisfy their husbands' sexual needs and for their own reproductive capacity. Marriage in Indonesia focuses on reproduction. The success of marriage is measured by the presence of children. Lyn Parker (2008, 23) showed that there is a close connection between marriage, sexuality, and procreation as 'the ideal and the norm' in Indonesia. Therefore, a childless marriage is viewed as pitiful. It is assumed to be the woman's fault and may become an excuse for her husband to either divorce her or engage in polygynous marriage (Koentjaraningrat 1985).[1] Blaming the woman for an infertile marriage is a common phenomenon in Indonesia.

Previous and recent studies have reported that in Java, the rate of polygynous marriage is low (Geertz 1961; Koentjaraningrat 1985; Nurmila 2009; Wichelen 2009). However, it is not uncommon for men to practise polygyny through *nikah siri* (secret marriage), in order to keep their reputation as respectable men, especially if they have not obtained their first wife's permission. Thus, their polygynous marriage remains unknown. Having an affair (*selingkuh, nyeleweng*) is also a common phenomenon in Indonesia. However, these phenomena do not weaken the expectation to marry. In many cases, couples who engage in *selingkuh* take the further step of either engaging in polygynous marriage (for the man) or terminating the former marriage and entering into a new married life.

Bilateral kinship is the most common kinship system in Indonesia. Bilateral kinship considers that the family lines of both husband and wife are important and have equal status. In a patrilineal system, the family lines are based on the male line, while in matrilineal societies, such as the Minangkabau, family lines are based on the female line.

Ethnographic research on marriage in different regions shows a strong connection between Islam and *adat* (custom) (Blackwood 1995b; Idrus 2003; Platt 2017; Robinson 2001). However, the extent to which Islam has adapted to local custom and vice versa differs significantly across these regions. Maria Platt's (2017) research on marriage among the Sasak people in Lombok showed that Sasak Islam is unique and differs from the mainstream Islamic belief of other places in Indonesia. For example, in performing prayers (*shalat*), Sasak Muslims pray *Wetu Telu* (three times) while in other parts of Indonesia the conventional prayer regime of five times a day is the norm. Platt reports that many marriages are organised in accordance with *adat* and Islam instead of state regulations. Consequently, many marriages are not registered (Platt 2017). In these cases, Islam is continuously misused to justify men's conduct, especially in issues such as polygyny and divorce. Similarly, Nurul Idrus (2003) found that Islam has influenced *adat* in marriage patterns among the Bugis, but unlike in Sasak areas, Bugis marriages are regulated by the state.

The contribution of Islam to the understanding and regulation of marriage should be considered. In Indonesia, Islam's close engagement with social practices and the government, and now politics, has given it significant influence in policies and regulations. For example, the Indonesian Marriage Law of 1974 was influenced by Islamic texts in regard to man's authority in the household and permission to practise polygyny. Chapter VI, Article 31(3) of the Indonesian Marriage Law states that 'The husband is the head of the family, the wife is the mother of the family' and this point was influenced by the Qur'anic verse which states that 'Men are the protectors and maintainers of women' (4: 34).

As we enter the third decade of the twentieth century, as a result of improved education, opportunities for women in the workforce have improved, with women working not only as labourers but also as professionals (Ford and Parker 2008a; Sen 1998). Research by Krishna Sen (1998) advises that both class and gender need to be considered in examining women's participation in the workforce. Women's participation in paid work has contributed to family incomes, as claimed by Jutta Berninghausen and Birgit Kerstan (1992), Diane Wolf (1992), and Brenner (1998). Wolf's study (1992) revealed that daughters, although not contributing significantly to family finances, could pay their own expenses, thus lessening the burden of on her parent/s. Brenner (1998) provided another example of women's engagement in the market and in business which gives them economic strength and autonomy. However, as she further noted, this financial strength and autonomy does not, at the same time, give women high status.

Women's participation in the workplace enables them to contribute to household income; however, it does not mean they are excused from housework and child rearing or that men participate in housework duties. Women's domestic work is considered 'dirty' (Munir 2002, 196) and insignificant; this work is marginalised and undervalued (Ford and Parker 2008a). New Order gender ideology gives priority to the husband's primary roles as provider and head of the family, and therefore the housewife's role is considered to be subordinate.

West Java

There are a few studies that focus on gender relations in West Javanese society. There are even fewer addressing women, marriage, and sexuality. Several studies have been published that are concerned with—women as industrial and non-industrial workers (Grijns 1987; Grijns et al. 1994; Hancock 2001; Mather 1985; Silvey 2004; Warouw 2004); women's health issues (Iskandar et al. 1996; Shefner-Rogers 2004; Utomo 1996); the implementation of Islamic shari'a and its effect on women's wellbeing (Noerdin 2002; Suhadi 2004; Turmudi 2004); and the role of *ulama* and *tarekat* (Horikoshi 1976; Millie 2008; Millie and Syihabuddin 2005; Newland 2000).

The work of Peter Hancock (2001) provides a valuable contribution to the study of gender relations, as he analyses the impact of industrial development on women's status in West Java. He found that women who work in factories enhance their status within the family. They are more involved in family decision-making processes, more independent, and they contribute more to the family income than before they engaged in paid work.

Numerous studies have reported the problems women workers face in factories such as long working hours, low wages, sexual harassment, discrimination, and poor health and safety at work (Tjandraningsih 2000). Women who work in factories are perceived as dependants of their husbands or fathers and have inadequate workers' rights (Hancock 2001; Mather 1985; Warouw 2004; Wolf 1992). For example, unlike male workers, married female workers do not receive a family allowance (Tjandraningsih 2000). Indeed, companies prefer women workers who are young, single, and educated—those who have at least completed secondary school. Thus, lesser educated women and those who are married find it harder to get jobs in factories (Tjandraningsih 2000).

Some married women, who are unable to compete with young unmarried women in the factories, turn to family businesses with more flexible working hours where they can divide their roles as worker and caregiver. Alternatively, they give up paid work altogether (Grijns et al. 1994). Wolf (1992) and Robinson (2009) also found that married women often give up work because they cannot find a relative or childcare facility to take care of their children. There is no suggestion that married men give up work because they have to look after their children.

There is some research related to health issues in West Java, because this region, generally speaking, has poor health, especially maternal and infant health. Infant mortality rates are high in this area (Horikoshi 1976; Utomo 1996). Research by Budi Utomo (1996), in Indramayu, showed that mothers, during the first three months after birth, tended to delay initiation of breastfeeding, were unlikely to discharge colostrum, and often fed their babies formula, in preference to breast milk. This reluctance to breastfeed causes a high risk of mortality. The maternal death rate is also high. Meiwita Iskandar et al. (1996) found that some traditional beliefs are harmful to pregnant women, but many still choose the services of a traditional midwife in preference to a midwife for economic reasons. However, subsequent studies (Shefner-Rogers 2004) indicate that increased knowledge of complications in pregnancy and positive attitude towards skilled health care providers and midwives, with support of the husband, can prevent maternal deaths.

Most Sundanese people are Muslim, with different Islamic backgrounds ranging from conservative to liberal. Sundanese culture and Islam are inextricably bound together: Sundanese are as keen to identify themselves as Muslim as they are Sundanese (Kahmad 2006; Newland 2000). Islam was accepted by the Sundanese through education and *dakwah* (propagation) in the fifteenth and sixteenth centuries (Kahmad 2006). The role of *ulama* and *kyai* as Islamic experts is significant in Sundanese society. Sometimes, these men are not only religious leaders who teach Islamic knowledge and give advice in religious matters, but they are also social leaders who deal with the social and psychological problems of their congregation (Horikoshi 1976). They wield charismatic influence over local as well as neighbouring residents—as can be seen in attendances at weekly or monthly preaching events (Millie 2008).

32 Marriage and sexuality

Marriage in Sundanese society has social and religious significance. Marriage is strongly recommended, if not obligated, by social and religious norms. In West Java, as in many other regions in Indonesia, marriage establishes a person's place in social life as an adult and a full member of society (Grijns 1987; Wessing 1978). Marriage in West Java is considered a familial and communal event that not only unites families but also involves community members. Thus, in most cases, marriage in West Java is considered to be parental business (or a parental obligation) (Muchtar and Umbara 1977). Accordingly, the approval of a marriage partner by parents is important. Unlike the Sasak people of Lombok (Bennett 2005a; Platt 2017) or the Bugis, in South Sulawesi (Idrus 2003), where elopement is common and acceptable, among the Sundanese this practice is uncommon.

In West Java, the ideal marriage partner should have four good qualities: *bebet, babat, bobot,* and *bibit,* literally: personal character, social equivalence, economic capability, and family background (Muchtar and Umbara 1977). In arranged marriages, judgment regarding these qualities is made by parents with the aim of matching the future couple with a long-lasting and harmonious married life. However, some cases of arranged marriage are also forced and many end up in divorce. In recent times, arranged marriage has become less common, instead being replaced by romantic or love marriage. More opportunities for both sexes to gain education and employment have meant more chances for socialising between the sexes.

The search for romantic love, usually called *cinta* (Ind.) or *bogoh* (S.) begins at around 14–15 years of age, during secondary school. At this stage, it is usually called *cinta monyet* (puppy love) where the feeling of liking (*suka*)/loving (*cinta*) someone of the opposite sex is not yet serious (Smith-Hefner 2005). In Sundanese, this stage is known as *kikindeuwan*. When the feeling develops into 'passionate love,' usually at a more mature age, there is an 'intense attraction that involves the intrusive thinking about one person within an erotic context' (Jankowiak and Paladino 2008, 13). This uncontrolled feeling towards the loved one, in certain Indonesian cultural contexts, is sometimes associated with magic (Jennaway 2002, 2003; Rottger-Rossler 2008). Among the Sundanese, this heightened feeling is called *kabungbulengan* (confusion) and when the targeted person has the same feelings, they are referred to as a *bobogohan* (lover) (Muchtar and Umbara 1977).

Understandings of courtship and courting behaviour differ across ethnic groups as well as between rural and urban areas of Indonesia. In rural society where there is a strong adherence to *adat* and religion, as in West Sumatra, courtship is tightly controlled (Parker 2009). For example, some people think that holding hands with a girlfriend or boyfriend can arouse sexual desire that can lead to illicit sex (*zina*). In contrast, in urban and heterogeneous social contexts, like Jakarta, courtship behaviour is loosely monitored and pre-marital sex is reportedly common among youth (Utomo 2002).

In arranged marriages, love does not precede married life. Many couples hardly know each other before marriage. They are told by older people that love will grow gradually. The gradual development of love and affection in married life in Indonesia is well presented by Birgitt Rottger-Rossler (2008) in her research on arranged marriage among the Makassarese of South Sulawesi. She reports the gradual development of feelings from total strangeness with no emotion, to intense feelings of love and intimacy (*ammaling-maling*) and mutual respect (*sikatutui*) across the duration of married life (Rottger-Rossler 2008, 151). In Sundanese, next to love (*bogoh*), the highest level of feeling to develop between the couple is *nyaah* (affection), where the couple shows mutual caring and respect and they avoid hurting each other.

A brief explanation of the marriage process in Sunda is provided here. Sundanese marriages have several steps: *neundeun omong* (entrusting a message); *nyeureuhan* (symbolic acceptance); *lamaran* (marriage proposal); *seserahan* (assigning); and *ijab kabul* (marriage contract). Before an official marriage proposal, the boy's parents, represented by his father, informally ask the girl's parents about the possibility of proposing. This is called *neundeun omong* (Muchtar and Umbara 1977). When the girl's parents have agreed, the next stage is *nyeureuhan* (from *seureuh* (S.), lit. betel leaf), which symbolically means an acceptance.[2] Several weeks before the wedding day, the process of *lamaran* (marriage proposal) takes place, where the boy's family proposes officially. The exchange of rings may also take place as a symbol that the couple is already taken and no one can make another proposal. Some couples get engaged if they wish to be bonded to each other but are not ready yet to marry; it could take months or years until they decide to marry. By contrast, in *lamaran* the family sets the wedding date soon after the marriage proposal. The wedding feast is organised by the girl's family and mostly held in the girl's house. These days, many weddings, especially where the family is considered to be well off, are held in rented halls or hotel ballrooms.

On the wedding day, the rite begins with welcoming the groom and his family, known as *seserahan*. The marriage ceremony (*akad nikah* (Ind.), *rapalan* (S.)) is usually set at 9 a.m. with the presence of the official marriage registrar from the Office of Religious Affairs (KUA). *Akad nikah* is usually held either in the bride's house or in the mosque nearest to the wedding venue. Apart from the bride and the groom, the marriage registrar, the bride's guardian (*wali*) and two witnesses are required for a valid Islamic marriage. The offer and acceptance, called *ijab kabul,* takes place between the groom and the bride's guardian, usually the father, or a male agnate. The *ijab kabul* is made in Indonesian, Sundanese, or Arabic, depending on the ability of the groom and the guardian.

Following the validation of the marriage contract by the KUA officer, the couple signs the marriage book (*buku nikah*) that has been prepared by the marriage registrar. The marriage book comes in two colours: green for the bride and brown for the groom; the content is the same (see Figures 1.1 and 1.2). This ceremony ends with the *sungkeman* (getting the blessing) from both parents.

The bride and the groom are then seated together in a special chair to receive blessings from the guests. Some couples perform other rituals such

34 *Marriage and sexuality*

Figure 1.1 My husband's Indonesian marriage book (*buku nikah*).
Source: Photographed by the author, 29 June 2012.

Figure 1.2 My own (wife's) Indonesian marriage book (*buku nikah*).
Source: Photographed by author, 29 June 2012.

as *nyawer* (lit. sprinkling rice, turmeric, and coins as a blessing for fortune) and *huap lingkung* (feeding each other) as a symbol of togetherness (Muchtar and Umbara 1977). Nowadays, in West Java and in Central Java, these traditional rituals are less often practised because the couple tends to focus on Islamic requirements (Smith-Hefner 2005).

Traditionally, West Java was known for its high rate of early marriage, with girls marrying when they were between 10 and 13 years old and some even before the age of 10 (McDonald and Abdurrahman 1974). *Kawin gantung* (suspended marriage) was also practised in several areas in West Java, where the girl was married off by her parents before the age of 10, but remained living in her parents' house to prevent cohabitation until she was a proper age (McDonald and Abdurrahman 1974; Wessing 1978). In the second decade of the twenty-first century, as reported by many researchers, child marriage in West Java has become less common.

In the second half of the twentieth century, there were changes to marriage patterns in Southeast Asia in general and in Indonesia in particular (Jones, Hull, and Mohamad 2011). In Indonesia, the increased age of marriage, increased education, and women's participation in paid work are factors influencing this new marriage pattern (Jones, Asari, and Djuartika 1994; Jones, Hull, and Mohamad 2011). In general, this new trend of marriage in Indonesia shows that women tend to delay marriage and choose their own partners. Data reported by Gavin Jones and Bina Gubhaju (2011, 50) show that in 1971 the percentage of females who remained single at 20–24 years was 18.5 percent. This increased significantly to 35.7 percent in 1990 and 51.4 percent in 2005. Among females aged 25–29 years, the data also indicate an increasing trend of delayed marriage from 5.0 percent in 1971 to 11.2 percent in 1990 and 19.7 percent in 2005 (ibid). In West Java, the average age of marriage for women now is 22.9 years (Jones and Gubhaju 2011, 51). The trend for women to remain single at the age of 30 and over has been identified, not only among middle-class, educated, urban women, but also among the lower socio-economic class as reported by Augustina Situmorang (2011) in West Java. According to Jones and Gubhaju (2011), West Java is no longer the province with the earliest marriage age. They further argue that 'strong cosmopolitanising' in urban areas like Bandung and the migration of people from Jakarta to suburban areas surrounding it are influencing marriage patterns in West Java (Jones and Gubhaju 2011, 53).

West Java is also known for its high rate of divorce. Factors associated with this development are early marriage, infertility, low education, and low income (Jones, Asari, and Djuartika 1994, 407; McDonald and Abdurrahman 1974, 20, 26). Surveys in this province indicated that most divorces happen in the early years of marriage (Jones, Asari, and Djuartika 1994, 398; McDonald and Abdurrahman 1974, 20). However, as many researchers of West Java have reported (Jones, Asari, and Djuartika 1994; McDonald and Abdurrahman 1974; Zuidberg 1978), this does not mean that the institution of marriage is declining. Many divorces are followed by remarriage.

Currently, however, the divorce rate remains high in West Java, with most applications for divorce lodged by the wife. Data from the Religious Court of the city of Bandung shows that in 2003, of the 1,871 divorce cases lodged, 505 were submitted by husbands and 1,207 by wives. The number of divorce cases had increased significantly by 2013 with 5,134—1,130 cases were lodged by husbands and 3,440 by wives (Pengadilan Agama Kota Bandung 2013). Women activists may present this data as a positive indication that women are no longer content to stay in unhappy marriages. Significantly, women who file for divorce may be viewed by the community as transgressing the ideal of the submissive and obedient wife (Parker, Riyani, and Nolan 2015).

Gender and sexuality: the Indonesian context

The terms gender (*jender*) and sexuality (*seksualitas*) are new to Indonesian society (Blackwood 2010). They are usually associated with biological sex or *jenis kelamin* (lit. genitalia) (Bennett 2005a; Davies 2010). Unlike sex, which refers to biological aspects of being male and female, gender is a socio-cultural construction attributed to men and women that differentiates their 'roles, function and responsibilities' in a given society (Jauhola 2012, 20). Similarly, sexuality is a social and cultural construction embedded in the social and cultural context where it varies according to differing social and cultural contexts.

The term sexuality, as used in this book, refers to social constructions of sexuality. Sexuality, according to the social constructionists, is not merely a biological identification, but also a product of social, cultural, and historical processes (Weeks 1989). Sexuality refers to the quality of being sexual that involves feelings, desires, practices, values, beliefs, and behaviour (Jackson 1978; Oakley 1972).

In Indonesia, the attribution of gender and sexuality starts early—when a baby is born, and even while the baby is in the mother's womb. The child's clothes, toys, wrapped gifts, and even ceremonies show these differences. At different life stages, the child learns different social norms and values according to its gender. Girls learn how to behave gracefully, to talk softly, to dress modestly, to guard their chastity, to be shy, and to be silent. They also learn to do housework at an early age to help their mothers. Meanwhile, boys learn to be strong and brave and that it is acceptable to be a bit naughty (*nakal*). These processes are reinforced by encounters with people in the family, at school, in religious institutions, and in broader society. In this way, gender norms are strongly embedded and influence the daily practices and relationships of women and men.

In this research, I argue that the regulation of gender and sexuality in Indonesia is influenced by various discourses, narratives, and norms. The practice and categorisation of gender and sexuality vary among regions in Indonesia. Different interpretations of Islamic teaching tend to regulate gender and sexuality in various ways. Different Indonesian governments in different eras have employed different gender and sexual ideologies: the Old

Order of Soekarno (1945–66), the New Order of Soeharto (1966–98), and the *Reformasi* era (1998–). This book focuses on contemporary debates on gender and sexuality in the Reform era, with particular attention to Islamic influences on women's sexuality.

The notion that sexuality is connected to biology is powerful. This opinion dominates in many societies, including Indonesia. In Indonesia, the dominant gender discourses deployed by the New Order regime are situated within heterosexual practice (Blackwood 2010; Wieringa 2012). Heteronormativity is the term that 'informs the normativity of daily life, including institutions, laws, and regulations that impact on the sexual and reproductive lives of members of society as well as the moral imperatives that influence people's personal lives' (Wieringa 2012, 518). According to this norm, socially standards and normal sexual activity occurs only between a man and a woman. The woman should be passive and submissive, and sexual relations should be aimed at reproduction (Wieringa, Katjasungkana, and Hidayana 2007).

In the Indonesian context, (hetero) sexual relations are only sanctioned within marriage. This norm is backed through the media, educational institutions, family, and state regulations. Other expressions of sexuality such as gay, lesbian, *waria* (transgender), pre-marital, and extra-marital sex are considered deviant and are therefore stigmatised (Blackwood 2010; Wieringa 2012). Tom Boellstorff (2005) reports that gay men in Indonesia struggle between expressing their desires and surrendering to the standard norms; and gay Muslims fear their behaviour is sinful.

The institutionalisation of heterosexual relations has neglected the discussion and experience of women's sexuality in Indonesia. My book, therefore, tries to explore the experiences of married women in their sexual relationships with their husbands.

Many scholars argue that the gender ideology of the New Order era was taught systematically over its duration through school, family, community events, and government development programs and policies. During the *Reformasi* era, this gender ideology has been challenged by many gender activists promoting democracy and human rights. They demand more equal relations between women and men, and encourage women's participation in the public sphere, in politics, in education, in employment, and at home (Brenner 2011; White and Anshor 2004). Challenges to an earlier gender ideology have resulted in: the opportunity for a woman to become a president; the employment of women in various occupations; and the enactment of Law No. 23 on the Eradication of Domestic Violence, 2004 (UU PKDRT). However, along with this government support for democracy and human rights emerged a very conservative interpretation of Islam. The moderate groups who promote democracy and gender equality are 'facing serious new challenges' because the conservative movements threaten their efforts (Hefner 2008, 39). The conservative organisations influence politics and government regulations, for example, in the establishment of some shari'a-based local governments and Anti-Pornography Law No. 44, 2008

(Brenner 2011; Feillard and Doorn-Haeder 2013; Hefner 2008; White and Anshor 2004).

Religion has the potential to be one of the most influential institutions in transforming society. It is 'among the foremost of institutions which conserve society, encoding stabilizing worldviews and values and transmitting these from generation to generation' (Falk 1985, 15). Thus, it can also be a force for the reproduction of societal values and norms. In regulating gender and sexuality, religion also influences its adherents through its precepts. Islam, as the predominant religion in Indonesia, influences the organisation of gender and sexuality in Indonesia. This research aims to investigate the influence of Islamic teachings about sexuality on married women's perceptions and behaviour in their marital sexual relationships.

Research on sexuality in Indonesia

In Indonesia, research on sexuality has been conducted by several scholars from different perspectives. Scholars have addressed various topics such as: adolescent sexuality (Holzner and Oetomo 2004; Parker 2008; Simon and Paxton 2004; Utomo and McDonald 2009); same-sex relations (Blackwood 1998; Boellstorff 2003, 2005; Davies 2010; Howard 1996; Murray 1999; Oetomo 1996; Wieringa 1999); sexual violence (Bennett, Andajani-Sutjahjo, and Idrus 2011; Binahayati 2011; Idrus 2001); sexually transmitted diseases (STDs) (Kroeger 2000); prostitution (Hull, Sulistyaningsih, and Jones 1997; Murray 1991); and pornography (Bungin 2003).

Research on adolescent sexuality in Indonesia mainly examines changing sexual patterns of adolescents, from abstinence to more permissive engagement in pre-marital sex (Holzner and Oetomo 2004; Purdy 2006; Simon and Paxton 2004; Utomo and McDonald 2009). Iwu Utomo and Peter McDonald (2009) suggest that various influences (global media, education, and westernisation) have led to the changed attitudes and behaviour of youth. This permissiveness can result in unwanted pregnancies and illegal and unsafe abortions. Many youth in Indonesia have limited knowledge of safe sex as a result of limited services providing adolescents with information on sexual and reproductive rights (Bennett 2005a).

In contrast to the above-mentioned research on active adolescent sexuality in Indonesia, research by Parker (2008) and Linda Bennett (2007) presents a rather different picture. Apart from the fact that they are active sexual agents, adolescents in Indonesia also have something to offer as the next generation of this country; their dedication to education, morality, and religion. Parker (2008, 4) shows that 'something different happens' in Indonesian adolescence concerning their sexuality. She indicates that adolescents in Indonesia can be diligent, industrious, and ambitious in their study to work for a bright future.

Almost all the researchers agree that sex education in Indonesia is a crucial issue. Not only does it provide young people with useful information concerning their sexuality and rights, but it also enhances their understanding of their sexual responsibilities towards their partners, in relation to pregnancy and sexual diseases. Research by Utomo (2003) and Parker (2008) among school students shows that almost all respondents are keen to have sex education in their school curricula. Many school students have very little information concerning their sexuality, as parents do not usually provide it.

In providing sex education in Indonesia, Bennett (2007, 383) suggests that religious values and cultural norms should be considered. She says that the Indonesian government has the obligation to ensure 'the provision of comprehensive and religiously appropriate sex education for Indonesia's Muslim youth.' Bennett (2007) further reports that some *pesantren* have established sex education and reproductive rights in their curricula. Some of the organisations that actively promote sexual and reproductive rights in *pesantren* are the Society for *Pesantren* and Community Development (P3M), the National Commission on Violence against Women (Komnas Perempuan), the Forum for the Study of *Kitab Kuning* (FK3), and Rahima and the Fahmina Institute (Brenner 2011; Feillard and Doorn-Harder 2013; Rinaldo 2010; Sciortino, Marcoes-Natsir, and Masudi 1996; White and Anshor 2004).

Alternative sexualities in Indonesia have gained visibility since the 1980s (Blackwood 2007). Transgender identities are more visible than male homosexuality and lesbianism. Terms related to homosexuality, like *'lesbi'* and *'gay,'* have been borrowed from English through the media (Blackwood 1995a; Boellstorff 2003). Evelyn Blackwood (2007) argues that the representation of these alternative sexualities in Indonesia is stigmatised and even criminalised. Many gay and lesbian Indonesians consider themselves to be *'sakit'* (ill) (Blackwood 1998; Boellstorff 2005; Howard 1996; Murray 1999). Some gay Muslims associate their gayness with sin (Boellstorff 2005). This is the main reason that gays and lesbians hide their identity from their families and society (Offord 2003). However, research by Sharyn Davies (2010) on *calabai* (transgender males) and *bissu* (androgynous shamans) revealed that they are well recognised and accepted in the Bugis cultural context as they have traditional roles in the community, but *calalai* (transgender females) are less visible than *calabai*.

Research on women's sexuality in Indonesia is limited. Bennett (2005a) has made a significant contribution with her work on single Muslim women's sexuality in Lombok. She explored single women's identities, expressions of desire, relationships, and lifestyles prior to marriage. She reported that for single women, the social regulation of women's sexuality is emphasised by guarding their purity. Virginity is highly valued before marriage and guarding one's reputation is an important aspect of being a prospective wife (Bennett 2005a; on the Bugis see Idrus 2003). Dwi Rubiyanti Kholifah (2005) also examined the sexual experiences of single young women, particularly in the *pesantren* community. She showed that sexual fantasy and desire are common among them, but young female *santri* (students) try to ignore these fantasies and desires.

Likewise, research on married women's sexuality is quite limited. Sexual experiences and sexuality within the marital relationship in Indonesia are considered private. Lily Munir investigated power within the marital sexual relationship in Java. She found that Javanese marriage is a relationship based on hierarchy and that sexual relations are based on inequality (2002, 193). She noted that Javanese tradition and a gender-biased interpretation of Islamic teachings supported each other in promoting women's sexual subordination. In her book on polygyny, Nina Nurmila (2009) did not discuss sex in polygynous marriage at any length, but she did find that disgust and jealousy interfered with the sexual pleasure of women in polygynous marriages. Polygyny, as practised by Indonesian men, is merely about addressing men's sexual drive and ignores women's sexual needs (Wichelen 2010).

Sexual violence in marriage is reportedly common in Indonesia. Research by Idrus (2001), Linda Bennett, Sari Andajani-Soetjahjo, and Nurul Idrus (2011), and Rusyidi Binahayati (2011) found that many women experience violence in their marital relationships. Bennett, Andajani-Soetjahjo, and Idrus (2011, 156) reported that sexual abuse at home was high. Idrus (2001, 46) confirms that sexual violence within marriage is considered 'normal' and sometimes it is used as a way to show the man's superiority over his wife. She detailed marital rape in her research and reported that it placed women under threat and in a position that forced them to engage in sex with their husbands (Idrus 1999). Nevertheless, as Binahayati (2011) reported, although women experienced violence from their husbands, rarely did they report it despite the enactment of the law against domestic violence, as mentioned above.

Desire and pleasure are absent from academic discussions on women's sexuality. Taboo, shame, and silence characterise the discussion of female sexuality. Bennett (2005a) notes that it is not easy for women to explore sexual desires and pleasure in Indonesia. As Megan Jennaway reports (2003), women's desires are denied in the Indonesian cultural context.

In Indonesian culture, women's sexuality is controlled and regulated, with religion and the state both being significantly influential in controlling women's sexuality. In general, women are ordered to control their desire. In Makassar, where the majority of the population is Muslim, Idrus (2003) reported that daughters should be closely monitored and guarded by male family members to protect the family honour (*siri*). The women, therefore, were required to guard their behaviour, not flirt with men or engage in sex. Similarly, in Lombok, single women have to be polite and refined to avoid damaging their reputation as respectable, prospective wives (Bennett 2005a). In Bali, where most people are Hindus, single women should not act too aggressively. They must dress modestly and guard their chastity (Jennaway 2002), while married women should be 'neither seductive nor lustful' (Parker 2001, 182).

Religion, Islam in particular, in many instances, shares prescriptions with *adat* concerning women's sexuality (Bennett 2005a; Idrus 2003; Munir 2002;

Platt 2017). Adat and Islam reinforce each other to control women's bodies and sexuality. For example, the notion of *zina,* an Islamic term for illicit sexual relations, is focused more on women than on men. Men who commit *zina* are more tolerated than women (Bennett 2005b). Women maintain their good reputation in public by choosing appropriate dress, in this case, veiling. Wearing the Islamic headscarf (*jilbab*) is one form of controlling the female body and both male and female sexuality.

In the Reform era, one of the most contested debates concerning sexuality was the Anti-Pornography Law No. 44 of 2008. Instead of banning the production and circulation of pornographic material, the Pornography Law concentrates on public morality. It targets women's dress, women's bodies, and women's mobility (Feillard and Doorn-Harder 2013). It also criminalises a variety of sexual practices (Wichelen 2010). It seems that in the *Reformasi* era, the government is strongly influenced by more conservative Islamic groups aiming to control public morality (Brenner 2011; Wichelen 2010).

In the above literature, most scholarly attention is directed at issues concerning same-sex and pre-marital sexuality. Little attention is given to the study of women's sexuality within the marital relationship. Sexual relations in marriage are usually considered normal and therefore unproblematic. In Indonesia, a considerable amount of research has been done on same-sex relations and very little on 'hegemonic heterosexuality' (Parker 2008, para. 19). Although there are many studies on kinship, marriage, and family in Indonesia, the sexual life of the married couple has not been a focus of research. This book addresses this gap, contributing, as it does, to the understanding of women's sexual experiences in marriage and the influence of Islamic teachings on their sexuality.

Marriage and sexuality: Islamic perspectives

In this section, I explore marriage and sexuality in Islam. I explore the way Islam regulates marriage and sexuality and discuss the literature on these topics. I have divided the section into two parts. The first part discusses important topics associated with marriage such as the requirements of marriage, rights and duties, *mahar* (bride price), marriage partner preferences, and divorce. I also provide detailed discussion of polygyny, men's authority in marriage, and attempts at the reform of marriage law in Muslim societies. In the second part I explore sexuality issues in Muslim societies: female sexuality associated with *fitnah* and *'awra*, virginity, female circumcision, family planning, contraception, abortion, rape, and *zina*. I also present criticisms of Muslim scholars' attitudes towards traditional norms of sex and sexuality. These topics are central to the discussion of women's experiences of marriage and sexuality in the data chapters, as many women referred to Islamic perspectives as their guide.

The regulation of marriage and sexuality in Islam is derived from Islamic texts, and not necessarily taken from the Qur'an alone. Sources include the Hadith, interpretations of the Qur'an and Hadith, and Islamic law. Because there are various sources, it is worth addressing the diversity of understandings and practices of these topics in Muslim societies. In reality, the application of such understandings varies according to time and context.

The Qur'an is believed to be God's message verbatim and is the highest and the primary source of Islam. However, there are a huge number of interpretations recorded over a long period by many Muslim scholars (*ulama*). Along with Qur'anic interpretations, the *ulama* formed Islamic law in the eighth century (Hallaq 2009). Islamic law is a product of human history and socio-cultural understandings of Islamic texts. The development of Islamic law involved a dialectical process of interaction with particular cases of social, moral, and material conditions in social reality (Hallaq 2009). It is subject to change in accordance with changes in society. Diversity among the four schools of law (*madzhab*) in Islam shows this process of construction occurred in different places and times associated with different social, cultural, and political conditions (Mas'ud 2009). There are four schools of law (*madzhab*) in Sunni Islam, namely, Hanbali, Maliki, Hanafi, and Shafi'i— each named after its founder. The majority of Muslims in Indonesia follow the Shafi'i school.

Marriage in Islam

Marriage is highly recommended by Islam. It is related to guarding one's chastity (Q. 4: 25). Marriage in Islam is a contract between two parties as part of the *Sunnah* (practised by the Prophet Muhammad). Marriage according to Islam lies between an *ibadah* (religious duty) and a *mu'amalah* (social/private action). Thus getting married is not only a matter of social and inter-personal relations but also a matter of obeying one of God's commands. Thus, celibacy is unsupported in Islam. Many Islamic texts make this recommendation:

> Marry those among you who are single, or the virtuous ones among your slaves, male or female: If they are in poverty, Allah will give them means out of His grace: for Allah encompasseth all, and He knoweth all things.
>
> (Q. 24: 32)[3]

> Narrated Abdullah: We were with the Prophet while we were young and had no wealth. So Allah's Messenger said, 'O young people! Whoever among you is able to marry, should marry, because it helps him lower his gaze and guard his modesty (i.e. his private parts from committing illegal sexual intercourse etc.), and whoever is not able to marry, should fast, as fasting diminishes his sexual power.'
>
> (Al-Bukhari 1997, vol. 7, Hadith no. 5066, 21)

Traditional Muslim scholars have written extensively about marriage. Two *kitab* are referred to in discussing marriage: *Fiqh ala Madzahib al-Arba'a* from Al-Jaziry (2003) and *al-Fiqh al-Islam wa Adillatuhu* by Al-Zuhaily (1985), and they provide opinions from the four Sunni Muslim legal schools. Here I present some of the key issues in discussing marriage in Islam, mostly with reference to the Shafi'i school of law as the most preferred and followed *madzhab* in Indonesia (Feener 2007). This preference is significant to the discussion of my findings for this research, but in several places, I also provide different opinions from other schools.

Definition

Marriage in Islam is called *nikah*. Another word that is usually used with the same meaning is *zawaj*. The word *nikah*, originally, meant sexual intercourse (*wath', dlom'*) but it also referred to the marriage contract (Al-Jaziry 2003). The Qur'an uses both words (*nikah* and *zawaj*) to refer to both meanings.

Shafi'i jurists define *nikah* as 'a contract that grants [the two parties] a permissible sexual enjoyment (*milk wath'*) using the word *inkah* (n-k-h) or *tazwij* (z-w-j)' (Al-Jaziry 2003, 8). Definitions by other jurists have similar meanings, recognising *nikah* as a contract that allows a man (specifically) to enjoy a woman sexually (not limited to intercourse) (Al-Jaziry 2003).

The definition of marriage derived from the Muslim jurists implies that the primary purpose and meaning of marriage is a contractual deed to organise the sexual life of man and woman in a lawful manner to form a family in society. The contract has individual and social significance. It is the contract that permits two persons to engage in sex, which is otherwise forbidden to them, in accordance with social and religious consensus. However, as seen from the definition, this sexual engagement gives priority to a man to enjoy sex with a woman and not the other way around. This definition of marriage is usually used by men to claim that sex in marriage is the husbands' right.

From the definition, it also can be inferred that the purpose of marriage is procreation as a possible result of sexual activity. The Qur'anic verse (16: 72) mentions: 'And Allah has made for you mates (and companions) of your own nature, and made for you, out of them, sons and daughters and grandchildren, and provided for you sustenance of the best.' Marriage establishes the propagation of the human species. It also establishes the existence of the Muslim *ummah* (society) and easy recognition of those children born as legitimate in relation to guardianship and parentage.

The requirements for a valid marriage

According to the Shafi'i school, a valid marriage should meet five requirements: (1) prospective husband; (2) prospective wife; (3) guardianship; (4) two witnesses; and (5) the offer and the acceptance (*ijab* and *qabul*)

(Al-Jaziry 2003, 32). The *ijab* and *qabul* is performed between the prospective husband and the woman's guardian (*wali*). The woman's guardian should be from the male line and preferably the father, grandfather, brother, or uncle. Accordingly, a woman cannot perform marriage on her own behalf; it is invalid according to the Shafi'i *madzhab*. However, the Hanafi *madzhab* stipulates that an adult woman, single or widowed, can marry without a guardian acting on her behalf (Al-Jaziry 2003, 34).

In Indonesian Marriage Law (No. 1/1974), which is influenced by the Shafi'i School, the *wali* is essential for a valid marriage. There are two kinds of *wali*: first, the agnate *wali* includes father, grandfather, brothers, and uncles from the male line; and the second, a judge (*wali hakim*), in case there are no relatives available in the family because of death, absence or refusal. *Wali hakim* is the *wali* appointed by the government to perform the marriage. In Indonesia, the role is assigned to the head of the KUA in the district where the marriage takes place.

Another requirement that needs to be fulfilled during the marriage contract is the payment of *mahar*. Mahar (Ind. *mas kawin*) is a gift given to the bride from the husband by virtue of the marriage contract as a sign of love (Q. 4: 4, 20, 24, 25). Much of the literature discussing *mahar* translates the word as dowry, but it is best translated as bride price.[4] Many jurists consider the payment of the bride price (*mahar*) as an exchange for the husband's sexual access to his wife based on the interpretation of Q. 4: 24 and 2: 237:

> Seeing that ye derive benefit from them, give them their dowers (at least) as prescribed; but if, after a dower is prescribed, ye agree mutually (to vary it), there is no blame on you, and Allah is All-knowing, All-wise.
> (Q. 4: 24)

Almost all schools of law in Islam agree that *mahar* is a kind of compensation paid by the husband for his sexual enjoyment of his wife (Al-Zuhaily 1985, 99).

Kecia Ali (2006, xxv) criticises this classical jurisprudent regulation of marriage as the jurists tend to classify it under the term *milk*, which means 'ownership, dominion, or control,' as the basis for lawful sexual activity. In the jurists' opinion, the bride price is an exchange for *milk nikah*: the husband's exclusive dominion over his wife. Ali says that this kind of logic is used to justify the assumption that the wife should be sexually available to the husband.

When the contract is valid, it assigns certain duties and rights to each of the married couple. The husband's duties become the wife's rights and vice versa, which will be discussed below.

Rights and obligations

The allocation of rights and obligations in marriage for both partners varies from one jurist to another. Different schools of law state different rights and obligations and seem to expand beyond what is stated in the Qur'an. However, two basic duties and rights that are believed to be complementary have almost become the consensus among the majority of jurists. They are *nafaqa* (Ind. *nafkah;* maintenance) for the husband and *ta'at* (obedience) for the wife. *Nafaqa* is material support that the husband is obliged to provide when he enters married life. This idea is referred to in the Qur'anic verses 2: 233 and 4: 34 (I will explain the latter verse in more detail below). *Ta'at* is considered to be a wife's duty towards her husband. Most of the jurists agree that because a husband gives *nafaqa,* he deserves her obedience (Al-Zuhaily 1985). The mutual duties and rights as stated in the Qur'an are: (1) to treat each other adequately (Q. 4: 19); (2) to create marriage in mutual love and affection (Q. 30: 21); and (3) to protect the family from any harm and misconduct (Q. 66: 6).

Marriage partner

In finding a marriage partner, Islam prescribes which partners are permissible and which are forbidden. The preferred marriage partners, based on the Qur'an, are single, virtuous people who are believers (*mu'minin*) (Q. 24: 32; 4: 25). While seeking partners from among *musyrikun* (a worshipper of idols) is forbidden for Muslim men and Muslim women (Q.2: 221), inter-religious marriage with 'people of the Book' (*ahl kitab*) is permissible for Muslim men only (Q. 5: 5).[5] The Qur'an also lists several types of persons one is forbidden from marrying. They are called *mahram,* and are prohibited because of blood relationship, affinity, or by fosterage.[6]

The Hadith also provide criteria for selecting a marriage partner. The term *kafa'ah* (*kufu'* (A.), (*sepadan* (Ind.), equivalence) is an important aspect in selecting a mate. There are four *kafa'ah* criteria that should be considered, namely, wealth (*maal*), beauty (*jamal*), lineage (*nasb*), and religion (*diin*).[7] These criteria were set to avoid a significant relational gap in married life—though, in practice, these criteria are not always applied.

Polygyny

Polygyny is a hot topic in discussions on Islamic marriage. The issue emerged in relation to Q. 4: 3: 'If ye fear that ye shall not be able to deal justly with the orphans, marry women of your choice, two or three or four; but if ye fear that ye shall not be able to deal justly (with them), then only one.' In fact, this passage is concerned with the treatment of orphans, not polygyny (Nurmila 2009; Wadud 1999). The practice of polygyny is not without strict requirements, as stated in the above Qur'anic verse. Many progressive scholars believe that God's permission to marry up to four women is not to be practised in general but only in very strict and special cases (Abu Zayd 2000; Al-Hibri 1982; Shahrur 1994; Wadud 1999). In addition, some commentators link polygyny to another verse—Q. 4: 129[8]—which states that men will never be able to do justice to several wives. They argue that this verse should be interpreted as indicating that polygyny is impossible to practise (Wadud 2006).

In practice, however, many Muslim men understand Q. 4: 3 as giving them permission to practise polygyny. The polygyny proponents seem to ignore the conditions associated with polygyny. In Indonesia, as reported by Euis Nurlaelawati (2013), the courts grant permission for husbands who wish to practice polygyny on the grounds that their sexual desire is high. Asma Barlas (2002) argues that this verse does not serve a sexual function, but that in fact the polygyny verse should be seen as a restriction of polygyny, to be practised only when a special requirement (i.e. justice for orphans) is to be satisfied; it was not intended primarily to satisfy sexual desire.

Divorce

Islam gives both parties the right to report for divorce (Q. 2: 229). Dissolution of marriage, apart from death, can take three forms: *thalaq* (lit. release), *khulu'* (lit. compensation), and *fasakh* (lit. annulment).

Thalaq is repudiation by the husband to terminate the marriage and is unilateral. According to the Muslim jurists' consensus, the husband can simply pronounce 'I divorce you' and it is considered a valid form of divorce. In many Muslim countries, this practice has been restricted by regulating that a divorce is valid only when it is registered with the court.

Thalaq can be divided into two categories: revocable (*thalaq raj'i*) and irrevocable (*thalaq ba'in*) (Al-Jaziry 2003, 282). *Thalaq raj'i* is when the husband pronounces divorce once or twice. In *thalaq raj'i* the husband can take back the wife either during the *'iddah* (waiting period after divorce) or after *'iddah*. *Thalaq ba'in* (irrevocable divorce) is when the husband pronounces triple divorce at one time ('I divorce you, I divorce you, and I divorce you') or he divorces his wife for the third time (after twice reconciling with her). When the husband pronounces *thalaq ba'in*, he cannot return to his former wife unless after she has married another man, consummated the marriage, and she is then either separated by divorce or death from her second marriage (Q.2: 230).

The Qur'an, in fact, permits divorce only twice and does not encourage a third divorce. Most jurists also reject a third divorce. The purpose is to prevent the uncertainty of divorce by a man towards his wife and to encourage men to be careful in pronouncing divorce. However, in some Muslim societies, many cases show that the husband pronounces the triple *thalaq* in one sitting, with or without the intention to do so (because he is drunk or angry) (Arshad 2010).

The second form of divorce is called *khulu'*. *Khulu'* is dissolution of marriage requested by the wife with the husband's consent, by giving the husband certain compensation (Al-Jaziry 2003, 346). The compensation can be either to return the *mahar* or to pay him financial compensation agreed to by both parties (*iwadh*) as stated in Q. 2: 229.

The third form of divorce is *fasakh*. *Fasakh* is annulment of the marriage for reasons such as failure to fulfil marriage requirements or other

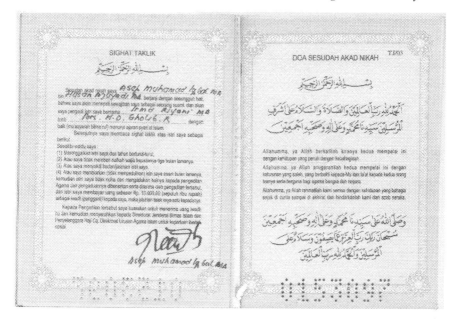

Figure 1.3 Shighat Taklik Talak.

Source: Photographed by the author from the back of her marriage book, 29 June 2012.

circumstances deemed harmful to the marriage. The verdict should take place in the court and be made by a judge. Conditions that enable both parties to report for divorce include failure by the husband to pay maintenance, desertion and maltreatment. In Indonesia, these three conditions are called *shighat taklik talak* (see Figure 1.3) and are printed at the back of the marriage book (*buku nikah*).

'Iddah and maintenance after divorce

'Iddah is a waiting period, after the dissolution of a marriage either by divorce or by death. The *'iddah* for divorced women is three menstrual cycles (Q. 2: 228). The idea of this *'iddah* is to give time for both parties to consider reconciliation of the marriage, and to ascertain that the woman is not pregnant from her previous husband in order to prevent disputes over lineage and guardianship of possible children. Within this period the wife should not marry another man, except if the husband wants to reunite. If the divorce took place while the wife was pregnant, then the waiting period for her is until delivery (Q. 65: 4). *'Iddah* does not apply to divorcees who have not had sexual intercourse with their husband (Q. 33: 49). The *'iddah* for women who no longer menstruate or who have not yet started to menstruate is three months (Q. 65: 4). By contrast, there is no certain *'iddah* assigned

48 *Marriage and sexuality*

to men after divorce, meaning that they can marry other women as soon as they please. In the case of marital separation by death, *'iddah* for both sexes is four months and ten days (Q. 2: 234).

During the period of *'iddah*, the divorced woman is entitled to maintenance in a suitable manner (Q. 2: 241). The divorced pregnant woman is entitled to maintenance and housing until she delivers the baby. If she breastfeeds the baby, they are both entitled to maintenance. In the case that the ex-wife cannot nurse the baby, with mutual consent the parents can hire another woman to breastfeed the baby (Q. 2: 233; 65: 6); when the former husband has died, his heir is responsible for taking care of his ex-wife and the baby. The widow can spend time in her husband's house and she is entitled to maintenance for one year. The family of her husband should look after her and treat her kindly (Q. 2: 240).

The concept of men's authority over women

> Men are the protectors and maintainers of [*qawwamun 'ala*] women, because Allah has given the one more (strength) [*faddala*] than the other, and because they support them from their means. Therefore, the righteous women [*shalihaat*] are devoutly obedient [*qanitat*], and guard in (the husband's) absence what Allah would have them guard. As to those women on whose part ye fear disloyalty and ill-conduct [*nushuz*], admonish them (first), (next), refuse to share their beds, (and last) chastise them [*idribu*] (lightly); but if they return to obedience, seek not against them means (of annoyance): For Allah is Most High, Great (above you all).
>
> (Q. 4:34)

There are three key terms in this verse that represent three themes: *qawwam, nushuz,* and *idribu*, often translated respectively as men's authority, women's disobedience, and the striking of one's wife. There have been various translations, interpretations, and understandings of this verse from Muslim scholars since the first time the verse was revealed.

The word *qawwamun* has been translated into English translations of the Qur'an as 'in charge of' (Pickthall 1930), 'maintainers' (Maulana M. Ali 1973), 'protectors and maintainers' (Ali 2000), 'the support' (Ahmed Ali 1993), and 'take full care' (Asad 2003). The traditionalist interpretation of this verse can be traced back to Al-Thabari (839–923), one of the well-known classic Qur'anic interpreters, and his interpretation is considered to be the most cited to date (Dunn and Kellison 2010). According to Al-Thabari, men's authority over women is limited to financial matters, as the verse states clearly (Al-Thabari 1992). Other traditionalist interpreters after Al-Thabari like Ibnu Kathir, Al-Zamakhsyari, and Al-Razi expanded the term *qawwam* to other aspects, such as mental and physical superiority of men over women, stating that men are more rational and stronger than women, who are considered weaker and more emotional (Dunn and Kellison 2010). Azizah al-Hibri (1982, 217) objected to this kind of interpretation and considered it as 'unwarranted' because there is nothing in the verse to support this argument.

The reformist Muslim scholars understand this verse differently. Amina Wadud (1999) argues that Muslims should read this verse within its context (i.e. the first time it was revealed) and understand it hermeneutically, according to the time when it was practised by Muslims. In understanding the term *qawwam,* Wadud (1999), alongside Al-Hibri (1982), argue that the men's *qawwam* towards women can only occur if two conditions are met, as stated in the verse above: first, men have more means or more prominence than women; and second, men spend their wealth on supporting women. Wadud (1999), Al-Hibri (1982), and Nasr Hamid Abu Zayd (2000) conclude that these privileges and responsibilities are conditional and that this *qawwam* can be applied to both men and women in marriage as they are partners and their responsibilities are interdependent. For this reason, Khaled Abou el Fadl (2001a) argues that when both wife and husband contribute to the family income, they share the guardianship of each other.

Al-Thabari interpreted *nushuz* as a wife's disobedience towards her husband, which may include refusing sexual intercourse. Reformist Muslims like Wadud (1999) reject this interpretation, because the term *nushuz* also applies to men as mentioned in Q. 4: 128. She argues that *nushuz* is better translated as 'disruption of marital harmony' (Wadud 1999, 74). In this case, three solutions are offered by the Qur'an: first, verbal advice; second, sleep in separate beds (a cooling down process); and third, and only in a severe case, severe punishment (*idribu*). In her later book, *Inside the Gender Jihad* (2006), Wadud argues that it is not possible to tolerate a man striking a woman. Although the text says so, the Muslim community cannot tolerate any violence towards women because this is against the spirit of Qur'anic justice as a whole (Wadud 2006). In understanding the word *idribu,* Barlas (2002) suggests that it means a symbolic action and the Qur'an uses it as a restrictive rather than prescriptive command, as *idribu* is considered as a last resort in dealing with marital disorder.

Riffat Hassan (1990) argues that this verse (Q. 4: 34) should be understood as a functional relationship between men and women in the Muslim community designed to build harmony. If men support women materially then women should also fulfil their duties that are related to child bearing (Hassan 1990). Barlas (2002) and Asghar Engineer (2005) also note that this verse obligates men to support women economically and this obligation does not at the same time appoint men as head of the family.

Sa'diyya Shaikh (2007, 70) takes a different approach in understanding this verse, which she called '*tafsir* through praxis.' This *tafsir* (interpretation), according to her, is based on the real experiences of ordinary women (in South Africa) dealing with their husbands' violence, and relates to the texts and Islamic ethics. These women's abusive experiences forced them to develop their own religious identity to defend them against such violence. They argue that God is just and does not tolerate any violence towards other human beings (Shaikh 2007).

Ayesha Chaudhry, Rachel Muers, and Randy Rashkover (2009), however, have a different understanding of this verse (Q. 4: 34). According to them, God seems to give more preference to men and supports the patriarchal system through text. After reading this verse, they consider the Qur'anic text as 'primarily patriarchal and without emancipatory potential for women reading the text today' (Chaudhry, Muers, and Rashkover 2009, 202). Their biggest fear is that no matter how hard Muslim reformists try to find alternative interpretations to avoid men's absolute superiority over women, the dominant understanding of most Muslims who read this verse is literal, and in practice this verse will always be used to legitimate men's violence in the name of religious doctrine.

Attempts to reform marriage law in Muslim societies

Islamic revivalism, modernity and the rise of Islamic feminism have brought new perspectives to the discussion of Muslim family law in many Muslim countries. Demands for reform of the legal system have been made in countries like Egypt, Morocco, and many others in the Middle East, as well as in Muslim societies in Asia. These reform attempts certainly invite heated debate about revised formulations of the law amongst various political and ideological interests (Hallaq 2009).

In these countries, several aspects of marriage have been subject to reform, including registration and documentation of marriage, divorce, and inheritance; prevention of child marriage including punishment for those who practise it; restriction of polygyny;[9] and raising the age of marriage for girls and boys (Esposito and DeLong-Bas 2001; Welchman 2007).

In Indonesia, issues surrounding marriage were the abiding concern of the women's movement after independence in 1945. Limited reforms were codified in Indonesian Marriage Law (No. 1/1974) such as requiring the registration of marriage, reporting divorce to the court, setting the minimum marriage age to 16 years for girls and 19 for boys,[10] and restricting polygyny. Further reforms have been proposed to amend the existing law to regulate marriage so it is a more equal relationship. This process was initiated in 2003 by the Institute for Legal Aid (LBH APIK) and the Jaringan Kerja Prolegnas Pro Perempuan (JKP3), the National Working Network of Pro-Women's Legislation).

In accordance with this attempt to amend the 1974 Marriage Law, a team lead by Musdah Mulia proposed several changes to the Compilation of Islamic Law (KHI) to establish a more egalitarian marital relationship. Considerations for change to the KHI included a minimum marriage age of 19 years for both men and women, each party being free to contract his or her own marriage (taking into account the Hanafi *madzhab,* as described above), and many others. Unfortunately, this draft was ultimately withdrawn from consideration in 2005 due to objections from a large number of Islamist organisations (Mulia and Cammack 2007).

Apart from reform attempts in Muslim countries, progressive Muslim scholars have also made efforts to criticise and re-examine existing laws and the interpretation of Islamic sources. Progressive Muslim scholars, like Wadud, Barlas, Fatima Mernissi, Kecia Ali, Engineer, Abou el Fadl, and many others, raise awareness by applying new methods of interpretation of the Qur'an, and by paying attention to the context, the message of the Qur'an as a whole, and the ethics and justice of the Qur'an. With regards to the marital relationship, they refer to the Qur'anic spirit of mutuality in marriage, as in the following:

> And among His signs is this, that He created for you mates from among yourselves, that ye may dwell in tranquillity with them, and He has put love and mercy between your (hearts): verily, in that are Signs for those who reflect.
>
> (Q. 30: 21)

> Permitted to you, on the night of the fasts, is the approach to your wives. *They are your garments and ye are their garments.* Allah knoweth what ye used to do secretly among yourselves; but He turned to you and forgave you; so now associate with them, and seek what Allah hath ordained for you [my emphasis].
>
> (Q. 2: 187)

From the above verses, marriage should be seen as a mutual contract between a couple and inferiority is not assigned to one or other of the parties (Goolam 2006). Attempted reforms of legal systems and of Qur'anic understanding are promising steps towards more equitable marital relationships.

Sexuality in Islam

There are shared beliefs among Muslims in many Muslim countries concerning sexuality in Islam. These beliefs may include that Islam views sex positively, which means that it recognises sex as part of human nature (*fitrah*). However, sexual relations should only be conducted within married life. Sex outside the marital bond is considered *zina.* Heterosexual relations are the norm. Any sexual practices and identities outside this norm are considered deviant. Men's sexual desire is privileged, while women's sexual desire is feared. Islam also recognises the purpose of sex within marriage as not only for procreation but also for pleasure.

Today's writings on sexuality in Islam challenge several beliefs that are considered to contradict human nature and neglect certain aspects of sexuality practised by Muslims around the globe. However, traditional attitudes towards sexuality in Islam are still thought to be the standard and dominant beliefs among Muslims in many countries. Below, I review certain works on Islam and sexuality covering female sexuality in relation to the concepts of *fitnah*, *'awra*, virginity, female circumcision, family planning, contraception, abortion, rape, *zina,* and some criticisms of traditional beliefs on sexuality.

Female sexuality in Muslim societies

Addressing sexuality, especially female sexuality, is still considered taboo and dangerous in Muslim societies. In fact, according to Evelyne Accad, the issue of female sexuality in developing countries is related to resisting male domination. Her research among Muslim women in Tunisia and Lebanon showed that 'women experience so much pain in remembering past events in their lives connected with sexuality' (2000, 40).

Research in other Muslim societies, like Iran, showed that women knew little about how their body works and were responsible for maintaining purity by controlling their bodily movements. Most of the women learned what is socially acceptable and unacceptable through experience (Bauer 1985).

Pinar Ilkkaracan (2000) and Haideh Moghissi (1999) both argue that the oppression of female sexuality in Muslim societies should not be seen as a result of the misunderstanding of religious teachings as such, but other aspects should also be taken into consideration such as economic inequality and political interests. However, in many cases, religion is considered an effective tool for controlling female sexuality and verifying male domination (Ilkkarachan 2000).

Mernissi (1987, 32) argues that female sexuality in Muslim societies is seen in two contradictory categories which she called 'explicit theory' and 'implicit theory.' The first theory is the belief that women's sexuality is passive while men's is active. By contrast, the second theory views women as having potent sexual desire, which is therefore dangerous. Both theories are applied in Muslim communities: on one side the Muslim community regulates female sexuality by describing female sexuality as inferior to men's sexuality, so women should be submissive in their sexual relations with their husbands. But at the same time, the community fears female sexual potency and considers it dangerous and liable to cause social disorder (*fitnah*) (Mernissi 1987, 32).

The concepts of fitnah *and* 'awra

Fitnah originally meant a trial from God, as stated in the Qur'an (Q. 21: 35). The term *fitnah* in the Qur'an has nothing to do with women nor is it associated with women as a source of disturbance of the faith. Unfortunately, this term has deviated from its original meaning and, when it is attributed to women, the meaning incorporates the sense that women are a source of social disorder. Women are then seen as a 'sexually driven and lustful species and a potent source of disorder and hence need to be segregated so that men can be protected from temptation' (Riaz Hassan 2008, 171). This expansion of the concept was derived from several traditions that provided legal and normative justification. For example, the report attributed to Ali, the fourth Caliph, stated that 'God created sexual desire in ten parts; then nine parts are given to women and one to men' (Brooks 1996, 39–40).

Abou el Fadl (2001a) criticises this *fitnah* concept as having been invented by some Muslim jurists to protect men with an overactive libido, who are impious and ill mannered. Rather than dealing with out-of-control men, women were sacrificed by being secluded and segregated. He calls for a faith-based protest against this 'presumed *fitnah*' because it violates the higher moral values of justice and fairness promoted by the Qur'an.

The discussion of *fitnah* is often linked to the concept of *'awra* (Ind. *aurat*) in Islam although they are different issues. *'Awra* in the Arabic dictionary means 'the pudendum of a human being that is abominable to uncover' (Lane 1984, 2194). In *fiqh* discussions, *'awra* refers to the body parts that should be covered from public sight, because they are 'considered private' (Abou el Fadl 2001b, 354). Muslim jurists mention *'awra* in their discussion of what should be covered in prayer for men and women. The *'awra* of man is between his navel and his knee, and for woman is considered to be her entire body except her face and hands (Al-Qaradlawi 2001; Abou el Fadl 2001a). In early Islamic discussion, *'awra* was never associated with *fitnah*. Since then, the regulation of *'awra* in prayer for woman has become applicable to her life outside prayer. In fact, the appropriateness of showing body parts is culturally diverse. Every society has different norms and behaviours in their dress codes and perceptions of appropriateness.

In fact, in the Qur'an, both women and men, *not just women,* were instructed to lower their gaze to control their own sexual desire (Q. 24: 30–31). Thus, women's dress code and the prohibition of women from participating in public life is the result of an unreasonable view of women as a source of *fitnah,* which is based only on assumption (Riaz Hassan 2008).

Virginity

Muslim societies highly value women's virginity and require that all women should be virgins at the time of their first marriage. By contrast, men's virginity at first marriage is absent from the discussion. In fact, virginity for both sexes should be required because it is related to the discussion of *zina;* any sexual relations outside the marital bond are forbidden. Mernissi (1982) criticises the demand that requires virginity for women and she advises that if men respect virginity, then they too should refrain from having sexual contact before marriage.

Muslim patriarchal society never questions men's sexual behaviour and men's sexual activity before marriage is never condemned as transgressive.

54 *Marriage and sexuality*

These points are excluded from discussions that demand women stay virgins until their wedding nights.

Female circumcision

The debate surrounding female circumcision, usually referred to as *khitan* or *khifadl* in Islam, or in recent discourse as female genital mutilation or cutting (FGM/FGC), is about whether this practice is an Islamic or a cultural practice. In African Muslim countries, it is usually associated with cultural influence because it is also practiced among tribes that are not categorised as Islamic. In Egypt, female circumcision is practised by both Muslims and Coptic Christians (Berkey 1996). In addition, some Muslim countries, such as Turkey and Iran, do not practice female circumcision and in the Maghreb it is unknown (Bouhdiba 1985).

Regardless of the debate, female circumcision is usually associated with Islam. In the Qur'an, in fact, there is no text supporting female circumcision. The proponents of female circumcision usually refer their argument to the Hadith under the authorisation of Abu Dawud:

> Circumcision is *sunna* [recommended] for men and *makruma* [noble act, honourable] for women. Another Hadith referred to the story of Umm Athiya [a woman who used to perform circumcisions in Medina], the Prophet (Peace Be Upon Him) said to her: 'Do not go to extremes in cutting, for that is better for the woman and more liked by the husband.'
> (Dawud, 2008, Hadith no. 5271, 486–87.)

According to Abu Dawud, these Hadith are considered weak because they have a weak chain of transmission (Kecia Ali 2006; Berkey 1996). However, they are still used as reference for the practice of female circumcision. According to proponents of circumcision, this Hadith advises the practice of female circumcision with the condition that the cutting should not be excessive. Apparently, the practice of female circumcision in Muslim countries is used to control woman's sexuality by reducing her sexual desire (Kister 1994; Giladi 1997; Berkey 1996). This notion is also linked to the idea of *fitnah;* that woman has an insatiable sexual desire and can cause social disorder.

In Indonesia, female circumcision is part of the rites of passage in some groups. The work of Andrée Feillard and Lies Marcoes (1998, 338) provides a comprehensive historical survey of the practice of circumcision in Indonesia, revealing that it first appeared in certain areas in 1670 and how it was practiced in secret as a part of the rite of entry into the Islamic community. Recent reports show regional variations in female circumcision across Indonesia. Lynda Newland (2006) observed that the practice of female circumcision in rural West Java is part of birthing rituals; a symbolic circumcision to position a child within the Islamic community that involves only scratching the prepuce with no actual cut, just to get rid of dirt. Research by Basilica Putranti (2008, 27), however, showed that an actual cut exists in certain areas of Indonesia like Madura and Yogyakarta with the aim of the child becoming a 'true' Muslim.

Although at first this practice seems to be merely a way of incorporating children into the Muslim *ummah* in Indonesia, currently the practice appears to be more about controlling female sexuality than social identity (Haworth 2012). This was reiterated in a *Kompas* article, 'MUI tolak larangan sunat perempuan' (MUI rejects the prohibition of female circumcision), published on 13 January 2013. In this article, Huzaimah (Yahido Tanggo), one of the board members of the MUI (Indonesian Council of Ulama), stated that female circumcision is a religious obligation and is to stabilise the sex drive (*menstabilkan syahwat*). In addition, the ritual aspect has decreased because of the medicalisation of the operation,[11] and the commercialisation of the practice—as part of a birthing package. In the process, female circumcision has become an obligation rather than a choice (Feillard and Marcoes 1998; Haworth 2012; Newland 2006; Putranti 2008; and the Kompas 2013 article mentioned above). This is misleading because there is no authoritative reference for this practice. Thus, the practice should be a choice, if not banned altogether, and it should be made public that there is no religious consequence if parents do not conform to the practice. Beliefs surrounding the association of female circumcision with women's sexual desire are but one aspect of patriarchal control over women's sexuality in the name of religion.

Zina *and rape*

Zina is illicit sexual activity outside of marriage. It is 'consensual or voluntary sexual intercourse between men and women not married to each other' (Al-Zuhaily 1985, 26). In Islam, *zina* is considered a crime that is subject to punishment (Q. 24: 2) and Islam permits sexual relationships only within marriage. The Qur'an even mentions that Muslims should avoid acts that may lead to *zina* (Q. 17: 35). Unmarried women and men going out together (unchaperoned),[12] flirting, hand holding, embracing, and kissing are forbidden in traditional Islam.

In many Muslim countries, however, the application of the *zina* ordinance overlaps with rape cases; there is a blurring of the distinction between the two terms (Imam 2005; Sidameh 2001; Zia 2000). Rape is unlike *zina*. Rape, in Islamic law, is categorised as *zina* by force (*zina bil ikrah*) because it is perpetrated on the woman without her consent, carried out by force, and committed under threat (Al-Kasani 1986.). Rape is also discussed under *hirabah* (forcibly taking or highway robbery). Sayyid Sabiq identified *hirabah* as a 'single person or group of people causing public disruption, killing, forcibly taking property or money, attacking or *raping women,* killing cattle or disrupting agriculture [my emphasis]' (1997, 309–10). Sabiq further notes that rape is a violent crime using sexual intercourse as a weapon, and one that has the worst impact on women of any crimes under *hirabah*. Muslim authorities dealing with rape cases under *zina* law fail to discuss *zina* within the context of *hirabah* or *ikrah* (duress). Indeed, it is a mistake to correlate rape with *zina* because they are different matters.

Family planning and contraception

In classical Islamic law, most legal schools permit contraception for the prevention of pregnancy. Abdel-Rahim Omran (1992, 152) identified that eight out of nine Muslim jurists permit contraception. In the Qur'an there is no text discussing family planning specifically. The Muslim scholars derive their opinion of contraception from the Hadith of *'azl* (coitus interruptus):

> Narrated Ibn Jabir Ibn Abdullah, he said: 'We [the Companions of the Prophet] used to practice coitus interruptus [*'azl*] during the lifetime of Allah's Messenger while the Qur'an was being revealed.'
> (Al-Bukhari 1997, vol. 7, Hadith. no. 5209, 97.)

> Another version of the same Hadith by Muslim stated: It was narrated that Jabir said: 'We used to engage in *'azl* [coitus interruptus] at the time of the Messenger of Allah. News of that reached the Messenger of Allah and He did not forbid us to do it.'
> (Muslim 2007, vol. 4, Hadith no. 3561, 86)

> On the authority of Abu Huraira the Prophet said *al'azl* is not allowed without the consent of the (free) wife. Authenticated by Abu Dawoud.
> (Omran 1992, 125)

These Hadith suggest that *'azl* was a method used to prevent pregnancy in the early days of Islam and that the practice of *'azl* requires the wife's permission. The wife's permission is important for two reasons: the wife has the right to experience sexual pleasure, and she has the right to offspring, if she so desires (Musallam 1983; Omran 1992; Shaikh 2003). It is important to remember these Hadith because they acknowledge that sexual activity in married life is shared and that decisions concerning family planning should be discussed between wife and husband (Shaikh 2003). The majority of Muslim scholars of most legal schools agree that the permission of the wife is conditional in relation to the practice of *'azl* (Musallam 1983, 31). On the contrary, Shafi'i scholars argue that the wife's permission is not needed for practising *'azl*.

In Indonesia, there are intense debates about family planning between moderate Muslim organisations such as the Nahdlatul Ulama (NU) and Muhammadiyah and more conservative groups like the PKS (Prosperous Justice Party) and the HTI (Hizbut Tahrir of Indonesia). Moderate Islam supports family planning to improve the quality of life in terms of the health, education, and prosperity of the family. In contrast, conservative Islamic groups state that family planning is forbidden and they associate it with a Western conspiracy to limit Muslim population growth (Tim Yayasan Rumah Kita Bersama 2013).

Abortion in Islamic law

There are two main opinions concerning abortion in Islam: those jurists who prohibit abortion for any reason and jurists who allow abortion at certain stages of pregnancy, with a valid reason. Before presenting these two main juridical views, it is relevant to explain the development of the foetus according to Islam, because this topic is central to jurists' arguments on abortion.

In the Qur'an, several verses discuss the creation of human beings. For example Q. 22: 5 states:

> O humankind! If ye have a doubt about the Resurrection, (consider) that We created you out of dust; then out of sperm [*nutfa*], then out of a leechlike clot ['*alaqa*], then out of a morsel of flesh [*mudgha*], partly formed and partly unformed.
>
> (Q. 22: 5)

Hadith also explain the development of human beings, as the Prophet said:

> It was narrated that 'Abdullah said: "The Messenger of Allah – and he is the truthful, the one who is believed – told us: 'The creation of any one of you is put together in his mother's womb for forty days, then, he is during that (period) an *'Alaqah* [a piece that hangs, clings or is suspended] for a similar period. Then he becomes a *Mudghah* [like a chewed lump of flesh] for a similar period. Then Allah sends to him an angel who breathes the soul into him, and is enjoined to write down four things: His provision, his lifespan, his deeds and his misery or happiness.'"
>
> (Muslim 2007, vol. 7, Hadith no. 6723, 15)

Referring to the verse and Hadith above, most of the jurists argue that abortion is prohibited after the angel breathes the soul into it. However, different Schools make different interpretations about the stage at which the angel breathes life into the soul (Musallam 1983). The Hanafi jurists permit abortion until the end of the fourth month of pregnancy. They grant the pregnant woman the right to ask for abortion even without her husband's permission but only for a valid reason (Musallam 1983). The Shafi'i jurists' opinions on abortion are divided into three groups: some jurists allow it before 120 days of pregnancy; some allow it until the fortieth day of pregnancy; and the famous jurist, Al-Ghazali, prohibits abortion at any time (Anshor 2006; Riyani 2005).

In the case of saving the mother's life, Muslim jurists unanimously allowed abortion with the reason that a mother is the source, the origin of life, so her life and wellbeing is given priority. Several other medical conditions under which abortion is permissible include the risk of genetically transmitted diseases, evidence of a congenital defect, severe foetal abnormality incompatible with survival, and a breastfeeding mother whose baby is in need of her nutritious milk (Rispler-Chaim 1993, 14–15).

Some criticisms of traditional Islamic sexuality

There are some criticisms attributed to traditional Islamic views of sexuality, particularly on the issue of privileging male sexuality over female sexuality.

Fatna Sabbah (1984) for example criticised the orthodox discourse of sexuality that privileges men's over women's sexual desire. Within this discourse, according to her, sexuality is 'domesticized and hierarchized' (Sabbah 1984, 98). Sexual activity is only permitted in the domestic arena and castrates women's sexuality, forcing women to submissively wait on men's demands for sexual satisfaction. Sabbah then argues that female sexuality is curtailed by the inscription 'tattooed' on women's body as silence, immobility, and obedience (Sabbah 1984, 5). She urges a decoding of this message by calling for strikes against oppression and stupidity.

A similar criticism is offered by Moghissi (1999, 22). She notes that women's sexuality has rarely found freedom of expression, because the main concerns of Islam are fear of women's seductive capacity and sexual conduct. These fears have raised the issue of curbing women's sexual potency and governing women's moral conduct through surveillance by father, brother, family, the public, and the state through the law (Moghissi 1999, 20). Moghissi underscores Sabbah's argument that orthodox Islam established the sexual hierarchy and identified woman as a mere sexual object whose primary duty is to serve her husband's sexual needs.

The work of Kecia Ali is significant in voicing and criticising the male bias and political struggles in regulating sexuality. Ali argues that sexuality, as described in the Qur'an, is based on 'mutual consent and reciprocal desires surrounding lawful sexuality' (2006, xxv), but is now perverted by many Islamic jurists as based on a hierarchical relation between husband and wife in married life. She criticises the *fiqh* texts on marriage and sexuality under the term *milk*—ownership, dominion, and control. Jurists view the marriage contract as 'an exchange of lawful sexual access for dower, and continued sexual availability for support' (Moghissi 1999, 13).

Reviewing the literature on marriage and sexuality in Islam, I found that the traditional Islamic law regulating marriage and sexuality is still the dominant influence in many Muslim countries, including Indonesia, but there have been a large number of recent attempts to reform the law in contemporary Muslim countries. I certainly agree with most progressive Muslim thinkers who suggest that marriage reform is needed to accommodate egalitarian relationships between the sexes. In terms of sexuality research, it is time to open up the discussion on sexuality, to consider diverse practices among Muslim societies, and to ensure fairness for both sexes. A comprehensive and integrated approach to re-examining and reinterpreting religious texts is necessary to build new understandings of the subject matter, particularly in relation to married women's sexuality.

In this general overview of the academic literature on marriage and sexuality in Indonesia and Islam, I have articulated several important conclusions. There has been increased research on sexuality in Indonesia; however, the focus has been mainly on adolescent sexuality and alternative sexualities. Women's sexuality, in particular married women's sexuality, is still given little attention. My book explores women's sexual experiences in married life. While, research on marriage and sexuality in Islam has been concentrated in Middle Eastern countries, marriage and sexuality in Islam in Indonesia and in Southeast Asia in general, have been usually overlooked in academic discussions (Hefner 1997; Offenhauer 2005). The small amount of research related to women's sexuality in Indonesian Islam means that this book is important in starting to breach the lacuna. This book builds upon existing studies already conducted in Indonesia on women's sexuality, particularly by investigating the sexual experiences of married women and linking these experiences to the influence of Islam.

Notes

1. The absence of a child in a marriage is a justification for a man to marry polygynously. See Indonesian Marriage Law (no. 1/1974) chapter VIII: 41a.
2. *Nyereuh* or *nyeupah* is chewing a betel leaf after putting lime and areca nut inside the leaf. Previously, in Sundanese tradition, *nyeureuh* or *nyepah* was widely practised by men and women alike at celebrations (Muchtar and Umbara 1977). This tradition no longer exists in Sundanese culture except in very limited rural areas.
3. As it is most widely used worldwide, for the Qur'anic translation I use Abdullah Yusuf Ali's English translation, *The Holy Qur'an,* Kashmiri Bazar, Lahore: Shaik Muhammad Ashraf. I used the 2000 version.
4. The two terms bride price and dowry are often confused. Bride price can be defined as 'property or money presented by a bridegroom to his bride's relatives in recognition of the marriage' (*Macquarie Dictionary* 2009, s.v. bride price) while dowry is 'the money, goods, or estate which a woman brings to her husband at marriage' (ibid., s.v. dowry). Dowry is often familial property transferred from parents to daughter upon marriage, and is typical of South Asian societies (Goody 1973; Tambiah 1973).
5. The Qur'an distinguishes between *musyrikun* and *ahl kitab*: the former refer to those who worship gods other than one God and the latter associate with Christian and Jews (Gimaret 1997).
6. Those persons who are considered *mahram* include: mothers, daughters, sisters, paternal and maternal aunts, brothers' and sisters' daughters, foster sisters, mothers-in-law, step daughters who are under one's protection, and father's wife.
7. The criteria are derived from Hadith narrated by Abu Huraira: The Prophet said, 'A woman is married for four [things], i.e., her wealth, her family status, her beauty and her religion. So you should take possession of [marry] the religious woman [otherwise] you will be a loser' (Al-Bukhari 1997, vol 7, Hadith no. 5090, 32–33).
8. 'You will never be able to treat your wives with equal fairness, however much you may desire to do so, but do not ignore one wife altogether, leaving her suspended [between marriage and divorce]' (Q. 4: 129).

60 *Marriage and sexuality*

9. An exception is Tunisia, where polygyny is prohibited: it is said to be part of 'a criminal infraction' because it is impossible for a man to do justice to more than one wife (Hallaq 2009, 464).
10. Indonesia has been successful in raising the age of marriage to 19 years for both females and males based on the amendment to the Indonesian Marriage Law, no. 16/2019, specifically chapter 7 point 1.
11. In 2010, the Ministry of Health, together with the Ministry of Law and Human Rights, issued a Regulation on female circumcision (*sunat perempuan*) no. 1636/MENKES/PER/XI/2010 that legitimates the practice of female circumcision under the authorisation of medical professionals. This regulation has been revoked by the regulation of Ministry of Health (no. 6/2014). This regulation does not explicitly prohibited female circumcision.
12. A relevant Hadith on this is narrated by Ibn Abbas: the Prophet said: 'No man should stay with a lady in seclusion except in the presence of *Dzu-Mahram*' (Al-Bukhari 1997, vol. 7, Hadith no. 5233, 108). *Dzu-Mahram* means a woman's relatives that are categorised as *muhrim* (someone it is forbidden to marry).

References

Abou el Fadl, M. Khaled. (2001a). *Speaking in God's Name: Islamic Law, Authority and Women*. Oxford: One World.

Abou el Fadl, M. Khaled. (2001b). *The Search for Beauty in Islam: Conference of the Books*. Lanham: University Press of America.

Abu Zayd, Nasr Hamid. (2000). *Dawair al-khawf: Qira'at fi khitab al-mar'a* (Circles of fear: Reading the discourse about women). Beirut: al-Markaz al-Thaqafi fi al-Arab.

Accad, Evelyne. (2000). 'Sexuality and sexual politics: Conflicts and contradictions for contemporary women in the Middle East.' In Pinar Ilkkaracan (ed.), *Women and Sexuality in Muslim Societies*, 37–50. Turkey: Women for Women's Human Rights (WWHR).

Adamson, Clarissa. (2007). 'Gendered anxieties: Islam, women's rights, and moral hierarchy in Java.' *Anthropological Quarterly*, 80(1), 5–37, DOI: 10.1353/anq.2007.0000.

Al-Bukhari, Muhammed Ibn Ismaiel. (1997). *The Translation of the Meanings of Shahih al-Bukhari: Arabic–English, vol. 7*. Muhammed Muhsin Khan (trans.). Riyadh, Saudi Arabia: Darussalam, available from: https://archive.org/stream/TheTranslationOfTheMeaningsOfSahihAl-Bukhari-Arabic-English9Volumes/Sahih%20Al-Bukhari-Arabic_English_Volume-7-Ahadith-5063-5969#page/n9/mode/2up (accessed 15 January 2020).

Al-Hibri, Azizah. (1982). 'A study of Islamic herstory: Or how did we ever get into this mess?' In Azizah Al-Hibri (ed.), *Women and Islam*, 207–19. Oxford: Pergamon Press. Also available from: *Women's Studies International Forum*, 5(2), 207–19, DOI: 10.1016/0277-5395(82)90028-0.

Ali, Ahmed. (1993). *Al-Qur'an: A Contemporary Translation*. Princeton, NJ: Princeton University Press.

Ali, Abdullah. Yusuf. (2000). *The Holy Qur'an*. London: Wordsworth Edition Ltd.

Ali, Kecia. (2006). *Sexual Ethics and Islam: Feminist Reflections on Qur'an, Hadith, and Jurisprudence*. Oxford: One World.

Ali, Maulana Muhammad. (1973). *The Holy Qur'an* (rev. ed.). Chicago, IL: Specialty Promotion.

Al-Jaziry, Abd al-Rahman. (2003). *Al-fiqh ala madzahib al-Arba'a: Juz 4* (Islamic jurisprudence of four schools: vol. 4). Beirut: Dar al-Kutub al-Ilmiyah.

Al-Kasani, Imam Alauddin. (1986.). *Bada'i al-sana'i fi tartib al-shari'i*. Cairo: Mathba'ah al-Imam.
Al-Qaradlawi, Yusuf. (2001). *The Lawful and Prohibited in Islam*. Cairo: Al-Falah Foundation, available from: http://www.usislam.org/pdf/Lawful&Prohibited.pdf (accessed 9 January 2020).
Al-Thabari, Muhammad ibn Jarir. (1992). *Tafsir Jami al-bayan 'an ta'wil ayat al-Qur'an* (Collection of statements on interpretation of verses of the Qur'an). Beirut: Dar al-Kutub al-Ilmiyya.
Al-Zuhaily, Wahbah. (1985). *Al-fiqh al-Islami wa adillatuhu* (Islamic jurisprudence and its proofs). Damascus: Dar al-Fikr.
Anshor, Maria Ulfah. (2006). *Fikih aborsi: Wacana penguatan hak reproduksi perempuan* (The fiqh of abortion: Discourse strengthening the reproductive rights of women). Jakarta: Kompas.
Arshad, Raffia. (2010). *Islamic Family Law*. London: Sweet & Maxwell.
Asad, Muhammad. (2003). *The Message of the Qur'an*. Gibraltar: Dar al-Andalus.
Barlas, Asma. (2002). *'Believing Women' in Islam: Unreading Patriarchal Interpretations of the Qur'an*. Austin: University of Texas Press.
Bauer, Janet L. (1985). 'Sexuality and the moral "construction" of women in an Islamic society.' *Anthropological Quarterly*, 58(3), 120–29, DOI: 10.2307/3317918.
:::Bennett, Linda Rae. (2005a). *Women, Islam and Modernity: Single Women, Sexuality and Reproductive Health in Contemporary Indonesia*. London: Routledge Curzon.
Bennett, Linda Rae. (2005b). 'Patterns of resistance and transgression in Eastern Indonesia: Single women's practices of clandestine courtship and cohabitation.' *Culture, Health & Sexuality*, 7(2), 101–12, DOI: 10.1080/13691050412331291397.
Bennett, Linda Rae. (2007). 'Zina and the enigma of sex education for Indonesian Muslim youth.' *Sex Education*, 7(4), 371–86, DOI: 10.1080/14681810701635970.
Bennett, Linda Rae, Sari Andajani-Soetjahjo, and Nurul I. Idrus. (2011). 'Domestic violence in Nusa Tenggara Barat, Indonesia: Married women's definitions and experiences of violence in the home.' *The Asia Pacific Journal of Anthropology*, 12(2), 146–63, DOI: 10.1080/14442213.2010.547514.
Berkey, Jonathan P. (1996). 'Circumcision circumscribed: Female excision and cultural accommodation in the Medieval Near East.' *International Journal of Middle East Studies*, 40(4), 535–40, DOI: 10.1017/S0020743800062760.
Berninghausen, Jutta and Birgit Kerstan. (1992). *Forging New Paths: Feminist Social Methodology and Rural Women in Java*. London: Zed Book.
Binahayati, Rusyidi. (2011). 'Perceptions and attitudes towards violence against wives in West Java, Indonesia.' PhD dissertation, State University of New York, Albany.
Blackburn, Susan. (2001). 'Gender relations in Indonesia: What women want.' In Grayson J. Lloyd and Shannon L. Smith (eds.), *Indonesia Today: Challenges of History*, 270–82. Singapore: Institute of Southeast Asian Studies, DOI: 10.1355/9789812305114-027.
Blackwood, Evelyn. (1995a). 'Falling in love with an-other lesbian: Reflections on identity in fieldwork.' In Don Kulick and Margaret Wilson (eds.), *Taboo: Sex, Identity, and Erotic Subjectivity in Anthropological Fieldwork*, 5–75. London: Routledge, DOI: 10.4324/9780203420379_chapter_2.
Blackwood, Evelyn. (1995b). 'Senior women, model mothers, and dutiful wives: Managing gender contradictions in a Minangkabau village.' In Aihwa Ong and Michael G. Peletz (eds.), *Bewitching Women, Pious Men: Gender and Body Politics in Southeast Asia*, 124–58. Berkeley: University of California Press.

Blackwood, Evelyn (1998). 'Tombois in West Sumatra: Constructing masculinity and erotic desire.' *Cultural Anthropology*, 13(4), 491–521, DOI: 10.1525/can.1998.13.4.491.

Blackwood, Evelyn. (2007). 'Transnational sexualities in one place: Indonesian readings.' In Saskia E. Wieringa, Evelyn Blackwood, and Abha Bhaiya (eds.), *Women's Sexualities and Masculinities in a Globalizing Asia*, 181–99. New York: Palgrave Macmillan, DOI: 10.1057/9780230604124_10.

Blackwood, Evelyn. (2010). *Falling into the Lesbi World: Desire and Difference in Indonesia*. Honolulu, HI: University of Hawai'i Press.

Boellstorff, Tom. (2003). 'The perfect path: Gay men, marriage, Indonesia.' In Robert J. Corber and Stephen Valocchi (eds.), *Queer Studies: An Interdisciplinary Reader*, 218–36. Malden: Blackwell Publishing.

Boellstorff, Tom. (2005). *The Gay Archipelago: Sexuality and Nation in Indonesia*. Princeton, NJ: Princeton University Press.

Bouhdiba, Abdelwahab. (1985). *Sexuality in Islam*. London: Routledge, DOI: 10.4324/9780203706916.

Brenner, Suzanne A. (1998). *The Domestification of Desire: Women, Wealth and Modernity in Java*. Princeton, NJ: Princeton University Press.

Brenner, Suzanne. (2011). 'Private moralities in the public sphere: Democratization, Islam, and gender in Indonesia.' *American Anthropologist*, 113(3), 478–90, DOI: 10.1111/j.1548-1433.2010.01355.x.

Brooks, Geraldine. (1996). *Nine Parts of Deaire: The Hidden World of Islamic Women*. New York, NY: Anchor Books.

Bungin, Burhan. (2003). *Pornomedia: Konstruksi sosial teknologi telematika dan perayaan seks di media massa* (Pornomedia: The constitution of telematica social technology and sex in the mass media). Bogor: Kencana.

Chaudhry, Ayesha Siddiqua, Rachel, Muers, and Randy, Rashkover. (2009). 'Women reading texts on marriage.' *Feminist Theology*, 17(2), 191–209, DOI: 10.1177/0966735008098723.

Davies, Sharyn Graham. (2010). *Gender Diversity in Indonesia: Sexuality, Islam and Queer Selves*. London: Routledge, DOI: 10.4324/9780203860953.

Dawud, Abu. (2008). *Translation of Sunan Abu-Dawud*, Nasiruddin al-Khattab (trans), Riyadh: Darussalam, available from: https://ia800905.us.archive.org/3/items/SunanAbuDawudVol.111160EnglishArabic/Sunan%20Abu%20Dawud%20Vol.%205%20-%204351-5274%20English%20Arabic.pdf (25 January 2020).

Dunn, Shannon and Rosemary B. Kellison. (2010). 'At the intersection of scripture and law: Qur'an 4: 34 and violence against women.' *Journal of Feminist Studies in Religion*, 26(2), 11–36, DOI: 10.2979/fsr.2010.26.2.11.

Engineer, Asghar Ali. (2005). *The Qur'an, Women and Modern Society* (2nd ed.). Berkshire: New Dawn Press.

Esposito, John L. and Natana J. DeLong-Bas. (2001). *Women in Muslim Family Law*. Syracuse, NY: Syracuse University Press.

Falk, Nancy. (1985). 'Introduction.' In Yvonne Yazbeck Haddad and Ellison Banks Findly (eds.), *Women, Religion, and Social Change*, xv–xxi. Albany, NY: State University of New York Press.

Feener, R. Michael. (2007). *Muslim Legal Thought in Modern Indonesia*. Cambridge: Cambridge University Press, DOI: 10.1017/CBO9780511495540.

Feillard, Andrée and Lies Marcoes. (1998). 'Female circumcision in Indonesia: To "Islamize" in ceremony or secrecy.' *Archipel*, 56, 337–67, DOI: 10.3406/arch.1998.3495.

Feillard, Andrée and Pieternella van Doorn-Harder. (2013). 'A new generation of feminists within traditional Islam: An Indonesian exception.' In Jajat Burhanuddin and Kees van Dijk (eds.), *Islam in Indonesia: Contrasting Images and Interpretations*, 139–59. Amsterdam: Amsterdam University Press, DOI: 10.2307/j.ctt46mwqt.12.

Ford, Michele and Lyn, Parker. (2008a). 'Introduction: Thinking about Indonesian women and work.' In Michele Ford and Lyn Parker (eds.), *Women and Work in Indonesia*, 1–16. London: Routledge, DOI: 10.4324/9780203932360.

Ford, Michele and Lyn, Parker (eds.). (2008b). *Women and Work in Indonesia*. London: Routledge, DOI: 10.4324/9780203932360.

Geertz, Hilda. (1961). *The Javanese Family: A Study of Kinship and Socialization*. New York: Free Press of Glencoe.

Giladi, Avner. (1997). 'Normative Islam versus local tradition: Some observations on female circumcision with special reference to Egypt.' *Arabica*, 44(2), 254–67, DOI: 10.1163/1570058972582489.

Gimaret, Daniel. (1997). 'Shirk.' In C. E. Bosworth, E. V. Donzel, W. P. Heinrichs, and G. Lecomte (eds.), *The Encyclopaedia of Islam* (new ed.). Leiden: E. J. Brill.

Goody, Jack. (1973). 'Bridewealth and dowry in Africa and Eurasia.' In Jack Goody and S. J. Tambiah (eds.), *Bridewealth and Dowry*, 1–58. Cambridge: Cambridge University Press.

Goolam, Hafiz Nazeem. (2006). 'Gender equality in Islamic family law: Dispelling common misconceptions and misunderstandings.' In H. M. Ramadan (ed.), *Understanding Islamic Law: From Classical to Contemporary*, 117–34. Lanham: Rowman & Littlefield.

Grijns, Mies. (1987). 'Tea-pickers in West Java as mothers and workers: Female work and women's jobs.' In Elsbeth Locher-Scholten and Anke Niehof (eds.), *Indonesian Women in Focus*, 104–19. Leiden: KITLV Press.

Grijns, Mies, Inez Smyth, Anita van Velzen, Sugiah Machfud, and Pudjiwati Sajogyo (eds.). (1994). *Different Women, Different Work: Gender and Industrialization in Indonesia*. Aldershot: Avenbury.

Hallaq, Wael. B. (2009). *Shari'a: Theory, Practice, Transformations*. Cambridge: Cambridge University Press, DOI: 10.1017/CBO9780511815300.

Hancock, Peter. (2001). 'Gender empowerment issues from West Java.' In Susan Blackburn (ed.), *Love, Sex and Power: Women in Southeast Asia*, 75–88. Clayton, Vic.: Monash Asia Institute.

Hassan, Riaz. (2008). *Inside Muslim Minds*. Carlton, Vic.: Melbourne University Press.

Hassan, Riffat. (1990). 'An Islamic perspective.' In Jeanne Becher (ed.), *Women, Religion and Sexuality: Studies on the Impact of Religious Teaching on Women*, 93–128. Geneva: World Council of Churches.

Haworth, Abigail. (2012). 'The day I saw 248 girls suffering genital mutilation.' *Guardian*, 18 Nov., available from: https://www.theguardian.com/society/2012/nov/18/female-genital-mutilation-circumcision-indonesia (accessed 14 October 2014).

Hefner, Robert W. (1997). 'Islam in an era of nation-states: Politics and religious renewal in Muslim Southeast Asia.' In Robert W. Hefner and Patricia Horvatich (eds.), *Islam in an Era of Nation-States: Politics and Religious Renewal in Muslim Southeast Asia*, 3–40. Honolulu, HI: University of Hawai'i Press.

Hefner, Robert W. (2008). 'A conservative turn in Indonesian Islam? Genesis and future.' In Luthfi Assyaukanie, Robert W. Hefner, and Azyumardi Azra (eds.), *Muslim Politics and Democratisation in Indonesia*, 33–50. Annual Indonesian Lecture Series, 28. Clayton, Vic.: Monash Asia Institute.

Holzner, Brigitte M. and Dédé Oetomo. (2004). 'Youth, sexuality and sex education messages in Indonesia: Issues of desire and control.' *Reproductive Health Matters*, 12(23), 40–49, DOI: 10.1016/S0968-8080(04)23122-6.

Horikoshi, Hiroko. (1976). 'A traditional leader in a time of change: The 'kijaji' and 'ulama' in West Java.' PhD thesis, University of Illinois, Urbana, Champaign.

Howard, Richard Stephen. (1996). 'Falling into the gay world: Manhood, marriage, and family in Indonesia.' PhD thesis, University of Illinois, Urbana, Champaign.

Hull, Terence H., Endang Sulistyaningsih, and Gavin W. Jones. (1997). *Pelacuran di Indonesia: Sejarah dan perkembangannya* (Prostitution in Indonesia: Its history and development). Jakarta: Pustaka Sinar Harapan and Ford Foundation.

Hull, Valerie J. (1982). 'Women in Java's rural middle class: Progress or regress?' In Penny van Esterik (ed.), *Women of Southeast Asia*, 100–23. DeKalb, IL: Centre for Southeast Asian Studies, Northern Illinois University.

Idrus, Nurul Ilmi. (1999). *Marital Rape: Kekerasan Seksual dalam perkawinan (Marital rape: Sexual violence in married life)*. Yogyakarta: Universitas Gadjah Mada.

Idrus, Nurul Ilmi. (2001). 'Marriage, sex and violence.' In Susan Blackburn (ed.), *Love, Sex and Power: Women in Southeast Asia*, 43–56. Clayton, Vic.: Monash Asia Institute.

Idrus, Nurul Ilmi. (2003). '"To take each other": Bugis practices of gender, sexuality and marriage.' PhD thesis, The Australia National University, Canberra.

Ilkkaracan, Pinar. (2000). 'Introduction.' In Pinar Ilkkaracan (ed.), *Women and Sexuality in Muslim Societies*, 1–15. Istanbul: Women for Women's Human Rights.

Imam, Ayesha M. (2005). 'Women's reproductive and sexual rights and the offence of *zina* in Muslim laws in Nigeria.' In Wendy Chavkin and Ellen Chesler (eds.), *Where Human Rights Begin: Health, Sexuality, and Women in the New Millennium*, 65–94. New Brunswick, NJ: Rutgers University Press.

Iskandar, Meiwita B., Budi Utomo, Terence Hull, Nick G. Dharmaputra, and Yuswardi Azwar. (1996). *Unraveling the Mysteries of Maternal Death in West Java: Reexamining the Witnesses*. Depok: Center for Health Research, Research Institute, University of Indonesia.

Jackson, Stevi. (1978). *On the Social Construction of Female Sexuality*. Exploration in FeminismSeries, 4. London: Women's Research and Resources Centre Publications.

Jankowiak, William R. and Thomas Paladino. (2008). 'Desiring sex, longing for love: A tripartite conundrum.' In William R. Jankowiak (ed.), *Intimacies: Love and Sex Across Cultures*, 1–36. New York: Columbia University Press.

Jauhola, Majaana. (2012). '"Natural" sex difference? Negotiating the meanings of the sex, gender and kodrat through gender equality discourse in Aceh, Indonesia.' *Intersections: Gender and Sexuality in Asia and the Pacific*, 30(Nov.), available from: http://intersections.anu.edu.au/issue30/jauhola.htm (accessed 20 September 2015).

Jay, Robert R. (1969). *Javanese Villagers: Social Relations in Rural Mojokuto*. Cambridge: MA: The MIT Press.

Jennaway, Megan. (2002). *Sisters and Lovers: Women and Desires in Bali*. Lanham, MD: Rowman & Littlefield.

Jennaway, Megan. (2003). 'Displacing desire: Sex and sickness in North Bali.' *Culture, Health and Sexuality: An International Journal for Research, Intervention and Care*, 5(3), 185–201, DOI: 10.1080/136910501172985.

Jones, Gavin W., Yahya Asari, and Tuti Djuartika. (1994). 'Divorce in West Java.' *Journal of Comparative Family Studies*, 25(3), 395–416, DOI: 10.3138/jcfs.25.3.395.

Jones, Gavin W. and Bina Gubhaju. (2011). 'Regional differences in marriage patterns in Indonesia in the twenty-first century.' In Gavin W. Jones, Terence H. Hull, and Maznah Mohamad (eds.), *Changing Marriage Patterns in Southeast Asia: Economic and Socio-Cultural Dimensions*, 49–61. London: Routledge.

Jones, Gavin W., Terence H. Hull, and Maznah Mohamad. (2011). 'Marriage trends in Insular Southeast Asia: Their economic and socio-cultural dimension.' In Gavin W. Jones, Terence H. Hull, and Maznah Mohamad (eds.), *Changing Marriage Patterns in Southeast Asia: Economic and Socio-Cultural Dimensions*, 1–10. London: Routledge.

Jones, Gavin W., Terence H. Hull, and Maznah Mohamad. (eds.). (2011). *Changing Marriage Patterns in Southeast Asia: Economic and Socio-Cultural Dimensions*. London: Routledge.

Kahmad, Dadang. (2006). 'Agama Islam dan budaya Sunda' (Islamic religion and Sundanese culture). In Ajip Rosidi, H. Edi S. Ekadjati, and A. Chaedar Alwasilah (eds.), *Konferensi International budaya Sunda* (International conference of Sundanese culture), vol. I. Bandung: Yayasan Kebudayaan Rancage.

Kholifah, Dwi. Rubiyanti. (2005). 'Contesting discourses on sexuality and sexual subjectivity among single young women in pesantren (Muslim boarding schools), West Java, Indonesia.' MA thesis. Mahidol University, Thailand.

Kister, M. J. (1994). '"...and he was born circumcised...": Some notes on circumcision in Hadith.' *Oriens*, 34, 10–30, DOI: 10.1163/19606028_032_02-22.

Koentjaraningrat. (1985). *Javanese Culture*. Singapore: Oxford University Press.

Kroeger, Karen A. (2000). 'Risk, boundary making and the social order: Understanding the social construction of AIDs and sexuality in Indonesia.' PhD thesis, Washington University, St Louis, MS.

Lane, E. W. [Edward William] (1984). *Arabic–English Lexicon*. Cambridge: Islamic Texts Society.

Mas'ud, Muhammad Khalid. (2009). '*Ikhtilaf al-Fuqaha*: Diversity in fiqh as a social construction.' In Zainah Anwar (ed.), *Wanted: Equality and Justice in the Muslim Family*, 65–91. Selangor: Musawah, available from: http://arabic.musawah.org/sites/default/files/Wanted-MKM-EN.pdf (accessed 9 January 2020).

Mather, Celia. (1985). "Rather than make trouble, it is better just to leave": Behind the lack of industrial strikes in the Tangerang region of West Java.' In Haleh Ashfar (ed.), *Women, Work, and Ideology in the Third World*, 153–80. London: Tavistock.

McDonald, Peter and E. H. Abdurrahman. (1974). *Marriage and Divorce in West Java: An Example of the Effective use of Marital Histories*. Jakarta: Lembaga Demografi Fakultas Ekonomi Universitas Indonesia.

Mernissi, Fatima. (1982). 'Virginity and patriarchy.' In Azizah Al-Hibri (ed.), *Women and Islam*, 183–91. Oxford: Pergamon Press.

Mernissi, Fatima. (1987). *Beyond the Veil: Male-Female Dynamics in Muslim Society* (rev. ed.). Bloomington, IN: Indiana University Press.

Millie, Julian. (2008). 'Non-specialists in the *pesantren*: The social construction of Islamic knowledge.' *Review of Indonesian and Malaysian Affairs*, 42(1), 107–24.

Millie, Julian and Syihabuddin. (2005). 'Addendum to Drewes: The burda of al-Busiri and the miracles of Abdulqadir al-Jaelani in West Java.' *Bijdragen tot de Taal-, Land- en Volkenkunde*, 161(1), 98–126.

Moghissi, Haideh. (1999). *Feminism and Islamic Fundamentalism: The Limits of Postmodern Analysis*. London: Zed Books.

Muchtar, R. H. Uton and Ki Umbara. (1977). *Modana*. Bandung: Mangle Panglipur.
'MUI tolak larangan sunat perempuan' (MUI rejects the prohibition of female circumcision). (2013). *Kompas*, 21 Jan., available from: http://nasional.kompas.com/read/2013/01/21/13404468/MUI.Tolak.Larangan.Sunat.Perempuan (23 May 2011).
Mulia, Siti Musdah and Mark E. Cammack. (2007). 'Toward a just marriage law: Empowering Indonesian women through a counter legal draft to the Indonesian compilation of Islamic law.' In R. Michael Feener and Mark E. Cammack (eds.), *Islamic Law in Contemporary Indonesia: Ideas and Institutions*, 128–45. Cambridge: Harvard University Press.
Munir, Lily Zakiyah. (2002). '"He is your garment and you are his ..." : Religious precepts, interpretation, and power relations in marital sexuality among Javanese Muslim women.' *SOJOURN: Journal of Social Issues in Southeast Asia*, 17(2), 191–220, DOI: 10.1355/SJ17-2C.
Murray, Alison J. (1991). *No Money, No Honey: A Study of Street Traders and Prostitutes in Jakarta*. Singapore: Oxford University Press.
Murray, Alison J. (1999). 'Let them take ecstasy: Class and Jakarta lesbians.' In Evelyn Blackwood and Saskia E. Wieringa (eds.), *Female Desires: Same-Sex Relations and Transgender Practices across Cultures*, 139–56. New York: Columbia University Press.
Muslim, Imam. (2007). *English Translation of Shahih Muslim*, trans. Nashiruddin al-Khattab. Riyadh. Saudi Arabia: Darussalam.
Musallam, B. F. [Basim] (1983). *Sex and Society in Islam: Birth Control before the Nineteenth Century*. Cambridge: Cambridge University Press.
Newland, Lynda. (2000). 'Under the banner of Islam: Mobilising religious identities in West Java.' *The Australian Journal of Anthropology*, 11(2), 199–222, DOI: 10.1111/j.1835-9310.2000.tb00056.x.
Newland, Lynda. (2006). Female circumcision: Muslim identities and zero tolerance policies in rural West Java. *Women's Studies International Forum*, 29(4), 394–404, DOI: 10.1016/j.wsif.2006.05.005.
Noerdin, Edriana. (2002). 'Customary institutions, s*yariah* law and the marginalisation of Indonesian women.' In Kathryn Robinson and Sharon Bessell (eds.), *Women in Indonesia: Gender, Equity and Development*, 179–86. Singapore: Institute of Southeast Asian Studies, DOI: 10.1355/9789812305152-021.
Nurlaelawati, Euis. (2013). 'Managing familial issues: Unique features of legal reform in Indonesia.' In Jajat Burhanuddin and Kees van Dijk (eds.), *Islam in Indonesia: Contrasting Images and Interpretations*, 123–38. Amsterdam: Amsterdam University Press, DOI: 10.2307/j.ctt46mwqt.11.
Nurmila, Nina. (2009). *Women, Islam and Everyday Life: Renegotiating Polygamy in Indonesia*. London: Routledge.
Oakley, Ann. (1972). *Sex, Gender and Society*. London: Maurice Temple Smith.
Oetomo, Dédé. (1996). 'Gender and sexual orientation in Indonesia.' In Laurie J. Sears (ed.), *Fantasizing the Feminine in Indonesia*, 259–69. Durham: Duke University Press, DOI: 10.1215/9780822396710-012.
Offenhauer, Priscilla. (2005). *Women in Islamic Societies: A Selected Review of Social Scientific Literature*. Washington, DC: Federal Research Division Library of Congress, available from: http://www.loc.gov/rr/frd/pdf-files/Women_Islamic_Societies.pdf (accessed 11 November 2014).
Offord, Baden. (2003). *Homosexual Rights as Human Rights: Activism in Indonesia, Singapore, and Australia*. Oxford: Peter Lang.

Omran, Abdel-Rahim. (1992). *Family Planning in the Legacy of Islam*. London: Routledge.
Parker, Lyn. (2001). 'Fecundity and the fertility decline in Bali.' In Margaret Jolly and Kalpana Ram (eds.), *Borders of Being: Citizenship, Fertility and Sexuality in Asia and the Pacific*, 178–203. Ann Arbor: University of Michigan Press, DOI: 10.3998/mpub.23538.
Parker, Lyn. (2008). 'Theorising adolescent sexualities in Indonesia – Where "something different happens".' *Intersections: Gender and Sexuality in Asia and the Pacific*, 18(Oct.), available from: http://intersections.anu.edu.au/issue18/parker. htm (accessed 27 April 2011).
Parker, Lyn. (2009). 'Religion, class and schooled sexuality among Minangkabau teenage girls.' *Bijdragen tot de taal-, land- en volkenkunde*, 165(1), 62–94, DOI: 10.1163/22134379-90003643.
Parker, Lyn, Irma Riyani, and Brooke Nolan. (2015). 'The stigmatisation of *janda* (widows and divorcées) in Indonesia and the possibilities for agency.' *Indonesia and the Malay World*, 44(128), 27–46, DOI: 10.1080/13639811.2016.1111677.
Pengadilan Agama Kota Bandung (City of Bandung Religious Court). (2013). 'Sistem informsi Penelusuran Perkara,' Mahkamah Agung Republik Indonesia: Pengadilan Agama Bandung, available from: http://pa-bandung.go.id/penelusuran-perkara (accessed 28 January 2020).
Pickthall, Marmaduke. (1930). *The Meaning of the Glorious Koran*. London: George Allen & Unwin.
Platt, Maria. (2017). *Marriage, Gender and Islam in Indonesia: Women Negotiating Informal Marriage, Divorce and Desire*. London: Routledge.
Purdy, Christopher H. (2006). 'Fruity, fun and safe: Creating a youth condom brand in Indonesia.' *Reproductive Health Matters*, 14(28), 127–34, DOI: 10.1016/S0968-8080(06)28256-9.
Putranti, Basilica Dyah. (2008). 'To Islamize, becoming a real woman or commercialized practices? Questioning female genital cutting in Indonesia.' *Finnish Journal of Ethnicity and Migration*, 3(2), 23–31.
Rinaldo, Rachel. (2010). 'The Islamic revival and women's political subjectivity in Indonesia.' *Women's Studies International Forum*, 33(4), 422–31, DOI: 10.1016/j.wsif.2010.02.016.
Rispler-Chaim. Vardit. (1993). *Islamic Medical Ethics in the Twentieth Century*. Leiden: E.J. Brill.
Riyani, Irma. (2005). 'Menimbang kembali hukum aborsi pada kasus kehamilan akibat perkosaan' (Rethinking Islamic law on abortion in the case of rape), *Jurnal Studi Agama dan Masyarakat (Journal of Religion and Social Studies)*, 2(2), 1–16.
Robinson, Kathryn. (2001). 'Gender, Islam and culture in Indonesia.' In Susan Blackburn (ed.), *Love, Sex and Power: Women in Southeast Asia*, 17–30. Clayton, Vic.: Monash Asia Institute.
Robinson, Kathryn. (2009). *Gender, Islam and Democracy in Indonesia*. London: Routledge, DOI: 10.4324/9780203891759.
Rottger-Rossler, Birgitt. (2008). 'Voiced intimacies: Verbalized experiences of love and sexuality in an Indonesian society.' In William R. Jankowiak (ed.), *Intimacies: Love and Sex across Cultures*, 148–73. New York: Columbia University Press.
Sabbah, Fatna A. (1984). *Woman in the Muslim Unconscious*. New York: Pergamon Press.

Sabiq, Sayyid. (1997). *Fiqh al-sunnah*. Cairo: dar al Fath li al A'lam al Araby.
Sciortino, Rosalia, Lies, Marcoes-Natsir, and Masdar F. Mas'udi. (1996). 'Learning from Islam: Advocacy of reproductive rights in Indonesian pesantren.' *Reproductive Health Matters*, 4(8), 86–96, DOI: 10.1016/S0968-8080(96)90305-5.
Sen, Krishna. (1998). 'Indonesian women at work: Reframing the subject.' In Krishna Sen and Maila Stivens (eds.), *Gender and Power in Affluent Asia*, 35–62. London: Routledge.
Shaikh, Sa'dyiia. (2003). 'Family planning, contraception, and abortion in Islam: Undertaking khilafah.' In Daniel C. Maguire (ed.), *Sacred Rights: The Case for Contraception and Abortion in World Religion*, 105–28. New York: Oxford University Press, DOI: 10.1093/acprof:oso/9780195160017.003.0005.
Shaikh, Sa'dyiia. (2007). 'A Tafsir of praxis: Gender, marital violence, and resistance in a South African Muslim community.' In Daniel C. Maguire (ed.), *Violence against Women in Contemporary World Religions: Roots and Cures*, 66–89. Cleveland, OH: Pilgrim Press.
Shahrur, Muhammad. (1994). *Al-kitab wa al-Qur'an: Qira'a mu'asira* (The Book and the Qur'an: Contemporary Reading). Damascus: Al-Ahali li al-Taba'a wa al-Nashr wa al-Tawzi'.
Shefner-Rogers, Corinne L. (2004). 'Pregnancy knowledge, attitudes and practices in Indonesia: Does husband's social support make a difference?' PhD thesis, John Hopkins University, Baltimore, MD.
Sidameh, Abdel Salam. (2001). 'Problems in contemporary applications of Islamic criminal sanctions: The penalty for adultery in relation to women.' *British Journal of Middle Eastern Studies*, 28(2), 187–204, DOI: 10.1080/13530190120083077.
Silvey, Rachel. (2004). 'Gender, socio-spatial networks, and rural migrants in West Java.' In R. Leinbach, (ed.), *The Indonesian Rural Economy: Mobility, Work and Enterprise*, 134–51. Singapore: Institute of Southeast Asian Studies, DOI: 10.1355/9789812305275-012.
Simon, Simon and Susan J. Paxton. (2004). 'Sexual risk attitudes and behaviours among young adult Indonesians.' *Culture, Health & Sexuality*, 6(5), 393–409, DOI: 10.1080/13691050410001680519.
Situmorang, Augustina. (2011). 'Delayed marriage among lower socio-economic groups in an Indonesian industrial city.' In Gavin W. Jones, Terence H. Hull, and Maznah Mohamad (eds.), *Changing Marriage Patterns in Southeast Asia: Economic and Socio-Cultural Dimensions*, 83–98. London: Routledge.
Smith-Hefner, Nancy J. (2005). 'The new Muslim romance: Changing patterns of courtship and marriage among educated Javanese Youth.' *Journal of Southeast Asian Studies*, 36(3), 441–59, DOI: 10.1017/S002246340500024X.
Suhadi. (2004). 'Perebutan wacana Islam kontemporer di Tasikmalaya' (The struggle of contemporary Islamic discourse in Tasikmalaya). In Kutut Suwondo, Nico L. Kana, and Pradjarta Ds (eds.), *Partisipasi dan demokrasi: Dinamika politik lokal di Indonesia* (Participation and democracy: The dynamics of local politics in Indonesia), 190–96. Jakarta: Ford Foundation.
Sullivan, Norma. (1994). *Masters and Managers: A Study of Gender Relation in Urban Java*. St. Leonards, NSW: Allen and Unwin.
Suryakusuma, Julia I. (1996). 'The state and sexuality in new order Indonesia.' In Laurie. J. Sears (ed.), *Fantasizing the Feminine in Indonesia*, 92–119. Durham: Duke University Press.

Tambiah, S. J. (1973). 'Dowry and bridewealth, and the property rights of women in South Asia.' In Jack R. Goody and S. J. Tambiah (eds.). *Bridewealth and Dowry*, 59–72. Cambridge: Cambridge University Press.

Tim Yayasan Rumah Kita Bersama. (2013). *Peta pandangan keagamaan tentang KB (Mapping religious opinions on family planning)*. Bekasi: Yayasan Rumah Kita Bersama.

Tjandraningsih, Indrasari. (2000). 'Gendered work and labour control: Women factory workers in Indonesia.' *Asian Studies Review*, 24(2), 257–68, DOI: 10.1080/10357820008713273.

Turmudi, Endang. (2004). 'Diskursus penerapan syariat Islam: Studi kasus di Tasikmalaya' (The discourse of Islamic shari'a implementation: Case study in Tasikmalaya). In Kutut Suwondo, Nico L. Kana, and Pradjarta Dirdjosanjoto (eds.), *Partisipasi dan demokrasi: Dinamika politik local di Indonesia* (Participation and democracy: The dynamic of local politics in Indonesia), 109–13. Salatiga: Pustaka Percik.

Utomo, Budi (1996). 'Health and social dimensions of infant feeding in Indramayu, West Java.' PhD thesis, The Australian National University, Canberra.

Utomo, Iwu Dwisetyani. (2002). 'Sexual values and early experiences among young people in Jakarta.' In Lenore Manderson and Pranee Liamputtong (eds.), *Coming of Age in Southeast Asia: Youth, Courtship and Sexuality*, 207–27. Richmond: Curzon.

Utomo, Iwu Dwisetyani. (2003). 'Reproductive health education in Indonesia: School versus parents' roles in providing sexuality information.' *Review of Indonesian and Malaysian Affairs*, 37(1), 107–34.

Utomo, Iwu Dwisetyani and Peter, McDonald. (2009). 'Adolescent reproductive health in Indonesia: Contested values and policy inaction.' *Studies in Family Planning*, 40(2), 133–46, DOI: 10.1111/j.1728-4465.2009.00196.x.

Wadud, Amina. (1999). *Qur'an and Woman: Rereading the Sacred Text from a Woman's Perspective*. Oxford: Oxford University Press.

Wadud, Amina. (2006). *Inside the Gender Jihad: Women Reform in Islam*. Oxford: Oneworld.

Warouw, Johannes Nicolaas. (2004). 'Assuming modernity: Migrant industrial workers in Tangerang, Indonesia.' PhD thesis, The Australia National University, Canberra.

Weeks, Jeffrey. (1989). *Sexuality*. London: Routledge.

Welchman, Lynn. (2007). *Women and Muslim Family Laws in Arab States: A Comparative Overview of Textual Development and Advocacy*. Amsterdam: ISIM/Amsterdam University Press.

Wessing, Robert. (1978). *Cosmology and Social Behaviour in a West Javanese Settlement*. Center for International Studies, Ohio University, Athens.

White, Sally and Maria Ulfah Anshor. (2004). 'Islam and gender in contemporary Indonesia: Public discourses on duties, rights and morality.' In Greg Fealy and Sally White (eds.), *Expressing Islam: Religious Life and Politics in Indonesia*, 137–58. Pasir Panjang, Singapore: Institute of Southeast Asian Studies, DOI: 10.1355/9789812308528-012.

Wichelen, Sonja van. (2009). 'Polygamy talk and the politics of feminism: Contestations over masculinity in a new Muslim Indonesia.' *Journal of International Women's Studies*, 11(1), 173–88.

Wichelen, Sonja van. (2010). *Religion, Politics and Gender in Indonesia: Disputing the Muslim Body*. New York: Routledge, DOI: 10.4324/9780203850657.

Wieringa, Saskia E. (1999). 'Desiring bodies or defiant cultures: Butch-femme lesbian in Jakarta and Lima.' In Evelyn Blackwood and Saskia E. Wieringa (eds.), *Female Desires: Same-Sex Relations and Transgender Practices Across Cultures*, 206–31. New York: Columbia University Press.
Wieringa, Saskia E. (2012). 'Passionate aesthetics and symbolic subversion: Heteronormativity in India and Indonesia.' *Asian Studies Review*, 36(4), 515–30, DOI: 10.1080/10357823.2012.739997.
Wieringa, Saskia E., Nursyahbani Katjasungkana, and Irwan M. Hidayana. (2007). 'Pengantar: Heteronormativitas dan pemberdayaan seksual' (Preface: Heteronormativity and sexual empowerment). In Wieringa, Katjasungkana, and Hidayana (eds.). *Hegemoni hetero-normativitas: Membongkar seksualitas perempuan yang terbungkam* (Hegemonic heteronormativity: Deconstructing the curbing of women's sexuality), xi–xxxii. Jakarta: Kartini Network.
Wolf, Diane L. (1992). *Factory Daughters: Gender, Household Dynamics, and Rural Industrialization in Java*. Berkeley: University of California Press.
Yusuf Ali, Abdullah. (2000). *The Holy Qur'an*. London: Wordsworth.
Zia, Afiya Shehrbano. (2000). 'Rape in Pakistan: *Zina* laws – legalities and loopholes.' In Pinar Ilkkaracan (ed.), *Women and Sexuality in Muslim Societies*, 328–38. Istanbul: Women for Women's Human Rights.
Zuidberg, Lida C. L. (ed.). (1978). *Family Planning in Rural West Java: The Serpong Project*. Leiden: Institute of Cultural and Social Studies, University of Leiden.

Legislation

Indonesian Law on Pornography (no. 44/2008), Undang-Undang Republik Indonesia, Nomor 44 Tahun 2008, Tentang Pornografi (UU tentang Pornografi), adopted 30 Oct. 2008, available from: http://www.dpr.go.id/dokjdih/document/uu/UU_2008_44.pdf (accessed 26 February 2020).
Indonesian Law on the Elimination of Domestic Violence (no. 23/2004), Undang-Undang tentang Penghapusan Kekerasan dalam Rumah Tangga (UU PKDRT), adopted 22 September 2004, available from: https://www.ilo.org/dyn/natlex/natlex4.detail?p_lang=en&p_isn=91238&p_country=IDN&p_count=611 (accessed 26 February 2020).
Indonesian Marriage Law (no. 1/1974), Undang-undang Republik Indonesia No 1 Tahun 1974 Tentang an, available from: https://www.scribd.com/doc/53066173/Undang-undang-Republik-Indonesia-No-1-Tahun-1974-Tentang-an (accessed 26 February 2020).
Indonesian Marriage Law no. 16 on amendment to the Indonesian Marriage Law, 2019, available from: http://www.koalisiperempuan.or.id/wp-content/uploads/2019/10/Salinan-UU-Nomor-16-Tahun-2019-.pdf (accessed 13 March 2020).
Indonesian Regulation no. 1636 on Female Circumcision (*sunat perempuan*) of the Ministry of Health and the Ministry of Law and Human Rights, 2010, available from: http://kesmas.kemkes.go.id/perpu/konten/permenkes/pmk-no.-1636-ttg-sunat-perempuan (accessed 13 March 2020).
Indonesian Regulation no. 6 on Annulment of Regulation on Female Circumcision of Ministry of Health, 2014, available from: http://kesmas.kemkes.go.id/perpu/konten/permenkes/pmk_no._6_ttg_sunat_perempuan_ (accessed 13 March 2020).

2 Situating sexuality in fieldwork

Sex research in anthropology is becoming more common and anthropologists have made significant contributions to the literature since the 1970s (Manderson, Bennett, and Sheldrake 1999; Markowitz 1999). This includes acknowledging the sex and sexuality of the researcher during the fieldwork.

Writing a diary of fieldwork experiences is a common practice among anthropologists, and many researchers have addressed the issue of their own sexuality during this time. For example, Evelyn Blackwood (1995) found it was impossible to reveal her sexual identity as a lesbian when conducting research in West Sumatra, Indonesia, where Islam and heterosexuality are central and powerful. In order to fit in with local expectations, she concealed her sexual identity and portrayed herself as heterosexual with a fiancé. Similarly, Diane Wolf (1996) pretended that she was a married woman to gain acceptance in the local community where she was doing research. However, this created a dilemma for these researchers who did not tell the truth about their identity (causing some difficulty and distress) (Blackwood 1995; Wolf 1996).

Wolf (1996) stated that doing fieldwork could create certain challenges for women. Because of their gender, local gender roles were applied to them so they needed to meet local expectations, especially in highly patriarchal societies. Further challenges faced by women who conduct research on sexuality in different places included being asked on dates, being proposed to in order to get married, being asked to engage in sexual activity, and being threatened with rape (Huseby-Darvas 1999; Jones 1999; Moreno 1995; Warren and Hackney 2000).

In Indonesia, many factors such as gender, marital status, ethnicity, and class may influence data gathering during fieldwork (Warren and Hackney 2000). This suggests that researchers will find different answers to research questions depending on whether the participant is male or female, single or married, insider or outsider, or high class or low class. To gain local access and acceptance, researchers should employ certain strategies in Indonesia, especially if researching a sensitive topic like sexuality. For example, same-sex interviewing is preferable in facilitating discussions in order to make participants comfortable with the process of exchanging information. Thus, mixed-gender focus-group discussions on sexuality are considered inappropriate (Hilber et al. 2010), and women should be accompanied by a male if they are interviewing a married man and vice versa. This accompanying male or female could be a male/female assistant but should preferably be a husband, father, wife, or mother. Alison Murray (1999), who did research in Jakarta, stated that it was quite helpful for her (with her foreign appearance) to ask direct questions of her participants concerning their sexual lives. Further, she noted that the participants were more open to answering questions posed by someone who was not part of their community (e.g. a foreigner) than someone they already knew (Murray 1999).

Being single is often an obstacle for female fieldworkers in Indonesia, as experienced by Blackwood and Wolf above. Lynda Newland's (2006) experience of being accepted as a single female conducting research in West Java appears to be quite exceptional. Certain privileges are given to married women (and men) accompanied by their spouses and their children when they are conducting fieldwork. Children are usually a passport to a close relationship with participants (Beatty 2009; Berninghausen and Kerstan 1992).

The above-mentioned descriptions are the experiences of 'outsider' researchers doing research on sexuality in Indonesia. During fieldwork, I also experienced certain issues when interviewing, especially around the often taboo topic of sexuality. Nevertheless, as an insider researcher, I did find some interesting stories while doing sexuality research in my own cultural context.

Positionality and reflexivity of the researcher/ participant in sexual research

> Turning in upon ourselves as researchers makes us look subjectively and reflexively at how we are positioned. Turning in upon ourselves prevents us from removing our selv(es) from our research process, from our connections with our informants, or from our written translation of data to text.
>
> (Chiseri-Strater 1996, 119)

This book is more than my academic journey. It encompasses my identity and my social life as a Sundanese, an Indonesian, and a Muslim woman. This book not only represents the research participants but in some part it also represents me. That is why I positioned myself in this research both as researcher and participant, in the same way as Anne Roald (2004) did when she was researching Muslim women in Europe. My research is about the sexuality of married Muslim women in West Java, Indonesia, and I am a married Muslim woman from West Java.

Unlike other topics which are commonly and openly discussed, such as how to raise children or how to manage daily expenses, sexual identity in relation to behaviour or practice is something that is not openly discussed in the family or in public in Indonesia. Although, sometimes a sex theme is used for making jokes, one's sexual life is still considered private. Discussing it with other people may cause shame or hesitation. With this in mind, I commenced my fieldwork feeling excited and wondering how it would be, as this was my first experience of field research. At the same time, I felt nervous. I was anxious about whether there would be anyone willing to participate in the study. Would they cooperate and would they share their stories?

Anticipating the challenge in this fieldwork, I equipped myself with strategies derived from my reading of feminist ethnography. Many feminists have adopted ethnography as an 'appropriate' way to approach feminist research because it emphasises the interaction between researcher and research and the reciprocity between them (Chiseri-Strater 1996; Jackson 1989; Stacey 1988). I was inspired by the feminist idea of the researcher/researched relationship and how it can be used to understand the experience of others with regard to mutuality, reduced hierarchy, and exploitation (Oakley 1981; Stanley and Wise 1983).

The interview model I used in this research was inspired by feminist research, especially Anne Oakley's article 'Interviewing Women' (1981). Oakley suggests that to interview in a less hierarchical and exploitative way, it is necessary to engage in a two-way communication process and to build a close relationship between the interviewer and interviewee. An in-depth and open-ended interview with the participants is considered 'a strategy for documenting women's own accounts of their lives' (Oakley 1981, 48) that would bring women's experiences to the surface. The feminist researcher should consider participants' experiences as 'new resources for research' and for knowledge references (Harding 1987, 7).

I was aware that conducting research on sexuality might be difficult; sensitive questions might affect participants' responses, or they might even refuse to answer questions or feel uncomfortable. To reduce this possibility, I applied what Ursula King described as a 'self-reflexive perspective' (King 1995, 26)—the representation of my own gender identity within my own culture and society—where I was born and grew up—in concert with a critical (i.e. thoughtful and self-conscious) examination of this representation. The strategy of self-reflexivity worked well during my fieldwork where I engaged closely with participants.

Reflexivity in qualitative research locates the self in the process of collecting data and makes the researcher conscious of the politics of representation (Macbeth 2001; Pillow 2003). When being reflexive, the researcher self-consciously interacts with the 'research world'—the self, the other, the context, and the text—to construct a mutual recognition of experiences, mutual understanding of the experiences, and mutual interpretations and representations of the research process (Chiseri-Strater 1996; Myerhoff and Ruby 1982; Wasserfall 1993). Reflexivity is also considered a suitable strategy for dealing with 'the complexity of fieldwork relations' (Dales 2007).

Elizabeth Chiseri-Strater (1996, 115) has asserted that 'researchers are positioned by age, gender, race, class, nationality, institutional affiliation, historical-personal circumstance, and intellectual predisposition.' The positions represented by the researcher influence the research process and are an integral part of the data (Altorki and El-Solh 1988).

In this research, I considered myself as an insider researcher doing research in my own culture (Okely 1996), and positioned myself not only as researcher but also as a participant in order to minimise the distance in the interpersonal exchange of experiences. Conducting research in my own culture meant I was part of the discussion on the topic being researched. I was both the researcher and the researched. As a researcher, I shared personal and emotional experiences with the participants of my study (Narayan 1989). Further, I expected that in these discussions I would put forward my own opinions in order to raise awareness of women's sexual rights and deepen my understanding of my own cultural and religious construction in relation to women's experiences (Okely 1996).

Since the 1960s, when researching one's own culture became popular, it has been increasingly argued that relevance, authenticity, and involvement in the production of knowledge are important. There are also challenges with respect to objectivity and pattern differentiation (Altorki and El-Solh 1988).

In conventional anthropology, fieldwork has meant conducting research in a place that is far away from 'home'—a place that is unusual and challenging. However, since the late-twentieth century, many anthropologists have conducted fieldwork in their 'home/own' cultures (Okely 1996). There are different challenges and experiences in conducting research in an 'other' and one's 'home/own' country. Scholars who conduct fieldwork in their 'home/own' country enjoy several advantages, such as a basic understanding of the cultural and social background, shared personal and emotional experiences, language assurance, and accessibility (Dyck 2000; Narayan 1993). However, doing fieldwork within my own cultural context, I had to be aware of possible challenges. I did not have to experience being forced to wear the veil, as experienced by Lyn Parker (2007), or convert to certain religious beliefs like Sylva Frisk (2009), but participants could criticise me for engaging with Western theory and ideas in analysing my/their own culture, as was shown in the cases of Virginia Mapedzahama (2007) and Suruchi Thapar-Bjorkert (1999). Similar complexities were addressed by Kirin Narayan (1993) in applying Western theory to her own cultural reality because of differences in experience, expectations, and analysis.

Certain considerations should be taken into account in doing fieldwork in one's 'home/own' realm, especially with the topic of sexuality. Many people in Indonesia still consider sexuality a private matter, and feel uncomfortable and fearful in discussing it. Personal sexual experience is a taboo subject for public discussion. However, as mentioned earlier, especially with regards to popular culture, there is much public discussion and concern about pre-marital and extra-marital sexuality, sexual promiscuity, and pornography. I believe that by conducting private, in-depth interviews with married women, and by presenting myself as an insider, I was able to conduct productive fieldwork.

When undertaking my fieldwork, I felt familiar with the site and knew where to go. Positioning oneself as an insider may not be better, however, than being an outsider—it depends on the context. As Laura Dales (2007) suggests, the insider/outsider position during fieldwork should be flexible in practice. During my fieldwork, most of the time, I enjoyed the privilege of shared gender, which enabled me to get close to women in relationships that were like those between friends, or that between mother and daughter. In this way, I shared life-story conversations as a fellow married Muslim woman.

In line with Warren and Hackney (2000) on factors that influence data gathering, in my experience there are three key factors: gender, marital status, and class. As a woman who had experienced the same gender socialisation as my research participants, it was easier to conduct interviews as a married woman, for whom it is more acceptable to discuss sex than it is for single women. Participants from lower social classes were quite open in their information about their marital sexual relationships compared to higher class women who tended to protect their image. Before beginning an interview, I always introduced myself as an academic who worked in a higher educational institution near the field site. Many of my participants were familiar with my place of work. I was surprised that most of the women were willing to cooperate and disclose their marital sexual experiences, though there were several who were reluctant to reveal their experiences.

As a researcher, there were many times when I was asked to disclose personal information to the female participants. In the interviews, it was not always me who asked the questions. The female participants asked questions as well, mostly about my personal identity or marital experiences; they even wanted to know what I would do in their position. Some women wanted to know my opinion of certain Qur'anic verses and Hadith. I often referred them to books or other reading materials.

Exercising self-reflexivity during my fieldwork was unavoidable for me. During the interviews, which were conversational, personal information was exchanged. Through the reciprocity of sharing personal information, we built mutual understanding and empathy. The resulting closeness and trust that developed further opened up the interaction.

There could be three possible reasons the participants were so willing to disclose their marital sexual experiences with me. First, I situated the sexual conversations within the framework of marriage, of which sex is a part. Second, I started the interview by asking about their marital history; asking them to remember when they first met their husband, which eased the topic into the conversation. Third, I assured them about the confidentiality of the research and that I would protect their identity. Confidentiality was a common issue raised during the interviews. Many of the participants (about 70 percent) had never previously revealed their stories to anyone.

I was honoured, but at the same time felt that it fell upon me to tell their stories appropriately.

During the interviews, when questioning the participants about their sexual experiences, I was very conscious of the need to consider appropriateness. Giggling and/or covering of the mouth were common when the women were answering my questions about their sexual perceptions or practices. These expressions indicated to me that the women were shy (*malu*) in talking about their sexual thoughts or behaviours. A few of the women would simply reply to these questions by saying 'something like that' (*nya kitu wae lah, neng*). On one occasion, a woman also asked me about my marital status, which suggested to me that she felt I was too forward in my discussion of sexual matters. When I said I was married, she looked satisfied. In Indonesia, discussion of sexual matters is not to be shared with unmarried women.

Several of the women cried in the middle of the interviews and their voices were trembling with emotion. For some women, participating in this study was a chance to pour out their feelings (*curhat: curahan hati,* lit. to overflow one's heart) about their marital experiences. For others, it was an opportunity to seek advice about marital problems. Some saw me as a marriage counsellor. In some cases, I could not avoid answering questions or giving advice in relation to their situations. However, when the problem was serious I referred them to professional help for further advice or advocacy. This experience contradicted the advice of Martin Forsey (2013, 17), who states that a 'research interview is NOT a therapy session.' In my case, although I did not, of course, intend to provide therapy in the interviews, there was a therapeutic aspect to the interviewing process. After finishing the interview, many women expressed gratitude for the opportunity to address the issues related to their experiences and to me for listening to their stories. Many felt a heavy burden had been lifted when they shared their marital problems. I realised that it is important for women to have someone to listen to them regarding their wishes, hopes, and expectations in marriage and their lives in general.

As gender significantly influences the analysis and interpretation of data, my understanding of those women's stories is also shaped by my own personal experience, my empathy for the women's experiences, and my feminism. Exercising reflexivity also enabled me to respect whatever opinions the women held.

This ethnographic research was aimed at understanding women's perceptions of marital sexual relations and how cultural and religious teachings influenced their perceptions and guided their practice in marriage. In understanding women's experiences, employing feminist ethnography and self-reflexivity enabled me to engage in very productive fieldwork. I enjoyed the fieldwork. It has enriched and deepened my understanding of my own society (especially women's everyday lives) but, more importantly, it has increased my consciousness of being an active member of the community. Michael Jackson once reminded us: 'Our understanding of others can only proceed from within our own experience, and this experience involves our personalities and histories as much as our field research' (Jackson 1989, 17).

References

Altorki, Soraya and Camillia Fawzi El-Solh. (1988). *Arab Women in the Field: Studying Your Own Society*. New York, NY: Syracuse University Press.
Beatty, Andrew. (2009). *The Shadow Falls in the Hearth of Java*. London: Faber & Faber.
Berninghausen, Jutta and Birgit Kerstan. (1992). *Forging New Paths: Feminist Social Methodology and Rural Women in Java*. London: Zed Book.
Blackwood, Evelyn. (1995). 'Falling in love with an-other lesbian: Reflections on identity in fieldwork.' In Don Kulick and Margaret Wilson (eds), *Taboo: Sex, Identity, and Erotic Subjectivity in Anthropological Fieldwork*, 5–75. London: Routledge, DOI: 10.4324/9780203420379_chapter_2.
Chiseri-Strater, Elizabeth. (1996). 'Turning in upon ourselves: Positionality, subjectivity, and reflexivity in case study and ethnographic research.' In Peter Mortensen and Gesa E. Kirsch (eds), *Ethics and Representation in Qualitative Studies of Literacy*, 115–33. Urbana: National Council of Teachers of English.
Dales, Laura. (2007). 'Feminist fieldwork in Japan (and beyond).' Outskirts: Feminisms along the Edge. *Online Journal*, 17, available from: http://www.outskirts.arts.uwa.edu.au/volumes/volume-17/dales (accessed 8 January 2020).
Dyck, Noel. (2000). 'Home field advantage? Exploring the social construction of children's sports.' In Vered Amit (ed.), *Constructing the Field: Ethnographic Fieldwork in the Contemporary World*, 32–53. London: Routledge, DOI: 10.4324/9780203450789_chapter_3.
Forsey, Martin. (2013). 'Qualitative research interviewing for the uninitiated.' *Lecture*, 20 June. Graduate Research School, University of Western Australia.
Frisk, Sylva. (2009). *Submitting to God: Women and Islam in Urban Malaysia*. Seattle, WA: University of Washington Press.
Harding, Sandra. (1987). *Feminism and Methodology*. Indiana: Indiana University Press.
Hilber, Adriane Martin, Terence H. Hull, Eleanor Preston-Whyte, Brigitte Bagnol, Jenni Smit, Chintana Wacharasin, and Ninuk Widyantoro. (2010). 'A cross cultural study of vaginal practices and sexuality: Implications for sexual health.' *Social Science and Medicine*, 70(3), 392–400, DOI: 10.1016/j.socscimed.2009.10.023.
Huseby-Darvas, E. V. (1999). 'Deconstructing and reconstructing my desexualized identity.' In Fran Markowitz and Michael Ashkenazi (eds), *Sex, Sexuality and the Anthropologist*, 145–58. Urbana: University of Illinois Press.
Jackson, Michael. (1989). *Path toward a Clearing: Radical Empiricism and Ethnographic Inquiry*. Bloomington, IN: Indiana University Press.
Jones, Rose. (1999). 'Husband and lovers: Gender construction and the ethnography of sex research.' In Fran Markowitz and Michael Ashkenazi (eds), *Sex, Sexuality and the Anthropologist*, 25–42. Urbana: University of Illinois Press.
King, Ursula. (1995). 'Introduction: Gender and the study of religion.' In Ursula King (ed.), *Religion and Gender*, 1–38. Oxford: Blackwell.

Macbeth, Douglas. (2001). 'On "reflexivity" in qualitative research: Two readings, and a third.' *Qualitative Inquiry*, 7(1), 35–68, DOI: 10.1177/107780040100700103.

Manderson, Lenore, Linda Rae Bennett, and Mark Sheldrake. (1999). 'Sex, social institutions, and social structure: Anthropological contributions to the study of sexuality.' *Annual Review of Sex Research*, 10, 184–209.

Mapedzahama, Virginia. (2007). 'The crisis of representation: An African researcher's dilemmas in doing feminist cross-cultural fieldwork in Africa and in the West.' In *Outskirts: Feminism along the Edge*, 17, Available from: https://www.outskirts.arts.uwa.edu.au/volumes/volume-17/mapedzahama. (Accessed 30 July 2020)

Markowitz, Fran. (1999). 'Sexing the anthropologist: Implications for ethnography.' In Fran Markowitz and Michael Ashkenazi (eds.), *Sex, Sexuality and the Anthropologist*, 161–74. Urbana: University of Illinois Press.

Moreno, Eva. (1995). 'Rape in the field: Reflection from a survivor.' In Don Kulick and Margaret Wilson (eds.), *Taboo: Sex, Identity and Erotic Subjectivity in Anthropological Fieldwork*, 219–75. London: Routledge, DOI: 10.4324/9780203420379_chapter_8.

Murray, Alison J. (1999). 'Let them take ecstasy: Class and Jakarta lesbians.' In Evelyn Blackwood and Saskia E. Wieringa (eds.), *Female Desires: Same-Sex Relations and Transgender Practices across Cultures*, 139–56. New York: Columbia University Press.

Myerhoff, Barbara and Jay Ruby. (1982). 'Introduction.' In Barbara Myerhoff and Jay Ruby (eds.), *A Crack in the Mirror*, 1–35. Philadelphia, PA: The University of Pennsylvania Press, DOI: 10.9783/9781512806434-003.

Narayan, Kirin. (1993). 'How native is a "native" anthropologist?' *American Anthropologist*, 95(3), 671–86, DOI: 10.1525/aa.1993.95.3.02a00070.

Narayan, Uma. (1989). 'The project of feminist epistemology: Perspectives from a nonwestern feminist.' In Alison M. Jaggar and Susan Bordo (eds.), *Gender/Body/Knowledge/: Feminist Reconstructions of Being and Knowledge*, 256–69. New Jersey: Rutgers University Press.

Newland, Lynda. (2006). 'Female circumcision: Muslim identities and zero tolerance policies in rural West Java.' *Women's Studies International Forum*, 29(4), 394–404, DOI: 10.1016/j.wsif.2006.05.005.

Oakley, Ann. (1981). 'Interviewing women: A contradiction in terms.' In Helen Roberts (ed.), *Doing Feminist Research*, 30–61. London: Routledge & Kegan Paul.

Okely, Judith. (1996). *Own or Other Culture*. London: Routledge, DOI: 10.4324/9780203973790.

Parker, Lyn. (2007). 'Of faith and feminism: Imagining discursive feminist space for Muslim.' *Outskirts: Feminism along the Edge*, 17, available from: http://www.outskirts.arts.uwa.edu.au/volumes/volume-17/parker (accessed 24 November 2011).

Pillow, Wanda. (2003). 'Confession, catharsis, or cure? Rethinking the use of reflexivity as methodological power in qualitative research.' *International Journal of Qualitative Studies in Education*, 16(2), 175–96, DOI: 10.1080/0951839032000060635.

Roald, Anne Sofie. (2004). 'Who are the Muslims? Questions of identity, gender and culture in research methodologies.' In Tina Beattie and Ursula King (eds.), *Gender, Religion and Diversity: Cross Cultural Perspectives*, 179–80. London: Continuum.

Stacey, Judith. (1988). 'Can there be a feminist ethnography?' *Women's Studies International Forum*, 11(1), 21–27, DOI: 10.1016/0277-5395(88)90004-0.

Stanley, Liz and Sue Wise. (1983). *Breaking Out: Feminist Consciousness and Feminist Research*. London: Routledge.

Thapar-Bjorkert, Suruchi. (1999). 'Negotiating otherness: Dilemmas for a non-western researcher in the Indian sub-continent.' *Journal of Gender Studies*, 8(1), 57–69, DOI: 10.1080/095892399102823.

Warren, Carol A. B. and Jennifer Kay Hackney. (2000). *Gender Issues in Ethnography* (2nd ed.). Thousand Oaks, CA: SAGE Publications.

Wasserfall, Rahel. (1993). 'Reflexivity, feminism and difference.' *Qualitative Sociology*, 16(1), 23–41, DOI: 10.1007/BF00990072.

Wolf, Diane L. (1996). 'Situating feminist dilemmas in fieldwork.' In Wolf (ed.), *Feminist Dilemmas in Fieldwork*, 1–55. Boulder: CO: Westview Press, DOI: 10.4324/9780429493843-1.

3 Women's perceptions and expectations of marriage and sexual relations

In this chapter, I explore the perceptions and expectations of women about marriage and sexual relations in West Java. In this context, understanding women's perceptions and expectations of marriage and sexual relations should be situated within the framework of an active relationship between Indonesia's imposed state gender ideology and other authoritative texts and local traditions, including religious texts and traditions. The gender ideology deployed during the Soeharto era (1966–98) influenced the construction of women's subjectivity. Islam, through its teaching, has strengthened the state gender ideology and contributed to the construction of women's subjectivity.

Most women I interviewed were aware that marriage brings happiness as well as unhappiness. They were made aware of this through the marriages of their parents, neighbours, and friends. Marriage was an important life stage for these women. As in many other regions in Indonesia, marriage in West Java establishes a person's place in social life as an adult and a full member of society (Grijns 1987; Wessing 1978). However, research by Hiroko Horikoshi (1976) mentioned that marriage did not necessarily grant a woman full adulthood until she had delivered a baby. Horikoshi's finding confirmed Marilyn Strathern's (1993, 42) observation that a woman gains 'less-than-full social status' compared to a man even after she has performed certain rites (like puberty or marriage), because she is seen in terms of her biological function rather than her social function. In the Sundanese community described by Horikoshi (1976), a woman is seen to gain full adulthood through fertility and she is considered an 'incomplete' human being until and unless she marries and bears a child (Strathern 1993, 42).

This 'incomplete' woman's social status is strengthened by both cultural and religious gender stereotypes. For example, in the Sundanese community it is said that *'awewe mah dulang ti nande'* (women are like a big rice bowl waiting to be filled), which means that a woman has to wait and follow her husband. Another saying, *'awewe mah pondok lengkah'* (women's footsteps are short), means that women's movements are limited. These stereotypes influence sexual and labour divisions within the family and society, limiting women's participation in the public sphere. An ideal Sundanese wife is expected to stay in the house waiting for her husband to return from work and she is expected not to go outside (to work or visit relatives/friends) except with the permission of her husband.

The participants in my study wished to get married at least once in their lifetime. Accordingly, they would prepare for their marriage carefully. As I observed during the interviews, women with higher levels of education considered it important to know their partner's character, family background, and friends prior to getting married, in order to avoid a miscast marriage and to minimise marital conflict. In contrast, women with lower educational backgrounds did not seriously take into consideration such factors. In general, partners from similar cultural backgrounds were preferred in order that they could easily adapt to each other.

The idea that a man was the head of the household and the breadwinner was deeply embedded in the minds of the women in this study when they came to select a marriage partner. Many women perceived that for them, marriage is about serving their husbands, reproduction and obedience. Regardless of their educational background, most women agreed that it is a wife's duty to serve her husband, including having sexual relations. These women perceived this submissive sexual activity as a naturally conceived duty in the marital relationship. This perception of a hierarchical relation in married life was strong, and is supported by state law (the 1974 Indonesian Marriage Law) and religious texts (the Qur'an, Hadith, and *fiqh*).

Listening to women's voices and recognising their experiences of daily life, I realised that in practice the women employed various strategies so they could meet their expected roles and duties in marriage. In this chapter, I demonstrate how the women in this study understood and reacted to the reality they experienced; how they interacted with other members of society, and how they negotiated certain conditions to form their own consciousness within the established social, cultural, and religious expectations directed at them.

Marriage as social, cultural, and religious obligations

Marriage is an ideal norm in Indonesian society in general. In West Java, the prestige associated with marriage is also directed towards the parents of the married couple. In Sundanese culture, marriage of one's children is considered a parental responsibility (Muchtar and Umbara 1977; Suhamihardja 1984). Consequently, parental blessing is an important aspect of marriage. Previously, underage (teen) marriage was common in West Java (Jones 2001; Jones, Asari, and Djuartika 1994). Nowadays, according to Gavin Jones and Bina Gubhaju (2011), West Java is no longer the province with the earliest marriage age. However, the practice of early marriage has not disappeared altogether. It is still practised by many, especially in rural areas (Iswarini 2011; Jones 2011). This practice in several areas in West Java, as in Cirebon, Sukabumi, and Bogor as reported in a monograph series published by Yayasan Rumah Kita Bersama, is associated with tradition, misinterpretation of Islamic texts, and the economy (Agustinah 2016; Ali 2016; Syatibi 2016). In Sunda, parents feel secure when they marry off a daughter early; it means that their daughter was marriageable (*laku*). Parents acknowledged that it was more difficult with daughters than sons when it came to the consequences of any sexual activity. The parents' biggest fear was that their daughters might engage in illicit sex or be raped, which would damage their reputation. In reality, though, rape is not a common threat in daily life. Contrary to this perceived threat, Atsushi Sano (2012) reports that many teenage girls in Indramayu, in the coastal area of West Java, were forced by their parents to undertake sex work in order to contribute to the household income, even to the extent of sacrificing their education.

Women experience greater pressure to marry than men. Gendered double standards require women to remain virgins and abstain from sexual encounters before marriage. Failure to demonstrate modesty and virginity will attribute a young woman with less value as a prospective wife and mother. Research in Lombok, another region in Indonesia, showed that preserving a good sexual reputation was important for women before marriage (Bennett 2005). This also applies elsewhere in Indonesia. Marriage also signifies the recognition of women's role in society and the nation. A woman is identified according to the binary opposition of man/woman, public/domestic. The labelling of women as *jomlo* (without partner) or *perawan tua* (old maid) can cause embarrassment to the woman herself and to her whole family. Similar standards do not apply to men.

Three factors influenced the decision to get married among my participants: parental and community pressure, age, and living in with a non-parental guardian. The primary reason for marriage was parental and community pressure. Most parents who demanded their daughter get married were seen as responding to community pressure, wherein neighbours and villagers would repeatedly ask parents when their daughter was going to get married. The social convention that says that women must marry is quite strong in West Java. A single woman is the target of gossip and sometimes mockery around the neighbourhood. The quotation below is one example indicating this pressure.

> Being the only single person aged 24 in the village at the time, I had to deal with so many fingers pointing at me. They [the neighbours] said that I was too picky, demanding only a man with a university degree for a husband—and there was not even one available in the village. In fact, I had simply not found the right one.
>
> (Ida, aged 36)

Another factor for getting married was age. Although many Indonesian women nowadays marry at a later age that previously, in some cases, when they are over 30, many women panic as they age and are likely to consider any already existing candidates for marriage. In several circumstances, women in this study had to forget about romantic love or getting to know the personality of their partners prior to marriage. This rushed decision, meant that women risked unpleasant treatment or marital abuse from their husbands. This was experienced by Sofi (aged 39) who was forced to marry by her parents because she was 34 at that time. When her uncle introduced her to a man, Sofi agreed, although she was unsure about marrying someone unfamiliar. Sofi experienced abusive treatment from her husband during the short duration of their marriage.

The third reason for women marrying was to remove themselves from living arrangements under non-parental guardianship. When parents' divorce and enter into another marriage, they sometimes leave their children to be taken care of by relatives or grandparents. Several women I interviewed, who lived in such situations, felt uncomfortable and decided to leave as soon as possible. Getting married is one way they can do this. This was the experience of Rani (aged 40) whose parents died when she was two years old. She was raised by her eldest sister for 19 years. She had no other choice but to accept the first man who proposed to her. She said:

> If it were not for the fact that I did not want to burden my sister any more, I would not have accepted my husband's proposal to marry. I was not ready to get married, I was not even thinking about it. Besides, I still wanted to choose a partner who had a better job and was rich.

Marriage is also seen as a religious requirement. In Islam, it is considered part of *sunnah,* practiced by the Prophet Muhammad. Muslims are encouraged to get married as marriage is also perceived as *ibadah* (part of worshipping God).

Recent studies of marriage in Indonesia indicate that there are changing attitudes towards marriage (Jones 1994, 2011). Delayed marriage and self-arranged marriage have become trendy among women, especially in urban areas (Situmorang 2011). Increased opportunities in education and paid work for women have strongly influenced this attitude (Jones 1994).

Social attitudes towards marriage, then, are expected to alter following changes in marriage patterns. Women should be given the opportunity to decide what is best for themselves—when, whom, and how to marry, or whether to marry or not. Cheryl Rampage (2002) suggests that it is time for the institution of marriage to adapt and this would include changes to the marriage law, as discussed above.

Women's dreams, expectations, and the reality of marriage and sex

For most women that I interviewed, an ideal marriage partner was a man with a good physical appearance (*berbadan tegap*), who is handsome (*ganteng*), and wealthy (*kaya*). In reality, however, many of these women could not find a man who could meet their criteria. In many cases, they had only a limited choice about whom they could marry. Parental and social pressure for marriage, age, and non-parental living arrangements, as explained above, pushed them to marry the first available candidate, without having much time for further consideration.

After marriage, women changed their criteria for ideal marriage partners. For example, Maya (aged 41), after she was married, said: 'An ideal marriage partner—it's not only about his physical appearance, which I used to dream of, but the most important thing is a mutual understanding of each other's limitations and weaknesses.' Rani (aged 40) also said: 'Before, my ideal marriage partner was someone who was handsome and wealthy. Nowadays, being good-looking is not what matters, but providing rice every day to survive.'

One interviewee, though, described her ideal marriage partner quite differently. Brought up in a devoted religious family who owned a *pesantren*, Hera (aged 28) wished to be married just like the daughters of her relatives, whose husbands were chosen by their parents and without courtship. She felt that she had been rebellious because she had not followed these processes. She told me that, 'I wished my husband was a *santri* (student in a *pesantren*), with good religious knowledge. But he [the husband] is not.' Later in their marriage, Hera's husband did become keen to improve his religious knowledge.

After marrying, several women also gave up their paid work, especially when the first baby arrived. Many of the couples did not delay in having children. The wife would get pregnant two or three months after the wedding. This pregnancy was also seen as proof of woman's reproductive capability.

Several women did have expectations of their partners within marriage. They set criteria and shared those with their partners before and within marriage. Some women expected that their partners comprehend and appreciate both parties' interests throughout the marriage. Mia (aged 25), for example, was keen to know whether her partner would support her either to work or to pursue further studies after they married. It was a difficult process to convince her partner before marrying. However, Mia continued her negotiations until they finally reached an agreement.

Other women expected that their future husbands would have a great sense of responsibility and independence. They anticipated that within marriage, their husbands would become leaders of their families. Consequently, they thought that it was important to marry a man who had a great sense of responsibility and independence and was not dependent on his parents. Leli (aged 29) decided to end her engagement with her fiancé because of his dependency on his mother when making decisions. Leli predicted that the parent would likely interfere with their marital affairs. Relationships with in-laws are important in West Java, especially for women who have their habits and behaviour monitored. Mala (aged 40), for example, was questioned by her mother-in-law and sister-in-law because she allocated housework to her husband, and her mother-in-law was not pleased that her son did housework.

Women from low educational and economic backgrounds usually did not place too many expectations on their marriage partner. Economics was one reason for getting married. Anah (aged 30) told me that she experienced better economic conditions after marriage:

> Before marriage, if I wanted to buy something like clothing or shoes I could not afford to buy these things. I did not dare to ask my parents as they were having difficulty in providing our daily expenses. After marriage, my husband provided what I needed.

Nowadays, with more opportunities for women in education and paid work, women's expectations of marriage and their partners have also gone up. As women participate more in paid work, they tend to expect their husbands to be more involved with housework and child rearing. However, in practice, this is not easy to manage because in marriage women are perceived to be primarily responsible for the domestic domain. Intensive communication is essential to make equal marriage arrangements possible. Some women taught their husbands to do housework such as sweeping the floor, washing the dishes, and taking care of the baby. Mala (aged 38) said:

> I hated to see my husband sit and watch TV while there were dirty dishes waiting to be washed. And I was too tired to do all that stuff after working all day. I began to talk to my husband about the household division of labour.

At first, her husband refused to participate, but after Mala told him she really needed help with all the housework, her husband grudgingly agreed (*terpaksa*).

This shift in women's expectations of marriage requires men to be more willing to participate in daily household affairs. Several women in my study managed to ask their husbands to participate more in domestic work, but men's level of engagement in housework is still low.

In terms of sexual relations, there was also a significant change among the younger women in my study. Rarely did older generations communicate about what kind of sexual relationship they would like to have, or how many children they wanted. The younger generation, in contrast, managed their marital relationship through intense communication about children and sexual relations. Most participants, those who married after 1995, mentioned that their husbands gave them the freedom to choose how many children to have, based on the wives' readiness to have more children or not. However, men still dominated in terms of initiating sex. Women only rarely invited their husband to have sex. Detailed discussion of the couple's sexual relationships is provided in Chapters 5 and 6.

There are indications of a more democratic relationship in marriages in West Java in contemporary times. This suggests a shift towards more flexible gender roles, especially in the sharing of duties and responsibilities between the partners. This could be traced to women who have acquired knowledge about marriage and sexuality, which has significantly influenced women's perceptions and expectations of marriage and sexuality. I will interrogate this empowerment of women in more detail in the next section.

Sources of knowledge about marriage and sexuality

> Women came to their marriage beds with ... very little exact knowledge of sexual relations or the way their bodies worked.
>
> (Bauer 1985, 121)

This quote describes the condition of women on their wedding night in Iran 35 years ago, as reported by Janet Bauer (1985). The observation is also relevant to the contemporary Indonesian context where many women have limited (if any) knowledge concerning sexual relations in marriage.

Data from my study suggest that no formal information is given to women about life within marriage or about sexual relations in marriage. The government of Indonesia is still reluctant to offer formal sex education in the school curriculum despite many studies suggesting there is high demand.[1] As a result, many women, prior to marriage, have to search for information about marital life, including sex. Preliminary knowledge may already have been obtained through observing their parents' practices and cultural values. They gain further information from reading books, attending religious meetings, or talking with friends; even so some women have no information concerning marriage and sexuality before marriage. They are even less likely to obtain information on sexual relations than they are on marital life due to the taboo and shame associated with public discussion of sex in Indonesian society in general. In the following section, I explain how women in the study gained information concerning marriage and sexuality.

There are four main sources considered influential in providing information on marriage and sexuality according to the women I interviewed: marriage and sex manual books, *pengajian* (religious gatherings), peer conversation, and socially and culturally learned behaviour.

Of the 42 women interviewed, 33 accessed information on marriage and sexuality from books that they read; 13 women learned from discussions about marriage but not about sex; 15 women learned from religious gatherings; 8 received information on marriage and sexuality from friends; 4 learned from parents about marriage; and 2 respondents obtained information on sex from their parents as well. This data suggests that women commonly gain information from a combination of sources. Seven respondents mentioned that they did not know anything about marriage and sexual life in marriage prior to the event. However, I would categorise them as having knowledge from observing their parents or neighbourhood marriages even though this might not have been an intentional process.

Islamic marriage and sex manuals

According to the Oxford Dictionary (Stevenson 2010, s.v. manual), a manual is 'a book giving instructions or information.' A marriage and sex manual is a book that contains instructions and information concerning marriage and sex. It is a practical guide to sex and married life. For this study, I differentiate this type of manual from self-help books on marriage and sex. Self-help books advocate 'the use of one's own efforts and resources to achieve things without relying on others' (Stevenson 2010, s.v. self-help). A self-help book on marriage and sex presumes self-motivation and self-reliance to improve the quality of one's married life and sex life. The difference between manuals and self-help books on marriage and sexuality is that the former give instructions and guidance for people who are getting married while the latter provide advice to married couples to improve the quality of married life, sometimes with 'therapeutic ideas and values' (Grodin 1991, 405). Arlie Hochschild (2003, 13) reports that in America the self-help 'advice book' related to intimate life has become more popular than the traditional advice of families or religious authorities. In Indonesia, the self-help book genre has flourished since the mid-1990s (Hariyadi 2013).

Most of the participants in this study referred to marriage and sex manual books to find information concerning marriage and sexuality. Therefore, I categorise two types of books that provide information on marriage and sexuality, as mentioned by participants. First are books related to marriage and sexuality in the Indonesian language, which are available in many bookstores (Figures 3.1 and 3.2). Marriage manual books are popular and can easily be obtained from bookstores in a city centre. Several participants noted that they read this kind of book before marriage, and some of them continued to read them after marriage. Second, there are classical Islamic books (known as *kitab kuning*) on marriage and sexuality that were read by my participants while they were studying at *pesantren* (Islamic boarding school) (Figures 3.3–3.5).

Marriage manuals generally contain instructions or advice on marriage, from marriage preparation, the wedding ceremony and the first night, through to duties and rights for couples when raising children. Some books of both categories discuss sexual life in more detail than others. Most of the books referred to by the participants were written from Islamic perspectives. Thus, I consider this type of book as an Islamic marriage and sex manual. In this section, I will review five books that have been read by several of my participants as representative of the above-mentioned descriptions.

88 *Women's perceptions and expectations*

Figure 3.1 Islamic Marriage and Sex Manual, Book 1.

Source: Photographed by author, 16 November 2012.

Examples of the first category of marriage and sex manual books are as follows: The first book, *Kado Pernikahan untuk Istriku* (Marriage gift for my wife) (1999), was written by a famous author, Muhamad Fauzil Adhim. This book is a compilation of his three books on marriage.[2] It contains information on the engagement, the wedding ceremony, the wedding night, sexual

Figure 3.2 Islamic Marriage and Sex Manual, Book 2.

Source: Photographed by author, 16 November 2012.

etiquette in Islam, marital adjustment, and raising children. The author starts by strongly encouraging marriage in Islam, but, in a disproportionate way, he depicts unmarried people as having no place in Islam. For example, he devalues all good deeds done by unmarried people and says that the deeds of the unmarried are never better than those of married people (Adhim 1999, 3).

In the discussion of *malam zafaf* (the wedding night), the author explains the rituals that both partners should undertake before this night in order that it is unforgettable. Grooming before spending the night together for the first

Figure 3.3 Uqud al-Lujayn.

Source: Photographed by the author, 16 November 2012.

time is important in order to give a good impression. He also suggests that the couple should make ablutions and pray together. Before intercourse, certain prayers (*do'a*) should be recited. Further, the book suggests that the husband should be aware of the readiness of the wife to have intercourse for the first time: he should approach her gently and never force her. Foreplay (*muqaddimah*) is encouraged, to achieve mutual orgasm with touching and kissing. The wife is also encouraged to be active and attractive (Adzim 1999, 127–144).

The second book is *Seks Tak Sekedar Birahi: Panduan Lengkap Seputar Kesehatan Reproduksi: Tinjauan Islam dan Medis* (Sex is not just lust:

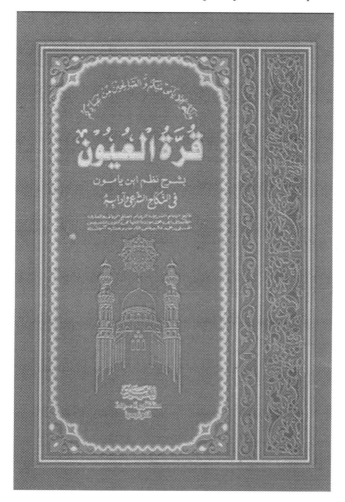

Figure 3.4 Qurratul 'Uyun.

Source: Photographed by the author, 16 November 2012.

Comprehensive guide on reproductive health from Islamic and medical perspectives) (2006) written by two authors: Hanny Ronosulistyo, an obstetrician and gynaecologist in Bandung, and Aam Amiruddin, a famous preacher in Bandung. This book brings together comprehensive information on reproductive health and sexuality from Islamic and medical perspectives. The book aims to end the taboo on discussions about sex between wife and husband to increase knowledge on this matter and to intensify intimate relationships between the wife and husband. The book contains 13 chapters that begin with definitions of sex and health, and go on to elaborate

Figure 3.5 Al-Liqa baina al-Zawjayni.

Source: Photographed by the author, 16 November 2012.

on adolescence sexuality, sexual intimacy in marriage, sexual and reproductive health, sexual rights, and tips on how to avoid sexual and reproductive problems (Ronosulistyo and Amiruddin 2006, xvi). There are many medical terms but these are accompanied by simple explanations that can be easily understood. The Islamic understanding comes from a moderate perspective that emphasises mutual recognition of sexual rights for both sexes. Compared to the first book, this book is more comprehensive, because it provides information on the human body and how it works to maximise health and encourage sexual relationships with religious support.

These two books also provide information about many of the practices of the Prophet Muhammad and his companions, and cite many religious texts on the subject. However, their claims are not always valid. Many books on marriage and sex manuals are written by male authors. It is hard to find books of this kind written by female authors. Based on my exploration of three big publishing companies in Indonesia (Gramedia, Mizan, and Gema Insani Press), most of the books on this genre are written by men. In my opinion, this relates to the issue of male authority. Men are seen in a patriarchal society such as Indonesia as having authority in giving guidance, especially in marriage and sexual matters. Explaining from a man's perspective, the first book displays the traditional ideology of the wife–husband relationship based on values in traditional Islam; men have the power to control married life, including sexual relations. In sexual relations, although this book recognises the wife's sexual desire and need for satisfaction, the husband is still the one who controls it and his sexual desire deserves more attention than that of the wife. The second book presents more balanced information and particularly emphasises the mutual rights of husband and wife in the sexual relationship.

The second category of marriage guidance manuals contains the classical Islamic books (*kitab kuning*) read in *pesantren*. Those on marriage and sex are: *Kitab Uqud al-Lujayn fi Bayan al-Huquq al-Zawjayn* (Marital bonds: Explanation of the rights of the wife and the husband) (Figure 3.3); *Qurratul 'Uyun fi al-Nikah al-Syar'iy wa Adabihi* (2005) (the comfort of the eyes: Shar'i marriage and its etiquette) (Figure 3.4); and *al-Liqa baina al-Zawjayni* (Sexual congress between wife and husband: Perspectives of the Qur'an and Sunnah) (1980) (Figure 3.5), all of which are written in Arabic and some are familiar among *santri* (*pesantren* students).

The most popular book referred to by my respondents was *Kitab Uqud al-Lujayn (Uqud)* (n.d.). This *kitab* was written in 1878 by Syeikh Nawawi al-Bantani, a famous *ulama* from Banten. This *kitab* is very popular in the Nahdlatul Ulama (NU) *pesantren* community and has become the main reference dealing with the marital relationship (Bruinessen 1995). This book explains the traditional Islamic viewpoint of the husband–wife relationship on duties and rights. It suggests that women pray at home, gives instruction about the prohibition on looking at the opposite sex, and advice about the behaviour of women. Most of the explanations in this *kitab* position woman as second to man in marriage and give the wife more duties than her husband. The main rule is that the wife should be obedient to the husband and provide him with sexual services. One striking feature of this *kitab* is that the author listed several conditions under which the husband is permitted to hit his wife, namely: when she refuses to beautify herself or to have sex; when she leaves the house without his permission; or when she insults him (Al-Bantani 2005, 12). In fact, Al-Bantani's opinion on violence towards wives has no basis in Islamic texts; it is only his opinion. This book's main focus is to provide information about how the wife should behave in relation to her husband and not vice versa. It depicts women's behaviour as routinely defiant, ill-mannered, and stupid. According to Al-Bantani, it is the husband's duty to teach his wife, thus suggesting that the woman has inferior intellectual and religious abilities. The author emphasises the physical and intellectual superiority of men over women.

Kitab Uqud has been criticised by progressive Muslims in Indonesia because it establishes the patriarchal order through promoting an unequal marital relationship. This *kitab* is believed to have influenced many Indonesians in their marital relationships. Several women in my study referred to this *kitab* as the guide they use in their marital relationships. The Study Forum of *Kitab Kuning* (Forum Kajian Kitab Kuning, FK3) established by Sinta Nuriyah—wife of former Indonesian President Abdurrahman Wahid—initiated a critique of this *kitab*. The critique aimed to trace the validity of the Prophetic reports and to clarify women's position in Islam. According to FK3, many Hadith cited in *Kitab Uqud* have no validity in relation to having been reported by the Prophet and have just been fabricated (Forum Kajian Kitab Kuning 2005, 34). The group has published two books containing criticisms of *Kitab Uqud*,[3] but, unfortunately, the critiques of *Kitab Uqud* are not yet widely known, and students (*santri*) do not read these books alongside the *Kitab Uqud*.

Another *kitab* that is important in giving information about marital sexual relations in Indonesia is *Qurratul 'Uyun,* written by Imam Abu Muhammad al-Tihami (2005). This book contains a sex manual based on detailed Islamic etiquette. The *kitab* starts by encouraging readers to marry and expounding on the benefits of marriage. Then, it presents guidance on sexual relationships as follows: favourable and unfavourable times to have sex; rituals to undertake before intercourse (ablution, praying, and reciting prayers); foods that increase and decrease sexual desire; the importance of foreplay; the recommended position for sex (missionary position) with detailed steps on how to achieve the most exciting sexual intercourse for both partners (Al-Tihami 2005, 28 - 51).

Kitab Qurratul 'Uyun is also popular among *santri* (students) in *pesantren* but less popular than *Kitab Uqud*. This *kitab* is considered to be suitable for an advanced level in giving information on marital sexual relationships in *pesantren*. Only *santri* who are mature and are preparing for marriage can read this *kitab*. Only two respondents mentioned having read this *kitab* compared to 13 women who had read *Kitab Uqud*.

Kitab Uqud is usually learned in *pesantren* at the intermediate level. Most of the women I interviewed mentioned that when they read it they did not understand its content because at that time they were still a long way from considering marriage. Some women (Ida and Sandra) assessed *Kitab Uqud* and the explanations given by the teacher (*ustadz*) as indecent (*jorok*) because of the detailed explanations of intercourse and the sexual organs.[4] Many of my research participants were still significantly informed and influenced by *Kitab Uqud* and referred to this *kitab* in their daily sexual relationships.

The third *kitab* is *Al-Liqa baina al-Zawjayn (Liqa)*. It was written by Abdul Qadir Ahmad 'Atha from Cairo in 1980. This *kitab* aims to give information about wife–husband relationships based on the Qur'an and Sunnah and it includes information on bodily cleanliness that can increase the couple's intimacy. The book begins by explaining the meaning of certain Arabic words in the Qur'anic verses about the conjugal relationship, such as the word *sukun* (tranquillity), *mawaddah wa rahmah* (love and mercy) (Q. 30: 21)[5], and *libas* (garment) (Q. 2: 187).[6] The author explains that the word *sukun* means free from any worry and fear and the couple will feel full of love, safe, and confident. The word *libas* means covering each other's limitations by complementing each other. When two people unite in one body during intercourse, both of them feel joy and satisfaction in exploring each other's bodies. The word *libas* is mentioned in the Qur'an interchangeably between wife and husband to show that there is mutuality and tenderness between the couple in word or deed (Ahmad 'Atha 1980).

Kitab Liqa is promising in giving information on marital sexual relationship as it puts emphasis on the couple's mutual sexual satisfaction. Foreplay, like sweet words and kissing (not limited to lips and face), is strongly recommended for both partners to achieve pleasurable sex. This *kitab* also dismisses the assumption that it is forbidden to be fully naked during intercourse (several women in this study said they believed this to be so). The author showed that the Hadith that support this assumption are *dla'if* (weak/unreliable). The author also provided the *shahih* (valid/reliable) Hadith that states it is fine to be fully naked during intercourse and to see each other's naked body (Ahmad 'Atha 1980, 92). Unfortunately, *Kitab Liqa* is not yet popular among *santri* in *pesantren*. Based on my observations and interviews with the *kyai* in Eastern Bandung, only one *pesantren* uses this *kitab* and the *kyai* claimed that no *pesantren* besides his own includes this *kitab* in the curriculum (Interview with the *kyai* of al-Khomis *pesantren*, 13 July 2012).

From the above observation, we can conclude that the second and third *kitab* are quite promising in giving information on sexuality within a less hierarchical marital relationship, and where the emphasis is on mutual satisfaction in sex. These last two books, which advocate equality between the couple, are preferable to the *Kitab Uqud,* and it may be that the *Kitab Uqud* should in fact no longer be read. Nevertheless, this review confirms that sex education has been initiated within *pesantren*.

Pengajian (religious study gatherings)

Other sources that respondents identified as being influential in giving information about marriage and sexual relations were *pengajian* (religious gatherings) or *majlis ta'lim* (women's religious gatherings).[7] These gatherings are usually attended by married women, most of whom are elderly. The themes are various but generally and foremost the (mostly male) preachers explain about the marital duties of women in relation to their husbands. The women I interviewed referred to some of the themes they had covered in *majlis ta'lim: ta'at* (being obedient to the husband); never refusing a husband's satisfaction of his sexual needs; how to behave towards the husband; and encouraging women to be patient (*sabar*) and forgiving (*pemaaf*) if they experience problems within the marriage.

Through *pengajian*, married women are given spiritual solutions to the problems they experience during marriage, but these 'solutions' usually consist of convincing them that they will be rewarded in the hereafter—not an immediate solution for their real, this life problems. The *pengajian* are influential in imposing religious messages because the messages are delivered repeatedly during weekly or monthly gatherings and because they are backed up by '*dalil*' (religious argument or proof-texts). One of my participants, Rani (43), said that since she had been actively engaged in *majlis ta'lim*, she had been influenced by the messages given by the preacher: 'We have to obey what is said in *pengajian* because there is *dalil* supporting the suggestion from religious texts; whether we like it or not.' Her example was that whenever she couldn't be bothered having sex with her husband, she felt she had to do it because it was her duty, whether she enjoyed it or not. Lies Marcoes (1992, 22) has described how topics relating to women's position are discussed in *majlis ta'lim,* but they do not empower the audience with the knowledge that women have certain rights in Islam. Instead, many preachers (including women preachers) emphasise the duty of women to be obedient to and serve their husbands.

Peer conversations

Friends who are already married were considered reliable sources of information on marriage and sexual relations. Through informal conversations, they shared their experiences of life in marriage and sometimes that included sexual relations. The women I interviewed, explicitly referred to their friends as sources of information on marriage. This conversation usually took place during special gatherings, while 'hanging out' or in home visits.

Maya (aged 41) and Ina (aged 33) shared their experience of gaining information from their friends. Ina said:

> My friend said that in marriage you will experience happiness and unhappiness. The happy side is that you will have someone at your side who can protect you and share everything with you, but the sad side of it is when you quarrel with your husband or when a 'third' person interferes in the marriage.

According to Maya and Ina this 'third' person can be the mother-in-law, a relative or 'another woman.'

Friends also share common beliefs about how marital relationships should be. For example, they believe that a wife should serve her husband in every aspect of married life, take care of the children, and never refuse sex to her husband. Nanda (aged 36) explained: 'My friend told me that when you are married, you should never refuse your husband's sexual demands if he asks for it.' Heni (aged 51) also explained:

> One thing that I remembered about the conversation with friends was that a wife should give full service towards the husband. I myself consider that I still cannot provide full service to my husband because I also work. In my opinion, it depends upon the couple's agreement in the arrangement of the house. My friend also shared about the wedding night, about how the husband will be pleased if the bride is a virgin.

Virginity is highly valued in Indonesian society. Although most women are virgins at the time of their first marriage, as a result of abstinence imposed by the *zina* concept, there are of course many cases where a couple married because of pre-marital sex that caused pregnancy. In Indonesia, this situation usually referred to by the joke acronym, MBA (married by accident).

The workplace is also where experiences about marriage are shared, but only among close friends. These friends might also share their sexual experiences, but usually only among other married friends and not among singles. Married women keep such matters secret from single women and lower their voices when talking. They will giggle and even laugh out loud when they consider a story amusing. However, occasionally, sexual experience might be shared with single women who are approaching marriage. This happened to Wiwi (aged 50) and Ikah (aged 30) who were told by their married friends about marital and sexual experiences. At that time, they were single but were getting married soon. Ikah said:

> My friend scared me by mentioning that during the first night, on the wedding night, the first intercourse will hurt, and if you refuse him, he will force you to have sex. I felt scared at that time, but luckily, my husband is not that kind of person, he is gentle and kind.

Learned behaviour

Some of the women I interviewed depended on learned patterns of behaviour for their knowledge of marriage. They looked to cultural patterns—most of which were parental practices and behaviours that they observed in the neighbourhood. This meant that they observed the behaviours of persons around them and these behaviours became their reference point for their own situations.

Observation of and learning from parental and neighbours' behaviour was the most common source of knowledge for my respondents. It was possible for parental marriage practices to become inspirational in either motivating women to emulate a certain pattern or to avoid an unwanted pattern. Sandra (aged 57) said:

> I observed my mother's attitude towards my father. My mother always served my father satisfactorily; she dressed nicely in front of him; was at home when he arrived; and obtained permission before leaving home. I do that too for my husband.

Parental and neighbourhood marital disharmony and divorce were also lessons some women learned, so as not to experience failure in marriage. Sinta (aged 40) said, 'I hate seeing divorce in other people's marriages, because I am a victim of my parent's divorce and I did not like it.' Mala (aged 40) said:

> I observed the marriages of people in my neighbourhood. In most of them I saw negative experiences of failed marriages. Television also contributed to showing negative images of marriage by exposing celebrities' marital conflicts publicly. This concerned me as I planned to get married.

It seems that parents failed to give adequate information on marriage and sexuality to their children who were preparing for marriage. Only four women mentioned that they were informed by their parents about marriage prior to their wedding day; two of them said that their mothers gave them some information about sexual relations in marriage. Leli (aged 29) said that, 'My mother told me to be cautious in my relationship with my parents-in-law; to always maintain a good relationship with them. Being married to their son does not mean that I possess him completely.' In terms of sexual relations, her mother also told her, 'As a wife it is OK to be sexually active (*agresif*) towards the husband as if you are a prostitute. A prostitute is sexually active in unlawful sex; you are sexually active in lawful sex.'

Several women also said that they were informed by their elders about traditional values of marital relationships. However, several said that these values had less influence on their marital life than Islamic teachings. Maya (aged 41) simply said, 'I ignored teachings like *istri mah dulang ti nande* (that women should always wait for their husbands' instruction). There should be mutuality in a marital relationship.' Similarly, Ida (aged 36) told me that her mother-in-law mentioned certain customs that she needed to adhere to or not, but she simply ignored this advice.

Learning by doing

Prior to getting married, several women I interviewed had no information about marriage, let alone about sexual relations in marriage. The reasons for this situation are various and may include not having access to available sources or simply not wanting to think about it. Some argued that this knowledge is something that you can only gain through experience; you learn something while doing it. In my opinion, though, these women have acquired preliminary knowledge about marriage through observation, but they were simply unaware of their own knowledge.

Some of the participants mentioned that they were unaware of the concept of marital and sexual knowledge. Others were simply inattentive to all matters related to marriage. Rosa (aged 44) said: 'I did not want to think of marriage. I just waited until I experienced it.' Based on the above, some women acquired knowledge of marriage and sexuality through reading books, attending *pengajian,* peer conversation, and learning from the behaviour of parents and neighbours. Other women simply thought that they would learn about marriage through being married.

To conclude, this chapter showed that women are under pressure to get married as a social and religious obligation. As a result, women experience uncertainty between holding to their own expectations of marriage and attending to social expectations. Unfortunately, this pressure does not give women appropriate access to the knowledge they need about marriage and sexual relations. Some of the sources the women mentioned in this study do not provide adequate knowledge and understanding.

The only program that gives information to a couple prior to marriage is at the Office of Religious Affairs (KUA), where marriages are validated and registered. My participants see this program as ineffective. Detailed discussion of this program, which is called *SUSCATIN* (*Kursus Calon Pengantin,* pre-marital information session), will be provided in the next chapter.

Notes

1. For further discussion concerning research on sex education see for example Lyn Parker (2008) and Iwu Utomo (2003).
2. Muhamad Fauzil Adhim's three books are: *Kupinang Engkau dengan Hamdalah* (I propose to you with *hamdalah*) (1997); *Mencapai Pernikahan Barakah* (Reaching the blessing of marriage) (1997); *Disebabkan oleh Cinta, Kupercayakan Rumahku Padamu* (In the name of love, I entrust my house to you) (1998).
3. There are two versions of this publication: (1) Forum Kajian Kitab Kuning (Forum for the Study of Kitab Kuning, FK3). (2001). *Wajah Baru Relasi Suami Istri: Telaah Kitab Uqud al-Lujayn* (The new face of the marital relationships: The study of Kitab Uqud al-Lujayn). Yogyakarta: LKiS; (2) Forum Kajian Kitab Kuning (Forum for the Study of Kitab Kuning, FK3). (2005). *Kembang Setaman Perkawinan: Analisis Kritis Kitab Uqud al-Lujayn* (The flower garden of marriage: Critical analysis of Kitab Uqud al-Lujayn). Jakarta: Kompas.
4. In Indonesian, the word *jorok* originally means dirty, but it is also used metaphorically as lewd (*cabul*). See *Kamus Besar Bahasa Indonesia Online* (KBBI Online). (2012), available from: https://kbbi.web.id/.
5. 'And among His Signs is this, that He created for you mates from among yourselves, that ye may dwell in tranquility [*sukun*] with them, and He has put love [*mawaddah*] and mercy [*warahmah*] between your [hearts]' (Q. 30: 21).

6. 'Permitted to you, on the night of the fasts, is the approach to your wives. They are your garments [*libas*] and ye are their garments [*libas*]' (Q. 2: 187).
7. I will discuss *majlis ta'lim* in more detail in Chapter 8.

References

Adhim, Mohammad Fauzil. (1999). *Kado Pernikahan untuk Istriku* (Marriage gift for my wife). Yogyakarta: Mitra Pustaka.

Agustinah, Aminah. (2016). *Mending Janda Ketimbang Jomblo: Studi Kasus Perkawinan Anak di Kabupaten Sukabumi* (Being divorced is better than an old maid: The case study of child marriage in Sukabumi). Bekasi: Yayasan Rumah Kita Bersama.

Ahmad 'Atha, Abdul Qadir. (1980). *Al-Liqa baina al-Zawjayni* (The congregation between wife and husband: The Qur'an and Sunnah perspectives). Cairo: Dar Al-Turats al-Araby.

Al-Bantani, Nawawi. (2005). *Uqud al-Lujayn fi Huquq al-Zawjayn* (Marital bonds and the explanation of wife and husband's rights). Indonesia: Al-Haromain Jaya.

Ali, Mukti. (2016). *Yang Penting Halal: Studi Kasus Perkawinan Anak di Bogor* (Halal is that matter: The case study of child marriage in Bogor). Bekasi: Yayasan Rumah Kita Bersama.

Al-Tihami, Abu Muhammad. (2005). *Qurratul Uyun fi al-Nikah al-Syar'i wa Adabihi* (The comfort of the eyes: On Shar'i marriage and its etiquette) (2nd ed.). Indonesia: Al-Haromain Jaya.

Bauer, Janet L. (1985). 'Sexuality and the moral "construction" of women in an Islamic society.' *Anthropological Quarterly*, 58(3), 120–29, DOI: 10.2307/3317918.

Bennett, Linda Rae. (2005). *Women, Islam and Modernity: Single Women, Sexuality and Reproductive Health in Contemporary Indonesia*. London: Routledge Curzon.

Bruinessen, Martin van. (1995). *Kitab Kuning, Pesantren, dan Tarekat: Tradisi-tradisi Islam di Indonesia* (Classical Islamic texts, Islamic boarding schools, and Sufi orders: Islamic traditions in Indonesia). Bandung: Mizan.

Forum Kajian Kitab Kuning (Forum for the study of *kitab kuning*, FK3). (2001). *Wajah Baru Relasi Suami Istri: Telaah kitab Uqud al-Lujayn* (The new face of marital relationships: The study of Kitab Uqud al-Lujayn). Yogyakarta: LKiS (Lembaga Kajian Islam dan Sosial, Institute for Islamic and Social Studies).

Forum Kajian Kitab Kuning (Forum for the study of *kitab kuning*, FK3). (2005). *Kembang Setaman Perkawinan: Analisis terhadap Kitab Uqud al-Lujayn* (The flower garden of marriage: Critical analysis of Kitab Uqud al-Lujayn). Jakarta: Kompas.

Grijns, Mies. (1987). 'Tea-pickers in West Java as mothers and workers: Female work and women's jobs.' In Elsbeth Locher-Scholten and Anke Niehof (eds.), *Indonesian Women in Focus*, 104–19. Leiden: KITLV Press.

Grodin, Debra. (1991). 'The interpreting audience: The therapeutics of self-help book reading.' *Critical Studies in Mass Communication*, 8, 404–20, DOI: 10.1080/15295039109366806.

Hariyadi. (2013). 'Islamic popular culture and the new identities of urban Muslim young people in Indonesia: The case of Islamic films and Islamic self-help books.' PhD thesis. Perth: The University of Western Australia.

Hochschild, Arlie Russell. (2003). *The Commercialization of Intimate Life: Notes from Home and Work*. Berkeley, CA: University of California Press.

Horikoshi, Hiroko. (1976). 'A traditional leader in a time of change: The "kijaji" and "ulama" in West Java.' PhD thesis. Urbana, Champaign: University of Illinois.
Iswarini, Sri Endras. (2011). 'Underage marriage and poverty in West Java, Indonesia.' In Gavin W. Jones, Terence H. Hull, and Maznah Mohamad (eds.), *Changing Marriage Patterns in South East Asia: Economic and Socio-Cultural Dimensions*, 73–82. London: Routledge.
Jones, Gavin W. (1994). *Marriage and Divorce in Islamic Southeast Asia*. Kuala Lumpur: Oxford University Press.
Jones, Gavin W. (2001). 'Which Indonesian women marry youngest and why?' *Journal of Southeast Asian Studies*, 32(1), 67–78, DOI: 10.1017/S0022463401000029.
Jones, Gavin W. (2011). 'Teenage marriage trends and issues in insular Southeast Asia.' In Gavin W. Jones, Terence H. Hull, and Maznah Mohamad (eds.), *Changing Marriage Patterns in Southeast Asia: Economic and Socio-Cultural Dimensions*, 29–46. London: Routledge.
Jones, Gavin W. and Bina Gubhaju. (2011). 'Regional differences in marriage patterns in Indonesia in the twenty-first century.' In Gavin W. Jones, Terence H. Hull, and Maznah Mohamad (eds), *Changing Marriage Patterns in Southeast Asia: Economic and Socio-Cultural Dimensions*, 49–61. London: Routledge.
Jones, Gavin W., Yahya Asari, and Tuti Djuartika. (1994). 'Divorce in West Java.' *Journal of Comparative Family Studies*, 25(3), 395–416, DOI: 10.3138/jcfs.25.3.395.
Jones, Gavin W., Terence H. Hull, and Maznah Mohamad (eds). (2011). *Changing Marriage Patterns in South East Asia: Economic and Socio-Cultural Dimensions*. London: Routledge.
Kamus Besar Bahasa Indonesia Online (KBBI Online). (2012), available from: https://kbbi.web.id/ (accessed 8 January 2020).
Marcoes, Lies. (1992). 'The female preacher as a mediator in religion: A case study in Jakarta and West Java.' In Sita van Bemmelen, Madelon Djajadiningrat-Nieuwenhuis, Elspeth Locher-Scholten, and Elly Touwen-Bouwsma (eds.), *Women and Mediation in Indonesia*, 203–28. Leiden: KITLV.
Muchtar, R. H. Uton and Ki Umbara. (1977). *Modana*. Bandung: Mangle Panglipur.
Munir, Lily Zakiyah. (2002). '"He is your garment and you are his...": Religious precepts, interpretation, and power relations in marital sexuality among Javanese Muslim women.' *SOJOURN: Journal of Social Issues in Southeast Asia*, 17(2), 191–220, DOI: 10.1355/SJ17-2C.
Parker, Lyn. (2008). 'Theorising adolescent sexualities in Indonesia – Where "something different happens".' *Intersections: Gender and Sexuality in Asia and the Pacific*, 18(October), available from: http://intersections.anu.edu.au/issue18/parker.htm (accessed 27 April 2011).
Rampage, Cheryl. (2002). 'Marriage in the 20th century: A feminist perspective.' *Family Process*, 4(2), 261–68, DOI: 10.1111/j.1545-5300.2002.41205.x.
Ronosulistyo, Hanny and Aam Amiruddin. (2006). *Seks Tak Sekedar Birahi: Panduan Lengkap Seputar Kesehatan Reproduksi: Tinjauan Islam dan Medis* (Sex Not Just Lust: Comprehensive guidance on reproductive health from Islamic and medical perspectives). Bandung: Khazanah intelektual.
Sano, Atsushi. (2012). 'Agency and resilience in the sex trade: Adolescent girls in rural Indramayu.' *The Asia Pacific Journal of Anthropology*, 13(1), 21–35, DOI: 10.1080/14442213.2011.636064.
Situmorang, Augustina. (2011). 'Delayed marriage among lower socio-economic groups on an Indonesian industrial city.' In Gavin W. Jones, Terence H. Hull,

and Maznah Mohamad (eds.), *Changing Marriage Patterns in Southeast Asia: Economic and Socio-Cultural Dimensions*, 83–98. London: Routledge.

Stevenson, Angus (ed.). (2010). *The Oxford Dictionary of English*. Oxford: Oxford University Press, available from: http://www.oxforddictionaries.com (accessed 24 January 2015).

Strathern, Marilyn. (1993). 'Making incomplete.' In Vigdis Broch-Due, Ingrid Rudie, and Tone Bleie (eds.), *Carved Flesh/Cast Selves: Gendered Symbols and Social Practices*, 41–51. Oxford: Berg.

Suhamihardja, A.S. (1984). 'Organisasi dan struktur masyarakat sunda' (Organisation and structure in Sundanese community). In Edi Suhardi Ekadjati (ed.), *Masyarakat Sunda dan Kebudayaannya* (Sundanese community and its culture), 207–22. Bandung: Karya Nusantara.

Syatibi, Ibi. (2016). *Kelembagaan Terbuka dan Tersamar: Potret Kawin Anak di Cirebon* (Open and hidden institutions: The picture of child marriage in Cirebon). Bekasi: Yayasan Rumah Kita Bersama.

Utomo, Iwu Dwisetyani. (2003). 'Reproductive health education in Indonesia: School versus parents' roles in providing sexuality information.' *Review of Indonesian and Malaysian Affairs*, 37(1), 107–34.

Wessing, Robert. (1978). *Cosmology and Social Behaviour in a West Javanese Settlement*. Athens: Center for International Studies, Ohio University.

Legislation

Indonesian Marriage Law (no. 1/1974), Undang-undang Republik Indonesia No 1 Tahun 1974 Tentang an, available from: https://www.scribd.com/doc/53066173/Undang-undang-Republik-Indonesia-No-1-Tahun-1974-Tentang-an (accessed 26 February 2020).

4 Prelude to marriage
Finding the right *Jodoh* (soul mate) for life

Central to a woman's pathway to marriage is finding the right man: a partner to share life with in both happiness and unhappiness; a person who understands and accepts his wife's limitations and with whom she can share marriage goals; a partner with whom she is destined to be with. This person is often called *jodoh*. Selection of a partner can be a stage of excitement as well as complexity for a woman. She has to find someone who suits not only her own preferences but also those of her family, as well as meeting social and religious standards.

In this chapter, I explore the steps that Muslim women take in preparing for their journey prior to marriage. The steps include finding and selecting an ideal marriage partner, courtship, and the administrative process of registering the marriage. Some of the questions emerging in women's minds are: will they find the right person to be their *jodoh*? How will they find their *jodoh*? How do religion and culture influence their decision in selecting a mate?

The criteria for an ideal marriage partner

In the previous chapter, I explained that physical attractiveness, a good job, and wealth were the most significant criteria many of the women I interviewed used in selecting their mates. Apart from these criteria, women did list several other qualities that they considered to be equally important in choosing their future husbands. Specifically, there were three more characteristics that most women would like their future husbands to have: better religious knowledge, a good personal character, and a supportive personality.

Women considered that religious knowledge is important when choosing their future husbands, because these men are going to be leaders and *imam* (those who lead prayer) within the marriage. To be an *imam* he should have memorised Qur'anic verses and be fluent in reciting them. Ida (aged 36), for example, said that when her brother wanted to introduce her to a potential suitor, Ida refused right away because she knew that he came from a city that is known to be not particularly religious. Ida's brother convinced her that the man had graduated from an Islamic university, and assured her that he was a devoted Muslim. After several meetings, Ida agreed to marry him.

Hera (aged 28) also shared that she had been worried about her boyfriend's lack of religious knowledge, and she doubted that he would make a good family leader. On the contrary, Hera's boyfriend was impressed by her religious knowledge. They finally got married and Hera's husband is endeavouring to increase his religious knowledge. Mia (aged 25) also told me that her boyfriend did not want to let her go because she taught him things related to religion that he did not know.

The above-mentioned experiences confirmed that some women also have more religious knowledge compared to some men. Thus, it is misleading to assume that women lack religious knowledge and that a husband needs to educate his wife. Within marriage, sharing knowledge between wife and husband is necessary to improve the quality of the marriage and to achieve marriage goals together without demeaning either partner. Men and women have the same opportunities and capacities to gain religious knowledge and they have the same responsibilities to disseminate their knowledge (Q. 9: 71).

Another important quality for a future husband was that he possessed good personal character (*baik*). When a woman felt that the person basically had a good character and demonstrated this not only towards her but also towards her family, he was considered a suitable prospective partner. Mala (aged 40) and Aas (aged 28) shared similar experiences for mate preference.

> Everything is going well between our two families. We both feel comfortable with each other and we are getting closer each day. I know him and his family and so does my family. And there is strength between us to continue this relationship into marriage. I see him as a kind man.
> (Mala)

> He'd been so good to me, bringing me presents and involving me in many activities in the neighbourhood. At first, I did not love him but his kindness softened my heart and after that we courted [*pacaran*] for two years before we were married. My family also supported our relationship.
> (Aas)

Being supportive was also considered important in managing the relationship. Many women expected that their future husbands would support them after marriage whether they wanted to study, work, or engage in other activities. Mia (aged 25) said:

> It took some time to get to know each other better. I needed to know my boyfriend's ethnic background and his character. I found it difficult to trust people at the time because I was still traumatised by my previous fiancé who called off the wedding. So, I needed to know all about him in detail, and that included whether he would support me if I wanted to pursue further study or to work after getting married.

There are cultural and religious standards for choosing acceptable mates. Women have to deal with these preferred standards, sometimes by ignoring their own preferences. It is a common standard for a future husband to be a man who has a good job and is older than the woman herself. Augustina Situmorang (2011, 83) reports that traditional standards recommend women to 'marry up' and men to 'marry down' in terms of age, education, and wealth. According to her, this standard has left well-educated and older women, and poor men overlooked and it has resulted in the rise of singlehood. Two-thirds of the women I interviewed had husbands who were 2–12 years older than themselves. Heni (aged 51) stated that when her uncle introduced her to a man who was 10 years older than her, she accepted him. She mentioned that she preferred to have a husband much older than her in order that he could guide and care for her.

Although several women I interviewed had the opportunity to choose their own marriage partners, several others said they did not have much choice over whom they married or who courted them. It was usually the man who approached the woman for courting or marriage; it was considered inappropriate for a woman to initiate courtship or to tell a man she 'liked' or 'loved' him. However, there are various ways for a woman to select her partner and to get to know him better through courtship. In the following section, I explore different strategies used to find a marriage partner.

Courtship: self-choice, and a God-given *jodoh*

A common way of selecting a mate is through courtship. There are many different forms of courtship in Indonesia, from traditional courtship to a more modern way of mate selection. Linda Bennett (2002, 96) explains that there are three courtship categories in Lombok, namely '*midang* (customary courtship) in a woman's natal home, *pacaran modern* (modern courtship practices), and *pacaran backstreet* (secret courtship).' In West Java, there is a type of courtship similar to *midang*,[1] a traditional courtship in Lombok as explained by Bennett above, called *nganjang* (*bertamu/bertandang*) means 'to pay a visit' (Rigg 1862, 39) or *apél* (modern use, originally meant ceremony) where a man visits a woman in whom he is interested in her house. Unlike in Lombok, *apél* only takes place on Saturday night (*malam minggu*). It is usually an exciting time for women on *malam minggu*, waiting for their boyfriends to come; but for those who have no boyfriend, *malam minggu* can be a painful time. Situmorang (2011) reported that for single men who still live with their parents, staying at home on a Saturday night was uncomfortable, as they were interrogated by their parents. Clearly, the expectation is that on Saturday nights young men will be out courting.

In contemporary times a new courtship pattern has emerged, which allows the couple to occupy a freer space away from parental sight. In this stage, the boyfriend picks up his girlfriend from her house or they simply make an appointment to meet in a certain place. In urban areas, they then go to venues such as shopping malls, recreational areas, pubs, and restaurants.

106 *Prelude to marriage*

Many women among my participants met their boyfriends at school, their workplace, somewhere in the neighbourhood, or at local festivities.[2] For example, Acih (aged 49) who owns a small kiosk mentioned that she first met her husband when she watched a *wayang golek* (wooden puppet)[3] performance in a neighbouring village. Another woman, Eha (aged 29) said that she met her husband in a *kuda renggong*[4] (a dance horse) performance; he was one of the performers.

Many women who have the opportunity to pursue further education start their relationships with men as friends. Many of them attend the same school and university, where they are allowed to interact regularly. Feelings develop from friends to lovers. Sari (aged 42) mentioned that she was in a relationship with her boyfriend for almost eight years, starting from their first year of undergraduate studies until they finished their master degrees.

Half of the women I interviewed chose their boyfriends and husbands for themselves, while the other half met their suitors through intermediaries arranged by a third party. A third party who arranges the meeting of the couple can be a family member—parents, brother/sister or uncle/aunt, or a friend. The process of arranged-mate introduction takes place directly (meeting both parties face to face) or indirectly, by giving each person the other's pictures or phone numbers. An initial meeting can be arranged by the third parties or the couple. Thereafter the process is left to the couple. During the initial period, the couple might exchange personal information. After this stage, they may consider seeing each other again and continuing their relationship to a further stage, or they might end it.

Arranged-mate selection by a family member sometimes led to forced marriage. Research in another area of West Java also showed that early and forced marriage still occurs, particularly in rural areas (Iswarini 2011). Arranged-mate selection by friends was more relaxed because the couples had more freedom to make their own decisions. Women were not forced to accept the candidates in this pairing process.

Siti (aged 40) preferred this pairing process because she was not interested in courtship. She said that she never thought of having a boyfriend and wanted to concentrate on studies instead. It was her brother who introduced her to his friend and they married soon after. Another respondent, Ani (aged 45), said that it was her friend who introduced her to her suitor. They met once and after that she prayed *istikharoh* to ask guidance from God.[5] Two weeks later, they decided to get married and sought approval from her mother.

Seven participants had their mates chosen for them by their family members. Rosa (aged 44) accepted her parents' choice of marriage partner. She already had a boyfriend at that time but it was not really a serious relationship. She agreed with her parent's proposal, as she was confident that her parents would choose the best partner for her. She said, 'I hadn't met him until a few minutes before the *akad* (marriage contract) took place. But luckily, he is a man with a good character, fine job, and is good looking too.' Minah (aged 50) at age 13 was introduced to a man seven years older than her by her parents. She said that she was interested in him and agreed to marry. Minah delayed the union with her husband for two months because she was not ready for a conjugal relationship. For the women whose mates and marriages were arranged, the process of getting to know one another could be quite short. Several women only had a chance to become acquainted one week prior to the marriage.

The courtship period enables the woman to examine the quality of her 'boyfriend' and decide whether he would make a suitable marriage partner. A certain period of courtship gives them time to decide whether the relationship might lead to marriage. A break-up early in the courtship process is common but break-ups after a long-term relationship can cause sadness and heartbreak, regardless of who broke it off. Several women I interviewed experienced trauma when their boyfriends called off the wedding.

In the process of finding the right mate, women often mentioned that the one who becomes the husband is their *jodoh* (Jennaway 2002). If the people are already destined to be matched (*berjodoh*), nothing can prevent them from being united (*kalau sudah jodoh tidak akan lari ke mana*). Even if, in the first place, one person thinks that they would never consider one another as their *jodoh*. If their fate is indeed to be together, then they will become a couple. Finding a *jodoh* involves matching feelings of *cocok* (suitability). Conversely, if the person is not destined to be her/his *jodoh*, no matter how hard they try to unite, it will never happen. They believe that God determines this pairing process—a common phrase is that *jodoh* is in the hands of God (*jodoh ada di tangan Tuhan*). Bennett (2005, 46) notes that *jodoh* is 'determined by destiny and spiritual compatibility and therefore requires religious consummation.' The couple is considered to be *jodoh* for each other until they are married. And if a person is destined to be one's *jodoh*, one should accept that unquestionably, otherwise one is denying God's will. Wiwi (aged 47), when asked why she stayed in her marriage even when she discovered after a year of marriage that her husband was a married man, said that he was already her *jodoh*: 'What can I do, he is my *jodoh* and I should accept him submissively [*pasrah*] and besides, it was too late [*sudah terlanjur*].' There is a famous Sundanese saying: '*Jodo, pati, bagja, cilaka kagungan Gusti Allah,*' which means that soul mates, death, happiness, and accidents are in God's command. People believe that humans cannot do anything about these things. This idea is also usually called *takdir*, or human fate.

A new type of romance was also reported by Nancy Smith-Hefner (2011). She wrote that university students who belonged to a conservative Islamic student organisation, (which promoted no courtship prior to marriage) tended to skip the courtship process—a process that is considered sinful according to their interpretation. If someone had the desire to marry, the organisation would arrange a candidate for him/her.

Intimacy in courtship: courtship behaviour and personal control

> Having conversation and going out together, just the two of us—we had already transgressed proper courtship behaviour.
>
> (Hera, aged 28)

In a society where virginity is highly valued for women, protecting women from 'uncontrolled' sexual behaviour is essential in the name of chastity. For the women I interviewed, preserving chastity was very important. The quote shows that for Hera, who was raised within a very religious family, her courtship behaviour was considered to exceed the limits of propriety. She quickly clarified that what she meant by exceeding the limit was talking to and going out with her boyfriend and no more than that. But still, she perceived that behaviour as transgressive. She vowed to abstain from further intimate courtship behaviour, but she was aware that she was sometimes unable to control her desire. She said, 'As a human who also has desires, I cannot avoid *Satan's* [evil] temptation.' To avoid any further transgression in courtship and any gossip from the community where she lived, she asked her boyfriend to marry her.

After the first meeting at her sister's house, Rani (43) and her suitor courted for six months. She mentioned that she was not officially 'courting,' as her sister was very strict and did not allow her to do so. There was no concept of *pacaran,* according to her sister, in Islam. During that period, they never touched one another physically, such as holding hands. Neither did they go out alone as a couple. Once, she mentioned, they went to the city centre (*jalan-jalan*), but they were accompanied by her niece.

There is a cultural expectation in Indonesia that women will be passive in courtship and marriage relationships. Passivity is considered a way of maintaining women's chastity and purity. In general, women are ordered to control their desire, especially by not engaging in pre- or extra-marital sex. But men are not subject to the same injunctions; it is common for them to engage in such behaviour. Men are not subjected to social or even legal punishment. Leli (aged 29) said that 'as a woman we were advised not to speak about our feelings openly to a man in advance. We should wait for a man to initiate it.'

Having a boyfriend is considered normal for many Indonesian women. However, many women also decide not to engage in such relationships. There are various reasons why women choose not to have a boyfriend or to be involved in courtship and these may be personal. Situmorang (2011) reports that for lower-class women workers, a long working day was the reason they had no time to look for a boyfriend. For other women, study and religion were two reasons among many others. Similar findings were reported by Parker (2009, 80–81) for young women in West Sumatra; having a boyfriend could disturb studies and was forbidden by religion. Some women in my study, like Leli, Mala, and Hera, had boyfriends but emphasised self-respect and self-control in their courtship behaviour. Parker reported that for senior school students in West Sumatra, school makes a significant contribution in imposing 'a curriculum of the body.' She argues that school rules about uniform, daily routines, and socialising behaviour are interrelated with the wider discursive context of moral and religious training for girls, in order that they maintain 'modesty, virtue, and virginity' (ibid., 79).

For women, to be valuable means always guarding their chastity as a sign of their self-respect. Not engaging in free sex means respecting their selves, and signifies their responsibility and commitment to their parents, community, and religion. Self-control and knowing the limits of proper behaviour in courtship are important for women. Any behaviour that they consider 'inappropriate' should be avoided as far as possible, such as conversing with a boyfriend, going out together as a couple (Hera), hand-holding (Rani) or kissing (Leli), and they may consider these behaviours as being close to *zina*. Similar findings were reported by Bennett (2007) and Parker (2009). Respondents associated intimate relations (other than intercourse), such as hand-holding, kissing, and embracing, as *zina*.

The religious concept of *zina* is central to women's perception of intimacy in courtship and they manage to avoid it as much as they can. The concept of *Satan* (evil) or temptation in courtship is also significant in their opinion. Religious texts mention that a man and woman who are not *muhrim* should never be allowed to be together without being chaperoned by a third party.[6] Bennett (2007) suggests that this concept of *zina* is central in promoting and implementing sex education in Indonesia.

Marriage preparation and registering the marriage

Marriage preparation: engagement, marriage proposal, and marital agreement

The next step of courtship, when the relationship has become stable, is either an engagement period or a marriage proposal. The women consider a relationship stable by several indicators, such as intense meetings, the development of romantic feelings, and close relationships with the family members of their fiancé/suitor.

The engagement process involves a meeting between both families (usually in the woman's house) to tighten the couple's relationship. The engagement is symbolised by an exchange of rings. The rings mean that the parties, although they may not be ready for marriage, are tied to each other and marriage is their goal. However, engagement does not always guarantee that the couple will end up married, as experienced by two of my respondents. Maya and Leli were both engaged for several years to men of their choice, but after some consideration they ended the engagements and instead married men they had known for just a couple of months. The reasons for breaking the engagements were different for the two women. Maya (aged 41), for example, ended her engagement because she met another man to whom she felt more connected and comfortable than her fiancé. Leli (aged 29) was engaged for one year and six months, but was not sure about marrying her fiancé as she noted that he was very dependent on his mother (*anak mami*). She met another man in her workplace—a man who was more mature and independent than her former fiancé.

A marriage proposal is submitted by the man and/or his family to his prospective wife's family. It is the man who asks the woman to marry and never otherwise, although sometimes the woman might urge the man to do so. During the process of courtship, parental approval is important for women. When a woman feels comfortable with a suitor, she will introduce him to her parents to seek approval. If the parents approve, the woman will then ask the man to propose formally. However, many suitors take a short cut. The man observes the woman and when he decides that she is the woman he is looking for, he will deal directly with the woman's parents instead of her. If the parents are interested, they will then ask their daughter whether she would accept him or not. It is the woman who decides after consultation with her parents. This process was experienced by Lina (aged 37) who stated:

> He [her suitor] had a conversation directly with my parents and asked my parents if he could marry me. Then, my parents asked me for my decision. I was still unsure about him, but I accepted him because of his kindness. I saw that he approached my parents directly, which meant he was serious, although I did not know his character. After a week, he proposed and then we got married. It was so quick.

When marriage is an ideal norm, pressure for marriage is high, especially for women. Thus, several women I interviewed accepted a proposal to marry regardless of their uncertain feelings towards the suitor. They equivocated for various reasons. Among the women I interviewed, there were five possible reasons, as follows: (1) pressure to marry; (2) the man showed kindness; (3) there had been only one serious proposal; (4) the woman was afraid that if she refused him there would be no other man who would take her as a wife; and (5) love (which came later in their relationship).

The pressure to marry for women can lead them to accept any available candidate who seems serious, and many said that it was better to accept any man than none at all. Several women mentioned their uncertain feelings towards their prospective husbands, even when they had agreed to get married. Various reasons for this uncertainty included: they had no romantic feelings for him (*tidak/belum cinta*) as experienced by Yuni, Ina, and Nisa; they did not know their suitor's personal character, noted by Iis, Lina, and Wida; they were not ready for marriage, experienced by Rani, Minah, and Acih; they were anxious about marriage, noted by Mala; and they had exceeded the marriage age as experienced by Sofi (aged 34), Yuni (aged 30), and Ani (aged 38)—their ages at their first marriage.

Yuni (aged 39) told me:

> I accepted him because I was 30 at that time. Although I felt distant from him because I still longed for my ex-boyfriend, I agreed to marry due to my age, *lillahi ta'ala* [all matters surrendered to God], feelings [of love/like] can develop later in marriage.

Other women observed:

> I married for the sake of my parents who urged me to get married. In fact, I was not that interested in my boyfriend and wanted to find the right person for marriage.
>
> (Ina, aged 33)

> The truth was I was not ready for marriage yet. If I heard the word marriage, I felt like an old lady. I still wanted to search for a rich and good-looking man. But, my husband was the only man who showed his sincerity towards me.
>
> (Rani, aged 43)

> We were very certain when we decided to get married. But when it got closer to the wedding day, I felt a strange feeling, a feeling of uncertainty and anxiety. Many questions emerged, is he the right person for me? Will he be a good husband? Will our marriage last forever? Will we accept each other's characters?
>
> (Mala, aged 40)

Apart from the above-mentioned experiences, around half of the women I interviewed felt confident in their decision to marry. The most commonly given reason included having romantic feelings for their prospective husbands. These women developed feelings of love/like during the courtship period. Care, attentiveness, and passion from their suitors were indications for continuing the relationship to the next level. Maya (aged 41) said 'The reason I decide to marry him is not because of his wealth, but because of his love and affection.' Maya and Aas (aged 28) also said that they loved their boyfriends because they were very attentive and cared for them.

For several women, before getting marriage, an agreement was made with their prospective husbands. Leli (aged 29) stated that before getting married she explained to her suitor that she had a sick mother and she was the one who supported the family. Her suitor agreed to take over her responsibilities to support her family financially after marriage. Thus, every month her husband sends money to Leli's family.

Registering the marriage

Indonesian marriage law

Marriage law in Indonesia is regulated by Indonesian Marriage Law no. 1/1974. This law was implemented a year after it was passed under Government Regulation of the Republic of Indonesia no. 9/1975. It was reported that the process of establishing this marriage law in Indonesia was highly political, with disputes among Muslims and other religions (Blackburn and Bessell 1997; Katz and Katz 1975). It is also worth noting the role of women's organisations, which made significant contributions in initiating the establishment of Indonesian Marriage Law no. 1/1974 (Katz and Katz 1975.).

Some important issues regulated in this marriage law include: the requirement to register the marriage and divorce; limitations to the practice of polygyny; the establishment of a minimum marriage age for men and women (19 years old); and regulations about marital property and the custody of children.

Despite the significant achievements in regulating family life in Indonesia, this law still posits unequal relations between a wife and husband. Although it states in Chapter VI, Article 31(1) that 'the wife has equal rights and position to that of the husband in marriage and social life,' another article differentiates their roles as follows: 31(3) 'the husband is the head of the family and the wife is the mother of the household (housewife).' Article 34(1) further mentions that 'husbands are responsible for protecting their wives and for providing all the necessities of life for the household, in keeping with their capability,' and Article 34(2) clearly lays out the wife's territory: 'wives are obliged to organise the household as well as possible.' This law has restricted women's role to the domestic sphere under the protection of the husband. In Indonesia, the gender role attached to women as promoted by the state in the New Order regime is that women's responsibility is at home. As wives and mothers they manage the household and take care of the children. Meanwhile, men's duty is in the public sphere as provider and protector (Robinson 2009; Suryakusuma 1996).

Unequal marital relationships promoted in the marriage law have resulted in criticism from several women's organisations, who demand changes to certain articles so that unequal relations between husband and wife can be addressed. Several women's organisations, initiated by the Lembaga Bantuan Hukum Asosiasi Perempuan Indonesia pro Keadilan (LBH APIK, Institution for Legal Aid for Indonesian Women's Association for Justice) and Jaringan Kerja Prolegnas Pro Perempuan (JKP3, National Network of Pro-women National Legislation Program) have prepared a draft amendment to Marriage Law No.1/1974 to accommodate gender equality. The amendments include the abolition of polygyny and also address the division of labour in marriage, and the establishment of equal rights and duties between husband and wife based on mutual agreement Chapter VI, Article 31(3) (Munti 2012;

personal communication with Nina Nurmila, representative of Alimat, one of the members invited to discuss the draft amendment, 24 July 2012).[7]

The role of the office of religious affairs (KUA)

Based on Indonesian Marriage Law no. 1 of 1974, Chapter I, Article 2(2) states that 'every marriage should be registered in accordance with the pertinent laws.' An institution for marriage registration has been established by the government.[8] For those who are Muslim, the marriage registration takes place in the Kantor Urusan Agama (KUA, Office of Religious Affairs), while, for non-Muslims, the registration can be carried out in the civil registration office (*kantor catatan sipil*). KUA is the operational unit of the Islamic Guidance division (Bimas: Bimbingan Masyarakat Islam) at the Ministry of Religious Affairs that has been established in each *kecamatan* (sub-district) across Indonesia. Its role is to provide marriage registration and reconciliation services and also to supervise other religious activities.[9] Previously, KUA also handled the divorce process (Nakamura 1983). Nowadays, KUA records a divorce only after it has been processed and the verdict delivered by the Religious Court.

The head of KUA serves as the Petugas Pencatat Nikah (PPN, marriage registrar), and is often selected from senior *penghulu*. *Penghulu* is the person in charge of conducting the marriage. PPN is responsible for supervising, registering, and concluding the marriage.[10] In their daily activities, the PPN appoints assistants, including other *penghulu* and a Pembantu Petugas Pencatat Nikah (P3N, the marriage registrar's assistant). A P3N is the assistant of the *penghulu* appointed in each village (usually a community leader) to help the PPN collect the data of people who are planning to get married but live far away from KUA.

For those who are planning to get married, there are certain documents that must be prepared for registering the marriage, namely: (1) a copy of the residential identity card (KTP); (2) a statement that the party has not yet married (for single women and men); or a statement that they are widowed or divorced verified by the local authority or by a divorce certificate; (3) a letter of information/recommendation concerning the marriage from the local authority; and (4) completed forms issued by the KUA which are called the N-forms.

All these documents should be lodged with the KUA at least 10 days in advance of the wedding. The marriage ceremony will also take place at the KUA. In West Java, as the wedding usually takes place in the woman's residential area, this requirement is lodged at the KUA in the woman's domicile. The PPN will then check all requirements (especially in relation to age), to determine whether the couple fulfils the requirements of marriage age according to the law, guardianship, and marital status. The *penghulu*[11] I interviewed explained that they have to be attentive in checking these three requirements as many cases have shown that couples give false information.

The KUA officer will cooperate with the P3N and local government to check the validity of information given by the parties.

Wiwi's husband submitted false information when he married Wiwi. Wiwi (aged 47) did not know that her husband was a married man. She found out one year into their marriage. Wiwi's husband told me during the interview that his reason at that time was that he wanted to practice polygyny (*ngawayuh* S.) but his first wife would not agree.

When all the requirements are accepted, the KUA will display the names of parties who are planning to marry along with information as to the time and place of the wedding ceremony on an information board in front of the office. Within these 10 days preceding the wedding ceremony, it is recommended that the couple will take part in a pre-marital information session held by the KUA. I will explain in more detail about this program in the next section.

On the day of the wedding ceremony, the *penghulu* visits the venue, often at the bride's house, mosque or hall, to record and conclude the marriage. The marriage contract (*ijab* and *qabul,* offer and acceptance) usually takes place between the groom and the bride's guardian, generally her father, in the presence of two witnesses. The bride is sometimes asked for her consent and the groom can be required to provide evidence of his identity, but sometimes the bride is not asked, and she may not even be present when the marriage contract takes place; she may be waiting in a separate room. After concluding the marriage contract, the bride will be seated side-by-side with the groom and the *penghulu* will give the couple the marriage book to be signed. The groom, then, is required to read out loud the *shighat taklik talak* printed on the last page of the marriage book.[12] A sermon will then be delivered to conclude the wedding ceremony. This sermon contains advice about married life.

The official payment for registering the marriage according to the regulation is 30,000 rupiah (equivalent to AUD 3.00; US 2.2) (Government Regulation/Peraturan Pemerintah (PP) Republik Indonesia no. 51/2000). However, in reality, the cost will vary according to the location of the KUA. In urban areas with 'high' income residents, the KUA will charge the couple much more than the amount required (approximately around 300,000–500,000 rupiah (AUD 32.00–54.00; US 22–36). In a newspaper article, 'Pemerintah gratiskan biaya nikah' (The government abolishes the cost of marriage registration), published in the *Antara News* on 23 May 2013, a statement was issued from the Minister of Religious Affairs abolishing the payment of marriage registration.

According to the Marriage Law, any marriage that is unregistered is subject to annulment and may even attract a fine from the government. Even the person who conducts the marriage may be liable for a fine. However, in many areas of Indonesia unregistered marriage is high (Platt 2017) due to incompatible roles between states and local culture, but also due to the inability of prospective couples to pay the fee. Thus, while registration is compulsory, it is not universal, and failure to register the marriage is not policed and the sanction stated above is ineffective.

Prelude to marriage 115

SUSCATIN: pre-marital information session

SUSCATIN is an abbreviation for the Kursus Calon Pengantin (Pre-marital information course). Originally it was designed as a course given by KUA for a couple requesting to be married. In other KUA this program is also called KBCM, which stands for Kursus Bimbingan Calon Mempelai (Pre-marital guidance course). This course is based on regulations issued by the Director General of Islamic Community Guidance/ Direktur Jenderal Bimas Islam at the Ministry of Religious Affairs No: DJ.II/491 Year 2009. This regulation requires all couples to participate in such a course as a requirement before registering their marriage. As proof of participation, the couple is given a certificate. In reality, many couples skip this session; some are not informed about the session while others have no time to attend.

The aim of the course is to give information to couples about married life. This course is intended to create a married life full of harmony (*sakinah*), love (*mawaddah*), and tenderness (*rahmah*). It also aims to decrease marital disharmony and divorce and to prevent domestic violence. According to the regulation, seven topics are covered in the course and the time allocated for each topic is as follows: (1) the administrative procedures of marriage (2 hours); (2) Islamic religious knowledge (5 hours); (3) governmental regulations on marriage and family matters (4 hours); (4) rights and duties of husband and wife (5 hours); (5) reproductive health (3 hours); (6) family management (3 hours); (7) marital and family psychology (2 hours). There are 24 hours in total allocated for this program.

If the course is delivered effectively and according to the regulation stated above, the program would contribute significantly to a couple's knowledge about marriage. However, not every KUA runs this program in accordance with the regulation. For example, not every topic stated above is covered in the KUA where I conducted an interview. In addition, in terms of time, it often takes only an hour or two to present the 'session' rather than the recommended 24 hours for the full course.

Based on the information from *penghulu* in three KUA in my study site, within the 10 days prior to marrying the couple should participate in a pre-marital information session. These KUA have their own schedules for providing the session, but mostly adapt to the couple's availability. Most information given in this session is based on Islamic law on marriage in accordance with the Marriage Law and the module provided by the Department of Religious Affairs. There are also references from classical Islamic books commonly used in each KUA such as *Kifayat al-Akhyar* (Taqiyuddin Abu Bakar Bin Muhammad al-Husaini al-Hishni) and *I'anat al-Thalibin* (Sayyid Bakri bin Muhammad Syatha al-Dimyati) for *fiqh*. This are also references from a Hadith compilation book *Riyad al-shalihin* (Yahya bin Syaraf al-Din al-Nawawi). These books are popular and widely read in *pesantren* in Indonesia (Bruinessen 1995).

The session will vary in time according to the educational level of the engaged couple. The method employed in this session, according to *penghulu*, is a combination of preaching, sharing, and dialogue. For couples from lower educational backgrounds, the session will take place over about half an hour. The couple usually just listens to the advice given by *penghulu*. By contrast, couples with a higher education actively engage in discussion during the session.

Advice given by *penghulu* in these KUA is related to information on the Islamic etiquette of sexual activity and the duties and rights in marriage. In KUA 2, the *penghulu* usually gives advice metaphorically to make it easier for the couple to understand the message. Here is an example:

> Marriage is like buying shoes. You go to the store, choose and buy them based on preference and your financial capacity. After two or three months, you go back to the shoe store and you will see that there are many new and great models available to choose from. That is what marriage is ... Marriage should be based on *ibadah* [religious duty] otherwise you will be disappointed, because after marriage you will find there are many men and women who may be better than your husband or wife. So, you should aim to base your marriage on *ibadah* in order that you are not dissatisfied.
> (Interview, 6 June 2012)

The *penghulu* in KUA 2 also mentioned that there is a duty in marriage to maintain harmony. In marriage, there is no first person or second person; both are equal partners in building a long-lasting marriage. To make this happen, they need a willingness to work together and a readiness to forgive one another.

The section in KUA that runs the pre-marital information session is the Badan Penasihatan, Pembinaan dan Pelestarian Perkawinan (BP4, The advisory body for developing and maintaining marriage). BP4 is a professional organisation affiliated with the Department of Religious Affairs to promote the establishment of harmonious marriage. In its first formal establishment in 1960, the abbreviation of BP4 stood for Badan Penasihat Perkawinan dan Penyelesaian Perceraian (The body of marriage counselling and divorce settlements). In 2009, after the National meeting of XIV, the BP4 abbreviation was changed to Badan Penasihatan, Pembinaan dan Pelestarian Perkawinan (The advisory body for developing and maintaining marriage) (Zainuddin 2009). This change was made with the stipulation that the KUA was no longer responsible for divorce proceedings.

During in-depth interviews with my primary participants, most women reported that they did not attend the pre-marital information session. Of 40 participants, only 7 attended the session while 33 did not. Various reason were given for not attending the session: they worked in another city; they had an assumption that they were already educated on the topic; or they were not informed about the information session. Several participants who did attend pre-marital information sessions commented positively saying they provided preliminary information on marriage life. Several others said that the session was ineffective because it was delivered over a short time and used a lecturing method that did not allow for a question time. Such negative comments were also reported by Derek Boylen (2012) among couples who participated in Catholic Marriage Education Services for the Archdiocese of Perth, Australia. He stated that before attending the pre-marriage education the couple already assumed that the session would be dogmatic and doctrinal as it was run by the church. However, after attending the program, they gave positive feedback on the session because it provided comprehensive information on marriage.

It is worth considering the recommendation from one focus group discussion (FGD) during my fieldwork that the session cover more comprehensive topics and that the KUA collaborate with other governmental department like the Health Department in giving information related to marriage (FGD 1, mixed-sex kindergarten teachers, 9 June 2012).

Each KUA allocated time for this session based on the couple's availability in regard to their working hours and the distance they needed to travel. For these reasons, the session was sometimes given individually or in groups, depending on how many couples were requesting weddings at the time. The instructor of the session is a *penghulu* who is also on the board of BP4.

The *penghulu* from the three KUA interviewed generally believed in equality within marriage. Their role is important in teaching gender equality in married life; hence, it is essential for the *penghulu* to understand gender equality. In considering the importance of the *penghulu's* understanding and promotion of gender equality during pre-marital information sessions, Rahima, an NGO based in Jakarta concerned with gender equality in Islam, has taken steps to establish a program to train *penghulu* in Indonesia on gender equality in Islamic marriage.[13] This program is supported by the Centre for Research and Development of Religious Affairs at the Department of Religious Affairs. This training aims to educate *penghulu*, instructors, and counsellors of BP4 on the promotion of harmonious marriage (*keluarga sakinah*) based on a gender equality perspective (Rahima 2012; personal communication with Rahima Director, Aditiana Dewi Eridani, 10 July 2012).

Considering the regulation on this pre-marital information session and the sources relating to knowledge of marriage and sexuality as outlined in my previous chapter, I would argue that SUSCATIN is an important program for the government in disseminating information on marriage and sexuality. This formal information should be organised in a more serious and comprehensive way involving not only BP4 in KUA but also in collaboration with other government departments such as the Health Department and the Law and Human Rights Department, to properly address important issues in marriage. In 2019, an attempt to optimise the pre-marital information session was initiated by the Coordinating Ministry of Human Development and Culture of the Republic of Indonesia (Kementrian Koordinator Pembangunan Manusia dan Kebudayaan—Kemenko PMK) to minimise child marriage, domestic violence, child sexual abuse, poverty,

118 *Prelude to marriage*

and stunting (impaired growth of the children because of poor nutrition) (Humas Kemenko PMK, 2019).

This chapter concludes with the suggestion that there are various ways for a woman to find her *jodoh*. Some women were able to meet their ideal marriage partner while others were not. Courtship allowed the couple to get to know each other better, and the women could evaluate the sincerity of their partners. Women, who had no chance for courtship, met their partner shortly prior to marriage. In a society where marriage is a social norm, women are persuaded to marry to avoid marginalisation as a result of unfulfilled social expectations. Several women in this study sacrificed their own interests in consideration of others.

Prior to marriage, the couple is required to fulfil the administration procedures associated with registering the marriage in accordance with state regulations. An important requirement for entering married life is attendance at a pre-marital information session provided by KUA. This session is significant in providing the couple with preliminary information on marriage.

Notes

1. *Midang* also appears in the Sundanese language with a different meaning. *Midang* in Sundanese literally means to exhibit, good performance; active participation; or to go about for pleasure (Rigg 1862, 36).
2. New trends show that women acquaint with their partners through social media like Facebook, Instagram or Twitter and the like.
3. *Wayang golek* is a Sundanese traditional wooden puppet show; usually performed during *hajatan* (wedding or male circumcision celebrations) or on Agustusan (Indonesian Independence Day celebration, 17 August).
4. *Kuda renggong* is a Sundanese traditional cultural performance originally from Sumedang and still commonly performed in Eastern Bandung—the site where I conducted fieldwork. It involves traditional music such as the *kendang* (drum), gong and flute accompanied by a song from a *sinden* (singer). It is performed mostly to accompany a circumcised boy who rides on a dance horse and is paraded along the village's main road.
5. Praying *istikharoh* usually occurs when someone is uncertain about something and they need guidance about whether it is good or bad. By performing it, it is believed that God will send a sign of a possible choice in various ways, allowing one to make the best decision. It is also used for choosing which person is best for one's future husband/wife.
6. *Muhrim* refers to close relatives of the opposite sex, whom a Muslim may not marry.
7. One of the amendments proposed that has been successfully approved is raising the age of marriage for girls from 16 to 19 years old; the same age as for boys.
8. Based on Governmental Regulation/Peraturan Pemerintah (PP) Republik Indonesia no. 9/1975 tentang pelaksanaan undang-undang nomor 1 tahun 1974 tentang perkawinan (on the implementation of Marriage Law no. 1/1974).
9. Based on the Regulation of Ministry of Religious Affairs/Peraturan Menteri Agama (PMA) no. 39/2012 of the organisation and work procedures of KUA.
10. Based on the Regulation of Ministry of Religious Affairs/Peraturan Menteri Agama (PMA) no. 11/2007 on PPN (marriage registrar).

11. There are three *penghulu* that I interviewed during my fieldwork in three KUA. I will refer to them as KUA 1, 2, and 3.
12. Detail of *shighat taklik talak* is provided in Chapter 1.
13. There are seven regions participated in this training namely: Sukabumi, Yogyakarta, Bangkalan, Medan, Palembang, Bandar Lampung, and Tanjung Pinang (personal communication with Director of Rahima, 10 July 2012).

References

Bennett, Linda Rae. (2002). 'Modernity, desire and courtship: The evolution of pre-marital relationships in Mataram, Eastern Indonesia.' In Lenore Manderson and Pranee Liamputtong (eds.), *Coming of Age in South and Southeast Asia: Youth, Courtship and Sexuality*, 96–112. Richmond: Curzon.

Bennett, Linda Rae. (2005). *Women, Islam and Modernity: Single Women, Sexuality and Reproductive Health in Contemporary Indonesia*. London: Routledge Curzon.

Bennett, Linda Rae. (2007). 'Zina and the enigma of sex education for Indonesian Muslim youth.' *Sex Education*, 7(4), 371–86, DOI: 10.1080/14681810701635970.

Blackburn, Susan and Sharon Bessell. (1997). 'Marriageable age: Political debates on early marriage in twentieth-century Indonesia.' *Indonesia*, 63, 107–41, DOI: 10.2307/3351513.

Boylen, Derek R. (2012). 'Unexpected benefits: The long term perceived experience for remarrying couples who have participated in a pre-marriage relationship education program.' MA Thesis, Perth: Notre Dame University.

Bruinessen, Martin van. (1995). *Kitab Kuning, Pesantren, dan Tarekat: Tradisi-tradisi Islam di Indonesia* (Classical Islamic texts, Islamic boarding schools, and Sufi orders: Islamic traditions in Indonesia). Bandung: Mizan.

Humas Kemenko PMK. (2019). *Kemenko PMK [Kementrian Koordinator bidang Pembangunan Manusia dan Kebudayaan] Gelar Rakor Peningkatan Kuantitas dan Kualitas Bimbingan Pra Nikah* (Coordinating Ministry for Human Development and Culture organized meeting on quantity and quality of pre-marital information session), available from: https://www.kemenkopmk.go.id/artikel/kemenko-pmk-gelar-rakor-peningkatan-kuantitas-dan-kualitas-bimbingan-pra-nikah (accessed 31 January 2020).

Iswarini, Sri Endras. (2011). 'Underage marriage and poverty in West Java, Indonesia.' In Gavin W. Jones, Terence H. Hull, and Maznah Mohamad (eds.), *Changing Marriage Patterns in South East Asia: Economic and Socio-Cultural Dimensions*, 73–82. London: Routledge.

Jennaway, Megan. (2002). *Sisters and Lovers: Women and Desires in Bali*. Lanham, MD: Rowman & Littlefield.

Katz, June S. and Ronald S. Katz. (1975). 'The new Indonesian marriage law: A mirror of Indonesia's political, cultural, and legal systems.' *The American Journal of Comparative Law*, 23(4), 653–81, DOI: 10.2307/839240.

Munti, Ratna Batara. (2012). *Draft Amandemen UU Perkawinan*. Jakarta: Asosiasi LBH APIK-JKP3.

Nakamura, Hisako. (1983). *Divorce in Java: A Study of the Dissolution of Marriage among Javanese Muslims*. Yogyakarta: Gadjah Mada University Press.

Parker, Lyn. (2009). 'Religion, class and schooled sexuality among Minangkabau teenage girls.' *Bijdragen tot de taal-, land- en volkenkunde*, 165(1), 62–94, DOI: 10.1163/22134379-90003643.

Platt, Maria. (2017). *Marriage, Gender and Islam in Indonesia: Women Negotiating Informal Marriage, Divorce and Desire*. London: Routledge.

Rahima. (2012). 'Ketika Penghulu, Penyuluh dan Konselor BP4 Berworkshop Keluarga Sakinah' (Workshop of harmonious marriage for marriage registrars, instructors and counsellors of BP4), available from: https://swararahima.com/2018/08/29/ketika-penghulu-penyuluh-dan-konselor-bp4-berworkshop-keluarga-sakinah/ (accessed 17 January 2020).

Rigg, Jonathan. (1862). *A Dictionary of the Sunda Language of Java*. Batavia: Lange & Co., available from: https://en.wikisource.org/wiki/A_Dictionary_of_the_Sunda_language (accessed 9 January 2020).

Robinson, Kathryn. (2009). *Gender, Islam and Democracy in Indonesia*. London: Routledge, DOI: 10.4324/9780203891759.

Situmorang, Augustina. (2011). 'Delayed marriage among lower socio-economic groups on an Indonesian industrial city.' In Gavin W. Jones, Terence H. Hull, and Maznah Mohamad (eds), *Changing Marriage Patterns in Southeast Asia: Economic and Socio-Cultural Dimensions*, 83–98. London: Routledge.

Smith-Hefner, Nancy J. (2005). 'The new Muslim romance: Changing patterns of courtship and marriage among educated Javanese youth.' *Journal of Southeast Asian Studies*, 36(3), 441–59, DOI: 10.1017/S002246340500024X.

Suryakusuma, Julia I. (1996). 'The state and sexuality in new order Indonesia.' In Laurie. J. Sears (ed.), *Fantasizing the Feminine in Indonesia*, 92–119. Durham: Duke University Press.

Zainuddin, Muhammad. (2009). *Anggaran Dasar dan Anggaran Rumah Tangga BP4 hasil Munas XIV/2009* (Statutes and Bylaws of BP4 based on National Conference XIV/2009), available from: https://www.scribd.com/document/121269012/Anggaran-Dasar-Dan-Anggaran-Rumah-Tangga-BP-4-Tahun-2009 (accessed 17 January 2020).

Legislation

Governmental Regulation/Peraturan Pemerintah (PP) Republik Indonesia no. 9/1975 tentang pelaksanaan undang-undang nomor 1 tahun 1974 tentang perkawinan (on the implementation of Marriage Law No.1/1974), available from: http://hukum.unsrat.ac.id/pp/pp_9_75.htm (accessed 28 February 2020).

Government Regulation/Peraturan Pemerintah (PP) Republik Indonesia no. 51/2000 on the Rate of Payment for non-taxable national income in the Religious Affairs Department, available from: http://hukum.unsrat.ac.id/pp/pp_51_2000.pdf (accessed 28 February 2020).

Indonesian Marriage Law (no. 1/1974), Undang-undang Republik Indonesia no 1 Tahun 1974 Tentang an, available from: https://www.scribd.com/doc/53066173/Undang-undang-Republik-Indonesia-No-1-Tahun-1974-Tentang-an (accessed 26 February 2020).

Regulation of Ministry of Religious Affairs/Peraturan Menteri Agama (PMA) no. 39/2012 on the organisation and work procedures of KUA.

Regulation of Ministry of Religious Affairs/Peraturan Menteri Agama (PMA) no. 11/2007 on PPN (marriage registrar).

Regulations of the Ministry of Religious Affairs no. DJ.II/491/2009 on the pre-marital information course.

5 Marital adjustment and household management

In this chapter, I explore the experiences of women during the adjustment period of marriage and the ways in which they learn to manage the household. This chapter contains two sections. The first section addresses several adjustments that the women have to deal with in the first stages of marriage, and the second section examines the arrangements made by the couples in managing the household. Included in this section is a discussion of how women deal with marital conflict and dissolution.

Marriage creates a new reality and a new family. Both partners need to cooperate with each other and rely on each other to make this new reality work. Marriage assigns new roles as wife and husband, which in turn gives each of them certain rights and responsibilities. Role theory, as used in this chapter, follows the definition of Daniel D. Martin and Janelle L. Wilson. It is a means of 'examining the linkages between social organization, culture, and the performances that humans give while engaged in interaction' (Martin and Wilson 2005, 651). In particular, sex role theory is significant in analysing marital adjustments and household management. According to this theory, each sex is assigned different roles with associated expected behaviours. This theory is criticised for differentiating roles solely based on biological function (Connell 1987), and limiting the potentialities of individuals and the variation of cultural gender experiences (Parker 1997). Nevertheless, employing role theory for this chapter is significant because it is useful for analysing gender relations in marriage by exploring the linkages to social institutions, and culture and state gender ideology in the Indonesian context.

Marital adjustment

> In my first year of marriage, there were tensions [*ketegangan*] between us. We felt uncomfortable [*kaku*] and tense [*tegang*]: we weren't comfortable with our level of openness [*keterbukaan*] yet. I was puzzled [*bingung*] about how to communicate everything related to our marriage arrangements. We just observed each other silently.
>
> (Mala, aged 40)

The quote above is the experience of a woman I interviewed in her first year of marriage. Mala was 29 years old when she married a man of the same age. Both came from a middle-class family background, and both had a good education and jobs before marriage. This background similarity did not help bring a smooth adjustment in their first year of marriage. Their short period of acquaintance before marriage could have contributed to their uneasiness. Mala had only known her husband for three months prior to their marriage. Tension had arisen as the date of her wedding day approached, and she was beset with increasing uncertainty and fear that she was marrying the wrong person.

Mala's experience suggests that the two factors that have upped the age of marriage—prolonged education and enhanced employment opportunities, especially for women—do not necessarily affect the adjustment process in the early years of marriage. Rather, I suggest that cultural factors such as family origin, upbringing, ethnic background, age, and personality do affect the marriage adjustment process.

Family origin and upbringing

Differences in the way a family raises children contribute to the process of adjustment after marriage. The family plays a significant role in encouraging certain habits and values that shape one's behaviour. Some problems may arise if these habits and values are not the same as those of the partner.

Mala (aged 40) experienced this difference. For example, her husband would criticise her for not wearing sandals whenever she walked on the ground in the backyard or the front yard. She said:

> My husband considered me weird [*aneh*] and dirty [*jorok*)] because I didn't wear thongs outside, in the backyard or front yard of the house. His family never encouraged him to do so; while in my family having bare feet was common. I have done that since I was a little girl when I played with my friends.

Other women also shared this difficulty in adjusting to their husband's habits. Nanda (aged 36) and her husband had different styles of upbringing. Nanda was brought up in a religious family which was very concerned with the behaviour and attitudes of the children, including how to dress. However, her husband came from a musician's family that was more relaxed in their behaviour, especially in relation to appearance and dress code; he had long hair and often wore untidy clothes. Her family did not even give their permission for her to marry him. These differences negatively affected Nanda's adjustment in her marriage.

When the habits and values of the family of origin coincide with the partner's expectation of how one should behave, there will generally not be tension between the couple. On the contrary, when the habits and values of the natal families are different, it may be problematic and lead to marital conflict. To guard against this, couples came to certain agreements. For example Ani (aged 45) said:

> My husband and I are different in several aspects: I am concerned with education whereas my husband is interested in music; my husband never has breakfast while I always have breakfast in the morning; my husband always prays [*shalat*] on time while I usually can't be bothered doing that.

Ani and her husband made several adjustments to overcome these differences: Ani's husband changed his breakfast habits, so that he eats breakfast every morning; and Ani follows her husband's schedule of praying on time.

Ethnic background

Many Sundanese prefer to marry someone from the same ethnic background so that they can adapt easily. In practice, however, couples of the same ethnicity can also have different habits and social manners. Sandra (aged 57), for example, married a man from her neighbouring district. Both are Sundanese, but Sandra mentioned that when she first visited her husband's family after her wedding day, she felt disturbed by their manners (*tata krama*). For example, her husband's family talked to her in a language that she considered coarse and inappropriate (*tidak sopan*). After a while, she understood that it was their custom and had nothing to do with them looking down on her. On the contrary, her husband's family welcomed her with open arms and showed their affection for her.

Sundanese women who married someone from a different ethnic background, such as a Batak, Minang, or Acehnese, said that they needed to learn and familiarise themselves with these differences. There are also stereotypical presumptions about certain ethnic groups. Sinta (aged 40) complained about the way her husband, who is Batak, talked. Batak are said to have a louder tone of voice and a hot temper, while Sundanese have a softer character. At first, she felt unhappy and could not accept this difference, but after a while she managed to accept it.

A rather different story of adaptation was told by Mira (aged 50), who married an Acehnese man. She had no difficulty in adapting to Acehnese custom. In fact, she became one of her mother-in-law's favourites. She has the ability to mingle with her husband's family and gain sympathy from them. She suggests, 'Do not be afraid of ethnic differences in marriage. All you need to do is to show your good behaviour to your husband's family and know how to adapt intelligently.'

Age, class, and education gaps

In Indonesia, as reported by Augustina Situmorang (2011), women tend to marry up in terms of age, class, and education. These differences affect women's adjustment in their marriage. Big gaps in age, class, or educational background can be difficult for women; if they are younger, and feel inferior to their husband, it can be difficult for them to convey their opinions. In this case, the role of the husband is significant in bridging this gap. Several of the women interviewed have difficulty in coping with these differences in their marriage.

Twelve of the women that I interviewed had varying age gaps with their husbands (between 6 and 12 years). Dian (aged 23) said:

> In the first year of my marriage, there was social and educational inequality between us. I felt inferior [*minder*] in front of my husband and my husband's friends. I have been to university but only up to second semester, while my husband has a master's degree and is a civil servant.

Education aside, there was also a big gap in terms of age: Dian was 20 years of age while her husband was 29. During their first year of marriage, conflicts often occurred: Dian got easily upset (*mudah tersinggung*) if something unpleasant occurred between them. In their second year, the couple managed to talk about their relationship and rectify their mistakes towards each other and to be better people.

Personality

One of the biggest challenges in marital adjustment was dealing with a partner's personality. Every individual has a different and unique personality. Common expressions from women I interviewed were: 'It is difficult to unite two heads' (*Menyatukan dua kepala itu susah banget*) (Tia); and 'Different head, different opinion' (*Beda kepala, beda pemikiran*) (Hera). It seems to be important to have someone who will give in (*mengalah*)—whether it be the wife or the husband. However, when both have a persistent and domineering character, it is quite difficult for them to adjust. Hera (aged 28) indicated that:

> In the early years of marriage, we often had fights, especially about my husband's attitudes. Sometimes, my husband did not agree with what I wanted. On the other hand, I wanted him to change to be a better person. Maybe because we are both the youngest in our families, we always insisted that we were right and were inconsiderate of the other. However, my husband usually cedes to my opinion.

Sofi (aged 39) also found it difficult to adjust to her husband's personality in her first three months of marriage. She said: 'He seldom spoke; he did not work; and he did not pray and fast. This triggered fights between us but I always gave in to what he wanted. I am trying to be an obedient wife.'

Managing the household

Gender and sex roles

Marriage signifies the recognition of the role of the couple in society and the nation, each component of which is specified according to gender. Indonesian Marriage Law no. 1/1974 (Chapter 6, Article 31), alongside New Order gender ideology, has clearly mapped out the household arrangement based on gender roles. In practice, although there are variations in household management in Indonesia, the primary responsibility of women as the main household managers is almost universally prescribed. Even in families where women also contribute to the household income, women felt (and are expected to be) responsible for household affairs.

Most couples were aware of their respective expected roles when entering married life, that is, that the wife's duty is to manage the household while the husband is obliged to provide financial support. These internalised expected roles have an immediate affect when a couple enters married life, unless an alternative agreement has been made between the couple before the marriage. Several women I interviewed directly conformed to this ascribed role—wives who served their husbands and managed the household. Many who were in paid employment before marriage gave up their jobs to stay at home to be an 'ideal' wife. Although, among my participants only eight considered themselves to be full-time housewives, and 34 others participated in paid work, they all considered serving their husbands, doing housework, and child rearing to be their main job.

For example, Nanda (aged 36) and Tia (aged 36) quit their jobs prior to getting married. However, Tia (aged 36) found that staying in the house all day was boring and a waste of time. She said:

> Since marrying, I quit my job as a teacher and moved to new place where my husband works. I was bored being at home all day. I told my husband that I wanted to apply for a job at his workplace, but he didn't allow it. So, I tried to find another job, and I was lucky to meet a friend who helped me establish a school for early learning. Since then, I have been teaching and dedicating myself to the development of this school.

In her first year of marriage, Sandra (aged 57) was also anxious that marriage would not be in accordance with her expectations. Her husband was busy with his own studies while she was left alone doing the housework—providing for his needs and rearing the children. She felt like she was his servant not his wife, especially when her husband left to pursue his studies overseas. She kept wondering why he did this. Later, when her husband had finished his studies she realised that he had wanted to focus on his education and did not want to be disturbed. Once he obtained his degree, he paid attention to her and his children, although he still did not participate in housework. They already had their assigned roles; she considers herself 'the home affairs minister' and her husband 'the foreign minister.'

Thus, the above-mentioned experiences of my participants suggest that while the majority of women conformed to their role as wives, they resisted being the sole guardian of the household and negotiated to actualise themselves by taking up various occupations in the public sphere.

Housework negotiation

In Indonesia, domestic work is believed to be the main job of the wife. Women contributing to the family income through paid work have to work extra hard: in addition to paid work, they have to serve their husbands, clean the house, and care for the children. To alleviate this double burden, assistance from the husband is important in the distribution of work around the home. Although several of the respondents were able to negotiate their position, it was unlikely to be easy.

Mala (aged 40) explained, 'It was necessary for me to bargain with my husband about who does what around the home.' She says that it was not easy and took some time to finally reach an agreement. Her husband was a much beloved son who had never done any housework. It was hard for her to tell him to contribute on a daily basis and he was initially reluctant. However, Mala kept reinforcing the necessity for him to be involved and taught him what she needed him to do. Nowadays, when they get home to find the house untidy, it is the job of whoever is less tired, not necessarily Mala, to do the work. A further challenge came from her mother-in-law, who objected to seeing her son doing housework. Her husband then explained to his natal family about the household arrangements in his marriage so they could understand and respect it.

Like Mala's husband, Edah's husband was raised in a family that assumed that housework is women's work. In her marriage, it was always Edah (aged 43) who was busy working around the house, especially when her first baby was born. Dissatisfied with this situation, Edah told her husband that building a marriage required two people, not one, so it was unfair if she did all the work. She started asking for his participation whenever she was cleaning the house or caring for the baby. She said it was more helpful for her to ask her husband to help her while she was doing the housework rather than telling him to do the job himself. In the end, her husband got used to doing these jobs by himself whenever she was absent, tired, or sick. The greatest challenge, as experienced by Mala, was the objection from her mother-in-law who protested (*tidak rela*) that her son was doing 'women's work.'

There are also several other husbands of interviewees who became used to doing housework, and would routinely participate in daily chores. Ani (aged 45) mentioned that her husband was skilful in cooking and sewing. Halimah (aged 31) also said that she and her husband did the housework together. Whenever she woke up late in the morning, her husband would have already washed the dishes and clothes. He used to sweep and mop the floor. During her first pregnancy, when Halimah had to have bed rest, her husband would do all the housework. Although, she noted, during this time her husband often broke glasses while doing the washing. But she would ignore this matter and thank her husband for his help.

However, the majority of the women in this study noted that their husbands still assume that housework is the work of wives. Husbands' participation in housework is low compared to wives' significant participation in paid work and women remain predominantly responsible for the housework. Many women do not label this as inequality, as they believe that housework is their main duty. The husband's participation in housework, in many cases, is necessary because the wife does other (paid) work. Nevertheless, women's education and participation as income earners does not seem to contribute significantly to equal gender relations within marriage. Many women and men in Indonesia would argue that it is fine to be a career woman as long as the household affairs are not neglected.

Household finances

Managing the household finances was also quite an issue among several women I interviewed. Mala (aged 40), for example, said she and her husband earned their own salaries but both still kept their income for themselves after marriage. Mala used her own money for her daily expenses and her husband did the same. This stand-off continued for about one year until their first child arrived. Since then they have started discussing everything related to their household affairs, as indicated in the quotation below:

> When I was pregnant with my first child I dare to communicate with my husband on how we would manage the household. The first thing we discussed was matters related to the wellbeing of the baby like the cost of the delivery, clothes, and food. Since then we have openly shared and discuss everything related to managing the household. That includes negotiating our roles in housework.
>
> (Mala aged 40)

In certain cases, where family income was insufficient due to the husband's unemployment or unstable income, wives decided to take side jobs in order to contribute to household expenses. In fact, many wives contributed significantly to the household income; they would find alternative jobs to provide backup income whenever their husbands failed to perform as provider. From 40 respondents, only eight could be considered 'real' housewives, while 32 took various jobs, with many even working several jobs a day. For example, in addition to working as teachers, Iis (aged 40) and Sinta (aged 40) took other jobs such as working in the rice field, cooking for other families, or cleaning other families' houses.

Acih (aged 49) is also an example of a wife who has played the role of economic provider throughout her marriage, as well as caring for the family. Her husband had no stable job and was often unemployed for long periods. Acih found her own income source for her daily needs, mostly by finding firewood in the forest or weeding her neighbour's garden. Compared to her husband, she is a hard worker. Continuous pregnancies (12 during the marriage) and domestic violence made her burden even heavier. She mentioned that she often had to work in the garden while she was heavily pregnant and was carrying another baby on her back. The husband's lack of commitment to his role as economic provider imposed upon his wife the, often simultaneous, burdens of reproducing, nurturing, and income earning.

Uum (aged 35) had a similar experience with a husband who had never given her financial support. After marriage, Uum quit her job as a teacher and stayed in her husband's parents' house. Her husband had no stable employment and often left Uum for periods of four to six months. During his absence, he left her without sufficient financial support. Uum had to support herself and their daughters. She would work in the rice field or help her in-laws in managing mosque activities.

Many cases showed that women's participation in paid work is not usually accompanied by men's participation in housework and child rearing. This situation leaves women working a double shift: outside and inside the house. Arlie Hochschild (1989) described this phenomenon in her studies of men and women's contributions to family life in America. She reported that the majority of men do not share domestic work, meaning that women work longer hours than men. For women who work in paid labour, this means working double shifts: 'one shift at the office or factory and a "second shift" at home' (Hochschild 1989, 4). Hochschild noted that these double shifts resulted in women being physically tired, getting easily upset, and feeling anxious—all of which influenced the quality of their marital relationships. The double shift experienced by my informants required women to have physical and emotional stability. Many women said that they had to be physically strong as they had many things to do around the house.

Marital conflict and marital dissolution

Adjustments are important within marriage, and through this process problems that can potentially trigger conflict may appear. A couple's failure to resolve problems may lead to marital disruption, separation, or divorce.

Among the 42 women I interviewed, 5 were divorced, 4 were widowed, and 1 was separated from her partner. The third category (separation) fits with the description given by Terence Hull (2011) of one type of marital disruption: separate residence, not in a relationship together, and where one of the spouses is engaged in another relationship. In my example, the woman continued to share a house with her husband, but she was no longer in a relationship with him because he had another relationship.

Of the three women who had remarried: one remarried her former husband; the other two married other men. One of them has been married five times. Three of the widowed and divorced women stated that they did not think about remarriage, and one of them had been a widow for 18 years. The widow's decision not to remarry was to show loyalty to her former husband (Idrus 2011; Zuidberg 1978) and dedication to the wellbeing of their children.

Conflict

In this section, I explore marital disruption as it was experienced by the women in the study. The section is divided into two parts. The first part discusses conflicts that emerged in the women's marriages and how, and if, they managed to resolve them. The second part examines divorce cases and the stigma attached to women following divorce.

Many women I interviewed were aware that marriage is not always about happiness. Unhappiness, as they describe it, is where a problem presents itself and leads to possible conflict with the husband. Marital conflict can be classified into various categories, according to the respondents: infidelity, economic difficulty, outsider interference, domestic violence, abandonment, and childlessness. Conflict occurring in marriage is not necessarily the result of a single cause. The women I interviewed identified multiple causes of conflict, as categorised above. For example, some women experienced conflict because of their husbands' infidelity, lack of responsibility, and continuous abusive behaviour. Couples who faced these conflicts did not necessarily end up divorcing. Many couples were able to resolve their marital conflicts, be considerate of each other's expectations, and achieve mutual understanding, while others decided to terminate the marriage.

Infidelity is the most common cause of conflict between spouses, based on women's experiences. Eight of my respondents said conflicts began when their husbands had affairs with other women or wanted to have another wife. Four of the women decided to get divorced because of their husband's infidelity, two others resolved the problem, and the other two were still negotiating.

Iis (aged 40), for example, managed to resolve the problem caused by her husband's affair. When she accidentally discovered his affair, Iis called the woman, asked her to end the relationship, and explained that her husband was already married with children. The woman told Iis that she did not know and apologised. Similarly, Acih (aged 49) found out, after one year of marriage, that her husband already had a wife who lived in another province. She was angry at the time and left her husband for a month. But then she went back to her marriage and accepted her husband's status. Indeed, three of my respondents found out after about one year of marriage that their husbands were already married. This phenomenon, where husbands hide or falsify their marital status, is common in Indonesia.

Nisa (aged 37) had a different story. The conflict between her and her husband began when her husband insisted on practising polygyny. Nisa refused to accept it. Her husband tried to force his opinion on her and provided her with some religious readings that support polygyny. Her husband even gave her an ultimatum. If, within a certain period, she did not permit him to take another wife, he would divorce her. After interviewing Nisa, I provided her with alternative readings on polygyny that differed from those of her husband, to provide her with balanced information concerning polygyny in Islam.

Ilah (aged 59) and her husband had been separated for almost six years. It all started when her husband had an affair with another married woman from the same village. This affair was publicly known and people felt pity for Ilah. Ilah felt sad, embarrassed, and helpless. Since the affair, her husband had not given Ilah and her children any financial support. They still live in their small house together with their married daughter, but they do not talk to each other. Ilah's husband wants a divorce, but Ilah does not. The reason is that if her husband divorces her, he will sell the house, which will mean that she and her married daughter will have nowhere to live. Divorce is not an option for her but a reunion is also unlikely.

Many conflicts in marriage also result from economic difficulties as a result of the husband failing to play his role as income earner. For example, Rani (aged 43) and Sinta (aged 40) have similar experiences. From the time they got married, Rani's husband had not had a stable job and they often fought over it. At the time of my interview with Rani, however, her husband had got a stable job and their marriage was more harmonious.

Sinta and her husband, who did not have a stable job, often fought over money. According to Sinta, her husband did not try hard enough to find work and she considered he was too picky. Meanwhile, Sinta always took any available job in the neighbourhood. Her husband often asked her for money or borrowed from a neighbour to try to run his own business—a business that he did not manage wisely, which resulted in debt. Once, her husband got very angry when he asked her for some money. She was unable to give it to him because she did not have any. She told her husband to find it himself. Her husband then threw a helmet at her. She was shocked and frightened because she was not expecting such a reaction. She returned to her father's house because she was afraid that her husband would try to harm her again. Her father stepped in and confronted Sinta's husband, advising him to stop being violent towards his daughter.

Childlessness can also trigger conflict within a marriage. Tia (aged 36) had been married for 12 years and she and her husband did not have any children. They argued a lot about the reasons, with Tia finally consulting a doctor after getting pressure from her husband.

Interference from outsiders can also create marital tension. Outsiders include immediate family like parents, in-laws, extended family, or even neighbours. These outsiders may interfere in matters such as household affairs, or they may provoke conflict between the spouses. Maya (aged 41) and Siti (aged 40) had different strategies in countering outsiders' meddling. Maya preferred to fix the problem right away, while Siti preferred to ignore interference from her husband's family. She tried not to be provoked because she felt that a response from her might create further conflict.

In this study, the women tended to keep their marital conflicts to themselves. They tried to resolve the issues without involving others. Indeed, they had been told by their mothers that they should not talk about their marital problems outside the house and endeavour to solve the problem themselves. However, if the problem became too complicated and they could not handle it, they could ask their parents to step in and help. During the interviews, several women, who felt that their marriages were in trouble, asked my advice about how to resolve their problems. They wrongly assumed I was a marriage counsellor. I suggested that they could go to the KUA (Religious Affairs Office) to ask for advice. I was informed by one of the marriage registrars that KUA, in association with Badan Penasehat, Pembinaan dan Pelestarian Perkawinan (BP4, The advisory body for developing and maintaining marriage), deals with marital complaints and issues.

Divorce

Many researchers have reported that divorce in West Java is high (Horikoshi 1976; Jones 2001; Jones, Asari, and Djuartika 1994; McDonald and Abdurrahman 1974). Until recently, divorce in West Java remained true to trend as the data shows increasing divorce cases in the Religious Court of Bandung city: 5,200 cases in 2016; 5,414 in 2017; 5,669 in 2018; and 6,085 cases in 2019 (Pengadilan Agama Kota Bandung 2017).

In contrast, for the women I interviewed, divorce is unlikely to be their choice, even when they know their husbands are having affairs, have other wives, or are violent. Kate O'Shaunghessy (2009, 21) has reported that the 'discourse of shame' constructed by the state towards divorce has made it an unfavourable option (for women). Nisa (aged 37), for example, whose husband insists on being polygynous, told me that:

> I do not want to get divorced, but I also do not want my husband to practise polygamy. I am not ready yet. But my husband is forcing me to agree to his decision. He has given me some time to think about it, but he said that if I still could not give him permission by a certain time, he might divorce me. Being divorced would not guarantee that my circumstances would improve.

Ita (aged 59) also said that:

> I actually wouldn't mind my husband having another wife, as long as he asked my permission first. I do not want to get divorced, because I am

concerned about the possible impact on my youngest daughter's psychological state, her position at school, and also our social and career status. In fact, my husband has already another wife secretly and his new wife is insisting that he divorce me.

Equally significantly, however, two other women stated that they would prefer to be divorced than to stay in the marriage when they found out that their husbands had had affairs with other women or were violent. Iis (aged 40) said:

I want to get divorced from my husband because of his violent behaviour in my marriage, and I have had enough. But my husband does not want this to happen. On the other side, there is no sign from him that he is becoming a better person.

Minah (aged 50) also said that when she found out that her husband was having an affair, she asked directly for a divorce. She said she found out where the woman lived, and when she caught the husband there she said to the woman, 'I am here not to fight over my husband or to take him back. You can have him. I am here just to ask my husband to divorce me.' A similar thing happened to Nanda (aged 36), who asked for a divorce from her husband when she found out that her husband had had an affair and the woman had got pregnant.

The factors classified as reasons for divorce may vary across the West Javanese region. Previous researchers have reported that common reasons for divorce were: the husband's irresponsible behaviour such as alcoholism and gambling in Indramayu (Jones, Asari, and Djuartika 1994); economic difficulties in Sumedang (Jones, Asari, and Djuartika 1994) and Garut (Horikoshi 1976); marital disharmony in Serpong (Zuidberg 1978), infidelity (or polygyny) (Nurmila 2009; Platt 2017); infertility and sub-fecundity in the highlands of Bandung (McDonald and Abdurrahman 1974). For the women I interviewed, the most frequent factors causing divorce were infidelity, polygyny, desertion, and their husbands' unstable emotional and psychological characters.

However, even following divorce, several women were unhappy, disappointed, and even in distress as described in the following divorce cases.

Ita (aged 59): 'between love, humiliation, and anger'

Sometimes I feel empty and disappointed knowing that 30 years of marriage had no meaning for him, as he turned to another woman. There are uncertain feelings inside me—between love, humiliation, and anger—after divorce.

Ita was married for 30 years and had five children. The conflict started when her husband took another wife secretly (*nikah siri*).[1] In fact, Ita would not have opposed her husband taking another wife but she did wish he had asked her permission first. She felt that he had completely ignored her existence. In the end, her husband's second wife forced him to divorce Ita if he wanted to continue with the marriage and Ita's husband agreed. Ita's husband was strategic in how he went about dissolving the marriage in order that the divorce would seem to have been initiated by Ita. He did not go home (to Ita) for long periods and abandoned his family. But Ita was quick to realise what was going on and did not react; she did not complain or make a fuss about his absence. She recognised that if she was the one who initiated the divorce, she would not be entitled to post-divorce spouse-and-children support from the husband. And her husband wanted his financial commitment to end.

In 2009, her husband finally lodged the application for divorce to the Court. In the end, although divorce was not her choice and she felt betrayed by her husband, she felt better: 'since my divorce, I feel more relaxed and no longer afraid.' However, Ita often wonders how her husband could divorce her after 30 years together and turn to another woman he had just met. After the divorce, Ita was entitled to the house and several properties they had acquired during the marriage, as compensation because her husband refused to give her alimony and child support.

Uum (aged 35): entangled

Uum's marital conflict began when she had a six-month-old baby and her husband left them for several months. Later she found out that her husband had a wife before he married her. She said that if her child had been a boy, she would have asked for a divorce right away. But, because she had a daughter, she stayed in her polygynous marriage for the sake of her daughter. In fact, she dared to visit her husband's first wife and introduce herself as his second wife and the first wife accepted her. But the conflict did not end; her husband often abandoned her for long periods, giving her no financial support for up to six months at a time. Whenever he was around, he limited her movements, abused her, and then left her for further months on end. This happened repeatedly, because every time he returned to her he promised her all kinds of things, which she believed, and let him back into her life again. They subsequently had three daughters. Uum's mother stepped in, brought Uum home and advised her to get divorced.

Another problem was that Uum had married her husband secretly and their marriage was not registered (*nikah siri*), thus she had no documentation to prove that she had ever married her husband. It was difficult for her to ask for a divorce because her husband not only refused to divorce her, but was hard to locate. Uum then asked her husband's elder brother to witness and sign, on behalf of her husband, the letter that she had written concerning the divorce. She returned the ring that had been used as a bride price (*khulu'*) to her husband's brother. Her husband's brother promised to take responsibility for the divorce process.

Nanda (aged 36): acquiescent

Nanda married her husband without the blessing of her family. Her parents already noted the differences between them, particularly the large age gap (18 years) and differing family backgrounds. Her husband worked in music production where, according to her family, it is very easy for a man to have an affair. However, Nanda ignored the warnings given by her family and insisted on marrying him. After several years of marriage, her husband indeed had an affair with another woman in his workplace and the conflict began. He seldom came home, stopped giving her financial support, and neglected the children. Nanda, who at first wanted to become a housewife, was forced to support herself and her twin daughters. She took whatever jobs were available to prevent her children from having to quit school.

Then one day her husband came to her in tears and told her that the woman whom he had had an affair with was pregnant and had asked him to marry her. Nanda was upset and slapped her husband. Her husband asked her forgiveness for his mistake; he even kissed her feet. Nanda said to her husband, 'Alright, marry her and divorce me.' Her husband then divorced Nanda once (revocable). Her family wanted her to ask for a third divorce (irrevocable) for what he had done to her. But Nanda did not agree; she explained that her decision was for the sake of her daughters, as they would need their father's guardianship later when they were married. Nanda's ex-husband divorced his second wife and Nanda remarried him in 2010; again her decision was opposed by her family.

Sofi (aged 39): confused

Sofi divorced her husband after only a very short period of marriage—three months. She told me that her three-month marriage was disastrous. She had been forced by her parents to marry because she was 34 years old at that time. Her uncle introduced her to a previously drug-addicted man. Although Sofi was unsure about marrying someone unfamiliar, she accepted the proposal and married him. Before getting married, she told her prospective husband that she wanted to continue teaching after marriage and he agreed. After marrying, Sofi moved to her husband's residence and from that time the conflict began. Her husband would not allow her to work as he had agreed, but he was not working himself; his parents subsidised all his daily needs. Furthermore, Sofi noted that her husband had an unstable emotional character and Sofi suspected that this was the result of his previous heavy drug addiction.

In the third month of their marriage, her husband divorced her while she was pregnant with their first child. Sofi was shocked because she was not ready for divorce, especially when she was pregnant. She was in so much distress that it affected her pregnancy. She experienced serious bleeding and lost her baby.

Much research about the dissolution of marriage in Indonesia focuses only on divorce cases and not widowhood. Four women among my respondents were widowed. One of them, Tuti (aged 55), had been a widow for about 18 years. She said that she focused on taking care of her children and had not considered remarrying. Another woman (Lela, aged 65) said that when her husband died she felt that he had abandoned her because he died too soon, and at that time she still needed him. Feelings of loss, sadness, and uncertainty were experienced by women after their husbands died.

Ani (aged 45) had been a widow for two years. After seven years of marriage, her husband died from a serious illness. She grieved deeply for her husband because she realised only after he left how much she loved him. After he died, Ani bought and read many books on topics related to death to find out about the afterlife. Ani never stopped praying (*berdoa*) for him. She believed that if she prayed regularly he would visit her in her dreams. She told me that she often sees her husband in her dreams. Only recently has she been able to start her activities again. However, she said that not many people in her workplace knew that her husband had passed away. She informed only her close friends. She said that this was to avoid gossip concerning her status, because she would feel unsafe if she revealed her status as a widow. Feeling unsafe and subject to gossip was also experienced by divorced women, because Indonesian society stigmatises *janda* (divorcees and widows).

Stigma

One of the social impacts of being *janda* (a divorcee or a widow) is social marginalisation. Marriage in Indonesia is an ideal social norm and the breakdown of marriage is considered pitiable and troubling. *Janda* are usually the target of gossip in the neighbourhood and suspected of sexual availability because they have experienced sex and are assumed to want to experience it again. Other married women fear that they might steal their husbands and *janda* are also targeted by 'naughty' husbands and young men who want to experience sex. In the case of 'wandering' husbands, the *janda* is perceived as being a threat to the equilibrium of married life and society. However, the stigma is only experienced by women and not men. Thus, the stigmatisation of *janda* in Indonesia is a gendered, moral experience (Parker, Riyani, and Nolan 2015). Citra (aged 50) noted: 'When my husband passed away, one of the senior male lecturers in my workplace advised me to remarry soon to avoid gossip among my workmates.' Uum (aged 35) said that her friends became suspicious about her sexual life after divorce:

> I swear to God [*demi Allah*], I never have illicit sex. I never even have time to think about it. I am busy with my life. My focus right now is caring for my daughters and studying hard. I do not want to make the same mistake again and to experience failure again in my study and my marriage. So, I am working hard to achieve a better life for my future.

136 *Marital adjustment and household management*

Sofi (aged 39) also stated:

> Being a divorcée is uncomfortable. No matter how good my behaviour is, people always suspect me, because I attract men. Married men often harass me and ask me to have affairs. Even married women in my neighbourhood often make unpleasant comments about me. Sometimes I just ignore them but sometimes I am just sick and tired of all these comments.

Many researchers also note that the high rate of divorce in West Java is followed by a high rate of remarriage (Jones, Asari, and Djuartika 1994; McDonald and Abdurrahman 1974). It is worth noting that this high rate of remarriage could relate to the stigmatisation of the status of divorcees/widows. Martin van Bruinessen (1988), whose research addresses some of the poorest urban migrants in Bandung, suggests that the demand for remarriage is most likely due to concern for women's reputations, rather than for economic reasons. Remarriage re-establishes one's position in the community as a respectable woman.

The status of *janda* is located beyond the normal category of married life. Thus many *janda* try to find a strategy to gain this 'normalcy' (Wieringa 2012, 518). They re-establish their position in the society as respectable women by becoming dedicated mothers and devoted Muslims. Several divorcees and widows in my research did not think of remarrying but rather focused on caring for their children and their education. Diah (aged 45) said:

> It is not easy to find a man who would accept me as a complete package: love me and at the same time love my children. So, I work hard to provide a better education for my children.

Another strategy to reclaim respectability and remove the stigma of being a *janda* is by regularly participating in religious gatherings (*pengajian*) to create a social network and increase religious knowledge. Lela (aged 65, widow) said:

> When my husband died, I started going from one *pengajian* to another. I didn't want to just stay at home all alone. Here [at *pengajian*] I can meet my friends, talk to them, and increase my spiritual knowledge.

To sum up, in this chapter I have provided a discussion of women's experiences of marital adjustment and household management. There are significant differences between individuals in how each person manages their daily life in marriage. In terms of the adjustments experienced by my participants, cultural differences were the main factors in this process. There also seemed to be a significant positive correlation between ease of adjustment and the length of the period of courtship, and between ease of adjustment and ease of communication. However, I discovered that women also need a communication strategy to convey messages to their husbands effectively. This strategy is important especially in managing the household and arranging domestic work between the couple. Cooperation between the couple in managing the household is important and could affect the longevity of married life and minimise marital disruption.

Marital disruption experienced by women in my study resulted from various factors such as infidelity, economic difficulty, outsider interference, domestic violence, abandonment, and childlessness. Several women managed to resolve these problems while several others ended up in divorce. In my study, avoidance of divorce is strong due to the stigma attached to being *janda*.

Note

1. *Nikah siri* is a marriage conducted by the couple secretly and without government registration. *Siri* is taken from the Arabic *sirrun-sirri*, meaning secret. In Indonesia, *nikah siri* is common with different terms used to indicate this kind of marriage: *nikah bawah tangan* (underhand marriage); *nikah syiri* (secret; some people in Indonesia spell this word by adding y to siri—syiri) (Iswarini 2011, 74); *kawin liar* (wild marriage) (Idrus 2011). In *nikah siri*, the couple fails to fulfil one or several of the requirements for a valid marriage, such as having a guardian (*wali*) or witness. In fact, *nikah siri* is risky for women, both socially and legally. The couple who perform *nikah siri* is subject to gossip, and legally a woman cannot claim the rights she is entitled to within marriage, e.g. it will be difficult to obtain documents such as birth certificates for children born from this type of marriage. Surprisingly, many people consider it to be *nikah secara agama* (religiously accepted). They need to make the differentiation between *nikah siri* and *nikah secara agama*. *Nikah secara agama* does not violate the requirements stipulated for a valid marriage, it is just not registered, while *nikah siri* violates the requirements needed for valid marriage. For example some poor people choose to keep their marriage unregistered, due to the expense of registration, but not necessarily secret, although they may fulfil all the requirements needed for a valid marriage. They would happily participate if KUA or certain other social organisations provided a *nikah massal* (mass wedding) where they could register their marriage for free.

References

Bruinessen, Martin van. (1988). '"Duit, djodoh, dukun": Observations on cultural change among poor migrants to Bandung.' *Masyarakat Indonesia*, 15, 35–65.
Connell, R. W. (1987). *Gender and Power*. Cambridge: Polity Press.
Hochschild, Arlie Russell. (1989). *The Second Shift: Working Parents and the Revolution at Home*. New York: Viking Penguin.
Horikoshi, Hiroko. (1976). 'A traditional leader in a time of change: The 'Kijaji' and 'Ulama' in West Java.' PhD thesis, University of Illinois, Urbana, Champaign.
Hull, Terence H. (2011). 'Statistical indices of marriage patterns in Insular Southeast Asia.' In Gavin W. Jones, Terence H. Hull, and Maznah Mohamad (eds.), *Changing Marriage Patterns in Southeast Asia: Economic and Socio-Cultural Dimensions*, 13–28. London: Routledge.

Idrus, Nurul Ilmi. (2011). 'Bugis marriage: State laws, Islam and local practice.' In Gavin W. Jones, Terence H. Hull, and Maznah Mohamad (eds.), *Changing Marriage Patterns in Southeast Asia: Economic and Socio-Cultural Dimensions*, 99–116. London: Routledge.

Iswarini, Sri Endras. (2011). 'Underage marriage and poverty in West Java, Indonesia.' In Gavin W. Jones, Terence H. Hull, and Maznah Mohamad (eds.). *Changing Marriage Patterns in South East Asia: Economic and Socio-Cultural Dimensions*, 73–82. London: Routledge.

Jones, Gavin W. (2001). 'Which Indonesian women marry youngest and why?' *Journal of Southeast Asian Studies*, 32(1), 67–78, DOI: 10.1017/S0022463401000029.

Jones, Gavin W, Yahya Asari, and Tuti Djuartika. (1994). 'Divorce in West Java.' *Journal of Comparative Family Studies*, 25(3), 395–416, DOI: 10.3138/jcfs.25.3.395.

Martin, Daniel D. and Janelle L. Wilson. (2005). 'Role theory.' *Encyclopedia of Social Theory, Vol II*. Thousand Oaks, CA: SAGE, DOI: 10.4135/9781412952552.n246.

McDonald, Peter and E. H. Abdurrahman. (1974). *Marriage and Divorce in West Java: An Example of the Effective use of Marital Histories*. Jakarta: Lembaga Demografi Fakultas Ekonomi Universitas Indonesia.

Nurmila, Nina. (2009). *Women, Islam and Everyday Life: Renegotiating Polygamy in Indonesia*. London: Routledge.

O'Shaunghessy, Kate. (2009). *Gender, State and Social Power in Contemporary Indonesia: Divorce and Marriage Law*. London: Routledge.

Parker, Lyn. (1997). 'Engendering school children in Bali.' *The Journal of the Royal Anthropological Institute*, 3(3), 497–516, DOI: 10.2307/3034764.

Parker, Lyn, Irma Riyani, and Brooke Nolan. (2015). 'The stigmatisation of *janda* (widows and divorcees) in Indonesia and the possibilities for agency.' *Indonesia and the Malay World*, 44(128), 27–46, DOI: 10.1080/13639811.2016.1111677.

Platt, Maria. (2017). *Marriage, Gender and Islam in Indonesia: Women Negotiating Informal Marriage, Divorce and Desire*. London: Routledge.

Pengadilan Agama Kota Bandung (City of Bandung Religious Court), 2017. 'Statistik Pengadilan.' Mahkamah Ugung Republik Indonesia: Pengadilan Agama Bandung, 10 April, available from: http://pa-bandung.go.id/tentang-pengadilan/statistik-pengadilan (accessed 4 February 2020).

Situmorang, Augustina. (2011). 'Delayed marriage among lower socio-economic groups on an Indonesian industrial city.' In Gavin W. Jones, Terence H. Hull, and M. Mohamad (eds.), *Changing Marriage Patterns in Southeast Asia: Economic and Socio-Cultural Dimensions*, 83–98. London: Routledge.

Wieringa, Saskia E. (2012). 'Passionate aesthetics and symbolic subversion: Heteronormativity in India and Indonesia.' *Asian Studies Review*, 36(4), 515–30, DOI: 10.1080/10357823.2012.739997.

Zuidberg, Lida C. L. (ed.). (1978). *Family Planning in Rural West Java: The Serpong Project*. Leiden: Institute of Cultural and Social Studies, University of Leiden.

Legislation

Indonesian Marriage Law (no. 1/1974), Undang-undang Republik Indonesia No 1 Tahun 1974 Tentang an, available from: https://www.scribd.com/doc/53066173/Undang-undang-Republik-Indonesia-No-1-Tahun-1974-Tentang-an (accessed 26 February 2020).

6 Women's experiences of marital sexual relationships

Sex as a duty

> If it [intercourse] was not my duty, I would be lazy [*malas*] about it.
> (Rosa, aged 44)

In this chapter, I explore women's experiences of marital sexual relationships with their husbands within the construct of female sexuality in Indonesia. The ideal femininity of married women requires them to control their desire, to show no interest in sex, and to be passive and submissive to their husbands. The asymmetric relationship in marriage between wife and husband, as stated in Indonesian Marriage Law no. 1/1974 and strengthened by religious prescription, has influenced sexual relations. Many women (and men) believe that sex in marriage is a woman's duty and man's right.

I demonstrate how the expected role of a woman's sexual relations in marriage makes her submissive to her husband's sexual desires, and confirms intercourse as a woman's duty rather than her right. In reading this chapter, the unique and diverse experiences among individual participants should be taken into account because the description might differ from the experiences of married Muslim women in other regions in West Java or in Indonesia in general. As a result, this representation is context-specific and the experiences are not necessarily able to be generalised.

The data in this chapter are analysed within the context of heterosexual relationships exploring married women's desire and the ways in which society and religion construct women's sexuality. The 'theory of scripts,' adopted from John Gagnon and William Simon (1973), Gagnon (1977), and Simon and Gagnon (1984) is useful in indicating how social behaviour follows certain scripts which guide one's action in a specific time and context (Gagnon 1977). In this book, the theory of scripts is a useful tool for analysing the ways in which women's marital sexual behaviours are guided by certain sexual scripts, governed by the state (regional and national government) through its laws. They are also prescribed by cultural discourse (particularly in the Sundanese cultural context) and by religious teachings (specifically, Muslim). This shared meaning of sexual behaviour is spread through family, school, religion, media, and many other institutions which influence individual personal relationships (Simon and Gagnon 1984).

140 *Women's marital experiences and sex as a duty*

I begin this chapter by exploring women's experiences in relation to: the initiation of sex on the wedding night; women's sex and reproductive experiences; and women's perception of sex in marriage as a duty. I also discuss the sexual violence experienced by some of my participants and how they have coped with this aggression.

Sexual initiation and perceived sexual roles

The 'first night' (malam pertama): between fear, shame, and desire

In a discussion of women's marital sexual relations, it is worth starting from their initiation into having sex on the *malam pertama* (lit. first night). *Malam pertama* is the night following the wedding day, when the couple is expected to have intercourse for the first time.

In Indonesia, with its predominantly Muslim population, sex is understood as an act restricted to marriage.[1] Promiscuous sex is unacceptable, and illicit sexual behaviour is stigmatised. Men and women are expected to be virgins on their wedding night. However, more pressure relating to virginity is directed towards women than men.

In Indonesia, information about sex and sexuality is not widely available. Consequently, women have limited, if any, information concerning sex and sexuality prior to marriage. To a certain extent, this affects their sexual interaction with their husbands, especially during their initiation into intercourse on the first night. Many women experience fear and anxiety about what will happen to them on that night. Many were informed that the first night would be painful. However, for men the wedding night is depicted as something that will be enjoyable.

During *malam pertama*, the newlywed couple will have their first experience of sexual intercourse, or at least they are expected to do so. However, several of my informants preferred to delay this first sexual experience, for several days, weeks, or even months after the wedding, due to their fear and anxiety at not knowing what to expect. Others felt obliged to submit to their husbands in the name of fulfilling what they perceived as their 'duty.' Yuni (aged 39; aged 30 at first marriage) said:

> The first night knocked me out for so many reasons: I was so tired because of the wedding reception all day, it made me feel weak, my face was pale and what's more, I was informed by my friends that the first night could be painful. These conditions stressed me. I was scared. We did not have sex that night as my husband also panicked, seeing my condition.

Mala (aged 40; aged 29 at first marriage) also mentioned:

> During our first night, there was stiffness [*kaku*] between us. We just stared at each other silently and did not do anything. I was scared and

shy. We fell asleep exhausted that night. When I woke up the next morning, I was surprised to see that I was sleeping with someone else. I felt scared. Then I realised that he was my husband now.

These feelings of fear, shame, and anxiety about the first night leave little room for a woman to explore her sexual desires or to focus on her sexual pleasure. Several women suggested that they preferred to delay their sexual initiation for days because of this anxiety and feelings of unreadiness. Dian (aged 23; aged 20 at first marriage) said:

On the first night I was scared and my body was shaking. A thought came to my mind at that time: what is my husband going to do with me? Because of that feeling, I did not have sex with him for two weeks after the wedding. I also did not have any information about the first night, what I should do or what might happen that night. However, after two weeks I did it, even though I was still unsure, I did it because I felt pity [*kasihan*] for my husband.

Wiwi (aged 47; aged 15 at first marriage) had a similar experience, and had sex with her husband two weeks after their wedding. She said:

I felt scared that night. That was why I did not have sex with my husband for about two weeks. After that, I realised that I was married to him legally so it was all right to have sex with him. I knew nothing about it, my husband guided me. I was scared but happy.

She mentioned that her husband guided her in her first sexual intercourse experience, because he had been married before and had already experienced sex. However, she informed me that she only found out that her husband had been previously married after one year of marriage. She was disappointed, but in the end accepted the way things were (*pasrah*).

Minah (aged 50; aged 13 at first marriage) described her first experience of intercourse as shocking. She was married off by her parents at 13, to a man 6 years older than her after only one week's acquaintance. Minah did not immediately live with her husband after their marriage. Two months later, her husband moved in to her parents' house and from that time she had sexual intercourse with him. She described it as 'creepy [*murinding*] and shocking [*gingiapeun*].'

Some husbands comply with their wives' disinclination to sexual initiation and understandably delay sexual intercourse on the wedding night. Others forcibly demand that their wives have sex on this first night. Eha (aged 29; aged 17 at first marriage) said that: 'My first night was painful, because my husband wanted to do it again and again.' She hesitated to say no to this unpleasant first experience of sex. Acih (aged 49) also experienced forced sex on the first night. At the time, she was only 13 and had not even experienced menarche. When I asked her husband about his violence, Rastam (aged 54) said to me laughing, 'What else could I do but to force her to have sex.' He was referring to his wife's lack of experience of sex. Forced sex at first intercourse was also reported by Sri Iswarini (2011) in other regions in West Java—a result of forced and underage marriage in the lower classes.

Women's lack of information about sex and about how their bodies work prevented them from exploring their own desires, let alone enjoying this sexual initiation with their husbands. Many women surrendered to having sex as a part of their assumed role as wives, which ascribes that sex in marriage is their duty. For example, Lina (aged 37; aged 21 at first marriage) said that 'on the first night I felt unsure and did not enjoy it because I had not accepted him wholeheartedly.' Siti (aged 40; aged 21 at first marriage) said, 'I did not enjoy my first night because I did not know anything about sex, or about my husband.' She described it as a 'cold' (*dingin-dingin saja*) night and she considered both of them ignorant (*bodoh*) about sex. It should be noted that many husbands were also anxious about 'first night' sexual activity, which many of them were to experience for the first time. In Indonesian society, men are assumed and expected to have more knowledge of sex than women.

Rani (aged 43; aged 21 at first marriage) also said:

> I did not have sex with my husband for a week after the wedding. Honestly, I still could not accept him as my husband. I even slept with my back against him and divided the bed with a pillow in-between us. A week later, I agreed to have sex, but only half-heartedly [*setengah hati*].

Rani told me that her sister noticed that she had not yet had sex with her husband because she had not washed her hair as a symbol of purification (*mandi wajib*),[2] which is required after intercourse in Islam. Ina (aged 33; aged 25 at first marriage) also said that: 'I had not accepted my husband 100 percent and that affected my sexual relations with him.'

Several women also experienced unfamiliarity with cohabitation. Some women felt strange and surprised the morning after their wedding, realising that they had woken up with a man beside them. On the first night, Ijah (aged 33; aged 20 at first marriage) felt surprised that she had shared her bed and blanket with 'someone else.' She had been used to sleeping on her own. She said that she needed a while to become accustomed to this change. Mala (aged 40) also felt surprised when she found out that she had shared her bed with 'a stranger' who happened to be her husband. This anxiety among women concerning a new husband can be understood as a function of a short courtship period and unfamiliarity with sharing their living space with men. In Indonesia, the norm regulates male-female interaction, thus limiting the open physical sharing of space between the sexes. Although in Indonesia strict segregation is not as clearly defined as in Middle Eastern countries, typically women and men are homosocial and self-segregate.

Delaying first sexual encounters for women on the wedding night is common for other reasons such as tiredness and embarrassment, as there are still many relatives in the house. The lack of privacy is an issue for couples who live in a small house with other family members. The couple's bedroom, which is usually decorated and situated in the front of the house, sometimes has just a curtain separating it from bamboo or timber-walled rooms. Nisa (aged 37; aged 24 at first marriage), for example, said, 'I felt shy on my first night. There were still many family members and relatives who spent the night at my home. Besides, I did not know anything about having sex.' By contrast, Nisa said that her husband seemed to know what to do that night. He prayed (*shalat*), a step to be fulfilled before intercourse, as indicated in Islamic guides. However, she did not have sex with her husband for about a week after the wedding due to her period.[3] After she finished menstruating, her husband asked her to spend the night at his place, a few blocks away from her house, and have sex.

Edah (aged 43; aged 24 at first marriage) also said:

> Although I read a sex manual, I still felt scared. We did not do anything that night. There were still many family members and relatives who slept just in front of my bedroom. I was shy that they would tease me in the morning. We were even very careful to move, to avoid any noise come from our bed. We tried to sleep quietly.

In Indonesian everyday life, males and females learn about shame (*malu*). *Malu* is associated with different categories: exposure of the naked body; self-exposure to strangers; and showing respect to the elderly and elites (Collins and Bahar 2000). As explained by Elizabeth Collins and Ernaldi Bahar (2000), *malu* supports hierarchical relations and shapes gendered responses. The meaning of *malu* also differs between boys and girls. For girls it relates to femininity (Blackwood 2010). Linda Bennett (2005, 25) further explains the term *malu* as it is associated with female sexuality and

> enduring notions of passive femininity ... Shame is therefore understood as a necessary emotion that enables the self-regulation of female sexuality, yet is also threatening when it derives from the public exposure of female sexual impropriety.

Malu was experienced by my participants in relation to exposing their naked bodies to their husbands, who, in many cases, were older than themselves. They were also *malu* about showing any interest in sex.

Many women mentioned that their sexual initiation on the first night happened naturally, including Rosa (aged 44; aged 20 at first marriage), Aas (aged 28; aged 21 at first marriage), and Tuti (aged 55; aged 19 at first marriage). They did not explain further whether this experience led to sexual enjoyment or whether they simply followed instructions from their husbands as most women did.

Apart from those experiences, many women I interviewed also had a successful first night. 'Successful' as explained by the women I interviewed, could mean mutual interest in sex, cooperation with the husband in having sex, enjoying intercourse, and an experience that was not painful. The rumour of a painful 'first night' arose partly because some men tended to rush sex that night, especially when it was also their first sexual intercourse, or when forced penetration occurred without proper foreplay. Lack of foreplay could also inhibit woman's sexual desire. In Islam, as explained in Chapter 1, foreplay is encouraged before sex to gain mutual orgasm. Ikah (aged 30; aged 18 at first marriage) mentioned that 'my friends told me that the first night would be painful and they said that if we refuse to have sex, our husbands will force us to do so. But, fortunately, I did not experience all those things. I did not feel pain, nor was I forced.' Tia (aged 36; aged 22 at first marriage) said, 'At first I felt shy, but I read in the classical Islamic book that I needed to respond and not just lie there passively. So, I responded to my husband's sexual intentions and enjoyed it.'

Ani (aged 45, 38 at first marriage) had a different story of her first night. It was not she who felt shy on *malam pertama*, but her husband. They had only met once and a week later decided to get married. On the wedding night, instead of sleeping in Ani's bedroom, her husband slept on the sofa in the living room. Ani pulled him into her bedroom and told him that they were already married and it would be embarrassing for her if her family found out that he slept on the sofa instead of 'their' bedroom. Her husband told her that he was shy and would join her if she turned the light off. Ani agreed and they finally shared the bed.

Other women cooperated with their husbands. While they initially experienced feelings of fear and shame, they enjoyed the sexual experience and felt happy, as Tia and Wiwi noted above. Some husbands tolerated their wives unpreparedness, but for a certain time only. Besides, family members would notice and suggest consummation. The women also already had a perception of their duty, so they felt obliged to fulfil it regardless of their (un)readiness.

Women's lack of information and knowledge concerning sex and sexuality influenced their first experience of sex. They did not know what to do during sexual intercourse, and therefore could not explore their desires and pursue pleasure and satisfaction. What they focused on was how to satisfy their husbands' sexual needs and desires—sex as duty. It seems from the women's experiences outlined above, the first sexual experience for women was not geared towards the goal of seeking pleasure, although many were curious about that.

Sex and reproduction

In this section, I discuss women's sexual desire as it is related to reproduction, which is an integral part of discussing women's sexuality. Here, reproduction encompasses menstruation, pregnancy, childbirth, infertility, and menopause which undoubtedly produce different states of desire for women.

Pregnancy, childbirth, and infertility

In Indonesia, procreation is still the primary aim of marriage. A successful marriage is considered to be when the bride falls pregnant soon after the wedding. Therefore, many couples do not attempt to prevent pregnancy in the first year of marriage. In addition, the older generation often imposes the belief that if the couple tries to prevent pregnancy in the first year of marriage by using contraception, the woman's womb may become dry, making it difficult to conceive. This 'story' was told to several women like Ikah (aged 30) and Aas (aged 28).

The majority of women I interviewed fell pregnant soon after their weddings. The interval between the wedding and the pregnancy ranged from weeks to a couple of months. The pressure to get pregnant quickly can cause social and psychological distress for a woman, because pregnancy confirms her existence within the extended family and the community where she belongs. Through marriage and having children, a woman will be considered an adult with the appropriate social status and the ability to participate in community activities (Grijns 1987).

Participants in this study had from two to six children, with most having two to four. Two of the women had 12 children. Before the implementation of the family planning program in Indonesia, which began in the 1970s, there was a tendency towards having a flexible number of children in West Java. Russell Darroch, Paul Meyer, and Masri Singarimbun (1981) reported that the desired number of children among the Sundanese was four to five. Poorer families tended to have more children (Bruinessen 1988) because of the economic contribution they could make to the family (Bruinessen 1988; Darroch, Meyer, and Singarimbun 1981). During the New Order (1966–98), the ideal was 'two were enough' (*dua anak cukup*) and this policy was quite firmly implemented (Niehof and Lubis 2003). In the Reform era, after 1998, the 'two-child' policy ceased being a strict regulation for Indonesian families. Among my participants, there was a tendency towards more highly controlled fertility in the hope that the parents could provide a better quality of health and education for the children and so they could enjoy their old age. Maya (aged 41) stated:

> I discuss everything with my husband, including how many children we want to have. At first we decided to have only two children but the third child arrived unexpectedly. We would like to prepare for their future: education and health with our limited funds. Besides, we also would like to enjoy our older age.

The idea of having a small family is no longer related to government pressure to control population, but rather it reflects self-reliance and an aspiration for 'quality' rather than size in family life.

Several of the women I interviewed experienced infant mortality. Six out of 42 of my female participants had experienced a miscarriage and five others experienced losing a child or children at birth, or a few weeks, months, or years after childbirth. The reasons for having a miscarriage were varied. Two of the women experienced stress because of their husbands' infidelity and the associated divorce process while they were pregnant (Ilah and Sofi). Others experienced bleeding after consuming high doses of non-prescription medicine for headaches (Rani), were exhausted (Edah), experienced a blighted ovum (Mala), an incompetent cervix (Ida), and ectopic pregnancy (Sandra).

Procreation is almost always the main aim of marriage; accordingly, those who have a childless marriage are pitied and this infertility can lead to divorce (McDonald and Abdurrahman 1974) or be used as a reason for polygyny (Indonesian Marriage Law, Article 4(2c).[4] Women are usually directly blamed for childlessness in marriage, regardless of which the spouse has fertility problems. Research conducted by Linda Bennett et al. (2012) report that a conservative estimate for infertility among those of reproductive age in Indonesia is between 10 and 15 percent, with men and women equally responsible. However, the impact of infertility is greater for women than for men because of the stigma of infertility, the elevated identity as *ibu* (mother), and the recognition of social adulthood that comes with childbirth. Two of my participants shared their experience of infertility. Tia (aged 36) said:

> It's been 12 years since we got married. But I haven't fallen pregnant yet. Conflict in my marriage between me and my husband is always about the absence of a child. So, I challenged my husband to visit the doctor to find out what has gone wrong. The result is that I was diagnosed as having a cyst in my womb, but there's still a chance I can have a baby. In the meantime, my husband was identified as lacking quality semen. After this consultation, I felt satisfied that my husband could not blame me any more for not having a baby, because I am not the only one who has fertility trouble. Then, we redefined the meaning of our marriage so having a child is not the only aim of our marriage.

Ina (aged 33) has a different story:

> By our ninth wedding anniversary, a baby had still not arrived. Sometimes I questioned myself as to why I wasn't pregnant yet. We did consult a doctor but the result was that there was nothing wrong with either of us. I talked to my husband sincerely about the absence of a baby in our marriage and I even told him to take another wife. My husband refused and he said that having or not having a child is in God's hands and he is not bothered if no child is present in our marriage.

When marriage means procreation, the woman is usually the one who is burdened by childlessness. Self-blame among women is common and in this situation a woman may sacrifice herself by letting her husband take another wife, as reported by Ina. Bennett (2015, 151) also indicated that 'incompleteness' is the feeling most women described in experiencing infertility.

Contraceptive use

There were several types of contraceptive methods used by my participants. The most popular method was Depo-Provera—an injection into the woman's arm or buttock. The second preference was having an Intra Uterine Device (IUD), and others reported using the contraceptive pill and Norplant. Only one couple used condoms. There were couples who practised 'traditional' methods for preventing pregnancy, namely using the periodic calendar and *'azl* (coitus interruptus; withdrawal).

It is evident from the interviews that unintended pregnancies frequently happened among the women. Several women told me that unintended pregnancies had occurred when they did not wish for additional children, but at the same time they did not want to use contraception. Accordingly, the term '*kebobolan*' (broken into, penetrated) emerged when talking about the number of children they had had.

Three women, two of whom had 12 children and one who had 5 children, decided not to practise contraception because they said that after trying different methods, not one was suitable and all caused health complications. Many women also complained about the side effects of contraception—both physical and psychological. One woman reported that her appetite changed and her libido was reduced when she was on the pill. Women who used Depo-Provera reported having irregular (or ceased) menses and they gained weight. Women who used an IUD experienced bleeding. Many of the women wished to be released from the burden of using contraception.

Halimah (aged 31) was among those who had experienced discomfort and pain after trying different types of contraception. She said:

> At first I used an IUD, but I experienced continuous bleeding. Then, I tried an implant [Norplant], but I experienced a swollen arm. When I told the doctor what had happened, s/he said that the midwife had inserted the implant incorrectly and when it was taken out half of the implant was still left inside my skin [she showed me the bump in her arm].

She further expressed her resistance to contraception and complained to her husband, saying:

> Why is it always me, the woman, who should suffer from all kinds of torture to my body? First, pregnancy, second, childbirth, and then I have to use contraception. These are all painful and uncomfortable.

Halimah's husband was concerned about her and wondered whether there was a contraceptive method that would not harm his wife. Halimah suggested that he use a condom, and subsequently they used condoms. Halimah's resistance to using contraception occurred only after she had tried several different types unsuccessfully. Although, in the end, her husband was sympathetic to his wife's condition, their story shows that the responsibility for reproduction is still mostly directed towards women.

In my research, the condom seemed unfamiliar as a contraceptive method to married couples in West Java. This was also reported by Karen Kroeger (2000) and Lynda Newland (2001). Condoms are more popular among single urban young adults so they can practise safe sex and avoid HIV-AIDS (Purdy 2006). There is a negative assumption related to condom use, in that it is usually associated with prostitution and disease prevention and not with contraception (Butt 2005). It is also said that using condoms can reduce enjoyment for men during intercourse, so they are resistant to using them. Several women I interviewed, who had experienced physical complications when trying different methods of contraception, did not mention condoms as an alternative method. In many cases, women lacked the power to suggest or negotiate with their husbands about the use of condoms. Halimah was the exception.

Male involvement in reproductive health is still low, even though their involvement in supporting family planning is important to facilitate women's reproductive choices. Several women I interviewed experienced discomfort with the cadre when they visited a *posyandu* (health service post), as they were criticised for having too many children with too short an interval between births. In fact, several women informed me that it was their husbands who forbade them from using contraception. Elis (aged 45) and Citra (aged 50) shared their stories, saying that their husbands prevented them from using contraception and thus, each year, they had to give birth. It was only after Citra had had her fifth baby and Elis had had her seventh that their husbands allowed them to use contraception. Citra said:

> At that time I was busy caring for the children and had no time for myself. I also quit my job because I did not have the time. In fact, my career was good at that time, and if I was still working I may already have a decent position now.

After childbirth, the women in the study often experienced an increase in weight. Weight gain has the propensity to decrease women's self-esteem and influence their sexual relationship. Thus, getting back into shape post-childbirth is popular in Indonesia.

In Indonesia, vaginal treatments and massage after giving birth are common practices. Traditional remedies like herbal concoctions (*jamu*), tea, and medical plants are consumed by women because they believe that these kinds of products tighten the vagina, reduce body size, enhance beauty, and increase their energy levels (Hilber et al. 2010; Roosita et al. 2008).

Sex

Women's experience with reproduction influences their interest in sex. In the study women reported that during pregnancy, they experienced anxiety about the ways their bodies were changing, hormonal instability, and the upcoming childbirth, especially when it was the first time. Rosa (aged 44) said:

> During the first trimester of my pregnancy I did not like my husband touching me, but when I reached four months of my pregnancy, my libido increased significantly and made me want to have sex often.

After childbirth, several women mentioned their decreased interest in sex. These women stated that they still felt pain around their vagina after birth or feared another pregnancy while they still had a small baby. Rani (aged 43) said, 'After giving birth I felt unwilling to have sex. I focused on my baby instead. I was afraid that if I had sex, I would get pregnant again while I still had a baby.'

Sometimes husbands were unable to wait to have sex with their wives after menstruation or giving birth. In Islam, it is forbidden to have sex during menstruation and for 40 days after giving birth (called *nifas*).[5] There is also a belief among some men that after birth the woman's vagina is tight, just like a virgin's. Therefore, they believe that the pleasure of intercourse (for men) 40 days after birth will be as good as on the first night. Rani and Sinta shared their stories:

> If my husband sees me washing my hair as a sign that I have finished my period,[6] he will directly ask to have sex. But I say that he needs to wait one more day after I have finished. Because, if he rushes to have sex, I usually experience more bleeding which makes my period last even longer.
>
> (Sinta)

> My husband was working in another city. After I finished my *nifas* period, my husband returned home and said he wanted to have sex. I refused to do so because I was afraid that I would get pregnant again. Also, I was not ready to use contraception. My husband was disappointed with my refusal. But later that night, when I had already fallen asleep, I felt warmth in my vagina. Then I realised that my husband had already penetrated me while I was sleeping. I could not do anything [to prevent it]. It had already happened.
>
> (Rani)

Rani was not pleased with what her husband had done that night. She was concerned that she would get pregnant again while her baby was still small. She wanted to focus on one child first before having another. One month after that night, Rani recognised that she was pregnant and she was really mad at her husband. She wanted to get an abortion because she was not ready to have another child. In her small city, there were no midwives or other health practitioners who would agree to perform an abortion. Rani then went to Jakarta to see her husband and they found a clinic where she got an abortion.

Seeking an abortion in Indonesia is not easy, especially without a 'valid' reason. In Islam, abortion is not strictly forbidden, and in certain circumstances many Muslim scholars give permission for abortion to be performed. The Indonesian Council of Ulama's (MUI's) fatwa in 2005 and Indonesia's current regulation on Abortion no. 61/2014 allows abortion not only when the physical state of the mother is jeopardised, but also when her psychological health is threatened, as in the case of rape and incest (Mudzhar 2014; Nasir and Asnawi 2011).[7]

Reproduction affects sexual pleasure. Sexual pleasure is also influenced by stereotypes and gender norms and is related to power and inequality. For the women I interviewed, lack of power relating to reproduction was an issue in terms of decision-making surrounding the use of contraception, health service accessibility, and partner support. Women were burdened with the responsibility of reproduction. Better information concerning different methods of contraception and their side effects is needed. Women should be given full rights to make decisions related to their bodies and be supported in this by their husbands, especially in reproduction issues. Women's experience of aging brings different challenges.

Aging and menopause

There were seven women in my sample in their late 40s and 50s and this section contains their stories in relation to their sexual experiences. Changes occur in women's bodies as they age. Experiencing menopause was much discussed by these women, although many seemed not to understand what it means. Discussion about menopause in Indonesia is limited and information concerning this stage of life is also rare. Fatigue, illness, and stiffness were the most common complaints that surfaced in the interviews. These factors certainly influenced women's sexual activity. Women referred to menopause when talking about their declining interest in sex. Research by Nurazzura Diah (2010) about the experience of menopause among urban middle-class Malaysians stated that women going through menopause experience hot flushes, night sweats, irregular menses, and vaginal dryness. In relation to their sexual activity, or otherwise, vaginal dryness was also one of the main concerns cited by my participants. It caused pain during intercourse. Many women said that the frequency of their sexual activity had decreased: some said it had decreased from three times a week to once a week; another said from twice a week to once a month or so, and another said she no longer had sex.

One woman (Rosa, aged 44) said, 'Nowadays, I have a really low interest in sex. It needs a really long time for me to be stimulated. I feel like my desire has died (*mati*). I was wondering could I be experiencing early menopause.' Wiwi (aged 47) said, 'I must admit that at my age I still have sex with my husband. But, because we are getting older and often feel tired we can only do it approximately every three months.' Ita (aged 59) complained about her husband's high sexual drive and said:

> I was frantic [*kewalahan*] to comply with my husband's sexual demands even at my age. He wants to do it whenever he feels like it. I often feel pain during intercourse because of vaginal dryness. My husband also complains because his penis hurts. Sometimes, he applies lotion to his penis before intercourse which I don't like.

This experience had serious consequences for her. She often felt pain when she had intercourse and so did her husband. Neither of them enjoyed their sexual relations. Ita could not enjoy sex because she always felt pain, and her husband, who always wanted to have sex because of his high sexual drive, found that sex with his wife did not satisfy him. Many times her husband forced her to have sex but Ita's body could not always comply with his demands because of fatigue, stiffness, and pain. One day, Ita discovered that her husband was cheating on her and had taken another wife secretly (*nikah siri*). Ita admitted that she could no longer serve her husband sexually as he demanded but his decision to secretly take another wife hurt her deeply.

The experience of Sandra (aged 57) was quite different from that of other women her age. She gave quite an interesting story about her sexual experience. She said, 'I still have regular intercourse (*didawamkan*) with my husband twice a week.' She explained that when she experienced menopause, she communicated to her husband that she desired to have regular intercourse. She argued that at her age, she could have experienced vaginal dryness and that regular intercourse could prevent this. And it seems she proved her theory; she never experienced any problems concerning her sex life. Sandra argued that she maintained this sexual relationship with her husband in order to keep a harmonious marriage. At the time of the study, Sandra and her husband were enjoying their life together and the companionship it provided. Sandra felt like she was re-living her courtship and she felt her relationship with her husband was closer than ever.

A different story is told by Minah (aged 50) who said:

> For five years I haven't had sex with my husband. We are old and weak. Especially my husband, he is 67 now and dislikes it if I touch him. He just wants to lie down undisturbed after a tiring day. We even sleep in separate beds.

Regardless of educational and economic backgrounds, many older couples mentioned that they consider themselves wiser now in their married relationships than they were when they were young. They said that they trusted each other and supported each other, especially after their children had left them to lead their own lives. They found their life more meaningful after so many years together.

Women experience sex in their older age and throughout menopause differently. They have developed their own strategies in relation to their changing bodies; in particular in relation to sexual activity. Vaginal dryness is the most commonly experienced factor that makes post-menopausal women uncomfortable having sex with their husbands because it causes pain. Some women manage this pain by applying gel or lubrication, but some try to avoid having sex. To avoid vaginal dryness, one woman continues to have regular sex and this works well for her. Fatigue, stiffness, and illness are other factors that cause older women to decrease sexual engagement with their husbands. Some older women reported that the most important aspect of marriage for them was companionship.

Marital sex as duty

Regardless of education and economic backgrounds, most of the women I interviewed stated that sex in marriage is their duty. Consequently, they try to provide this service whenever their husbands express a need. Information concerning the notion that sex is the wife's duty is acquired from various sources as mentioned in Chapter 3. Some said they learnt it from religious teachings that they read in certain *kitab* (Islamic classical texts) in *pesantren* (Islamic boarding schools), or heard it from *pengajian* (religious gatherings). Some said they acquired knowledge from reading sex manuals, while others said they acquired the knowledge from friends and cultural behaviours they observed around them.

Gender and sex role divisions between wife and husband in marriage, which are supported by the state and religious teachings, have given one gender power over the other. Assigned as head of the household, a man feels he is in charge of his wife and the entire household. This also applies in terms of sexual relations where women are expected to be sexually passive, submissive, and to fulfil men's sexual desires. Thus, in sexual relations the husband believes he deserves to be sexually fulfilled because marriage is understood to provide him with full access to his wife's body whenever he desires. This state and religiously inspired teaching gives men the power to decide when and how to have sex. Most of the time, marital sex is about satisfying the sexual desires of the husband not the wife. He decides the time and the position and his wife has to be ready, whether she is willing or not. This can be seen from the wives' expressions as follows:

> Whenever my husband wants to have sex I have to do it regardless of my unwillingness to do so, *because it is my duty*; whether I enjoy it or not [my emphasis].
>
> (Rani, aged 43)

> In my marriage, you know, my sexual satisfaction is unimportant. The most important thing is to make my husband satisfied [sexually]. Rarely

have I experienced orgasm during my marital sexual relations. *If it wasn't my duty*, I would be lazy [*malas*] about doing it [my emphasis].

(Rosa, aged 44)

If my husband wants to have sex, he will do it right away, no matter how sleepy and unwillingly I am; he even slaps me on the face to make me wake up and fulfil his desire.

(Ita, aged 56)

Some women's reluctance to refuse their husband's sexual demands is associated with cultural and religious proscriptions of *pamali* (taboo) and *dosa* (sin), or simply for fear of provoking the husband's anger and infidelity.

Since I have been going to *pengajian* [religious gatherings], I have heard the Islamic teaching that if the husband asks to have sex, you should do it even when you are doing the dishes;[8] you should stop doing [what you are doing] it and fulfil your husband's sexual desire.

(Rani, aged 43)

I was told not to refuse my husband's sexual need; it is *pamali* [taboo].

(Eha, aged 29)

I feel disturbed by my husband's sexual desires, as he always wants to have sex every day. I feel tired and unwell if we do it that often. But if I refuse him, I am afraid that he will betray me for another woman.

(Iis, aged 40)

I always fulfil my husband's request to have sex. I am afraid that he will get angry if I refuse him.

(Edah, aged 43)

When women have a chance to refuse sex, they associate it with feelings of guilt.

When I am tired or sleepy I just ignore him, but often, I can't get to sleep that night for fear of sin. I make sure that my husband is not angry and apologise to him in the morning.

(Sinta, aged 39)

Failure to provide sex may jeopardise a couple's marriage, especially if men seek sexual pleasure outside the marriage. Guilt often lingers in a woman's minds, as a sense of responsibility for her husband's infidelity or his finding another wife (Iis and Tia). Thus, wives are held responsible for their husbands' sexual satisfaction and it is their fault if he has an affair.

Alternatively, a husband does not always comprehend his wife's desire and she has less power than her husband to make him fulfil her needs. In fact, to express her desire, a woman has to gather all her courage and put aside her shyness and reticence. Rosa for example said:

> My sexual desire increased significantly during the fourth month of my pregnancy. But, my husband worked in another city and when I wanted to have sex and called him to come home, he did not come. Maybe [he didn't come] because it was not the weekend yet.

Leli also said:

> Once I asked my husband to have sex, but he refused. Maybe it was because he was not in the mood. I was really disappointed and irritated. To ask for it, I had to gather all my courage and when he refused, not only was I embarrassed, but also frustrated [*sakit hati*].

Although in the end, Leli's husband apologised to her for what had happened, Leli told herself that she would never ever attempt to initiate sex with her husband again.

When a husband refused his wife's sexual advances, she may try to rationalise his refusal as indicated above. Indeed, a woman has no language with which to speak out about her sexual needs because she is trained to silence her desires. A woman is not supposed to initiate sex, because it is the man's job to do so; a woman is expected to respond. When a woman initiates sex, it could be assumed to mean that she is taking control, which may damage her husband's pride. One woman said, 'My husband believes that man is in charge of woman [referring to *"arrijalu qawwamuna ala nisa,"* Q. S 4: 34] and that includes sexual activity' (Sandra, aged 57). Research by Lily Munir (2002) among Javanese women showed that inequality within sexual relations was influenced not only by Javanese tradition but also by Islamic precepts, including the verse cited above that claims male power over females.

Some women indicated that they had initiated sex, but that their husbands teased them about it, which made them embarrassed. Consequently, many women said that they tended not do so. Hera (aged 28) said, 'As a woman I am shy to ask for sex, so I'd rather not.' Many women have never initiated sex (nor do they intend to), for fear of their husbands' (unpleasant) perceptions of them as sexually experienced. Research in Bali, another region in Indonesia, also shows that married women are expected to be 'neither seductive nor lustful' (Parker 2001, 182).

Limited available information also influences women's expressions of desire. The discussion of sexuality is absent from government textbooks concerning sexuality for young adults (Parker 2008; Utomo 2003). In the Indonesian context, talking about sex and sexuality is still considered taboo and sensitive despite the display and accessibility of sex in this technological era. The discourse opposing sex education is morally justified on the grounds that it can encourage early sexual experimentation or permissive behaviour. This opposition ignores the fact that sex education is important so as to give comprehensive knowledge about sexuality, which enables young people to make better decisions concerning their bodies and sexuality.

Consequently, many women know very little, if anything, about how their body works. Many find out only through experience, for example, menarche and first intercourse on *malam pertama*. As a result, they never know what to do or what to expect. They do not know what bodily changes they might experience, the consequences of certain behaviours, or how to take care of their bodies in relation to cleanliness. During Focus Group Discussions (FGD) in my fieldwork, one woman told me that she was informed by her mother that she would experience menstruation, but there was no explanation of what it entailed. She wondered what it could be, until she experienced it herself (FGD I, 09 June 2012). A young man said, 'We were told by our teacher that one sign of puberty is that we (as males) will experience wet dreams [*mimpi basah*], but we were never told what it meant or what kind of dream it is' (FGD V, 20 July 2012).

However, based on my field research, the strength of the 'theory of scripts' does not mean that women do not want to experience pleasure in sex. Several of the women questioned and resisted their unsatisfying sexual experiences. Sandra (aged 57, aged 25 at first marriage), for example, in her first year of marriage, was a submissive wife who believed that sex in marriage was her duty. When she did not experience pleasure in sex with her husband, she did not complain. However, she always thought about it and wondered why this sex was not enjoyable for her. Only later in her marriage did she have the courage to communicate this problem to her husband. Now they enjoy mutual satisfaction in sex. Eha (aged 29) also mentioned, 'I felt disappointed if I could not reach orgasm. But what else could I do, I just accepted it.' She never told her husband. Indeed, only a few among my informants felt able to express their complaints, and most could not communicate their sexual preferences to their husbands. Many remained silent, accepting their unfulfilled sexual experiences with their husbands as their duty. They worried about whether or not it was appropriate for them to raise the issue, to even express it and demand something different. They doubted themselves. They were also concerned about their husbands' negative judgement if they raised the issue. For example, Nisa (aged 37) said, 'If I frequently ask him to have sex I am afraid that my husband will question why it is me who often asks for it.'

The above explanation shows that women's perceptions and behaviours in relation to their marital experiences are deeply influenced by 'sexual scripts,' either cultural norms or religious prescriptions. Women try to fulfil the sexual behaviour prescribed by these scripts by being submissive and obedient, prioritising 'duty,' and sacrificing their own desires. Within this parameter, the discussion of women's pleasure and choice is absent from the conversation.

Silencing women's desire

The term 'desire' in this book refers to 'the motivation to engage in sexual acts' (Schwartz and Rutter 1998, 2). It is a broad term and is not limited only to sexual intercourse. Especially for women in Indonesia, it is still considered difficult, if not dangerous, to discuss desire. In this book, I argue that three associated principles have had a significant influence in preventing and controlling the discussion of desire, namely cultural norms, state regulations, and religious prescriptions. Sex in marriage for women is associated with serving and satisfying their husbands' sexual desires. Thus, women's own sexual desires and satisfaction are unimportant and ignored.

Research in another area in Indonesia suggests that the same perceptions are related to women's desire. Megan Jennaway (2003) explains that Balinese society does not accommodate female desire and when young women express their desire, their actions are associated with hysterical illness. Bennett (2005) also reported that there is still little discussion about desire in research into women's sexuality in Indonesia.

The ideals of *malu* (shame) and *pasrah* (compliance) characterise appropriate women's behaviour so that chastity and modesty are maintained (Bennett 2005; Blackwood 2010). Women should maintain their desire in accordance with chastity and virginity ideals, and with an eye to being respectable and reputable future wives and mothers (Bennett 2005). Women who transgress this social script may be stigmatised or labelled as deviant. Women, who show their knowledge of sexual engagement and take control of it, risk having their appearance of modesty threatened and challenged which could lead to them gaining a bad reputation. This 'theory of scripts' prevents women from exploring and expressing their own desire as shown from the data above. Within these influential scripts, women develop their sexual selves as inferior/submissive sexual agents whose pleasure is unimportant compared to the service that they must provide for their husbands. In this context, male sexual pleasure is privileged. Women internalise the scripts which then become embodied in their relationships.

These scripts pass on from one generation to another and become internalised in women's minds, influencing their perceptions and guiding their behaviour in their sexual relations with their husbands. As women perceive that sex in marriage is their duty, they consider that their own sexual satisfaction in this relationship is unimportant. Their main priority is making their husbands happy and satisfied. Many women I interviewed confirmed this prescription and they acted in accordance with these common beliefs.

Because they are hesitant to discuss their sexual preferences with their husbands, some women lose interest in exploring their desires. Instead, they divert this sexual energy towards something (or someone) else—caring for the children or undertaking other activities. Research in Java, another region in Indonesia, suggests that compared to men, women are better able to control their desire (Brenner 1998). Perhaps, women are presumed better able to control their desires because their desires are made invisible.

The invisibility of women's desires is worsened by the typically hierarchical relationship between spouses in terms of age, education, and class which negatively affects women in negotiation processes and their ability to express their desires. Lessening the taboo associated with the discussion of sexuality and situating it within the topic of women's reproductive rights could open up awareness to women's desires. Furthermore, one might expect that the changing marriage patterns today, from parentally arranged marriages to self-arranged romantic and peer marriages, should lessen the hierarchical relationship between spouses.

The etiquette of intercourse in Islam

There are certain rules prescribed in Islamic discourse concerning sexual intercourse. The majority of women I interviewed were quite familiar with all these rules, while a few others were not. The women I interviewed mentioned various sources from where they obtained information about intercourse: classical *kitab*; marriage and sex manuals (Islamic); *kyai*; and *pengajian*. Several steps that a couple needs to do before having sex in Islam are explained below.

The women randomly mentioned the steps they performed before engaging in intercourse: ablutions (*wudhu*); praying (*shalat*); reciting certain verses from the Qur'an, *muqaddimah* (Arabic, lit. introduction; foreplay); reciting the special prayer before penetration. Most of the women who were familiar with these steps mentioned that in practice, they were unable do all these steps. Several women said, '[laughing] I had no time to do all those steps' (Hera, aged 28). However, they mentioned that if unable to do all the steps, at least reciting the prayer before penetration was a must. There is a special prayer assigned for intercourse, namely, 'Allahumma jannibna syaithan wa jannibi syaithan ma razaqtana ...' (O God, protect us from Satan and keep Satan away from the children You grant us). By reciting this prayer, the couples believed that they would not be disturbed by Satan who could lead them astray. Several other women declared that reciting the prayer before intercourse means that having sex is not just about lust (*nafsu*), but more importantly it means that God will bless the union.

Based on my interviews, it is evident that men and women did not have equal knowledge of the Islamic prescriptions concerning the etiquette of intercourse. Sometimes, only the wife knew the rules and the exact prayer before intercourse and instructed the husband to comply. Similarly, it may have been the husband who knew more about certain rules before intercourse. Mia (aged 25) for example said:

> My husband did not know about the Islamic rules of intercourse and I told him about that. But my husband complained because there are too many steps and he couldn't do all of them. I told him he should at

least recite the prayer before penetrating me, and I taught him the exact words of the prayer.

Another woman, Mira (aged 50), said, 'It is my husband who is concerned about Islamic rules of intercourse like reciting the prayer.' The common steps that many couples still take before intercourse are ablutions, praying (*shalat*), and reciting the prayer of intercourse.

Another Islamic convention familiar among the female participants was the necessity to cover their naked body while having intercourse. It is suggested in the Hadith attributed to the Prophet that it was narrated from 'Utbah bin 'Abd Sulami that the Messenger of Allah said: 'When anyone of you has intercourse with his wife, let him cover himself and not be naked like donkeys' (Ibn Majah 2007, vol. 3, Hadith no. 1921, 102).[9] Several women stated that their bodies must be covered while having sex with a blanket or other fabric (like a sarong). The women in the study had been told that Satan and the angels were watching so it was appropriate to cover the body during intercourse. However, Maya (aged 41) said:

> But I ignore this rule. I do not want to miss the aesthetic [*estetika*] of intercourse with my husband. I don't mind being fully naked in front of my husband. Sometimes my husband wants to see me naked and I want to see him too. So we do it.

She further explained that she heard this rule from an *ustadz* (religious teacher) a long time ago, and according to her his thoughts might be out of date. Four other women also mentioned this etiquette of covering the bodies with a blanket while having sex.

Another form of pre-intercourse etiquette is *muqaddimah* (Arabic, literally, introduction) or *pemanasan* (stimulation). The word *muqaddimah* refers to the importance of foreplay before intercourse and it is taken from the Prophet's report to his companion:

> One of you should not fulfil one's [sexual] need from one's wife like an animal, rather there should be a messenger between you. 'And what is that messenger?' they asked, and he replied: 'Kisses and [sweet] words.'
> (Al-Daylami, 1987, vol. 2, Hadith no. 55)

Many women said that for them it is important that their husbands stimulate them in order that they can enjoy sex without pain, and that he uses sufficient lubrication and so they could possibly reach orgasm. However, not many husbands of the women I interviewed indulged in foreplay before intercourse. Several women complained about the lack of foreplay by their husbands and said that lack of it could make intercourse painful. These same women said that it was easy to arouse their husbands and that by touching any part of his body they could stimulate him. Several women also said that if their husbands spent too long on foreplay, it would make them ejaculate early.

Another aspect of etiquette that the women identified was not having sex during menstruation and not having anal sex. Each of these is forbidden in Islam (Q. 2: 222–223 and from Hadith).[10] Following the practice of the Prophet Muhammad and his first wife (Khadijah), bathing together is an activity couples can indulge in prior to intercourse. One woman, Halimah, said that she often bathes together with her husband as she learnt this from *pengajian*. Furthermore, mutual orgasm between wife and husband is actually suggested in Islam. There is a Hadith suggesting that a husband should wait until his wife reaches orgasm.[11] However, this Hadith is not popular and seems to be ignored.

The majority of the women I interviewed were familiar with Islamic etiquette associated with intercourse; some of them mentioned certain related Islamic texts. Apart from the text that positions women as inferior to men in sexual relations, there are texts that support women's exploration of their sexual satisfaction. However, only a few women knew those particular texts.

'More than just lust': sex as ibadah

In Islam, sexual activity within marriage is considered not only a biological act but also a blessing and a part of *ibadah* (worship).

> It was narrated from Abu Dharr that some of the Companions [of the] Prophet said to the Prophet: 'O Messenger of Allah, the rich people have taken all the reward. They offer Salat as we offer Salat and they fast as we fast, but they give charity from their surplus wealth. He said, "Has Allah not given you something with which you may do acts of charity? Every Tasbihah is a charity, every Takbirah is a charity, every Tahmidah is a charity, every Tahlilah is a charity, enjoining what is good is a charity, forbidding what is evil is a charity, and (the intimacy of one of you with his wife) is a charity.' They said, 'O Messenger of Allah, if one of us fulfils his desire, will he be rewarded for that?' He said, 'Do you not see that if he did it in an unlawful manner, there would be a burden of sin on him for that? Similarly, if he does it in a lawful manner, he will be rewarded for it.'"
> (Muslim, 2007, vol. 3, Hadith no. 1006, 51–52)

Several women I interviewed considered that their sexual activity with their husband was *ibadah* and that it had a spiritual meaning. From the interviews, I observed there were two situations where women categorised sexual activity as *ibadah*. The first was related to the above-mentioned Hadith: that lawful sexual activity will receive God's blessing. For example, the women mentioned that if they recite a prayer before having sex, the act of sex was not merely an expression of lust between the spouses but an act of serving God. This is particularly the case when the sexual act is aimed at procreation. The couple hopes that the blessed act will produce children who will be good children (*anak shaleh/shalehah*). Mira (aged 50) said:

> Having sex according to Islam is not merely about lust, but also about how to have good children [*melahirkan anak-anak yang shaleh*]. And to do that, there are certain forms of etiquette in Islam that allow one to get a blessing from Allah.

Lina emphasised, 'If I recite a prayer before intercourse, there is more than just lust in our act. We will get a blessing from Allah; that is *ibadah*.'

The second category of *ibadah* in sexual activity is referred to as compensation; that is, a woman's compensation for her dissatisfaction with her sexual experiences with her husband. For many women, sex is about fulfilling their husbands' sexual demands, and if they refuse, they are afraid of certain religious consequences. In reality, not every time the husband asks to have sex does the wife also want to have sex. In this situation, many women submitted to their husbands' desire for sex and believed they would be recompensed in the Hereafter. Hence, performing sex as a duty is part of worship (*ibadah*). One woman, Rani, told me that at present she never refuses to have sex with her husband even when she feels unwilling to do so. She said:

> Sometimes, I can't be bothered to do it [intercourse], but, never mind, I just do it; it is my duty. Because by doing it I will get a reward from God. I consider it as my investment in the afterlife and to pay for my previous mistakes. Besides, afterwards, I feel I've made up for my mistakes [*lunas*].

Rani noted that in the early years of her marriage she often refused her husband's requests to have sex. These days, since she has been actively involved in *pengajian*, where she has been taught that serving her husband sexually is her duty and to refuse him is a sin, she never refuses him.

Another interesting story came from Halimah, who said, 'Sometimes, I feel unwilling to have sex. Nevertheless, I always offer it to my husband. I heard from *pengajian* that if the wife initiates sex, she will get a reward [*pahala*] from Allah.' Maya added some points relating to the discussion about sex as duty related to *ibadah*. She said:

> Because there is *dalil* [proof of texts] related to wife's duty to serve the husband sexually, we need to follow them. It implies that our entire act is not only for our earthly wellbeing [*kemaslahatan dunia*] but also for our heavenly welfare [*kemaslahatan akhirat*].

The respondents tried to follow the rules prescribed in Islam concerning their sexual relationships with their husbands. Several women who knew the Islamic etiquette of intercourse would practice it, though not fully. However, reciting the prayer of intercourse was considered a necessity in order to get a blessing from God. Many women associated the act of sex not merely with lust but also as part of worship (*ibadah*); if they performed their duty they would receive a blessing from God.

One dilemma among women related to serving their husbands sexually was that when they did not want to have sex, there was fear that religious consequences would be imposed if they refused. Sexual desire for these women was influenced by many factors, not only by biological urges, and they were unwilling to serve their husbands sexually every time. Women usually associated the act of serving their husbands as a sacrifice in this world, and an investment that would be rewarded in the Hereafter.

Concerning sex as *ibadah,* Nina Hoel and Sa'diyya Shaikh (2013, 81) suggest there resides a 'coercive inner logic' that women should not refuse the act of *ibadah*. This logic is also used by men as justification for sexual coercion.

Domestic and sexual violence

This section contains the stories of nine women who experienced abusive marital relationships; five will be presented in detail here. It was upsetting for these women to describe the violence they had experienced, as it revived unpleasant memories. Most of the women cried while telling their stories and lamented their fate. They considered that their life experiences were miserable. I referred the women who experienced the most serious abuse to professional services for further assistance. Most of the women I interviewed said that they had never told anyone else about their marital lives. After finishing their stories, these women mentioned that they felt free (*plong*) and released. They were thankful for having been able to relieve the heavy burdens that they had kept hidden for so long. They said they could not tell their stories to friends or families because they were afraid that they would become the subjects of gossip. But they felt safe talking to me because I assured them of anonymity and the confidentiality of their stories.

Four out of the nine women were divorced from their husbands, while the other five were still negotiating with their husbands about their violent behaviour. The women in these stories experienced various forms of violence from their husbands: verbal, physical, sexual, economic, and psychological violence. The definition of domestic violence presented here follows the recommendation of the UN Declaration on the Elimination of all Forms of Violence against Women (1994) which defines violence against women as any violence that results in physical, sexual, or psychological harm to women. Indonesia adopted this definition and in 2004 paid serious attention to domestic violence by issuing Law no. 23/2004 on The Eradication of Domestic Violence/UU PKDRT no. 23/2004 (Undang-Undang Penghapusan Kekerasan Dalam Rumah Tangga). In this law, domestic violence includes any act that constitutes violence; it is not limited to physical violence and includes sexual and psychological violence and abandonment of the marital relationship—all of which have been experienced by the nine female participants are introduced below. However, as will be seen in the discussion, most women associated domestic violence as physical violence.

Ita, 59, Master's degree, lecturer

Ita's husband was one of her suitors. The reason that she finally chose him was because she needed someone to protect her and avoid *fitnah* (gossip associated with illicit intimacy), although she later realised that he showed violent behaviour by forcing her to accept him.

Later in their marriage, Ita's husband's violent behaviour became obvious and excessive. He would get angry whenever he noticed the house was untidy or dirty. When he was angry, he often slapped Ita on her face or kicked her in the back. Ita said, 'I never stopped cleaning things around the house whenever my husband was at home and I would make sure that everything was clean and tidy.' However, her efforts did not prevent her husband from being violent towards her. This happened for a long time, and caused physical and psychological pain. She often felt her body shaking unexpectedly for no reason; she was unable to move her fingers properly, her backbone hurt, and she had difficulty swallowing food. Her doctor even commented about frequent visits related to her physical injuries.

Ita's husband also often abused her sexually. According to Ita, he had a high sexual desire and often wanted to have sex at all hours of the day. Whenever he arrived home late at night from work or from visiting another city and Ita was asleep, her husband would wake her up to serve him sexually. He never considered that Ita might be tired or unwilling to have sex; he would slap her face if necessary to make her fully awake and serve him. By the time she reached 50, Ita could not compete with her husband's sexual demands any longer. She often felt pain during intercourse because of the lack of vaginal lubrication, and she also experienced various other bodily pains. Meanwhile, her husband still wanted to have sex twice a night. Sometimes Ita felt stiff and numb and could not even move, yet had to do a second round. Ita did not enjoy having sex with her husband because he never considered how she felt. He was only concerned about his own satisfaction. Her husband even complained about Ita's physical condition saying that it decreased his pleasure in having sex.

Acih, 49, never finished school (year 2 elementary school), petty trader

Acih got married to her husband when she was 13. Her husband was 20 at that time. When Acih spoke about her husband's violent behaviour, she said, 'He would yell and scream at me when he was angry; he hit me on my face or my body. One day, he ran after me with a knife in his hand.' Acih's husband also forced Acih to have sex whenever he wanted it; for instance, on their first night (*malam pertama*). At that time Acih did not know anything about sex and was frightened. Her husband forced her to have sex with him. I had an opportunity to ask Acih's husband, who was present while we were doing the interview, about his violent behaviour. He said:

> At that time, I was still young and if I had a problem with a friend or experienced disappointment, I would vent my frustration and anger at home. And my wife was the target—who else? Because she was the one at home. And about our first night (*malam pertama*), she didn't know how to do it [intercourse], so what else could I do except force her to have sex [laughing].

Acih also suffered from economic violence. Her husband never provided financial support for her and their children. They had 12 children from the marriage. Acih always had to think hard about how to feed the children, while her husband never contributed any money to the household. While he was away and did not support her, Acih had to work hard to provide a daily income. Acih said, 'I often worked (weeding or collecting wood) with my baby on my back even while I was heavily pregnant. I usually work when I am ill too. I have to because my husband never brings home money.'

Acih's husband had been unemployed for several years. Research by Nurul Idrus (2001) in Sulawesi reported that violence from unemployed husbands was a way for them to show power within the marriage. According to Acih, since her fifth child, her husband's violent behaviour had been decreasing, and more especially now in his older age. Acih's husband confirmed that in their older age, he had become more aware of Acih's efforts in taking care of the children and her financial contribution to the household.

Iis, 40, completed high school, teacher at elementary school

When her husband proposed to her, Iis was unsure about her feelings for him. She did not know him well. However, she finally accepted him because she felt indebted (*berhutang budi*) to him for his kindness. It was only later in their marriage that Iis realised that he could be violent. Her husband would get angry whenever he had a problem outside the house—with his friends or at his work—and he would release his anger on her. Whenever he got angry, he said rude things to her, insulted her and hit her. He also smashed everything in the house. What made Iis confused was that whenever he finished banging or smashing things in the house, he would say: 'OK, I am finished now. Let's tidy up the mess,' as if nothing had happened. In addition, when he met the neighbours, he seemed so kind and friendly that people could not imagine his violent behaviour at home.

The worst abuse Iis experienced was when her husband hit her on her head with a thick wooden sandal until she bled. She had to go to the hospital. Her husband also once cut her hair when he was angry. Iis told her parents about her husband's violent behaviour and that she wanted to ask for a divorce. Iis's parents then warned the husband that if he continued being violent, it would be better for him to divorce Iis. However, while Iis's husband refused to divorce her, his violent behaviour did not change. Instead, he prevented Iis from visiting her parents.

The latest abuse happened one week before our interview, when her husband insulted her by saying 'You're stupid!' Iis could not accept his humiliating remarks any longer. She got angry and hit him. They quarrelled and brawled. But she could not compete with her husband's strength and was beaten by her husband.

Iis's husband also has high sexual desire, and often wants to have sex every day. Iis feels disturbed by her husband's sexual demands, but fears that refusing him will lead him to look for sex outside. Iis is confused (*serba salah*) about what to do about her husband's violent behaviour. There is a tendency towards decreasing violence but violent behaviour is still happening regularly in Iis's marriage.

Sofi, 39, completed high school, kindergarten teacher

Sofi was 37 when she first married. It was an arranged marriage. The abuse began at the time of their first intercourse. Her husband seemed to have a low interest in sex, but when they did have sex it was a nightmare for her. Sofi said:

> Whenever he wanted to have sex, he needed to watch a porn movie first. After that he would directly approach me and then put his fingers into my vagina forcefully. It really hurt. I don't know why he did that. And then he penetrated me.

Sofi described it in tears, such that I needed to stop the interview for a while until she was ready to talk again. There was a deep sadness in her eyes and she told me that when that happened, it was very painful for her. She further said that her husband never did foreplay to stimulate her desire but wanted to have sex directly and forcefully. She said:

> I never enjoyed having sex with my husband. I never experienced pleasurable sex [*surga dunia*] with my husband. On the contrary, I was terrified of it. Though actually, we rarely had sex during our short period of marriage.

Sofi's marriage lasted for three months and she said they only had sex three or four times. Her husband divorced her for no valid reason and that made her shocked and stressed. She experienced a miscarriage during the divorce process.

Uum, 35, completed high school, kindergarten teacher

Uum secretly married (*nikah siri*), a more senior student at college because her older sister did not agree to her marriage. During her marriage, Uum's husband often abandoned her and her daughter for long periods. While he was away, he never gave her financial support. Uum had to support herself and her daughter, doing whatever work was available. When Uum's husband returned home, he would limit Uum's movements outside the house and would not permit Uum to work. He often got angry for no valid reason. When he got angry, he would hit Uum across her face or kick her back. Uum was also whipped with a broom (*sapu lidi*) by her husband. This violence has left some marks on Uum's face, hands, and feet. She said:

> Luckily, I wear the head scarf so I can hide the scars and no one can see them. In fact, nobody knows, including my family, that my husband often abandons me and abuses me at home. I keep it to myself. I always lie to my family about his absence when I visit them.

Her husband was also sexually violent towards Uum. He forced her to have sex whenever he demanded it. He never considered Uum's feelings or health, or whether she was tired or ill. If Uum showed reluctance, he became irritated. For example, if Uum did not respond to him while having sex, he would get angry because it influenced his pleasure. If she refused to have sex, he would hit her, sometimes whip her, and he even toss burning cigarettes (*disundut rokok*) onto her lap. Her husband claimed that he has control in the marriage and that she should comply with his sexual demands. He even cited a Hadith text to justify his violence saying, 'The abuse that I did was nothing compared to what you will get later in the Hereafter if you refuse to have sex with me. The Hadith said that if you refuse me, the angels will curse you.'

However, Uum argued that power in marriage has limits, including in matters of sex. According to Uum, her husband was not entitled to use his power arbitrarily, especially after his desertion of her. She said, 'I never enjoyed being with my husband sexually, especially when I think about his bad temper and abandonment of me.'

Later on, Uum's mother noticed that Uum had been deserted by her husband and she ordered Uum to return to her mother's house. In 2009, Uum could not tolerate her husband's behaviour any longer and she got a divorce. She is now trying to manage her new life with her daughters and without her husband. She is actively involved in teaching and continues her study at university. She said:

> I am studying hard to achieve what I missed out on. My friends have all already got their degrees. I want to have a better future. My past has been miserable; now I'm trying to get my life back. I know it won't be easy but I am determined to do it. My life is like a broken glass; it is hard to put back together again, but that does not mean it's impossible.

Discussion

Several of the women presented above experienced multiple forms of violence from their husbands. Some of them experienced physical and sexual abuse, or physical, sexual, and economic abuse at the same time. Different types of physical attacks included being slapped, hit, kicked, dragged, having hard objects thrown at them, being whipped, and poked with live cigarettes. Psychological abuse involved the use of rude words, insults, yelling, and making threats. Economic abuse and abandonment resulted in some women being financially unsupported for long periods, while others were prevented from engaging in paid work. Sexual violence, such as forced sex, vaginal injury, and fear of Sexual Transmitted Infections (STIs), was experienced by some women in the study. Fear of STIs was experienced by Nanda whose husband was promiscuous and whenever Nanda had sex with her husband, she thought of possible transmitted diseases. She asked her husband to check with the doctor, but he refused.

A report from Komnas Perempuan (National Commission on Violence against Women) shows that the number of cases of violence against women reported to the court has increased significantly from 93,133 cases in 2010 to 263,285 cases in 2013 (Komnas Perempuan 2014, 20). The most common violence occurs in domestic life (71 percent of all violence) and is experienced in the form of psychological abuse (50 percent), economic abuse (40 percent), and physical abuse (2 percent). Other unspecified forms of abuse make up 8 percent of violent abuse in the home (Komnas Perempuan 2014, 23–24).

Ironically, almost all of my participants who experienced domestic violence (with the exception of two), preferred to stay in their abusive marriages rather than get divorced. Although four of them were divorced, the applicant for divorce in each of these cases was the husband. The reasons the women stayed in their marriages were mostly related to their children's wellbeing, keeping the marital property, and avoiding the label *janda* (widow or divorcee) which is stigmatised in Indonesia (Parker, Riyani, and Nolan 2015).

Women who experience an abusive marriage suffer from mental and physical harm perpetrated by their husbands. Psychologically, they feel nervous whenever their husbands are around. They try not to make them angry because that can lead to physical abuse. The women feel fear because they are subject to a range of threats, from the threat of physical violence to that of taking another wife. Physically, the women suffer from injuries that range from bruises and scars on their bodies to bleeding. These women try to hide their injuries from public eyes. None of the women had reported their husbands' violence to the authorities, even at the local level or to the police. They were not aware of the law on domestic violence. Their suffering in silence is related to internalised gender norms where women are advised, usually by their mothers, not to tell anyone else about marital problems or conflict within the marriage. It is considered an embarrassment to the whole family. The women are told they should keep it to themselves and if possible find a solution within the bounds of the marriage. My findings are in line with research conducted by Rusyidi Binahayati (2011) in West Java concerning perceptions and attitudes in relation to violence against wives. According to her research, women who experienced an abusive marriage refused to report the violence to the police and, curiously, they showed strong opposition to their husbands being punished or jailed (Binahayati 2011, 118). Other factors may include that the process of reporting the violence does not protect the women who report the cases. Many women who experienced sexual abuse did not report to the police because many times they became intimidated in the process of reporting. In this case, Komnas Perempuan and Forum Pengada Layanan (FPL)—Service Provider Forum have initiated a bill on the elimination of sexual violence since 2016. Included in this bill is the protection of women in the process of reporting (Nurmila, 2019).

In Indonesia, marital problems and marital violence are considered private matters. Outsiders or third parties are advised not to interfere. This perception makes it difficult to implement the Law on the Abolition of Domestic Violence (UU KDRT). Up until the end of the second decade of the twenty-first century, reporting on domestic violence had been irregular, even after the establishment of the UU KDRT. Many people were reluctant to report incidents of domestic violence and did not even know about the law (Hayati et al. 2013).

This research shows that domestic violence occurs across the social classes and among people of all educational backgrounds. It shows that abusive behaviour is not confined to poor and lower-class marriages. Abuse occurred in marriages with higher educational and economic levels (e.g. Ita's story) as well as in marriages of poor people with lower educational backgrounds (e.g. Acih's story). Based on research conducted by Komnas Perempuan (2002), these abusive marriages came about because of the strong patriarchal system in Indonesia—a system that positions women as inferior to men in the family and society (Komnas Perempuan 2002, 69). Religious belief also seems to strengthen this system and many men find justification for their violence in religious texts (e.g. Uum's case). The majority of violence in the home, therefore, is related to the husband's power over the wife. Challenging a husband's authority within the marriage can trigger further violence as reported by Siti Aisyah and Lyn Parker (2014) on domestic violence in Sulawesi.

From my interviews, many women associated violence only with physical abuse. Other forms of aggression such as verbal insults, forced sex, or economic abandonment were not considered to be violent behaviours. In fact, many women I interviewed, beyond the nine participants cited above, reported that their husbands sometimes asked them to have sex when they were unwilling to do so or without their full consent. A husband forcing himself upon his wife can be categorised as marital rape. In many cases, women acquiesced for fear of their husbands' anger or infidelity, and did not consider their actions as violent. Besides, Sari Andajani-Sutjahjo and Linda Bennett (2008), who research violence against women in East Java, suggest using a more culturally acceptable term in relation to sexually violent language. They found that the term 'unwanted sex' was more acceptable than 'forced sex' when attempting to uncover women's experiences of sexual violence (ibid., 28). It seems that reporting sexual abuse in marriage is a sensitive issue (Bennett, Andajani-Soetjahjo, and Idrus 2011). Similarly, in Komnas Perempuan's 2014 report, sexual violence was not the term used in many cases of domestic violence. However, Komnas Perempuan did suggest that sexual violence may be categorised under psychological abuse, such as polygyny, forced and underage marriage, and lack of harmony within the marriage. Besides, the Law on the Abolition of Domestic Violence (UU KDRT no. 23/2004) does not specifically discuss marital rape.

In this chapter, I have also demonstrated that the majority of the women interviewed consider that sex in marriage was their duty; that is, that they should comply whenever their husbands demand it. The women did not categorise unwanted sexual activity as sexual violence. Many women believe that they have committed a sin (*dosa*) or broken a cultural taboo (*pamali*) if they refuse to have sex and they fear cultural and religious consequences, such as being cursed by angels.

Notes

1. Explained extensively in Chapter 1.
2. The obligatory bath (Arabic. *gusl*) in Islam obliges people to become clean (*thahara*) after having: A wet dream (male); menstruation (female); intercourse (male and female); bleeding after birth (female). Bathing symbolises cleanliness and readiness to perform religious rites like praying, fasting, and reciting the Qur'an.
3. Having sex with a menstruating woman is prohibited in Islam.
4. The court will only grant the husband permission to take another wife if: (a) the wife cannot perform her household duties appropriately; (b) the wife has a bodily deformity or incurable disease; and (c) the marriage is infertile.
5. *Nifas* is the period after giving birth when woman experience bleeding—usually until 40 days. During this time, it is forbidden for a couple to have sex, until the bleeding stops.
6. In Islam, this is a purification that should be performed after menstruation (for women) or after having sex (for both partners). This purification includes pouring water over the body to wash it from head to toe.
7. Detail discussion on abortion is provided in Chapter 1.
8. This teaching is very popular in Indonesia, with many versions. I will explain this teaching and other Islamic teachings related to sexuality in Islam in more detail in Chapter 8.
9. As explained in Chapter 4, this belief is referred to in a Hadith that is considered weak (*dla'if*). The reliable Hadith (*shahih*) mentioned that it is permissible for couples to be naked and to see each other's private organs during intercourse.
10. 'They ask thee concerning women's courses. Say: They are a hurt and a pollution: so keep away from women in their courses, and do not approach them until they are clean. But when they have purified themselves, ye may approach them in any manner, time, or place ordained for you by Allah. For Allah loves those who turn to Him constantly and He loves those who keep themselves pure and clean' (Q. 2: 222). 'Your wives are as a tilth unto you; so approach your tilth when and how you will; but do some good act for your soul beforehand; and fear Allah. And know that ye are to meet Him (in the Hereafter), and give (these) good tidings to those who believe' (Q. 2: 223). This verse is usually interpreted as permission for a husband to approach his wife whenever and however

he wants, except for anal sex. The Hadith of An-Nu'man from Az-Zuhri adds: '... if he wishes, while she is lying on her front, and if he wishes while she is not lying on her front, so long as that is in only one opening [vagina]' (Muslim 2007, vol. 4, Hadith no. 3537, 77).
11. This Hadith was narrated by Annas bin malik, the Prophet said, 'If any of you have sex with his wife let him be true to her. If he attains his pleasure before her then he shouldn't hurry her away until she also attains her pleasure' (Abi Ya'la 1986, part VII, 208–9).

References

Abi Ya'la, Al-Imam. (1986). *Musnad Abi Ya'la. Juz VII* (A compilation of Hadith by Abi Ya'la: Part VII). Beirut: Dar al-Ma'mun li Turats.

Aisyah, Siti and Lyn Parker. (2014). 'Problematic conjugations: Women's agency, marriage and domestic violence in Indonesia,' *Asian Studies Review*, 38(2), 205–23, DOI: 10.1080/10357823.2014.899312.

Al-Daylami, Imam. (1987). Firdaws al-Akhbar (Paradise of Reports). Beirut: Dar al-Kitab al-Araby.

Andajani-Sutjahjo, Sari and Linda Bennett. (2008). 'Violence against new mothers in Indonesia: Cultural context, disclosure and the experience of unwanted sex in marriage.' *Women Against Violence: An Australian Feminist Journal*, 20, 23–32, ISSN: 1327-5550.

Bennett, Linda Rae. (2005). *Women, Islam and Modernity: Single Women, Sexuality and Reproductive Health in Contemporary Indonesia*. London: Routledge Curzon.

Bennett, Linda Rae. (2015). 'Sexual morality and the silencing of sexual health within Indonesian infertility care.' In Linda Rae Bennett and Sharyn Graham Davies (eds.), *Sex and Sexuality in Contemporary Indonesia: Sexual Politics, Health, Diversity and Representations*, 148–66. London: Routledge.

Bennett, Linda Rae, Budi Wiweko, Aucky Hinting, IB Putra Adnyana, and Mulyoto Pangestu. (2012). 'Indonesian infertility patients' health seeking behaviour and patterns of access to biomedical infertility care: an interviewer administered survey conducted in three clinics.' *Reproductive Health*, 9(24), 1–7, DOI: 10.1186/1742-4755-9-24.

Bennett, Linda Rae, Sari Andajani-Soetjahjo, and Nurul I. Idrus. (2011). 'Domestic violence in Nusa Tenggara Barat, Indonesia: Married women's definitions and experiences of violence in the home.' *The Asia Pacific Journal of Anthropology*, 12(2), 146–63, DOI: 10.1080/14442213.2010.547514.

Binahayati, Rusyidi. (2011). 'Perceptions and attitudes towards violence against wives in West Java, Indonesia.' PhD dissertation, State University of New York, Albany.

Blackwood, Evelyn. (2010). *Falling into the Lesbi World: Desire and Difference in Indonesia*. Honolulu, HI: University of Hawai'i Press.

Brenner, Suzanne A. (1998). *The Domestication of Desire: Women, Wealth and Modernity in Java*. Princeton: Princeton University Press.

Bruinessen, Martin van. (1988). '"Duit, djodoh, dukun": Observations on cultural change among poor migrants to Bandung.' *Masyarakat Indonesia*, 15, 35–65.

Butt, Leslie. (2005). 'Sexuality, the state, and the runaway wives of highlands Papua, Indonesia.' In Vincanne Adams and Stacy Leigh Pigg (eds.), *Sex in Development: Science, Sexuality, and Morality in Global Perspective*, 163–85. Durham: Duke University Press, DOI: 10.1215/9780822386414-008.

Collins, Elizabeth Fuller and Ernaldi Bahar. (2000). 'To know shame: *Malu* and its uses in Malay societies.' *Crossroads: An Interdisciplinary Journal of Southeast Asian Studies*, 14(1), 35–70, DOI: 10.2307/40860752.

Darroch, Russell K., Paul A. Meyer, and Masri Singarimbun. (1981). *Two are not Enough: The Value of Children to Javanese and Sundanese Parents.* Honolulu: East-West Population Institute and Yogyakarta: The Population Studies Centre, UGM.

Diah, Nurazzura Mohamad. (2010). 'Changing bodies, changing lives: Urban middle class Malay women's experiences of menopause.' PhD Thesis, The University of Western Australia, Perth.

Gagnon, John H. (1977). *Human Sexualities.* Dallas, TX: Scott, Foresman and Company.

Gagnon, John H. and William Simon. (1973). *Sexual Conduct.* Chicago, IL: Aldine.

Grijns, Mies. (1987). 'Tea-pickers in West Java as mothers and workers: Female work and women's jobs.' In Elsbeth Locher-Scholten and Anke Niehof (eds.), *Indonesian Women in Focus*, 104–19. Leiden: KITLV Press.

Hayati, Elli, Malin Eriksson, Mohammad Hakimi, Ulf Högberg, and Maria Emmelin. (2013). '"Elastic band strategy": Women's lived experience of coping with domestic violence in rural Indonesia.' *Global Health Action*, 6, 1–12, DOI: 10.3402/gha.v6i0.18894.

Hilber, Adriane Martin, Terence H. Hull, Eleanor Preston-Whyte, Brigitte Bagnol, Jenni Smit, Chintana Wacharasin, and Ninuk Widyantoro. (2010). 'A cross cultural study of vaginal practices and sexuality: Implications for sexual health.' *Social Science and Medicine*, 70(3), 392–400, DOI: 10.1016/j.socscimed.2009.10.023.

Hoel, Nina and Sa'diyya Shaikh. (2013). 'Sex as ibadah: Religion, gender, and subjectivity among South African Muslim women.' *Journal of Feminist Studies in Religion*, 29(1), 69–91, DOI: 10.2979/jfemistudreli.29.1.69.

Ibn Majah, Imam. (2007). *Sunan Ibn Majah*, trans. Nashiruddin al-Khattab. Riyadh, Saudi Arabia: Darussalam, available from: https://archive.org/stream/SunanIbnMajahVol.11802EnglishArabic/Sunan%20Ibn%20Majah%20Vol.%203%20-%201783-2718%20English%20Arabic (Accessed 4 August 2020).

Idrus, Nurul Ilmi. (2001). 'Marriage, sex and violence.' In Susan Blackburn (ed.), *Love, Sex and Power: Women in Southeast Asia*, 43–56. Clayton, Vic.: Monash Asia Institute.

Iswarini, Sri Endras. (2011). 'Underage marriage and poverty in West Java, Indonesia.' In Gavin W. Jones, Terence H. Hull, and Maznah Mohamad (eds.). *Changing Marriage Patterns in South East Asia: Economic and Socio-Cultural Dimensions*, 73–82. London: Routledge.

Jennaway, Megan. (2003). 'Displacing desire: Sex and sickness in North Bali.' *Culture, Health and Sexuality: An International Journal for Research, Intervention and Care*, 5(3), 185–201, DOI: 10.1080/136910501172985.

Komnas Perempuan (National Committee on Violence against Women). (2002). *Peta Kekerasan: Pengalaman Perempuan* (Mapping the violence: Women's experience). Jakarta: Ameepro.

Komnas Perempuan (National Committee on Violence against Women). (2014). *Kegentingan kekerasan seksual: Lemahnya upaya penanganan Negara* (The crisis of sexual violence: The government's weak handling the issue). Catahu Komnas Perempuan 2014 (Yearly report of National Committee on violence against women). Jakarta: Komnas Perempuan.

Kroeger, Karen A. (2000). 'Risk, boundary making and the social order: Understanding the social construction of AIDs and sexuality in Indonesia.' PhD thesis, Washington University, St. Louis, MO.

McDonald, Peter and E. H. Abdurrahman. (1974). *Marriage and Divorce in West Java: An Example of the Effective use of Marital Histories*. Jakarta: Lembaga Demografi Fakultas Ekonomi Universitas Indonesia.

Mudzhar, Muhammad Atha. (2014). 'Indonesian fatwas on bioethical issues: Cases of heart-valve transplantation and abortion.' Paper presented at the International Seminar on Comparative Studies of Islamic Reasoning on Health and Sexuality. Jakarta: State Islamic University.

Munir, Lily Zakiyah. (2002). '"He is your garment and you are his…"': Religious precepts, interpretation, and power relations in marital sexuality among Javanese Muslim women.' *Journal of Social Issues in Southeast Asia*, 17(2), 191–220, DOI: 10.1355/SJ17-2C.

Muslim, Imam. (2007). *English Translation of Shahih Muslim*, trans. Nashiruddin al-Khattab. Riyadh. Saudi Arabia: Darussalam, available from: https://archive.org/stream/TheTranslationOfTheMeaningsOfSahihMuslim-Arabic-English7Volumes/Sahih_Muslim-Arabic_English_Volume-4_Ahadith-3398-4518#page/n5/mode/2up (accessed 19 March 2020).

Nasir, Mohamad Abdun and Asnawi. (2011). 'The *majelis ulama's fatwa* on abortion in contemporary Indonesia.' *The Muslim World*, 101(1), 33–52, DOI: 10.1111/j.1478-1913.2010.01341.x.

Newland, Lynda. (2001). 'The deployment of the prosperous family: Family planning in West Java.' *NWSA Journal*, 13(3), 22–48, DOI: 10.2979/NWS.2001.13.3.22.

Niehof, Anke and Firman Lubis. (eds). (2003). *Two is Enough: Family Planning in Indonesia under the New Order (1968–1998)*. Leiden: KITLV Press.

Nurmila, Nina. (2019). 'Advokasi Komnas Perempuan dalam Kasus-Kasus Kekerasan Seksual (National Commission on Violence against Women's Advocation to sexual violence cases).' Slide presentation for Consolidation of Women Ulama in Responding to Sexual Violence Cases, Jakarta, 22 November.

Parker, Lyn. (2001). 'Fecundity and the fertility decline in Bali.' In Margaret Jolly and Kalpana Ram (eds), *Borders of Being: Citizenship, Fertility and Sexuality in Asia and the Pacific*, 178–203. Ann Arbor: University of Michigan Press, DOI: 10.3998/mpub.23538.

Parker, Lyn. (2008). 'Theorising adolescent sexualities in Indonesia – Where 'something different happens.' *Intersections: Gender and Sexuality in Asia and the Pacific*, 18(October), available from: http://intersections.anu.edu.au/issue18/parker.htm (accessed 27 April 2011).

Parker, Lyn, Irma Riyani, and Brooke Nolan. (2015). 'The stigmatisation of *janda* (widows and divorcées) in Indonesia and the possibilities for agency.' *Indonesia and the Malay World*, 44(128), 27–46, DOI: 10.1080/13639811.2016.1111677.

Purdy, Christopher H. (2006). 'Fruity, fun and safe: Creating a youth condom brand in Indonesia.' *Reproductive Health Matters*, 14(28), 127–34, DOI: 10.1016/S0968-8080(06)28256-9.

Roosita, Katrin, Clara M. Kusharto, Makiko Sekiyama, Yulian Fachrurozi, and Ryutaro Ohtsuka. (2008). 'Medicinal plants used by the villagers of a Sundanese community in West Java, Indonesia.' *Journal of Ethnopharmacology*, 115, 72–81, DOI: 10.1016/j.jep.2007.09.010.

Simon, William and John H. Gagnon. (1984). 'Sexual scripts.' *Society*, 22, 53–60, DOI: 10.1007/BF02701260.

Schwartz, Pepper and Virginia Rutter. (1998). *The Gender of Sexuality*. Lanham, MD: Altamira Press.

Utomo, Iwu Dwisetyani. (2003). 'Reproductive health education in Indonesia: school versus parents' roles in providing sexuality information.' *Review of Indonesian and Malaysian Affairs*, 37(1), 107–34.

Legislation

Indonesian Bill on Sexual Violence Eradication, 2020 (RUU PKS – Rancangan Undang-Undang Penghapusan Kekerasan Seksual) available from: https://www.dpr.go.id/doksileg/proses2/RJ2-20170201-043128-3029.pdf (accessed 28 February 2020). This bill has not yet been passed. A draft of the bill has been submitted to be discussed in the House of Representatives this year (2020).

Indonesian Law on Health (no. 36/2009), Undang-Undang Nomor 36 tentang Kesehatan, 2009, adopted 13 October 2019, available from: https://www.ilo.org/dyn/natlex/natlex4.detail?p_lang=en&p_isn=91185 (accessed 23 February 2020).

Indonesian Law on Health (no. 36/2009), Undang-Undang Nomor 36 tentang Kesehatan, 2009, adopted 13 October 2019, available from: https://www.ilo.org/dyn/natlex/natlex4.detail?p_lang=en&p_isn=91185 (accessed 23 February 2020). Implementing text: Regional Regulation concerning the Protection of Women and Children against Violent Acts (Regional Regulation of the Special Capital Province of Jakarta (no. 8/2011), adopted 14 November 2011.

Indonesian Law on the Elimination of Domestic Violence (no. 23/2004), Undang-Undang tentang Penghapusan Kekerasan dalam Rumah Tangga (UU PKDRT), adopted 22 September 2004, available from: http://hukum.unsrat.ac.id/uu/uu_23_04.htm (accessed 23 February 2020).

Indonesian Marriage Law (no. 1/1974), Undang-undang Republik Indonesia No 1 Tahun 1974 Tentang an, available from: https://www.scribd.com/doc/53066173/Undang-undang-Republik-Indonesia-No-1-Tahun-1974-Tentang-an (accessed 26 February 2020).

Regulation on Abortion (no. 61/2014) (Peraturan Pemerintah no. 61 tentang Aborsi, 2014) based on the 2009 Health Law.

UN General Assembly. Convention on the Elimination of all forms of Discrimination against Women (CEDAW), 1979, available from: https://www.un.org/womenwatch/daw/cedaw/cedaw.htm (accessed 18 February 2020).

7 Women's experiences of marital sexual relationships

Sex as a right

> I am a normal human being and I also want to experience orgasm.
> (Halimah, aged 31)

Women's experiences of marital sexual relationships with their husbands is the topic I explore in this chapter. Unlike the previous chapter which considered sex in marriage as a duty, several women in the study claimed that sex in marriage is also their right. With respect to women's diverse experiences, I explore women's desires and the way they find the agency with which to negotiate their need for sexual fulfilment with their husbands.

I suggest that socio-cultural, religious, and political influences shape the production and nature of desire. Social, cultural, religious, and political forces regulate the structure of desire and the context in which desire should and should not emerge. Pepper Schwartz and Virginia Rutter (1998) define 'normal' and 'abnormal,' appropriate and inappropriate sexual behaviours. Within this context, women adopt strategies to negotiate their sexual preferences in their marital sexual relationships.

Negotiating desire; exploring pleasure

The most important element in negotiating women's sexual desire, pleasure, and enjoyment is communication. Building good communication between spouses is important so that each knows and understands the preferences of the other when they engage in sex and what makes each of them feel comfortable during sex.

In practice, it is not that easy for the women I interviewed to discuss what they wanted or what they did not want with their husbands in relation to sexual preferences. As I mentioned earlier, the discussion of sex and sexuality is still considered taboo; women are wrapped up in their feelings of shyness and modesty and their subordinate position in the asymmetrical marital relationship prevents them from easily discussing sexual matters. Fear (*takut*), restraint (*segan*), and shame (*malu*) are feelings that prevent women from talking about sexual matters, even with their husbands.

However, several women in my study reported that they managed to discuss sex with their husbands—such as the position they use and when they schedule sex. Fifteen out of the 40 women I interviewed, mentioned that in most cases they communicated with their husbands about sex, although not in detail; six women stated that only sometimes or rarely did they communicate about sex, while the other 19 women never discussed sex with their husbands at all.

Sexual position

For many women I interviewed, the so-called missionary position with the man on top was the most popular and preferable position for intercourse. Their consideration was based on comfort. They called this position ordinary (*biasa*), simple (*sederhana*), or normal or uncomplicated (*tidak neko-neko*). Siti (aged 40) for example said: 'I told my husband to let us just do the ordinary position [missionary position] [*posisi biasa*] because we are respectable people and do not do weird positions like animals [referring to doggy style].'

Other women were willing to try different positions if they were asked by their husbands. Some of them felt surprised to learn that there were lots of different positions they had not known about before, but they complied with their husbands' instruction as long as it was not what they considered out of bounds (*melampaui batas*). One woman, Mia (aged 25), told me what she considered to be beyond the limit of acceptable sex, that is, what she thought was forbidden in Islam:

> I do not mind doing different positions as asked by my husband as long as it's not anal sex or sex while I have my period because these are forbidden in Islam. I also do not want to do it with the woman on top or in a sitting position because I heard that it would damage both spouses' renal systems.

Several other women confirmed that they would comply with different positions during intercourse except anal sex. Most women knew that anal sex is forbidden in Islam. However, when they felt uncomfortable having sex in unusual positions they would tell their husband afterwards, not while they were doing it. One woman, Edah (aged 43), told me, 'If I feel uncomfortable when in such positions, I tell my husband afterwards, not while we are doing it, because it usually ruins his desire.' Another woman, Aas (aged 28), also said that she usually discussed sex positions with her husband and if she felt uncomfortable having sex in some position, she would say to her husband, 'The position that we just did was not that enjoyable for me.' According to some women, trying different positions for sex was necessary, and was related to the duration of intercourse. They would communicate to their husbands the position that would make sex take longer and be more comfortable.

Sexual signs and schedules

The frequency of sex reported by the women ranged from every day to once a month. Couples where the husband had a high sexual desire mentioned that they have intercourse almost every day. For older couples, the frequency drops significantly for various reasons. Iis (aged 40) stated that:

> I am disturbed by my husband's sexual desire; he wants to have sex every day. I feel too tired and unwell to do it that often. I complain to him that he needs to control his desire and make a schedule for having sex. But he gets angry and accuses me of having an affair with another man instead. My husband states that if he misses having sex one day his body feels stiff and fatigued.

Iis said that having sex every day detracts from her worship time. Her husband tried fasting, as it is believed to decrease sexual desire, but it did not work.

The couples also used various ways to communicate about sex. Some easily talked to each other before or after having sex, some talked about it in a humorous way to avoid embarrassment, some wrote it down, while others used body language. Each couple had their own terms for intercourse. There are many Indonesian terms to refer to intercourse. Some words that the women I interviewed used are: *hubungan seks* (sexual relationship); *hubungan; berhubungan* (to have a relationship; bond); *berhubungan badan* (to have a body relationship); *bersetubuh* (to become one body). Several women used euphemistic terms like: to do 'that' (Ind. *itu*; S. *eta*), or to do 'that thing'; 'something like that' (*melakukan hal itu; hal seperti itu*). One example is Sinta (aged 40) and her husband, who had their own term for intercourse, '*nyunah*,' and they usually have sex on Thursday nights (*malam Jum'at*).[1]

Ani (aged 45) had a different story: she and her husband never had sex at night, when most couples do. In fact, Ani would really like to experience it at night. Nevertheless, she said that her husband forbade it because it might disturb his worship time (night prayer). Thus, usually, Ani takes a day off work on Fridays so she can stay at home with her husband.

Rani (aged 43) said:

> Nowadays, I have sex with my husband once a week; previously we did it about twice a week. My husband never speaks if he wants to have sex but I know when he wants it. Sometimes he looks intently at me from morning on, and he will buy my favourite food. And then, at night he waits until I have finished putting the kids to bed. Then he makes some noise to signal that he is waiting for me to have sex. When that happens, I say, 'So you want it?' And he nods, and then we have sex.

The above-mentioned experiences are only a small sample from the interviews in which women noted that their husbands did not directly or verbally ask to have sex but gave signals instead. In most cases, women had to comply whenever the husbands asked to have intercourse. Several women, however, found various strategies to excuse themselves from having sex with their husbands whenever they felt unwilling. Some of them pretended to fall asleep or went to bed earlier; some slept in their children's bed or wrapped themselves up tightly to prevent their husbands from having access to their lower half. Some reasons they gave for being unwilling to have sex were fatigue, being unwell, pregnancy, having recently given birth, conflict, economic difficulty, husbands' infidelity, and abusive behaviour. These factors influence women's desire.

Many women said that when they were tired after working all day, they would just go to bed early or sleep in the children's bedroom so that their husbands would not disturb them. Some of the husbands would notice and understand, while others would not. Those who noticed how their wife was feeling would restrain themselves from having sex that night, but some would be disappointed or complain. Others got angry and some would forcibly have sex without consent, even while the wife was sleeping.

One woman, Tia (aged 36) said, 'If I am tired, I fall asleep straight away, because I do not want to have sex.' Aas (aged 28) added that, 'If I do not want to have sex, my husband also does not want to do it because it will not be enjoyable for him if I do not respond.' Rani (aged 43) said:

> When I am tired I just go to bed early, but sometimes, in the middle of my sleeping, I feel warm in my vagina. I just realise that my husband has already penetrated me while I am sleeping. I am just too sleepy to respond so I just continue my sleeping and ignore what is happening.

Another woman, Ijah (aged 59), said, 'When my husband wants to have sex but I don't, I never respond to him. When he penetrates me, my body is stiff like a dead banana trunk [*gedebog cau*].'

Consent for sex is quite an issue among Muslim Indonesian women, who are expected not to refuse their husbands' intention to have sex regardless of their own desires. Those women who refuse their husbands risk transgressing both a cultural taboo and a religious sanction. Several husbands in this study claimed that they have the right to access their wives' bodies even without their consent.

Another factor that influenced women's sexual desire was associated with economic difficulties. Rani said, 'My sexual desire decreases whenever I am having economic difficulties. I do not think about sex.' Once she refused her husband who had returned empty-handed from looking for a job in the city. She said to him, 'No, no, go away. You'd better look for a job and bring me money instead.' She further said that when there is no income she becomes worried and dislikes her husband for not trying hard enough to find a job. But that night she saw her husband masturbating and questioned him. Her husband argued that because she did not want to have sex with him, he masturbated.

Abusive behaviour also affects women's interest in sex with their husbands. Several women whose husbands were bad tempered not only felt fear but also suffered from the violence. Sofi (aged 39) said: 'Every time I have sex with my husband, it really hurts and I never enjoy it.' Uum (aged 35) also said:

> My husband often forced me and was violent whenever we had sex. It affected me and I often lost my desire. But if I was unwilling to do it he would notice and get angry, then hit me. I never enjoyed being with my husband sexually.

A husband's infidelity also disturbs women's desire, especially when the wives notice that their husbands' affairs involve sex. This was experienced by Nanda (aged 36) whose husband had an affair with another woman. She knew that her husband had had sex with another woman because she felt that her husband was no longer interested in having sex with her when he came home. 'When I found out that my husband had had an affair and had had sex with her, I did not want to have sex with him, I felt disgusted.' Nanda often wonders, when she is having intercourse with her husband, if he is infected with sexual diseases that might be transmitted to her. She asked her husband to have himself checked, but he refused. Nanda asked for a divorce from her husband when she found out that his sexual partner had fallen pregnant. She let her husband marry the woman with whom he was having an affair, but the marriage did not last for long and ended in divorce. Her husband then asked Nanda to remarry and she agreed. After they became a couple again, Nanda remembered his infidelity whenever she had intercourse with him, and this affected her enjoyment. She cannot bear to imagine her husband ever doing it (having sex) with another woman. Sometimes her husband gets angry if he notices that Nanda is still thinking about his previous affair. Nanda has said to him, 'You might be forgiven but I've not forgotten what you've done to me.'

A different story is given by Nisa (aged 37), whose husband threatened that he would take another wife in polygyny. When she discovered that her husband wanted to practice polygyny and he told her that he might have an eligible candidate, Nisa became more possessive. She felt that if she asked for sex more than her husband and if he had another wife, she would miss out. Sexual jealousy was reported as the main concern in polygynous marriages (Nurmila 2009; Nurmila and Bennett, 2015).

Another factor that influences women's desire is when the woman cannot or does not love her husband. Sex, for these women, is not only about a physical union but it also should involve romantic feelings and intimacy. Ina (aged 33) said, 'Once I refused my husband when we were about to have intercourse because I suddenly didn't feel like it. I still could not love my husband and it affects me sexually.'

Lina (aged 37) also mentioned that, 'In my first years of marriage, I did not love my husband and it affected me when we had intercourse. I didn't fully desire to have sex with him.' Over time, she has grown to accept her husband and gradually to love him. Nowadays, according to her, their love is getting stronger. She now loves him wholeheartedly. She calls it love for the second time; a second puberty (*puber ke dua*) with her husband.

Ina and Lina's cases demonstrate that a sexual relationship is not just about a physical union but it also requires a romantic love relationship. Some other women associated desire with emotional intimacy and close relationships with their partners. However this desire and emotional intimacy did not necessarily end with sexual intercourse. Nida (aged 25) stated, 'Sometimes I only want to have a hug with my husband while watching TV or indulging myself in his arms, but he thinks that I want to have sex.'

Sexual activity for many of the women I interviewed means intercourse. For many, sexual intercourse is not only regarded as a biological urge, like the husbands suggest, but it is associated with many other factors that affect their desire.

Exploring desire

While many women might experience discomfort in sexual relations with their husbands, other women negotiate about how to experience pleasure. One woman argued: 'I am a normal human being and I also want to experience orgasm' (Halimah, aged 31).

To build a good understanding concerning sexual preferences, good communication is needed. Some couples are quite open in discussing sexual matters, but others are still hesitant. Leli (aged 29) would write down in their special communication book what she wanted from her husband concerning sex. For example, once she noticed that her husband seldom asked her to have sex. She shared it with him, writing about what she had learnt from the *pengajian* (religious gathering) about a verse in the Qur'an which states *'nisaukum hartsun lakum'* (Your wives are as a tilth unto you (to cultivate).[2] After reading her notes, her husband confirmed that it did not mean that he was not interested in sex but that he was concerned about Leli, that she might be tired or unwilling. She further said, 'My husband is a very understanding person. In terms of sex he does not want to have pleasure before I experience it. So, timing is very important for us, we never do it when one of us is tired.' Using a communication book is an effective way for them to communicate what they want and what they do not want, and can prevent misunderstandings between them. They can read each other's messages and then discuss them.

Tia (aged 36) also said, 'I told my husband that in sexual relations he should not think only about his sexual satisfaction but that he should hold it until I also reach a climax. That was a Hadith[3] I read in *pesantren*.' Tia's husband agreed and they even asked each other whether they felt satisfied that night. While Maya (aged 41) said, 'We discuss what I want and what he wants [sexually]: there is time to give and to get.'

Orgasm does not happen every time women have intercourse. Several women in the study mentioned that they sometimes reached orgasm while others said they rarely or never experienced it. Several women indicated that to reach orgasm they needed their husband to indulge in foreplay. It depended on the husband's skill in stimulating their wives in the beginning as to whether they achieved mutual pleasure. Some couples watched BF (Blue Films, movies that contain many sex scenes) before intercourse. Women who rarely experienced orgasm or pleasure mentioned that if they did not feel like having sex this prevented vaginal lubrication and made intercourse painful. Some wives noted that if they asked their husbands to engage in foreplay, the husbands would ejaculate sooner. Other women had their own strategies when their husbands could hold their desire no longer. Aas (aged 28) would give her husband quick sex. As she said to me during the interview, 'just let it go' (*yang penting bucat*). Several other women suggested that another factor preventing them from reaching orgasm was that their husbands had certain diseases or illnesses that affected their stamina. Diabetes was the most frequently noted medical cause of husbands' premature ejaculation.

There were also times when wives desired to have sex. Initiating sex verbally is still considered taboo for women. Most felt embarrassed (*malu*) if they were the initiators because, in Indonesia, gender perception suggests that a woman should not openly show her interest in sex, otherwise she would be negatively labelled. In Indonesia, *malu* associated with female sexuality refers to the learned feminine traits of passivity and submission (Bennett 2005; Blackwood 2010). However, many women developed strategies to make their husbands comprehend their desire without them having verbalise it. Most of the women said that in practice it was easy to attract their husbands to have sex. Sandra (aged 57), for example, said, 'Whenever I want to do it [intercourse], I dress up nicely, put on my make-up and perfume to attract him.' Another woman, Eha (aged 29), said, 'Whenever I want to have sex (*berhubungan*), I touch my husband's private parts and he understands.' Nisa (aged 37) said, 'If I want it, I give him a massage so that he understands what I want.'

An interesting story was told by Halimah (aged 31), who, without hesitation, would ask her husband to have sex. She would offer it to her husband: 'Do you want it?' (*Hoyong teu?*). Her husband would answer, 'Yes, I do, but I am tired right now.' Then, Halimah would reply, 'Just relax, you do not have to do anything, let me do the move [*biar mamah nu ngageol*].' Her husband would agree. Halimah said, 'I heard from *pengajian* that if the wife asks the husband to have sex, she will get *pahala* [a reward] from Allah.' Further, she said that sex in married life is very important for her. She wants to make the sex in her marriage special so that her husband will always long for it. Based on her experience, this works really well for her marriage. Her husband is affectionate towards her and spoils her with gifts.

Halimah's story is unique compared to the other women's stories. Other women considered sex in marriage to be relatively unimportant. Rosa (aged 44) said that sex in marriage was not that important for her. Another woman, Edah (aged 43), gave a metaphor about sex in her marriage: 'Sex in marriage is like a dessert, not a main course. Unlike a main course, which you need to have every day, with dessert, sometimes you have it and sometimes you don't.'

Some women expressed that sex in marriage was also their right. Sex is part of the married life that both spouses should enjoy mutually. Although there are several texts in Islam that encourage the couple to experience a pleasurable and mutual sexual relationship, rarely did the women refer to these texts. Only one woman (Tia) claimed that there are Islamic texts that speak of women's rights to experience pleasurable sex. Given that only one woman knew about these texts suggests that the notion of sex as a mutual right in Islam is not that well known compared to the idea that sex in marriage is a wife's duty.

The possibility of women's sexual agency

In this section, I explore the possibilities of agency among women in their sexual relationships with their husbands. Among the 42 women I interviewed, there were only 4 whom I consider confidently demonstrated their capacity to exercise agency. Following Laura Ahearn, I define agency as 'the socio-culturally mediated capacity to act' (2001, 112). In this case, the *possible* agency is the women's capacity to act and to negotiate with their husbands in three aspects: (1) lessening the husband's dominance in sexual relationships; (2) encouraging the husband to recognise women's desire; and (3) pursuing mutual pleasure.

In Indonesia, the marital relationship has been constructed as an asymmetric power relationship supported by state laws, cultural norms, and Islamic rules. Cultural norms and Islamic teachings are interrelated in regard to hierarchical relationships between men and women in Indonesia (Adamson 2007; Munir 2002). Men have the power to control women's desire by deciding when and how to engage in sex, and women are expected to comply and serve their husbands. However, the diversity of women's experiences and practices shows that some women are able to negotiate the prescriptions and conventions of marriage with their husbands. Within this context, agency is context-specific, in that it occurs in particular social circumstances that enable certain women to exercise agency and that agency may differ from one to another according to gender, class, or ethnicity (Parker 2005). It is only by considering the specific cultural context that one can gauge the meaning and importance of agency.

The heterosexual marital relationship is not always a relationship of dominance and subordination between husband and wife. Heterosexual relations also offer the possibility of the recognition and fulfilment of women's desires and pleasures. Through negotiation and strategising, a few of the women I interviewed found ways to resist domination and gain mutuality and satisfaction. It seems that the key way to achieve this agency is to build communication between the spouses. Halimah (31, bachelor's degree, kindergarten administrator) said:

> I always discuss sex with my husband: what I want and what I do not want. I am a normal human being and I also want to experience orgasm. So, my husband tries hard to make me experience that. Sometimes, I feel powerful when my husband gives up and fails to bring me to orgasm. Later I will ask for compensation in the way of new jewellery or money.

Sandra (57, master's degree, lecturer) also said:

> In my early years of marriage, I never experienced sexual enjoyment, and I felt down about it and I asked myself why. Then I talked about it to my husband and he understood and now we manage to achieve mutual pleasure.

Halimah's experience was quite exceptional compared to the other women in the study. There was ease of communication between Halimah and her husband concerning sexual matters. They were friends and got married after their university graduation. Halimah said that the key aspect of happiness in marriage is sex. Thus, sex is important in marriage. She and her husband always try to reach mutual satisfaction. Sandra, whose husband was also a friend from university days, was hesitant in her first years of marriage to talk to her husband about her disappointment because she did not experience sexual pleasure. However, Sandra often thought about it and eventually plucked up courage to talk to her husband. He conformed to her demands of mutual pleasure in sex. Having the opportunity to express desire and experience pleasurable sex allowed Halimah and Sandra to manage harmonious marriage relationships.

Agency takes form also by resisting normative social relations in marriage that position women as passive subjects whose duty is solely to fulfil their husbands' needs. A few women I interviewed resisted both cultural norms or religious prescriptions that advocate 'appropriate' sexual desire. These women demanded recognition of their sexual desire and the attainment of mutual pleasure in sexual relationships. Maya (41, bachelor's degree, kindergarten teacher) said:

> I do not agree with the Sundanese proverb, 'Istri mah dulang tinande' [A woman is like a big wooden rice bowl waiting to be filled]. A husband should pay attention to how his wife is feeling when he wants to have sex. There is togetherness in sexual relationships and both partners should experience pleasure.

This proverb is popular among Sundanese, suggesting that the wife should obey the husband. However, Maya refused to be like the image described in the proverb, saying that the husband cannot assume the bowl will always be there, ready, willing, and able to serve when he wants. Further she demanded mutuality in her sexual relationships.

Ida (36, finished high school, kindergarten teacher) also said:

> I do not agree with the discussion in this book [she was referring to *Kitab uqud al lujayn*][4] especially concerning sexual relations: it's indecent and shameful. I did not follow the guidance stated in this book for my marital relationships.

Ida, who read the *uqud kitab* in a *pesantren*, disliked the content of the *kitab* as well as the way the teacher explained it, especially as it privileges male sexual fulfilment in relationships. Tia (36, finished high school, teacher) even confronted her husband to claim her right to sexual fulfilment. She said:

> I told my husband that in sexual relations, he should not care solely about his own satisfaction, but he should hold it until I also reach climax. That was a Hadith I read in *pesantren*.

There were two steps in these women's resistance. First, they resisted the prescribed cultural and religious norms of appropriate women's sexual behaviour. Second, they operationalised their resistance by negotiating with their husbands so that the husbands acknowledged their wives desire so that the couple could achieve mutual satisfaction.

These women tried to negotiate gendered power relations that instantiated male-centredness in marital sexual relationships. These negotiation processes can be seen to follow what Deniz Kandiyoti called the 'patriarchal bargain' (1988, 275). Bargaining with patriarchy means the women's strategies to deal with male domination occurred within a particular context that enabled them to do so (Kandiyoti 1988). However, as she pointed out in a later article, this bargain has limitations because in many cases the normative discourse and hegemony remain dominant (Kandiyoti 1998). This is quite true for my study. There were only a few women who could exercise agency within the dominant discourse of normative gender ideology. Although replacing this dominant ideology is not easy, it does not mean that it is impossible. Women's consciousness and determination to resist unequal sexual relations can lead to a mutual recognition of desire and respect. The women speak up against the prevailing gender ideology and patriarchal structure to gain control over their bodies and to confirm their existence in their marital relationship as a subject and not merely as an object of male desire.

Halimah (aged 31) explained, 'I am not a product of the older generation who were told that it's inappropriate to express desire openly and taught to be shy and passive in sexual relationships with the husband.' Maya (aged 41) also said, 'I am no longer living in my mother's era. I was born in modern times and such "taboo" issues have been left behind. We discuss what I want and what he wants [sexually]: there is time to give and to get.' Halimah and Maya refused to follow the prescribed norms of femininity that suggest that women must be shy in relation to sex. In fact, they created their own sexual subjectivities in which they deserved to experience sexual pleasure and to make active decisions related to sexual choice in marital relationships. These few agentic women exercised a more muscular agency—the 're-signification or the displacement of hegemonic meaning to create space for subversive gender practices' (McNay 2008, 167).

In reality, the negotiation of power relations in marriage was not especially easy for the women who participated in this study. They needed courage and supportive conditions that enabled them to negotiate. This negotiation process affected women's personal feelings and they risked the possible reaction of their husbands—husbands who could either support or reject their overtures. Recognition of women's desire should mean that the husbands can accommodate women's self-expression. For example, when women express that they want to have sex, they should be free from being teased about their boldness (as experienced by Ina). They should not be rejected; neither should they be denied (as experienced by Leli), or experience embarrassment. Ina experienced being teased by her husband for initiating sex, while Leli felt rejected by her husband when she asked for intercourse. Although they said that their husbands did not mean to humiliate them, their experiences have made these two women reluctant to initiate sexual relations ever again. Thus, successful negotiation needs for males to participate in supporting changes in sexual relations—participation which recognises women's expressions of sexual desire, as well as their need for mutuality and respect. Several husbands have been able to comprehend how to satisfy their wives, as noted by Leli. She experienced being rejected when she initiated sex, but in terms of fulfilling her desires, she feels her husband is considerate. Leli (aged 29) said, 'My husband is a very understanding person. In relation to sex, he does not want to have pleasure before I experience it. So, timing is very important for us, we never do it when one of us is tired.' Siti (aged 40) also said, 'My husband will notice if I am in the mood or not, or when I feel tired or unwilling. He never forces me to do it [have sex].'

The partner's support is important in providing space for women to negotiate about their sexual preferences. A few women have emboldened themselves to take a chance and speak out to their husbands about their sexual relationships.

Based on the findings of my study, it is important to note the factors that facilitate the exercise of women's agency. Many of the more agentic women were educated and had known their husbands for quite some time before marriage. Thus, changing marriage patterns, that is the shift to peer, romantic, and self-choice marriage, and increased education, should contribute to restructuring the gender and sexual relations in marital relationships.

It is also important to promote the promising suggestion of Kecia Ali (2006) who proposed the construction of a just sexual relationship with two main concerns: (1) 'meaningful consent' and (2) 'mutuality' which will bring about respectful sexual relationships between the partners (Ali 2006, 151).

In this chapter, I have presented the views of several women who consider that sex in marriage is their right. They noted that they have sexual desires that should be attended to by their husbands. These particular women had the capacity to discuss and negotiate their preferences relating to sexual positions and schedules. They also resisted the prescribed cultural norms and religious teachings of normative femininity. From the above explanations, it is obvious that women associate desire not merely with physical urges but also with social and emotional factors.

I have explored the examples of agency that I had observed among a few women. The women I presented in this section exercised agency in their sexual relationships with their husbands and this capacity was 'interactively negotiated' (Ortner 2006, 151) in daily life. Nevertheless, the perceptions and behaviour of the women were still strongly shaped by cultural norms, legal regulations, and religious prescriptions. It has been important to present these few voices, with the hope that there will be a shift in beliefs and perceptions and a move towards acknowledging women's sexual and reproductive rights. This will facilitate women's ability to decide their preferences in sexual activities, to control their bodies, and to have their sexual desire and pleasure recognised.

Notes

1. The word *nyunah* is taken from *sunnah,* and is a way of referring to the practice of the Prophet. Muslims believe that Thursday night (*malam Jum'at*) is the most blessed night to have sex following the practice of the Prophet.
2. 'Your wives are as a tilth unto you; so approach your tilth when and how you will; but do some good act for your soul beforehand; and fear Allah. And know that ye are to meet Him (in the Hereafter), and give (these) good tidings to those who believe' (Q. 2: 223).
3. This Hadith was narrated by Annas bin malik. The Prophet said, 'If any of you have sex with his wife let him be true to her. If he attains his pleasure before her then he shouldn't hurry her away until she also attains her pleasure' (Abi Ya'la 1986, Part VII, 208–9).
4. This is a classic Islamic book taught in *pesantren* (Islamic boarding schools). It is about the marital relationship. The content mostly concerns how a wife should behave towards a husband: submissively and obediently. This is a very famous book and widely read in traditional *pesantren* in Indonesia. See Chapter 3 for a detailed discussion of the content of this *kitab*.

References

Abi Ya'la Al-Mawshili, Al-Imam. (1986). *Musnad Abi Ya'la. Juz VII* (A compilation of Hadith by Abi Ya'la: Part VII). Beirut: Dar al-Ma'mun li Turats. Available from https://perpustakaanislamdigital.com/index.php/fp/flip/hd_msd13#book/ (Accessed 3 August 2020).

Adamson, Clarissa. (2007). 'Gendered anxieties: Islam, women's rights, and moral hierarchy in Java.' *Anthropological Quarterly*, 80(1), 5–37, DOI: 10.1353/anq.2007.0000.

Ahearn, Laura M. (2001). 'Language and agency.' *Annual Review of Anthropology*, 30, 109–37, DOI: 10.1146/annurev.anthro.30.1.109.

Ali, Kecia. (2006). *Sexual Ethics and Islam: Feminist Reflections on Qur'an, Hadith, and Jurisprudence*. Oxford: One World.

Bennett, Linda Rae. (2005). *Women, Islam and Modernity: Single Women, Sexuality and Reproductive Health in Contemporary Indonesia*. London: Routledge Curzon.

Bennett, Linda Rae. (2015). 'Sexual morality and the silencing of sexual health within Indonesian infertility care.' In Linda Rae Bennett and Sharyn Graham Davies (eds.), *Sex and Sexuality in Contemporary Indonesia: Sexual Politics, Health, Diversity and Representations*, 148–66. London: Routledge.

Blackwood, Evelyn. (2010). *Falling into the Lesbi World: Desire and Difference in Indonesia*. Honolulu, HI: University of Hawai'i Press.

Kandiyoti, Deniz. (1988). 'Bargaining with patriarchy.' *Gender and Society*, 2(3), 274–90, DOI: 10.1177/089124388002003004.

Kandiyoti, Deniz. (1998). 'Gender, power and contestation: "Rethinking bargaining with patriarchy".' In Cecile Jackson and Ruth Pearson (eds.), *Feminist Visions of Development: Gender Analysis and Policy*, 138–54. London: Routledge.

Munir, Lily Zakiyah. (2002). '"He is your garment and you are his …": Religious precepts, interpretation, and power relations in marital sexuality among Javanese Muslim women.' *SOJOURN: Journal of Social Issues in Southeast Asia*, 17(2), 191–220, DOI: 10.1355/SJ17-2C.

McNay, Lois. (2008). *Against Recognition*. Cambridge: Polity.

Nurmila, Nina. (2009). *Women, Islam and Everyday Life: Renegotiating Polygamy in Indonesia*. London: Routledge.

Nurmila, Nina and Linda Rae Bennett. (2015). 'The politics of polygamy in Indonesian marriages.' In Linda Rae Bennett and Sharyn Graham Davies (eds), *Sex and Sexuality in Contemporary Indonesia: Sexual Politics, Health, Diversity and Representations*, 69–87. London: Routledge.

Ortner, Sherry B. (2006). *Anthropology and Social Theory: Culture, Power, and the Acting Subject*. Durham: Duke University Press, DOI: 10.1215/9780822388456.

Parker, Lyn. (2005). 'Introduction: The agency of women in Asia.' In Lyn Parker (ed.), *The Agency of Women in Asia*, 1–25. Singapore: Marshal Cavendish Academic.

Schwartz, Pepper and Virginia Rutter. (1998). *The Gender of Sexuality*. Thousand Oaks, CA: Pine Forge Press.

8 Women, Islamic texts, and knowledge construction

The process of acquiring Islamic knowledge among married Muslim women

This chapter focuses on Islamic texts on marriage and sexuality that affect women's perceptions and behaviour. In it, I explore how the women acquired those texts and the topics covered in them. For this purpose, I observed two sites considered authoritative in constructing and disseminating Islamic knowledge to the women, namely, *pesantren* (Islamic boarding schools) and *majlis ta'lim* (women's religious study groups). Most of the women mentioned these as the places where they had acquired the texts or knowledge of the texts (Millie 2011). By analysing these two sites, my aim is to discover which texts are selected to be delivered/studied. In this chapter, I also demonstrate how the dissemination of the texts is influenced by the personal and intellectual background of the preachers and the *kyai* (leader of the *pesantren*). I explore the link between the women's knowledge of Islamic teachings and their perceived behaviour in the broader context of the construction of Islamic knowledge in Indonesia.

This chapter is divided into three sections. The first discusses the places where most women learn about Islamic knowledge related to marriage and sexuality, namely, *pesantren* and *majlis ta'lim*. The second describes the Islamic texts mentioned by the women during their interviews and their understandings of these texts. I will also mention some texts related to the discussions that were rarely, or never, mentioned by my participants. I will show that there are relevant texts that are unfamiliar to them, with the aim of providing a counterbalance to the texts they mentioned. I will also seek to uncover why some texts are favoured over others, and the political interests of the Muslim authorities in the dissemination of Islamic teachings on marriage and sexuality in Indonesia. By political interest I mean the power relations involved in religious knowledge production (Foucault 1990); how knowledge and ideas are distributed in society, by whom and for what purpose. The third section of this chapter gives an alternative reading of Islamic texts on marriage and sexuality to provide a balanced understanding of them. I also provide an example of the role of a non-government organisation (NGO) in empowering a rural community in relation to reproductive and sexuality rights.

I employ an Islamic feminist hermeneutical approach to my interpretation of the Islamic texts. This approach emphasises the importance of interpreting texts by considering the socio-historical context in which they were revealed and written, rather than focusing exclusively on the texts themselves. Detailed discussion on the hermeneutical approach is provided in the Introduction.

I visited five *pesantren* and six *majlis ta'lim* near the site of my fieldwork in Eastern Bandung. I participated in the activities at the *majlis ta'lim*. At the *pesantren*, I interviewed the *kyai*.

Pesantren: the process of knowledge construction

My aim here is not to give a detailed history or description of *pesantren* (Dhofier 1980; Rahardjo 1985), but to document the transmission of knowledge in *pesantren* that involves women. The *pesantren* has an important role in knowledge production and the construction of Islamic teachings. The five *pesantren* I visited were established in the Dutch colonial period and date back to the 1930s.

These five *pesantren* are connected to each other by family lines, marriage, or student-teacher relationships. It is a tradition among *kyai* to construct a strong network among *pesantren* by marrying endogamously among the *pesantren* families (Dhofier 1980). A *pesantren* usually starts with a small group of people studying classical Islamic textbooks in a small *mushala* (praying hall) or mosque. Then the group grows, with participants coming from other regions and cities. As the group grows, the *kyai* build permanent housing, usually a dormitory, in which the students stay, near the *mushala*, and often the *mushala* becomes a fully-fledged mosque. The founders of the five *pesantren* around Bandung were people who had a strong commitment to Islamic education, had gained knowledge from other *pesantren* in nearby towns like Banten and Garut, and had a financial capacity.

Almost all the *pesantren* I visited are affiliated with Nahdlatul Ulama (NU, the largest and one of the most prominent Muslim organisations in Indonesia), although not so much with the organisational structure as with their religious practices. All of the *pesantren* can be categorised as *salafi-yyah*[1] (*pesantren salaf*; traditional) as opposed to *pesantren khalaf* (modern) (Lukens-Bull 2010, 10). *Pesantren salaf* continue the tradition of studying the classical Islamic textbooks known as *kitab kuning* (lit. yellow books, as they are printed on yellow paper). *Kitab kuning* are not uniquely Indonesian in origin. They were written on Arabic coloured paper and many were brought from the Middle East in the early twentieth century by *kyai* who visited Mecca for the pilgrimage (Bruinessen 1990, 1994).

In their early development, all the *pesantren* at the study site catered for male students (*santri putra*) only. The reason given was that there was limited dormitory space available. Elisabeth Jackson and Lyn Parker (2008, 27) provide data from the Ministry of Religious Affairs that shows the students enrolled in *pesantren* in 2005. At all levels, 53.2 percent were male and 46.8 percent were female. The higher ratio of male to female students in many *pesantren* can be traced back to the history of their first establishment that catered exclusively for males. Nowadays, four of the *pesantren* I visited also accepted female students (*santri putri*) and one *pesantren* was preparing to accept female students by the following year. In some *pesantren*, al-Robi' and al-Khamis, female students outnumbered males (75% female *santri* to 25% male *santri*).[2] Social change, along with the opportunity for women to pursue education, and the changing awareness of the *kyai* about the significance of education for women have all contributed to this increase in female students.

With the high demand for safe and affordable accommodation for university students, these *pesantren* have opened their doors to accept *santri* studying at university and each year these numbers have increased significantly. Recently, the majority of *pesantren* in my study site began accepting only those *santri* studying at university and, because of this, these *pesantren* are called *pesantren mahasiswa* (university student *pesantren*). These *pesantren* are located alongside universities—secular and Islamic, state owned and private in Eastern Bandung. Thus many students search for accommodation in *pesantren* rather than rented rooms/houses (*kamar kost/rumah kontrakan*). The reason these students choose to live in the *pesantren* is to deepen their religious knowledge, as well as to save on the cost of accommodation. Accommodation in the *pesantren* costs less than a rented room. For example, each month in *pesantren* al-Robi' the *santri* have to pay around 25,000–35,000 rupiah (AUD 2.75–3.86, USD 1.82–2.55) a month for electricity and maintenance, compared to 250,000–500,000 rupiah (AUD 27.54–55.07, USD 18.21–36.41) a month for a rented room.

Pesantren activities start in the evening around 6 p.m., with the communal *maghrib* prayer that lasts until 9 p.m., and then activities begin again in the early morning with the *subuh* prayer at 4.30 a.m., followed by study of the *kitab* until 6 a.m., when they prepare to go to university.

In terms of the curriculum in these *pesantren*, the *kyai* has the authority to decide which *kitab* should be learned and which should not, in accordance with the dominant and already established characteristics of *salafiyyah pesantren* in Indonesia and the *kyai's* interests and special expertise. However, as I observed, most of these *pesantren* have a similar curriculum of *kitab*. As in most other *pesantren salaf*, the subjects taught in these *pesantren* can be categorised into various Islamic disciplines (Table 8.1).

There are two methods of studying *kitab kuning* in these *pesantren*: *sorogan* (individual reading) and *balagan* (group reading). In *sorogan*, the person can choose any *kitab kuning* that s/he wishes to study and read. For the *balagan*, it is the *kyai* who chooses which *kitab* should be read.

The *pesantren* is a place where knowledge is produced and reproduced, with the aim of maintaining the tradition of *salafiyyah*. Oral transmission of knowledge is important in this learning process (Millie 2008). Criticism of

Table 8.1 Various Islamic disciplines

Subject	Names of the various kitab that were taught
Tawhid (Islamic monotheism)	*Tijan, Syu'bul Iman, Fathul Majid,* and *Jauhar al-tawhid*
Fiqh (Islamic jurisprudence)	*Safinatunnaja, Sulam al-tawfiq, Fathul Qarib, Fathul Mu'in, Iqna',* and *Kifayatul Akhyar*
Nahwu (syntax)	*Jurumiyyah, Imritti, Mutamimmah,* and *Alfiyah*
Sharaf (inflection)	*Amshillah Tashrif, Kailany,* and *Nadhom Maksud*
Akhlak/adab (morality/etiquette)	*Ta'lim Muta'alim, Sulamunnajat, Akhlaqu lil Banat,* and *Akhlaqu lil Banin*
Hadith	*Riyadl as-Salihin* and *Min Kunuzissunnah*
Tafsir al-Qur'an (Qur'anic exegesis)	*Tafsir al-Jalalain, Fathul Mu'in, Tafsir Munir, al-sya'rawi,* and *Sofwatuttafasir.*[3]

Source: Timetable schedule in each *pesantren* that I observed on 4, 7, 8, 18, and 29 June 2012.

the content of the *kitab* is avoided and is in fact taboo. The main concern is with the literal meaning which is ascertained by annotating the text word by word; this process is called *ngalogat*.

In each *pesantren*, the students are usually divided into three groups: Group A includes beginners (Arabic, *mubtadi'*) who have just started learning *kitab kuning;* Group B includes intermediate students (*mutawassith*), and the advanced learners (*muta'ally*) are in Group C. The teachers who teach and assist the learning process are usually the *ustadz* (teachers) who have dedicated themselves to that *pesantren,* or the more senior *santri* who are already at an advanced level.

Guidance related to marriage and sexuality is available in *fiqh* (jurisprudence) under the heading of *kitab/bab al-nikah* (chapter/section on marriage) and is only available in the intermediate to advanced levels. *Fiqh* is considered the main subject of *pesantren* curricula as it is related to everyday guidance (Bruinessen 1990). *Kitab fiqh* usually begins with the chapter of *thaharah* (purification) and the discussion of marriage is available in the second half of the *kitab*.

The popular *kitab kuning* in the *pesantren* that specifically discuss marriage and sexual relations are *kitab Uqud al-Lujain* by Nawawi al-Bantani and *Qurratul 'Uyun* by As-Somdani Abi Muhammad al-Tihami. These *kitab* are learnt by *santri* in the advanced level. *Kitab Uqud al-Lujain* is learned as a chosen *kitab* in three *pesantren:* al-Thani, al-Thalis, and al-Robi', and is offered by individual *ustadz* or at the request of students. Some students in *pesantren* al-Robi' and al-Khomis read *Qurratul Uyun* as *sorogan*. However, the *kyai* in *pesantren* al-Khomis teach a more recent *kitab* on marital sexual relations, called *Kitab Liqa Bainal al-Zawjayn* by Abdul Qadir Ahmad 'Atha, published in 1980. This *kitab,* according to the *kyai,* is quite new and no other *pesantren* use it. Interestingly, after I informed the *kyai* in *pesantren* al-Khomis about the topic of my study, he noted that: 'sexual satisfaction influences the intelligence of the child born.' He further explained that it is important to achieve sexual pleasure for both partners. In contrast to all other *kyai* in my area, the *kyai* of *pesantren* al-Khomis is quite progressive in his opinions about marital relationships, teaching methods, and the *kitab* used in his *pesantren*.

Kitab Uqud al-Lujain, which was written by *syaikh* Nawawi al-Bantani from Banten, is a popular *kitab* on marital relationships between wife and husband. During my fieldwork, many women I interviewed referred to this *kitab* as the Islamic guidance for their marital relationships. However, gender bias is clearly present in the content of this *kitab*, which privileges men over women in marital relationships and demands that women be completely submissive and obedient to their husbands. This *kitab* also emphasises that marital sex is the wife's duty and the husband's right. The wife should comply whenever the husband demands it, and never refuse him because refusal is considered a sin. *Kitab Qurratul 'Uyun* specifically discusses marital sexual relationships related to sexual positions, times, and foods to eat to increase sexual desire.[4]

Kitab that contain a gender bias are many and they are not criticised when they are read in *pesantren*. That is why *pesantren* are seen as maintaining the patriarchal system (Mas'udi 1993). Because of this, women learn a certain Islamic discourse of femininity. Critical thinking is not encouraged and discussion is not the main method in this learning process. Research by Eka Srimulyani (2007, 88), reports that in *pesantren* that cater specifically to girls, there is a strong emphasis on moral and religious values, including an interpretation of femininity that prepares a woman to 'morally and religiously be ... a good wife and a good mother for the future generation.'

It is quite difficult to break the patriarchal values embedded in the *kitab* text, although that does not mean it is impossible. Certain efforts have been initiated by gender activists with a *pesantren* background (female and male) to establish gender awareness in the *pesantren* (Doorn-Harder 2006). The *Kitab Kuning* Study Forum (FK3), the Association for the Development of *Pesantren* and Society (P3M), Rahima and the Fahmina Institute are examples of NGOs that promote gender equality in the *pesantren,* and some conduct critical discussions of the gender bias contained in the *kitab kuning*. Changes in *pesantren* concerning gender equality need to be started by members of the specific *pesantren*. In this case, the roles of *kyai, nyai* (*kyai's* wife), and the teacher are important in increasing the awareness of gender equality (Kholifah 2014; Smith and Woodward 2014; Srimulyani 2012). The *pesantren* is the main institution that promotes a traditional gender relationship, and it will remain as such as long as the traditional curriculum, with its *kitab kuning,* is read uncritically. In order to change this patriarchal tradition, critical thinking, rather than passive and receptive reading, should be employed.

The *pesantren* is an established Islamic institution in Indonesia that has contributed to the education system. In addition, it has provided progressive discussion on democracy and pluralism (Sirry 2010). However, *pesantren* also continue to promote and sustain normative gender relationships, especially marital relationships that promote the husband's authority and the wife's obedience. The so-called 'traditional' *pesantren* that specialise in *salafiyyah's* method of preserving the traditional chain of knowledge, with the *kitab kuning* as the main textbook corpus, survive despite the emergence of modern *pesantren* (*pesantren khalaf*) that adopt modern curricula and offer formal Islamic primary (Madrasah Ibtida'iyyah, MI), secondary (Madrasah Tsanawiyah, MTs), and high school (Madrasah Aliyah, MA) education. The *kitab kuning*, which are taught in 'traditional' *pesantren*, still have high status as the authority for Islamic learning that influences the knowledge construction of Muslim men and women in Indonesia. Reading these classical texts in a contemporary context should entail critical thinking about each text. *Kitab kuning* should be regarded as historical texts that emerged at a specific time and context. Thus, their authoritative status should be regarded as temporary and not absolute.

Majlis Ta'lim (women's religious study groups): exercising religious piety

In this section, I describe two different types of *majlis ta'lim* (women's religious study groups): *majlis ta'lim* that are attached to the *pesantren* and *majlis ta'lim* that are attached to specific mosques. I observed four *majlis ta'lim* attached to *pesantren* and two *majlis ta'lim* that functioned as part of mosque activities. In Sundanese, this religious gathering is also called *pangaosan* (Ind. *pengajian*), derived from *ngaos* (Ind. *ngaji*) which means 'recite,' specially to recite the Qur'an. The term *pangaosan*, however, can refer to any religious study gathering that involves an audience of men and women. Nevertheless, *majlis ta'lim* specifically refers to women's religious study gatherings (Marcoes 1992).

Majlis ta'lim is a common phenomenon that can be seen all over Indonesia, with different methods of learning and types of activity employed in an effort to increase women's religious knowledge. The most common method is listening to the preaching of the preacher/*kyai*, without taking notes about the message being delivered. Thus, oral transmission of knowledge is important in the *majlis ta'lim* learning process (Gade 2004; Millie 2011). The audience relies only upon their listening ability and their memory of the discussion. In other regions of West Java, *majlis ta'lim* is also called *bandungan* which means 'listening' (Ind. *mendengarkan*).

Pesantren are also involved in *majlis ta'lim* and *pangaosan rutin* (regular religious preaching) for the wider community surrounding the *pesantren*. *Pangaosan ibu-ibu* (*majlis ta'lim*) is scheduled in the morning, usually between 8 o'clock and 11 o'clock. The schedule of *pangaosan ibu-ibu* at each *pesantren* differs so that it does not conflict with the *pangaosan* schedule in other *pesantren*. For example in *pesantren* al-Thani, *pangaosan ibu-ibu* is conducted on Thursday (S. *Kemis*; Ind. *kamis*) so usually it is called *kemisan*. In *pesantren* al-Ula, it is held on Mondays; and in *pesantren* al-Robi' it is held on Fridays.

Having a different day for *pangaosan* in each *pesantren* allows participants to attend all of them. As I observed, the participants of one *pangaosan* are almost always the same people who attend other *pangaosan*. The distance between *pesantren* is about one kilometre along a busy street. Research by

Julian Millie (2011) also suggests that women attend four to five *pangaosan* per week, more than men.

The *pangaosan* usually begin with *sholawatan, yasinan* (recitation of the surah Yasin of the Qur'an), recitation of certain prayers, and the main program of preaching from the *kyai*. As I observed, in all *majlis ta'lim* the women read from a single textbook that they hold, which is called *majmu' syarief* (the compilation of the respectable). It is written in Arabic and some versions include its Latin script, with an Indonesian translation. *Majmu' syarief* is a compilation of Arabic texts containing selected Qur'anic *surah* and prayers accompanied by an explanation on the virtue (*faidah*) of reading those *surah* and prayers that are believed to have a beneficial effect in the daily life of the reader (*do'a-do'a mustajab*). *Sholawatan* are the prayers containing praise for the Prophet Muhammad. They are read rhythmically while waiting for latecomers to arrive. The women arrive at different times depending on when they can finish their housework. As all the recitations are in Arabic, many of the women do not understand the meanings as they recite by rote. These women memorised many prayers and verses from this *majmu'*. All of these activities are led by women of the *pesantren* family, either the *nyai* (the *kyai's* wife) or the *kyai's* sister. These activities take about two hours, until the main part of the *pengaosan* is started by the *kyai*. The *kyai* is the only one who delivers the sermon for the *pangaosan* each week.

The audiences of the *pangaosan* are Muslim women, mostly married, aged in their 40s and older. Most come from middle and lower socio-economic backgrounds and many are housewives. In my observations, only a few of the women were from middle or higher levels of the socio-economic ladder. These attendees could be identified by their dress and the respectful greeting of other attendees. Sometimes, the seating arrangements were arranged to accommodate them in the front rows or on the left or right side of the podium.

In *majlis ta'lim* the women sit on a carpet or mat (*tikar*) on the floor. Some of the women brought along goods to sell and they tried to sell these from where they were sitting among the attendees while (listening) to the recitation or preaching. The women offered various products: from different types of foods to clothes and accessories. For these women, *pangaosan* are seen not only as a way to increase religious knowledge but also as a place for economic gain. One *pesantren*, popular for its *pangaosan*, attracts around 300 attendees who come from all around the area. During this *pangaosan* (every Thursday), a temporary market (*pasar kaget*) is established by petty traders who come specially to trade in this location. The narrow road to the *pangaosan* venue becomes crowded with pedestrians, traders, and vehicles. There is a stark difference in the road to the *pangaosan* site between *pesantren* al-Thani on Thursday (Figure 8.1) when there is *pangaosan*, and other days (Figure 8.2).

During the *kyai's* message, I observed that some of the women would listen attentively to the content, some would be half asleep, others would hold conversations with the women next to them, while others tried to bargain and trade. The *kyai* requires good communication skills and strategies to

Figure 8.1 Road conditions outside the *pesantren* al-Thani on Thursdays.
Source: Photographed by author, 7 June 2012.

attract and keep the attendees' interest. The *kyai* reminds the attendees to keep focused and avoids boredom by making jokes, singing, and speaking in a loud voice. In research by Millie (2008, 2011) conducted in another region in West Java, the *kyai* also use *Sundanese tembang* (sung verse) of different stanza forms (*pupuh*) to attract the attendees' attention.

The ability of the preacher to communicate Islamic knowledge to the audiences is influenced by his educational background which impacts on his reputation. According to Lies Marcoes (1992, 212), a *kyai* who is well-liked by the audience is one who has the ability to '*ngadagel, ngadalil jeung ngadumel*' (to make jokes, to use appropriate scriptural quotations, and to voice social protest).

The topics of *pangaosan* are mostly related to *tawhid* (the oneness of God), *aqidah* (the belief system), *fiqh* (Islamic jurisprudence), and marital relationships. A *kyai* in *pesantren* al-Thani and al-Khomis mentioned that the main aims of the *pangaosan* are to strengthen the *tawhid* among the listeners and advise them on how to worship God correctly. The audience is also instructed that they should leave local animist practices behind.

Figure 8.2 Road conditions outside the *pesantren* al-Thani on days other than Thursday.
Source: Photographed by author, 7 June 2012.

Apart from increasing Islamic knowledge, the aim of the women attending the *pangaosan* is also to socialise with other women and to make new friends. One woman said, 'it is better to attend this kind of *pangaosan* than to sit at home and be overwhelmed by the complexities (*keruwetan*) of life.' Another woman compared her attendance at *pangaosan* to the way a plant needs to be watered to stay fresh and allow it to grow; similarly indicating that she was nourished by attending the *pangaosan*. Another woman beside her agreed, saying that the heart needs to be filled with spiritual knowledge to cool it down from the various problems faced in everyday life. This spiritual cleansing (*siraman rohani*) would make them strong and optimistic. The *pesantren* is a trusted place for ordinary people to acquire Islamic knowledge through regular *pangaosan*. Millie (2008) showed that this kind of *pangaosan* for *orang awam* (non-specialists) is a ritual event that establishes *pesantren* as the symbol of religious tradition and authority and as a place where ordinary people can express and strengthen their faith.

The *kyai* is the leader of the *pesantren* (in West Java *kyai* are also called *ajengan*) and has charisma and high social prestige in the community. The role of the *kyai* in the community is not merely as an expert in Islamic knowledge who gives advice on religious matters but, historically speaking, the *kyai* has also been seen as a leading figure in the Indonesian revolution against colonialism (Dhofier 1980). Hiroko Horikoshi (1976) reported on the various roles of the *kyai*, showing that the *kyai* in rural areas are charismatic characters who give guidance on spiritual and mystical issues. They are also expected to solve community problems in regards to social change. Clifford Geertz (1960, 234) also mentioned several roles of the *kyai*—'a cultural broker' who acts as 'spiritual advisor, magical curer, and social superior.' I observed, in *pesantren* in semi-urban areas that the charismatic figure of the *kyai* remains the key attraction for students and attendees of his *pangaosan*. All of the *kyai* I observed were also believed to be persons with the perceived 'authority' to cure certain diseases, prevent misfortune, and facilitate successful achievements for the members of the community around them.

Ngalap barakah (to gain divine good fortune) is what motivated *pangaosan* attendees to come from all areas surrounding the *pesantren*. They brought drinking water bottles to be put in front of where the *kyai* was expected to recite prayers. The attendees believed that by drinking that water their hopes would be realised. When the sermon finished, the women, especially those in the front rows, would approach the *kyai* and shake his hands, and pass him envelopes containing money.

At two of the *majlis ta'lim* I attended, these donations were not seen as a part of mosque activities. These two *majlis ta'lim* were organised by the same woman, Ibu Citra (aged 50), who is also the sub-district leader of *majlis ta'lim*. Unlike the *pangaosan* described above, this *majlis ta'lim* is well organised, involving all members of the *pengajian*. They are not passive attendees who just come, sit, recite, and listen. Each week, there are certain members appointed responsible for the assembly—one to be a master of ceremonies, one to recite the Qur'an, and one to read its translation. Each person takes a turn. Around 20–30 women attended these *majlis ta'lim*, fewer than for the *pangaosan* in the *pesantren* that attract 50–300 attendees. Unlike the *majlis ta'lim* attached to the *pesantren*, where the main preacher is the *kyai*, the preachers at these two *majlis ta'lim* come from diverse backgrounds and are not necessarily the *kyai*. Some of them are male and female scholars, lecturers, students, and community leaders.

According to Ibu Citra, there are various activities conducted in her *majlis ta'lim*, which emphasise not only learning and reciting the Qur'an, mainly done inside the mosque, but also activities outside the mosque such as running courses to increase skills for the members of *pangaosan*, nature exploration, charity events, and a Qur'an recitation competition for the members.

The sermons delivered in *majlis ta'lim* are mostly about worship, the afterlife, marital relationships, Islamic virtues, and social interactions. The material for the sermon is taken from various sources, many of which are from *kitab kuning* like *dzurratun Nasihin* (the compilation of advice), *safinatun najah* (Islamic jurisprudence), and many others. They explain praying (*shalat*), fasting (*puasa*), forgiveness (*memaafkan*), patience (*sabar*), acceptance (*ikhlas*), alms (*sedekah*), caring (*tolong menolong*), and repentance (*taubat*) for enhancing piety. Topics pertaining to marital relationships also dominate the preaching in *majlis ta'lim*, specifically related to parenting (caring for and educating children), organising the household, and wife-husband relationships. Advice about the proper conduct of these relationships is directed at women, as women are considered to be the safeguards of the family. The content of the sermons guide women on what they should do and what they should not do. One woman even said to me that she was disappointed at the topics delivered in *majlis ta'lim*, which mostly asked women to be *sabr* (patient), and *ikhlas* (accepting) in relation to the problems they face in marriage, for the sake of the children and peace in the community. These topics feature repeatedly in *majlis ta'lim*. The woman who complained wanted discussions more related to the problems of women in everyday life and ideas on how to solve these problems. Many *majlis ta'lim* promoted conventional female virtues justified by religious texts—modesty, obedience, and self-sacrifice in relation to children and family.

In a Focus Group Discussion (FGD), many women complained about this instructive message directed at them. One woman, Edah (aged 43) said:

> We (women) attend many religious gatherings that teach proper conduct related to the family: how to interact with our husbands, take care of the children, and maintain the household. We are fed up with that knowledge—we are already experts because that's what we do every day. By contrast, I am wondering whether men in their religious gatherings are also being advised to do the same—on how to behave with proper conduct toward the family, the children, and the household? I doubt it. If we want a harmonious family, the same knowledge should be given to husbands as well because many problems related to the household are also triggered by the husband.

A *kyai* of *pesantren* al-Ula also affirmed that:

> When I deliver sermons concerning marital relationships to the women of *pengajian*, it is ineffective, because the husbands are not given the same information. It is unbalanced. The best way is to give the same advice and knowledge to both partners on how to create a harmonious married life.

The *majlis ta'lim* generally represented marital relationship according to normative gender roles and relations: that the wife should obey her husband because of his role as breadwinner and head of the family (*kepala rumah tangga*). Research by Phillip Winn (2012, 19) suggests that *majlis ta'lim* in Leihitu, Ambon, work in 'reiterating normatively gendered forms of religious practice' besides mastering fluency in Arabic recitation. This is also true for *majlis ta'lim* in Eastern Bandung. I would argue they do not just *reiterate* but also *strengthen* gendered norms of religious practices and knowledge.

In Indonesia, women play an important role in religious life. Women are not exempt from public life or acquiring religious knowledge. They organise religious activities in the mosque through *majlis ta'lim*. There are various activities performed in *majlis ta'lim* including preaching, studying the Qur'an, reciting, praying, doing charity work, and so on. The activities vary from one *majlis ta'lim* to another. I would argue that there is no doubt that *majlis ta'lim* in Indonesia allow women to claim public space, enhance religious knowledge, and exercise religious piety, as noted by Sylva Frisk (2009) in Malaysia and Saba Mahmood (2001) in Egypt. In Malaysia, Frisk (2009) reported that these kinds of religious activities in the mosque give women space within the male-dominated environment and create agency, as they can shape women's opinions concerning such texts. Similarly, Mahmood (2001) argues that the women's mosque movement gives opportunities for women to experience Islamic piety—maintain their modesty and shyness and devotion as Muslims. The topics given in the mosque movement in Egypt like *sabr* (patience) and *taqwa* (righteousness) are taken up by the women as survival strategies for daily life.

However, in terms of the religious messages provided, particularly about marital relationships, *majlis ta'lim* promotes the ideal normative women's behaviour in patriarchal society justified by religious texts. Women are advised to sacrifice themselves for the sake of the family, with the lure of reward in the afterlife (*pahala*) for their patience and obedience toward their husbands. Submitting to God is the answer to the problems faced by women, and unluckiness is considered their fate (*nasib*), their destiny (*takdir*). It is hard, in this context, not to see *majlis ta'lim* as sustaining patriarchal values. It is true that through *majlis ta'lim* women have the opportunity to increase their religious knowledge, learn the Qur'anic text, master Arabic recitation, and exercise piety as Muslims. However, the analysis should go beyond just claiming the space, and extend to the content and value of religious prescription disseminated to women in the process of meaning construction that still privileges men's position in their daily lives. In this case, *majlis ta'lim* transmit and facilitate male bias by making use of religious texts as a way of strengthening the patriarchal chain. Nevertheless, *majlis ta'lim* offer temporary relief from women's unresolved problems through social interaction, and they perhaps gain comfort in their own piety. However, because of their inability to challenge the existing conditions, women cannot actually resolve their problems other than by acceptance and submission to God. Religion becomes an excuse for helplessness when no other solution is available. In my opinion this is un-empowered escape; an enforced surrender to religious devotion. In this case, women's piety is politicised or used as a means of strengthening the politics of patriarchy (Deeb 2010).

The difference in women's attitudes in regards to marriage, before and after attending the *pengajian*, is demonstrated by Rani and Tuti:

> Early in my marriage, I often refused to have sex with my husband if I wasn't in the mood. Nowadays, since I became actively engaged in

pengajian, even when I'm not keen on having sex, I don't refuse him, because it is my duty and I am afraid of sin (*takut berdosa*).

(Rani, aged 43)

I know from *pengajian* that refusing your husband's sexual need is a sin in Islam, I did not know about that until I attended *pengajian*. Before that, I often refused my husband if I was unwilling to [have sex].

(Tuti, aged 55)

Majlis ta'lim facilitated women's capacity to act, in terms of providing an opportunity to acquire religious knowledge. However, at the same time women were hindered because they were surrounded by religious teachings that advised them to safeguard the family by sacrificing their own desire in the name of 'silence, immobility, and obedience the key criteria of female beauty in Islamic culture' (Fatna Sabbah 1984, 3).

The role of *majlis ta'lim* is significant in disseminating Islamic texts on marital relationships, most of which subordinate women (Hamdanah 2005). Even female preachers promote such topics and rarely do they discuss the awareness of women's rights in Islam (see Marcoes 1992). I argue that there is a need to reformulate the topics and content of *majlis ta'lim* to make them provide more enlightened information for women. In addition, it is time for the preachers in *majlis ta'lim,* both male and female, to provide gender-balanced exegeses of Islamic texts, promoting the spirit of gender equality.

The Islamic texts on marriage and sexuality and women's understanding

In the following I discuss Islamic texts relating to marriage and sexuality that were mentioned by my female participants. As mentioned above, when I refer to 'texts' I am referring to various sources and not necessarily to a single Islamic written source. When bringing up Islamic sources, the women usually mentioned the books/*kitab* they had read, the *pengajian* they had attended or the *pesantren* (*kyai*) at which they had studied. Many of them could not differentiate between whether the texts they recited were from the Qur'an or the Hadith or if they were simply the opinion of the *kyai* or *ustadz*. They often just said vaguely, 'According to Islam it is said so and so ...,' or they said, 'In the Hadith it is said...,' but in fact it was the Qur'an. The women frequently mixed up the sources from where the texts were obtained.

It is understandable that these women quoted the source or the text incorrectly because many of them relied only on the oral transmission of knowledge that was used in *pengajian* or *pesantren*. In this chapter, I locate the texts mentioned by my participants in their correct source: the Qur'an, Hadith, or the words/opinions of local *kyai* and *ustadz*.

I analysed the religious texts related to marriage and sexual relations so that I can better understand how the women made use of these texts as their guide in their marital relationships and the importance of these texts in influencing their relationships.

The Qur'an

Several women cited Chapter 4 verse 34 of the Qur'an:

> *Men are the protectors and maintainers of women [Al-rijalu qawwamuna ala al-nisa]*, because Allah has given the one more (strength) than the other, and because they support them from their means. Therefore, the righteous women are devoutly obedient, and guard in (the husband's) absence what Allah would have them guard. As to those women on whose part ye fear disloyalty and ill-conduct, admonish them (first), (next), refuse to share their beds, (and last) chastise them (lightly); but if they return to obedience, seek not against them means (of annoyance): for Allah is Most High, Great (above you all) [my emphasis].[5]
>
> (Q. 4: 34)

The majority of women I interviewed unanimously mentioned that the husband is the head of the family and referred to this verse to augment their argument. However, many of them only cited the first part of the verse—the part I have italicised. This is the main piece of advice they received on their wedding day; it is stated in the marriage sermon. No matter how the wife contributes to the family income or what level of education she has achieved, the main principle of marriage for Indonesian women still applies—to serve her husband.

For example, Sari (aged 42, with a doctorate), a director of a study program at a university, mentioned, 'At home, I position myself as an ordinary housewife [*ibu rumah tangga biasa*]. I serve my husband, like getting him a drink when he returns home from work.' When I prompted her with the question, what would happen if she was also tired from working when she returned home. Would he ever get her a drink? She just said defensively that she usually came home earlier, meaning that it would be unusual for a husband to serve the wife. This is to imply that no matter how prestigious her public achievements, at home Sari's position is a mere housewife whose main duty is to serve her husband. Many Indonesians also believe that a career woman can be anything in public as long as she does not neglect her main role as a wife and mother (Nilan and Utami 2008).

Another woman, Sandra (aged 57), when referring to the verse mentioned above, stated that the authority of the husband is also related to the sexual relationship:

> In terms of our sexual relationship, I never initiate having sex, I feel embarrassed [*malu*] to do so because I am a woman. Besides, my husband believes that the verse '*Al-rijalu qawwamuna ala al-nisa*' [men are the protectors and maintainers of women] also applies to sexual relations.

The implication of her statement is that her husband would not be pleased if Sandra initiated sex, because, according to her husband, it is the job of the husband to initiate sex as the leader of the household.

Another woman, Mala (aged 40), also mentioned the same verse. However, she had an interesting comment:

> There are times when I regard my husband as the leader of the family, but there are also times when I considered him an equal partner [*mitra sejajar*] in married life. It depends on the situation.

Heni (aged 51) also has an alternative understanding of verse. She explained:

> Men are the head of the family under the conditions as stated in that verse. Thus, when the husband cannot provide financial support and the task is taken over by the wife, he is no longer the head of the family.

This verse is widely used by men and women alike to refer to and to justify an absolute authority of male over female, especially in marital relationships that oblige women to be obedient. However, many cited this verse partially—just the italicised text—and did not mention the rest of the verse which clearly states the conditions which enable a male to have authority over a female: *fadala* (preference) and *nafaqa* (maintenance).[6]

Iis (aged 40), who experienced domestic violence from her husband, had a different opinion about this verse and challenged the absolute power of the husband in marriage. She said:

> We should define first what kind of husband deserves obedience from his wife and what kinds of command should be followed. I do not always comply with what my husband orders me to do, it depends on the context. Just like in sex, Islam does not prescribe that a couple should have sex every day, like my husband demands. But, I also fear that if I don't obey his command, he will betray me for another woman. That's what I see in my neighbourhood.

Uum (aged 35) also resisted allowing the use of this verse as male justification for absolute power in marriage. She reported that whenever her husband demanded to have sex with her, but she felt unwilling to do so, her husband would say, 'I have power [*aku berkuasa*] over you.' At that time Uum could not refuse, but later on Uum declared that a husband's power in marriage has limits, including in sex. There should be no power for a husband who is violent or does not financially support his wife and the family—her husband was violent and non-financially supportive.

In practice, although women unanimously agreed that the husband is the head of the family and the wife is expected to be obedient to him in married life, the women could compromise, and even resist absolute guardianship and obedience. There are women who submit passively to the prescriptions, but many others resisted, arguing that the husband's power has limits under certain conditions—such as the inability to support the family, and bad or violent behaviour—such that the wife may not obey his commands. The reality faced by these women in their interactions with their husbands enhanced their understanding of this verse and caused them to argue against their husband's absolute authority. Iis and Uum challenged their husbands, who both used religious texts to justify their violent behaviour in claiming sex.

Another Qur'anic verse on marriage and sexuality that was usually used by males to justify their behaviour is about polygyny:

> If ye fear that ye shall not be able to deal justly with the orphans, *marry women of your choice, two or three or four;* but if ye fear that ye shall not be able to deal justly (with them), then only one, or (a captive) that your right hands possess. That will be more suitable, to prevent you from doing injustice [my emphasis].
>
> (Q. 4: 3)

Many men declared that this verse gives them permission to take another wife. This verse was used by Nisa's husband who insisted on practising polygyny. According to Nisa (aged 37), her husband argued that if she would not permit him to take another wife then she would be rejecting this verse as a command of God. Nisa felt disturbed by her husband's statement; she feared being labelled a disbeliever, but at the same time she could not agree to her husband taking another wife.

Many people quoted the verse about polygyny incompletely, only including the italicised phrase. This is because the men wanted to justify the act using an unassailable religious text. The verse on polygyny should be read completely, like any other verse in the Qur'an. By reading comprehensively, the directive can be understood correctly, including the conditions under which polygyny is permissible. The main Qur'anic requirement for polygyny is for men to practise justice, which, according to Amina Wadud (1999, 2006), is almost unachievable. Many progressive scholars, instead of seeing this verse as giving men permission to practise polygyny, believe that the verse is about limiting marriage to one wife only.[7]

Most of the women were also familiar with Islamic teachings about menstruation. During their periods, women are exempt from religious worship such as praying (*shalat*) and fasting (*puasa*). In addition, during a woman's period, it is forbidden to have intercourse. This is stated in Q. 2: 222:

> They ask thee concerning women's courses. Say: They are a hurt and a pollution: so keep away from women in their courses, and do not approach them until they are clean. But when they have purified themselves, ye may approach them in any manner, time, or place ordained for you by Allah. For Allah loves those who turn to Him constantly and He loves those who keep themselves pure and clean.

In fact the text only prohibits intercourse, not sexual intimacy. There are several Hadith that report that the Prophet used to be intimate (but not to have intercourse) with his wife Aisyah while she was menstruating. I make this point in order to discard the opinion that a woman's body is polluting (or polluted) during menstruation. The pollution refers only to discharged menstrual blood not to a woman's body.

Several women thought of the menstrual period as their free time—a time during which they were excused from having sex without feeling guilty. Many husbands understood as well that during this period they could not have sex with their wives. However, several others could not wait until their wives had finished their period.

Another text that regulates sexual relations in Islam that was quoted by my respondents is Q. 2: 223 on how to approach the wife. Sometimes, this verse is misunderstood to justify husbands' authority to decide when and how they wish to have sex.

> Your wives are as a tilth unto you; so approach your tilth when and how ye will; but do some good act for your souls beforehand; and fear Allah. And know that ye are to meet Him (in the Hereafter), and give (these) good tidings to those who believe.

Leli (aged 29), cited this verse in relation to feeling that her husband is uninterested in sex and rarely asked for intercourse. She shared what she knew about this verse with her husband: that it encouraged husbands to ask for sex without hesitation. Leli said that she is ready to serve her husband sexually whenever he wants. In the meantime, her husband is very considerate when asking for sex, fearing that she is tired after taking care of their son all day.

This verse also relates to the etiquette of intercourse and sexual positions based on the *asbab al-nuzul* (the specific socio-historical context following the revelation) of this verse. According to this verse the husband is permitted to have intercourse with his wife in a variety of positions as long as it is vaginal (not anal) sex. One Hadith related to the discussion is reported on the authority of Zuhri: 'If he likes he may (have intercourse) from behind or while facing her, but it should be through the vagina' (Muslim 2007, Vol. 4, Hadith no. 3537, 77).[8] Mia explained that she learned about this verse at the *pesantren,* saying that those engaging in anal sex would not be protected by God in the afterlife. She mentioned that at that time she could not imagine what anal sex was.

Another Islamic teaching that was mentioned by my participants is about *zina*. One of my respondents, Ai (aged 18), became pregnant before marriage. During the interview she said that she knew that premarital sex was prohibited in Islam, it is called *zina* (fornication; adultery). Although she personally had not read the text related to the prohibition, I provided it for her. Q. 17: 32; 24: 2–3 focuses on the prohibition from pre-marital sex and the punishment for the doer. Ai said:

When that happened [premarital sex], it was an evil temptation. I could not resist it. I was heartbroken [*sakit hati*] afterward and regretted what I had done. But, what could I do, it had already happened and I had to accept the risk of possible pregnancy. My boyfriend said that I should not worry about that because he would marry me and be responsible if I got pregnant. I believed him, and we were married a year later, after I delivered my baby.

Another Qur'anic verse related to marital sexual relationships is Q. 2: 187. It provides permission to engage in sexual activity on the nights of the fasting month (Ramadan) and the metaphor of wife-husband sexual relationships promoted in the Qur'an. This verse shows that the marital sexual relationship is a mutual relationship allowing both partners the right to gain mutual satisfaction. The metaphor used in this verse is that sexual activity between husband and wife is like a garment that covers each of their bodies. This implies mutuality in the relationship and recognition that both sexes have desires to be fulfilled.

> Permitted to you, on the night of the fasts, is the approach to your wives. *They are your garments and ye are their garments.* Allah knoweth what ye used to do secretly among yourselves; but He turned to you and forgave you; so now associate with them, and seek what Allah hath ordained for you [my emphasis].
>
> (Q. 2: 187)

Unfortunately, rarely did the women mention this verse as providing guidance in their sexual relations. This verse was unfamiliar compared to the Hadith about serving a husband's sexual needs or the verse about men's authority. Only once was this verse cited, during a FGD, without further elaboration on its meaning. In fact, this verse can be used to counter the teachings that suggest sex in marriage is the husband's right and the wife's duty, which mostly derive from the Hadith or *ulama's* commentary. On the contrary, this verse declares that both wife and husband have the right to sexual fulfilment and satisfaction.

Hadith

The women mentioned several of the teachings related to marriage and sexuality derived from Hadith. One of the most cited teachings suggests that marital sex is the wife's duty and husband's right and that she cannot refuse his demands:

> Narrated Abu Huraira: The Prophet said, 'If a man invites his wife to sleep with him and she refuses to come to him, then the angels send their curses on her till morning.'
>
> (Al-Bukhari 1997, vol. 7, Hadith no. 5193, 90)[9]

This text was well known among the women I interviewed. When describing their sexual relations, many women said that they should comply with their husband's request for sex and if they refuse, their refusal is associated with sin (*dosa*), being cursed (*dilaknat*), and being taboo (*pamali*). Several women could cite the content of the Hadith and were familiar with it as they knew it from *pengajian* or *pesantren*. Other women had only heard about the message that Islam forbids women to refuse their husbands. A few others who did not engage in religious study acquired this advice about *pamali* from local cultural norms passed on by their mothers or their elders, or it was already a widely held belief among people.

The content of this Hadith is familiar not only among women but also men. Several husbands used the Hadith to justify their sexual demands, and one even forced sex on his wife using the Hadith to legitimate his actions. Uum stated:

> Once I refused to have sex with my husband because I was fed up with his bad behaviour. I felt no sexual desire. My husband got angry and he poked my leg with a cigarette, burning it, and he beat me, and said, 'This pain, pointing to my wounds, is nothing compared to what you will get in the afterlife: the curse of an angel.' I stayed silent. I know that it is my duty to serve my husband and if I do not I am committing a sin.

However, Uum realised that her husband's violent behaviour was making her sick and she decided that enough was enough. She argued that a husband's power has limits, including in relation to sex and especially because he had been violent and abandoned her.

In regard to Uum's experience of violence from her husband during intercourse, she actually could counter her husband's acts by referring to other texts (Hadith) mentioning that the Prophet banned the husband from being violent towards his wife, but at the same time having intercourse with her: 'Narrated Abdullah bin Zam'a: The Prophet said, "None of you should flog his wife as he flogs a slave and then have sexual intercourse with her in the last part of the day"' (Al-Bukhari 1997, vol. 7, Hadith no. 5204, 96). Unfortunately, this Hadith is unfamiliar or unknown to most women. Though the flogging of a slave is not acceptable either, this Hadith shows us that the Prophet did not encourage husbands to be violent towards their wives.

There are several Hadith mentioned by my respondents which suggest positive attitudes towards marriage and sexuality. The Hadith that support women's sexual expression and satisfaction in their marital relationships were mentioned by several of the women I interviewed:

First, *mukaddimah* or *mula'abah*—the importance of foreplay

> Imam al-Daylami records a narration on the authority of Anas ibn Malik that the Messenger of Allah is reported to have said: 'One of you should not fulfil one's (sexual) need from one's wife like an animal, rather there should be a messenger between you.' 'And what is that messenger?' they asked, and he replied: 'Kisses and [sweet] words.'
>
> (Al-Daylami, 1987, vol. 2, Hadith no. 55)

Many women said that they would like their husbands to indulge in foreplay before intercourse, but this was not accommodated by several husbands. The respondents complained that while it is easy to arouse a husband's sexual desire, they (the wives) require time to be sexually aroused, and foreplay would help them to increase their sexual desire.

Second, a wife has the right to experience pleasurable sex. In one Hadith it is reported:

> Narrated by Annas bin malik, the Prophet said: 'If any of you have sex with his wife let him be true to her. If he attains his pleasure before her then he shouldn't hurry her away until she also attains her pleasure.'
> (Abi Ya'la, 1986, part VII, 208–9)

Only Tia mentioned this Hadith in the interview. She told her husband that in sexual relations he should not be focused only on his own pleasure but he should wait until she too experienced pleasure, and her husband agreed.

Third, a wife's invitation to sexual activity is rewarded (*pahala*). This is derived from an Islamic prescription suggesting that sexual activity is not only physical but also gains God's blessing because it is considered as *ibadah* (part of worship).

> It was narrated from Abu Dharr that some of the Companion[s of] the Prophet said to the Prophet: 'O Messenger of Allah, the rich people have taken all the reward. They offer Salat as we offer Salat and they fast as we fast, but they give charity from their surplus wealth. He said: "Has Allah not given you something with which you may do acts of charity? Every Tasbihah is a charity, every Takbirah is a charity, every Tahmidah is a charity, every Tahlilah is a charity, enjoining what is good is a charity, forbidding what is evil is a charity, and (the intimacy of one of you with his wife) is a charity." They said: "O Messenger of Allah, if one of us fulfils his desire, will he be rewarded for that?" He said: "Do you not see that if he did it in an unlawful manner, there would be a burden of sin on him for that? Similarly, if he does it in a lawful manner, he will be rewarded for it."'
> (Muslim, 2007, vol. 3, Hadith no. 2329, 51–2)

Only one woman, Halimah, would openly offer and initiate sex with her husband. She believed that she would gain rewards by initiating sex with her husband, in the same way that other women believed serving their husband sexually would gain them rewards in the afterlife. However, many other women were hesitant about initiating sex. They feared various repercussions if they did. Sandra thought it would irritate her husband because it would be as though she were taking control. Hera and Ina feared being teased by their husbands. Leli feared being rejected and Nisa and Leli feared being labelled as being too hungry for sex. Nevertheless, the reason most often given by my respondents for not initiating sex with their husbands was that they were shy (*malu*). *Malu* is an important learnt behaviour in Indonesian society that shapes daily interactions.

Many women have strategies for when they want to have sex but are embarrassed to say so openly to their husbands. They use indirect invitations such as they beautify themselves, or use perfume, or give a massage. The husbands notice these signs and happily acquiesce. One woman, Nida (aged 25), said 'My husband almost never refuses to take part.'

These three religious texts—the instruction to engage in foreplay before sex, to satisfy the wife in sex, and sex as *ibadah*—ascertain and acknowledge that women have sexual desires that need to be fulfilled and the right to experience sexual pleasure and satisfaction. Unfortunately, these texts are unfamiliar to women, men, and Muslim society in general.

Islamic texts can often be used to justify two points of view, and sometimes are contradictory in their advice concerning gender relations in marriage. From the above description of Islamic texts on marriage and sexuality, there are some texts that support women's desire, while several others seem to repress it. Unfortunately, in the teachings I observed and the women's opinions I heard the repressive texts dominated the other texts. It is the task of Muslim scholars to propose alternative insights in presenting and interpreting texts related to marriage and sexuality. Alternative readings of these texts, from a Muslim feminist theological perspective, are discussed below.

Rereading Islamic texts on marriage and sexuality

By Islamic texts, as I noted above, I am referring not to a single text but to various Islamic sources. These texts I categorised into three genres: the primary text, the Qur'an; the secondary text, the *Sunnah*, the Prophet's praxis including his sayings, actions, and approval of certain deeds that he knew about which are recorded in the Hadith; and tertiary texts, which are texts other than the above mentioned. They could be the sayings of the first generation *ulama* or of contemporary *ulama,* or simply the opinions of the *kyai* or *ustadz*.

Considering the many facets of the texts in Islam, this chapter employs a hermeneutical reading of Islamic texts offered by Islamic feminists as they analyse Islamic texts on marriage and sexuality.[10] This hermeneutical reading emerged from the fact that Islamic texts have been abused in Muslim communities to oppress people, especially women. Islamic feminists offer a liberatory and egalitarian exegesis of the texts through their anti-patriarchal reading of the Qur'an (Barlas 2002) and the sexist biases of the Arabic language (Wadud 2006).

In analysing the texts related to marriage and sexuality in Islam, most of which seem to position women as subordinate to men, Muslim scholars suggest that this analysis is linked to state power and politics. Many cases, as recorded in Islamic history, show a strong engagement of texts and knowledge production/construction that aims to sustain the state's power or to privilege certain groups—rich over poor, majority over minority and men over women. Pinar Ilkkaracan (2000, 13) concluded that 'the sexual oppression of Muslim women is not the result of the "Islamic" vision of sexuality, but a combination of political, social, and economic inequalities throughout the ages.' Unfortunately, religion is often misused as a powerful instrument of control by regimes that 'instrumentalise' religion to strengthen their legitimacy (Arkoun 2006, 33).

A person who is in a position of power exercises control over the production of knowledge: which texts should be learned and which ones should be hidden; which text sustains interest and which does not. In Mohammed Arkoun's (2006, 31) words, a person in power can decide which text is 'thinkable' and which is 'unthinkable.' According to Arkoun (2006), women are the main victims of the oppressive regime that has (mis)used religious texts that not only sustain women's subordination, but also repress, control, and criminalise women's sexuality under religious codes.

Islamic feminists aim to return 'thinking' to the Islamic principles derived from the Qur'an as the primary source. They argue that much inequality and discrimination in the name of Islam derives not from the Qur'an but from secondary and tertiary texts (Abou El Fadl 2001; Barlas 2002).

It is important to differentiate between the authoritative texts in Islam. Most Islamic feminists focus on the primary source of Islam that is the Qur'an, as the most authoritative text against other texts such as Hadith,[11] Qur'anic interpretations, or Muslim's scholars opinions (*ulama*). Islamic feminists argue that the Qur'an, in particular, promotes the equality of human beings. They first explain the ontological state of being human. According to the Qur'an, a human is created from a single self that has the same quality either before God or before other humans (Q. 4: 1).

The confusion between the primary text and other texts is not a new phenomenon in Islamic societies. Arkoun (1994) indicates that the primary text has been marginalised over secondary and even tertiary sources since the early days of Islam. The primary source became tertiary and the tertiary texts became the primary reference points for Muslim attitudes.

Indonesia is no exception to this misunderstanding of Islamic texts. In Indonesia, the sayings of the *ulama* or *ustadz* often become the primary authority and people are unfamiliar with messages derived from the Qur'an. There is a tendency in Indonesia to formalise the Qur'an as a mere Arabic text that needs to be read and memorised to gain prestigious achievement without given attention to its translation or meaning. From an early age, children are forced to memorise certain *surah* in the Qur'an. They are praised for how many *surah* they have memorised and parents invest in this expectation. However, it would seem to be better to emphasise meaning and understanding rather than merely memorisation.

Rarely did my respondents refer to the Qur'an in their explanation of marriage and sexuality in Islam. More commonly they referred to the Hadith and the *ulama's* opinions. Unfortunately, the teachings derived from these texts are those that do not support women's equality. For example, the Hadith cited by my respondents about serving a husband's sexual needs or being cursed by an angel are teachings that not only degrade women's position but also oppose the teachings of the Qur'an. In verses Q. 4: 1 and Q. 9: 71–72 the Qur'an states that woman is a full human agent on earth (*khalifah*) and has equal responsibilities and capabilities as men.

There is debate in relation to the Hadith about bringing down the curse of an angel:

> Narrated Abu Huraira: The Prophet said, 'If a man invites his wife to sleep with him and she refuses to come to him, then the angels send their curses on her till morning.'
> (Al-Bukhari 1997, vol. 7, Hadith no. 5193, 90)

Abdul Kodir (2012), a gender activist from a *pesantren*, proposes a *reciprocal* reading (*qiro'ah mubadalah*). Reciprocal readings of a text suggest that one text is always in relation to other texts and one should always rely on the universal Islamic principle of mutuality so as not to disgrace or disadvantage one party. Reading this Hadith reciprocally enables us to use three approaches.

In approach one, the linguistic approach, attention is paid to the literal meaning of the words used in the narration. The word *da'a*, used in the Hadith, in Arabic usually means to invite someone politely and with good manners. *Aabat* (lit. refuse) means to refuse someone impolitely (Abdul Kodir 2012, 43). And the word *la'ana* (lit. curse) should be interpreted metaphorically given the fact that angels are the creation of God—they have no desire and therefore would always be obedient. Thus, it seems quite contradictory that an angel would curse. Taken metaphorically, this passage means that refusal to have sex would cause a state of unease between the spouses. Using this approach the Hadith is suggesting that if a husband invites his wife to have sex politely or in a nice way but the wife rejects him impolitely, this would make their relationship uncomfortable for the whole night (Mas'udi 2000, 126).

Approach two refers to the principle of Islamic jurisprudence. By using the principle of Islamic jurisprudence (*ushul fiqh*) and applying the principle of *dilalah al-dilalah* (the meaning of meaning) or *mafhum mukhalafah* (contrary understanding; divergent meaning) one can conclude that there is a consequence of the act: if a wife invited her husband to have sex and he refused her, there would be religious consequences (Abdul Kodir 2012). There is a reciprocal need for sex in marriage between wife and husband so they should cooperate with one another and fulfil their desires mutually.

Islamic jurisprudence (*fiqh*) is the third approach. It is a fact that *fiqh* has strengthened the norm of sex as the wife's duty and the husband's right (Abdul Kodir 2007, 2012). In fact, if we look deep down to analyse the *fiqh*, there is room for negotiation of women's positions in sexual relationships. Referring to the Hadith above, some jurists suggest that the wife is permitted to refuse her husband's sexual invitation with valid reasons, such as the husband's violence (Al-Zuhaily 1985). In *fiqh* concerning marital sexual relations, Wahbah al-Zuhaily (1985, 106–107) mentions four famous jurists, most of whom (*jumhur ulama*)[12] declared that sex in marriage is the husband's obligation toward his wife, a sign of love and affection, because both spouses have the right to sexual fulfilment in marriage.

In relation to jurist opinions that support the wife's right to sexual fulfilment is the Hadith concerning *azl* (coitus interruptus) which most jurists (*jumhur ulama*, except Syafi'i) agree should only be done by the husband after he gets permission from the wife. Acquiring permission from the wife indicates that she has the right to sexual pleasure and the act of *'azl* may interrupt her sexual satisfaction.

> From the compilation of Abu Dawud, it was narrated from Abu Huraira that Umar bin Khattab said: 'The Messenger of Allah forbade practising *'azl* [coitus interruptus] with a free woman except with her consent.'
> (Dawud 2012, book 9, Hadith no. 2003)

Syafi'i jurists hold the opinion that sex in marriage is the husband's right. Thus, the husband can practice *azl* whenever he wants and without the wife's permission because she is not entitled to sexual fulfilment. Unfortunately, most Indonesian Muslims hold to the Syafi'i school of *fiqh* and their views on this matter dominate.

In relation to the verse on guardianship (Q. 4: 34), 'Men are the protectors and maintainers of women [*qawwam*], because Allah has given the one more (strength) than the other, and because they support them from their means,' progressive scholars argue that male guardianship is not absolute and is adjustable. Wadud (1999), alongside Azizah al-Hibri (1982), argues that the men's *qawwam* toward women can only occur if two conditions are met, as stated in the verse above, namely, the men have more means or more prominence than women and second, men spend their wealth to support women. If men fail to satisfy both conditions, they are not *qawwam* over women. Arguably, according to Khaled Abou El Fadl (2001), if a woman is the one providing financial support for the family, she is the one who is in the state of guardianship. Otherwise, if both spouses contribute to the family income, they share guardianship. It is flexible so long as the conditions stipulated in the verse are met by both partners.

One important aspect worthy of attention is that the Qur'an does not use the word 'obedience' or promote the obedience of the wife towards the husband. Many of the teachings related to women's subjugation in married life derive from secondary or tertiary sources like the Hadith and the opinions of *ulama*. The Qur'anic teachings about marital relationships promote a relationship of mutual love and satisfaction for both partners as indicated in the following verses:

> And among His Signs is this, that He created for you mates from among yourselves, that ye may dwell in tranquillity [*sakinah*] with them, and He has put love [*mawaddah*] and mercy [*rahmah*] between your (hearts): verily, in that are signs for those who reflect.
> (Q. 30: 21)

> Permitted to you, on the night of the fasts, is the approach to your wives. *They are your garments and ye are their garments.* Allah knoweth what ye used to do secretly among yourselves; but He turned to you and forgave you; so now associate with them, and seek what Allah hath ordained for you [my emphasis].
>
> (Q. 2: 187)

> O ye who believe! Ye are forbidden to inherit women against their will. Nor should ye treat them with harshness, that ye may take away part of the dower [bride price] ye have given them – except where they have been guilty of open lewdness; on the contrary *live with them on a footing of kindness and equity* [my emphasis].
>
> (Q. 4: 19)

These verses signify that the marital/sexual relationship should be built upon mutual love, respect, harmony, and fulfilment and indicate that both men and women have sexual desires that need to be fulfilled. By recognising marital sex based on mutuality, the Qur'an suggests that sex is not only for procreation but also for pleasure (Barlas 2002).

Annemarie Schimmel said that Qur'anic verse 2 (187) is an example of 'ideal gender relations' in Islam. She further explained the meaning of 'garment' in reference to ancient religious ideas. It is 'the *alter ego* of human beings [my emphasis]' (Schimmel 1992, ix):

> The garment can serve as a substitute for the person, and with a new garment one gains as it were a new personality. Furthermore, it hides the body, hinders the looking at the private parts, protects the wearer. According to this interpretation, husband and wife are so to speak each other's alter ego, and each of them protects the partner's honor. This seems to show how well the yang–yin principle works in marital relationships: husband and wife are equal in their perfect togetherness.

Asma Barlas (2002) also argues that the Qur'an does not prescribe a particular sexual identity that privileges only one sex. The Qur'an does not mention female sexuality as insatiable or passive. On the contrary, the Qur'an advises chastity for both sexes and suggests that sexual praxis should follow the moral limit prescribed in the Qur'an (Q. 24: 30–31). By applying the hermeneutical method, Barlas (2002, 25) arrived at the conclusion that the Qur'an is an egalitarian text that established the principle of equality of the sexes.

It is, then, important to provide both sides of the interpretation of texts—those that support women and those that seem to repress them—in order to provide women with a balanced knowledge, understanding, and guidance in relation to marriage and sexuality. The fact that some texts are more popular than others indicates that there are power structures that enable control of the circulation and dissemination of texts such that patriarchal norms of marriage and sexuality are sustained.

Learning from SAPA: reproductive and sexuality rights among rural Muslim women in Eastern Bandung

The SAPA Institute is an NGO established in 2005 from a small university circle discussion that focused on women's issues.[13] SAPA is located in a rural area of Eastern Bandung and aims to educate the community particularly with regard to three issues: reproductive and sexual rights, domestic violence, and economic empowerment.

During an interview on 11 July 2012, its founder and director told me that the recruitment methods employed by SAPA to attract community participation were: first, to approach community leaders and cadres; second, to visit houses and engage in conversation to address the problems faced by women in that community; and third, to promote active participation in *majlis ta'lim* so that messages about gender equality from an Islamic perspective could be heard.

Based on the issues identified in conversations, the director said that the main issues faced by women in the village were domestic violence, trafficking, maternal mortality, difficulty in accessing business capital, and lack of participation in village organisations. To discuss these issues further, SAPA then established what it called Bale Istri (Women's Shed), with regular fortnightly meetings. The number of women who participated in these meetings grew significantly, and came to include women from neighbouring villages. There are now eight villages participating in Bale Istri.

According to the director of SAPA, Islam is the basis for this empowerment because Islam is important in community life. The director said that identifying Islam as the basis for addressing issues of women's equality avoided the problem of the activists being accused of promoting a Western (feminist) agenda. She further said that discussions include understanding the meanings of Qur'anic verses and Hadith related to women's issues.

Nowadays, women can negotiate and claim their right to refuse sex under certain conditions, such as when they are unwell or forced, and this is supported by Islam. The NGO also enabled intense communication with husbands in relation to unwanted sex. The Bale Istri meetings concerning reproductive and sexual health have resulted in women becoming more aware of their rights and developing the capacity to bargain with their husbands.

This NGO attracts community participation because it not only provides information about women's issues but also skills, training, and assistance to members who are in need of help because of domestic violence and reproductive problems. Economic empowerment is also included in the training programs. Thus, women in these communities are now more ready to challenge discrimination against them and they have the ability and skills to resist. Many young women in these villages have begun to delay marriage until they reach 20 years of age, and those who are already married delay pregnancy until they reach 20 years of age.

SAPA also established Bale Laki-laki (Men's Shed) to increase men's awareness of women's issues. Although at first Bale Laki-laki gained scant attention, nowadays, more and more men participate and are concerned about women's issues. One of the director's strategies in Bale Laki-laki was to have participants map the daily division of housework between the wife and husband. Many husbands suddenly realised how their wives were overloaded with housework. In addition, the husbands also realised how this heavy burden affected their wives' health, with consequences such as miscarriages, difficult pregnancies, and even maternal death. The men who participated in Bale Laki-laki are now willing to share the housework.

SAPA became even more significant through its active participation in drafting local legislation on the health of mothers, babies and toddlers called *Perda KIBBLA* (*Peraturan Daerah tentang Kesehatan Ibu, Bayi baru lahir, Bayi dan Balita*) 2009 in Bandung district. SAPA also monitored its application in the community through establishing community-based monitoring. SAPA has made a significant contribution to empowering a rural community, particularly in relation to the reproductive and sexual health of women.

Conclusion

In this chapter, I have provided the link between certain Islamic texts and women's experience of sex within marriage. The women used certain Islamic teachings as guides and because they were considered sacred, it was clear that the teachings played an important role in shaping their sexual lives. Teachings on marriage and sexual relationships from Islamic texts are often contradictory. Unfortunately, the misogynist texts seem to be encouraged more actively than the texts that promote egalitarian relationships. *Pesantren* and *majlis ta'lim* are places that sustain the normative gender ideology in Indonesia through disseminating religious teachings. Many teachings emphasise the wife's obedience in marital relationships and thus maintain the patriarchal system through the process of knowledge construction. Women have internalised these religiously sanctioned prescriptions which have subsequently influenced their daily interactions with their husbands. Many women were not aware of the source of the teachings, because the knowledge was mostly transferred orally. Women referred to these teachings as Islamic (whether they were taken from the Qur'an, or Hadith, or were simply the opinions of *kyai*/*ustadz*) and just accepted the authority of the sayings. In formal teaching events, rarely was there time to discuss or elaborate upon the teachings or even criticise them.

Within this situation, however, there is an increasing number of *ulama* and activists who adopt a pro-female interpretation of Islamic texts, as explained above. At the community level, the SAPA Institut is a good example of an NGO that promotes women's sexual and reproductive rights from an Islamic perspective through *majlis ta'lim*. In this way a non-gender-biased interpretation is available.

Critical examination of the texts using an Islamic feminist hermeneutic approach is important in order to open the discourse to equity and social justice. The hermeneutic approach interrogates the domination of knowledge construction and distribution by certain authoritative religious powers and enhances the opportunities for other voices to contribute to the construction of knowledge and create new meanings. These critical methods address the use and abuse of Islamic teachings (see Azra 2005) that seek to preserve the status quo, and aim to end any discrimination that occurs in the name of Islam. These methods of re-reading the texts have the potential to transform Islamic social relations and practice.

Notes

1. The terms *pesantren salafiyyah* (*salaf*) should be differentiated from *pesantren salafi*. *Pesantren salafi* and the *salafi* movement follow the Wahhabi teachings of Saudi Arabia. The *salafi* movement is a fundamentalist Islamic movement which has recently gained popularity in Indonesian Islam. The *salafi* understanding of Islam is quite conservative, with an absolute and strict understanding of the Qur'an and *sunna* (Bruinessen 2008; Hasan 2007).
2. All of the *pesantren* and *kyai* names are pseudonyms.
3. For more detail and extensive discussion on *kitab kuning* used in *pesantren* in Indonesia, see Bruinessen (1990).
4. Detailed discussions of the content of these three *kitab* are provided in Chapter 3 in the section entitled Sources of knowledge about marriage and sexuality.
5. For the translation of the Qur'an I refer to Ali (2000) *The Holy Qur'an*.
6. Detailed discussion of this verse is provided in Chapter 1.
7. Detailed discussion of polygyny is provided in the section on marriage and sexuality in Islam in Chapter 1.
8. The English translation of Shahih Muslim by Nashiruddin al-Khattab (2007).
9. I use the English translation of Shahih Al-Bukhari by M. Muhsin Khan (1997).
10. This hermeneutical reading is particularly proposed by Amina Wadud (1999, 2006) and Asma Barlas (2002). Both of them offer comprehensive methodologies for reading the Qur'an hermeneutically. Detailed discussion on the hermeneutical approach is provided in the Introduction.
11. It should be checked in regard to authenticity and validity of the Hadith being reported by the Prophet.
12. *Jumhur ulama* refers to the majority opinion of *ulama* concerning certain cases which can be used as the basis for Muslims to follow. There are four law schools in Islam, thus *jumhur ulama* usually happens when three of the jurists have the same opinion and only one opposes, as in the above case, where the Syafi'i jurist dissented.
13. SAPA in Indonesian means greet.

References

Abdul Kodir, F. (2007). *Hadith and Gender Justice: Understanding the Prophetic Traditions*. Cirebon: Fahmina Institute.
Abdul Kodir, F. (2012). 'Pembacaan resiprokal terhadap isu-isu seksualitas dalam hadis' (The reciprocal reading of sexuality issues in Hadith). *Swara Rahima: Media Islam untuk Hak-hak Perempuan* (Swara Rahima: Islamic media for women's rights), 40(xii), 41–44.

Abi Ya'la Al-Maushili, Al-Imam. (1986). *Musnad Abi Ya'la. Juz VII* (A compilation of Hadith by Abi Ya'la: part VII). Beirut: Dar al-Ma'mun li Turats. Available from https://perpustakaanislamdigital.com/index.php/fp/flip/hd_msd13#book/ (Accessed 3 August 2020)

Abou El Fadl, Khaled. M. (2001). *Speaking in God's Name: Islamic Law, Authority and Women.* Oxford: One World.

Al-Bukhari, Muhammed Ibn Ismaiel. (1997). *The Translation of the Meanings of Shahih al-Bukhari: Arabic–English, vol. 7,* trans. Muhammed Muhsin Khan. Riyadh, Saudi Arabia: Darussalam, available from: https://archive.org/stream/TheTranslationOfT heMeaningsOfSahihAl-Bukhari-Arabic-English9Volumes/Sahih%20Al-Bukhari-Arabic_English_Volume-7-Ahadith-5063-5969#page/n9/mode/2up (accessed 15 January 2020).

Al-Hibri, Azizah. (1982). 'A study of Islamic herstory: Or how did we ever get into this mess?' In Al-Hibri (ed.). *Women and Islam,* 207–19. Oxford: Pergamon Press, DOI: 10.1016/0277-5395(82)90028-0.

Al-Hibri, Azizah (ed.). (1982). *Women and Islam.* Oxford: Pergamon Press.

Al-Daylami, Imam. (1987). *Firdaws al-Akhbar* (Paradise of reports). Beirut: Dar al-Kitab al-Araby.

Al-Zuhaily, Wahbah. (1985). *al-Fiqh al-Islami wa Adillatuhu* (Islamic jurisprudence and its proofs). Damascus: Dar al-Fikr.

Ali, Abdullah. Yusuf. (2000). *The Holy Qur'an.* London: Wordsworth.

Arkoun, Mohammed. (1994). *Rethinking Islam: Common Questions, Uncommon Answers.* Boulder, CO: Westview Press.

Arkoun, Mohammed. (2006). *Islam: To Reform or to Subvert?* (rev. ed.). London: Saqi Books.

Azra, Azyumardi. (2005). 'The use and abuse of Qur'anic verses in contemporary Indonesian politics.' In Abdullah Saeed (ed.), *Approaches to the Qur'an in Contemporary Indonesia,* 193–208. Oxford: Oxford University Press.

Barlas, Asma. (2002). *'Believing Women' in Islam: Unreading Patriarchal Interpretations of the Qur'an.* Austin: University of Texas Press.

Bruinessen, Martin van. (1990). '*Kitab kuning*: Books in Arabic script used in the pesantren milieu: Comments on a new collection in the KITLV library.' *Bijdragen tot de Taal-, Land- en Volkenkunde,* 146(2–3), 226–69, DOI: 10.1163/22134379-90003218.

Bruinessen, Martin van. (1994). 'Pesantren and Kitab Kuning: Continuity and Change in a Tradition of Religious Learning.' In Wolfgang Marschall (ed.), *Texts from the Islands: Oral and Written Traditions of Indonesia and the Malay World,* 121–46. Berne: The University of Berne Institute of Ethnology.

Bruinessen, Martin van. (2008). 'Traditionalist and Islamist *pesantrens* in contemporary Indonesia.' In Farish A. Noor., Yoginder Sikand, and Martin van Bruinessen (eds.), *The Madrasa in Asia: Political Activism and Transnational Linkages,* 217–45. Amsterdam: Amsterdam University Press, DOI: 10.1515/9789048501380-010.

Dawud, Abu. (2012). *Translation of Sunan Abu-Dawud,* Ahmad Hasan (trans), (11th ed.). Kalan Mahal: New Delhi, available from: https://archive.org/stream/SunanAbuDawudVol.2/Sunan%20Abu%20Dawud%2C%20vol.%203_djvu.txt (accessed 15 January 2020).

Deeb, Lara. (2010). 'Piety politics and the role of a transnational feminist analysis.' In Felippo Osella and Benjamin Soares (eds.), *Islam, Politics, Anthropology,* 107–20. West Sussex: Wiley-Blackwell, DOI: 10.1002/9781444324402.ch7.

Dhofier, Zamakhsyari. (1980). 'The pesantren tradition: A study of the role of the *kyai* in the maintenance of the traditional ideology of Islam in Java.' PhD thesis. The Australian National University, Canberra.

Doorn-Harder, Pieternella van. (2006). *Women Shaping Islam: Reading the Qur'an in Indonesia*. Urbana: University of Illinois Press.

Foucault, Michel. (1990). *The History of Sexuality, vol. I: An Introduction*. London: Penguin.

Frisk, Sylva. (2009). *Submitting to God: Women and Islam in Urban Malaysia*. Seattle, WA: University of Washington Press.

Gade, Anna M. (2004). *Perfection Makes Practice: Learning, Emotion and the Recited Qur'an in Indonesia*. Honolulu, HI: University of Hawai'i Press.

Geertz, Clifford. (1960). 'The Javanese *kijaji*: The changing role of a cultural broker.' *Comparative Studies in Society and History*, 2(2), 228–49, DOI: 10.1017/S0010417500000670.

Hamdanah.(2005). *Musim Kawin di Musim Kemarau: Studi atas Pandangan Ulama Perempuan Jember tentang Hak-Hak Reproduksi Perempuan* (Marriage season in the dry season: A study of women ulamas' perspectives on women's reproductive rights in Jember). Yogyakarta: Bigraf.

Hasan, Noorhaidi. (2007). 'The salafi movement in Indonesia: Transnational dynamics and local development.' *Comparative Studies of South Asia, Africa and the Middle East*, 27(1), 83–94, DOI: 10.1215/1089201x-2006-045.

Horikoshi, Hiroko. (1976). 'A traditional leader in a time of hange: The "kijaji" and "ulama" in West Java.' PhD thesis, University of Illinois, Urbana, Champaign.

Ilkkaracan, Pinar. (2000). 'Introduction.' In Pinar Ilkkaracan (ed.), *Women and Sexuality in Muslim Societies*, 1–15. Istanbul: Women for Women's Human Rights.

Jackson, Elisabeth and Lyn Parker. (2008). '"Enriched with knowledge": Modernisation, Islamisation and the future of Islamic education in Indonesia.' *Review of Indonesian and Malaysian Affairs*, 42(1), 21–53.

Kholifah, Siti. (2014). 'Gendered continuity and change in Javanese pesantren.' PhD thesis. Victoria University, Melbourne.

Lukens-Bull, Ronald. (2010). '*Madrasa* by any other name: *Pondok*, *pesantren*, and Islamic schools in Indonesia and larger Southeast Asian region.' *Journal of Indonesian Islam*, 4(1), 1–21, DOI: 10.15642/JIIS.2010.4.1.1-21.

Mahmood, Saba. (2001). 'Feminist theory, embodiment and the docile agent: Some reflections on the Egyptian Islamic revival.' *Cultural Anthropology*, 16(2), 202–36, DOI: 10.1525/can.2001.16.2.202.

Marcoes, Lies. (1992). 'The female preacher as a mediator in religion: A case study in Jakarta and West Java.' In Sita van Bemmelen, Madelon Djajadiningrat-Nieuwenhuis, Elspeth Locher-Scholten, and Elly Touwen-Bouwsma (eds.), *Women and Mediation in Indonesia*, 203–28. Leiden: KITLV.

Mas'udi, Masdar F. (1993). 'Perempuan di antara lembaran kitab kuning' (Women in kitab kuning). In Lies M. Marcoes-Natsir and Johan Hendrik Meuleuman (eds.), *Wanita Islam Indonesia dalam Kajian Tekstual dan Kontekstual* (Indonesian Muslim women in textual and contextual studies), 155–74. Jakarta: INIS.

Mas'udi, Masdar F. (2000). *Islam & hak-hak Reproduksi Perempuan: Dialog Fiqh Pemberdayaan* (Islam and reproductive rights: Dialog on fiqh of empowerment). Mizan: Bandung.

Millie, Julian. (2008). 'Non-specialists in the *pesantren*: The social construction of Islamic knowledge.' *Review of Indonesian and Malaysian Affairs*, 42(1), 107–24.

Millie, Julian. (2011). 'Islamic preaching and women's spectatorship in West Java.' *The Australian Journal of Anthropology*, 22, 151–69, DOI: 10.1111/j.1757-6547.2011.00132.x.

Muslim, Imam. (2007). *English Translation of Shahih Muslim*, trans. Nashiruddin al-Khattab. Riyadh. Saudi Arabia: Darussalam, available from: https://muslim-library.com/books/2018/010/en_The_Translation_of_the_Meanings_of_Sahih_Muslim_Vol_4.pdf (accessed 3 August 2020).

Muslim, Imam. (2007). *English Translation of Shahih Muslim*, trans. Nashiruddin al-Khattab. Riyadh. Saudi Arabia: Darussalam, available from: https://muslim-library.com/books/2018/010/en_The_Translation_of_the_Meanings_of_Sahih_Muslim_Vol_3.pdf (accessed 3 August 2020).

Nilan, Pamela and Prahastiwi Utari. (2008). 'Meanings of work for female media and communication workers.' In Michele Ford and Lyn Parker (eds), *Women and Work in Indonesia*, 136–54. Oxon: Routledge.

Rahardjo, Dawam (1985). *Pergulatan Dunia Pesantren: Membangun dari Bawah* (The struggle of the pesantern: Building from below). Jakarta: P3M.

Sabbah, Fatna A. (1984). *Woman in the Muslim Unconscious*. New York: Pergamon Press.

Schimmel, Annemarie. (1992). 'Foreword.' In Sachiko Murata, *The Tao of Islam: A Sourcebook of Gender Relationship in Islamic Thought*. Albany: State University of New York Press.

Sirry, Mun'in. (2010). 'The public expression of traditional Islam: The *pesantren* and civil society in post-Suharto Indonesia.' *The Muslim World*, 100, 60–77, DOI: 10.1111/j.1478-1913.2009.01302.x.

Smith, Bianca J. and Mark Woodward. (2014). *Gender and Power in Indonesian Islam: Leaders, Feminists, Sufis, and Pesantren Selves*. London: Routledge, DOI: 10.4324/9780203797518.

Srimulyani, Eka. (2007). 'Muslim women and education in Indonesia: The *pondok pesantren* experience.' *Asia Pacific Journal of Education*, 27(1), 85–99, DOI: 10.1080/02188790601145564.

Srimulyani, Eka. (2012). *Women from Traditional Islamic Educational Institutions in Indonesia: Negotiating Public Spaces*. Amsterdam: Amsterdam University Press, DOI: 10.26530/OAPEN_418531.

Wadud, Amina. (1999). *Qur'an and Woman: Rereading the Sacred Text from a Woman's Perspective*. Oxford: Oxford University Press.

Wadud, Amina. (2006). *Inside the Gender Jihad: Women Reform in Islam*. Oxford: Oneworld.

Winn, P. (2012). 'Women's *majlis taklim* and gendered religious practice in Northern Ambon.' *Intersections: Gender and Sexuality in Asia and the Pacific*, 30(November), available from: http://intersections.anu.edu.au/issue30/winn.htm (accessed 6 June 2015).

Legislation

Regional Regulation no. 8 on the Health of Mother, new born baby, infant and toddler (*Perda KIBBLA - Peraturan Daerah tentang Kesehatan Ibu, Bayi baru lahir, Bayi, dan Balita*), 2009, available from: http://jdih.bandungkab.go.id/uploads/2015/03/PERBUP-NO.-10-KIBBLA.pdf, (accessed 3 March 2020).

Conclusion

Throughout the chapters in this book I have argued that sexual perceptions and behaviours among married Muslim women in West Java are influenced in various ways by religious (Islamic) teachings. Cultural norms also influence their perceptions and behaviours. Religious teachings that refer to Islamic texts related to marriage and sexuality are derived from various Islamic sources: the Qur'an, the Hadith, the opinions of the Prophet's companions (*sahabat*) and their predecessors (*tabi'in* and *tabi'it tabi'in*), and the opinions of Muslim scholars (*ulama*). Cultural norms refer to cultural values related to marriage and sexuality in West Java in particular and in Indonesia in general. After Islam arrived in Indonesia, its teachings mingled with Indonesian cultures such that many Islamic teachings and cultural values became blended with those of Indonesia and, for many, no longer differentiable. Accordingly, in this book, Islamic teachings and cultural norms are inseparable but may be distinguishable from those of Indonesia. Indeed, the distinction between Islamic teachings and cultural norms is based on interviews I had with women, where the women themselves were unsure about the two.

I have demonstrated that religious teachings play a significant role in guiding women's perceptions and behaviour in everyday marital relationships, as explained in Chapter 3. The women acquired these teachings from various sources such as Islamic books on marriage, sex manuals, *kitab* (classical Islamic textbooks), *pengajian* (religious gatherings), and from conversations with their peers. These sources informed the women about ideal marital and sexual relationships. Several women who did not have access to *kitab* or did not have the opportunity to attend *pengajian* relied on their observations of the behaviour of their parents for their understanding of marriage. Some said that they learned only through experience. Generally, the women in this study knew very little about sexuality. The normative gender ideology prescribes that women be sexually passive in marriage and obedient to their husbands.

The Office of Religious Affairs (KUA) does provide a 'pre-marital information session,' for about-to-be-married men and women, but it was seen by many as ineffective because it gave only general information relating to married life in accordance with the normative gender ideology. If it was properly implemented, this program has the potential to be important in providing knowledge to couples prior to marriage, and more could be done, for example, to collaborate with other departments such as the Ministry of Health (*Kementrian Kesehatan*) and the Ministry of Law and Human Rights (*Kementrian Hukum dan Ham*) to inform prospective married couples about reproductive and legal aspects of marriage.

Since marriage in Indonesia is a social and religious norm—as part of *ibadah*—the women in the study looked forward to achieving this goal. They felt happy preparing for their marriage but at the same time they felt anxious. As explained in Chapter 4, finding the right person to be one's *jodoh* (soul mate) is complicated. Apart from physical attraction, wealth, and good character, the women looked for religious knowledge in a prospective partner. However, in many cases, women accepted a candidate who did not match their ideals. In reality, their own criteria for a husband were not much help for some women. Age and parental and social pressure to marry forced some women to accept the first available candidate who proposed. Equally important though, some of the women were able to choose and decide which partner they wanted to marry. With the growing tendency towards self-choice and romantic love, some couples managed a more 'democratic relationship' (Giddens 1992) than before. During the courtship period, the women were expected to maintain their chastity and not engage in pre-marital sex. Many women were aware of the danger of *zina* (illicit sex) and managed to stay away from it. In reality, however, some women could not avoid the pressure from their boyfriends or fiancés to engage in pre-marital sex.

Several women knew their husbands for only a short time prior to marriage. Several others had been friends for quite a long time before they married. A consequence of a short period of courtship was often difficulty in adjusting to marriage, especially in the first years. In Chapter 5, five differences were identified as factors associated with this difficulty, even for those who had known their husbands for quite a long time, namely, family origin and upbringing, cultural background, age gap, class gap, and personal character.

These factors also influenced the management of the household. All the men and women in this study believed that housework and child rearing were a woman's responsibility, while earning the household income was a man's job. Because of this division of labour, rarely did husbands help with the housework. Even in the cases of unemployed husbands and/or working wives, the husbands did not share the housework load. Only a few women managed to negotiate a distribution of housework with their husbands. Intense communication and understanding between the partners in regard to household arrangements was necessary to avoid tension and conflict in marriage.

Many researchers have documented changes in marriage patterns in Indonesia in the second half of the twentieth century (Jones, Hull, and

Mohamad 2011). Women, they argue, are increasingly choosing to marry at a later age, to make their own decisions about their marriage partner, to engage in romantic relationships, and even to remain single. However, it is still predominantly husbands who have more authority in marriage. Marital relationships in Indonesia are still characterised by a hierarchical relationship between wife and husband—a relationship that is supported by the state through the Indonesian Marriage Law of 1974 and religious prescription particularly (*al-rijalu qawwamuna ala al-nisa*, Q. 4: 34), both of which are strongly adhered to by Indonesians.[1] Many husbands of the female participants in my study showed their authority over their wives in matters such as prohibiting them from working, preventing them from using contraception, and forcing them to engage in sex.

The hierarchical nature of marital relationships extends to the sexual relationship between wife and husband. From the descriptions of women's experiences of marital sexual relations in Chapter 6, we can see that in most cases husbands still control wives' sexuality—when to have sex and how to do it. The man is still the one who expresses his love for the woman, the man is still the one who asks for a date, and the man is still the one who initiates sexual activity. Several women did indicate that they initiated sex, but very rarely. This suggests that there will always be exceptional practices among couples; however, the general norm is that the male takes the lead.

Many scholars who have done research on sex and sexuality in Indonesia (Bennett 2005; Blackwood and Wieringa 2007; Jennaway 2002; Parker 2008; Utomo 2003) have argued that women's sexuality is influenced by the normative gender ideology. This is also true for my female participants. The above-mentioned researchers focused on single women's sexuality, arguing that the normative gender ideology requires single women in Indonesia to contain their sexual desire and guard their chastity and virginity. My book has focused on women's sexual relationships within married life, but I found that married women, too, were indoctrinated by the normative gender ideology of 'good wife and mother.'

There are two main indicators of the sexual standard for married Muslim woman in Indonesia, namely, submission and servitude. The ideology of women's submissiveness and servitude in married life is strongly justified by religious prescription. The concept of *istri yang ta'at* (an obedient wife) lingers in women's minds when they describe the ideal of the good wife. The concept of *ta'at* (obedience) is given prominence as the core principle in married women's relationships with their husbands.

Marriage for a woman was also about serving her husband. The women in the study, whether willing or not, were expected to be ready at any time to attend to their husbands' sexual needs. This prescription is strongly influenced by Islamic teaching which makes women reluctant to refuse their husbands' sexual advances for fear of religious sanctions.

As the only sanctioned sexual relationship in Indonesia, marriage should be a place where women can express and explore sexual desires, which were repressed and forbidden when they were single. In reality, this is not easy to do, not only because they have already been trained not to express their sexuality but also because women find themselves subject to another strong norm concerning their sexuality in marriage—sex as a duty. Most of the female participants in this study described marital sexual relationships as their duty and their husbands' right. There is significant pressure on women when sex is seen as a duty instead of a right. In seeing sex as a right, the women would have the opportunity to discuss, negotiate, and express their own sexual desires so they could experience pleasurable sex. In contrast, if sex is a duty, a woman focuses on her husband's satisfaction and tends to ignore her own sexual needs, which are considered unimportant compared to servicing her husband.

The experience of sexual initiation on the first night after marriage, when couples are expected to have their first sexual encounter, varied among women. Most women felt fear and anxiety. Lack of information about sex (how to do it) and negative assumptions, such as that women experience pain in their first sexual encounter, increased their anxiety. However, the women were familiar with the Islamic etiquette of intercourse prior to getting married. Included in the steps ordained prior to intercourse is *mukaddimah* (introduction), where it is recommended that the husband engages in foreplay before having sex. This foreplay is necessary in order that a wife can experience an orgasm together with her husband. However, many of the husbands of wives in this study ignored this step.

Included in the concept of submission and servitude is the expectation of a wife's unconditional and eternal sexual availability. Because of this belief, women were reluctant to refuse their husbands sex whether they were willing or unwilling, and whether they enjoyed it or not. Religious teachings strongly influenced the understanding that refusing a husband's need to have sex is associated with sin. In the study there was also the underlying tension that refusing a husband results in being cursed, and is therefore *pamali* (taboo). Women created meaning by viewing their own sacrifice as a form of religious devotion and perceived their servitude as *ibadah* (worshipping God) that would gain them rewards in the afterlife.

There are different attitudes towards sex in marriage between women and men. For several women, sex was not that important in marriage compared to other aspects such as children and fulfilling the everyday needs of the household. Only a few mentioned that sex was an important aspect of married life. During the interviews, some women acknowledged that they had sexual desires. Unlike their husbands, many women associated sexual desire with emotional intimacy and a close relationship that did not necessarily culminate in sexual intercourse. Women's experiences of sexual desire were varied and were influenced by many factors such as their financial situation, fatigue, their husbands' abusive behaviour, reproductive status (pregnancy, childbirth, and menopause), their husbands' infidelity, and frequency of sexual activity. These factors variously caused women's sexual desire to increase or decrease. For men, sex was important in marriage and lack of it could be used, in many cases, as an excuse for divorce and the freedom to engage in another marriage. Put simply, men associated intimacy with the sex act.

Several women in this study experienced sexual abuse associated with domestic violence, in varying degrees from minor to severe. Unexpectedly, I found that some women who experienced domestic violence did not wish to get divorced and instead chose to stay in their abusive marriages. At the same time, they did not try to have discussions with their husbands to stop or decrease the violent behaviour. They argued that life after divorce would not guarantee them better conditions. Those women who did eventually divorce after leaving their violent marriages noted their changed attitudes: (1) self-awareness and transformed self-consciousness, such that a woman could empower herself in order that she could take responsibility for her own fate and avoid men's objectification; (2) self-reliance, and the ability to increase their skills or seek further education to improve their living standards and to achieve more; (3) self-reflexivity, to avoid making the same mistake by being careful in choosing a future marriage partner.

Religious texts provide two sets of teachings about sex in marriage for women, as a duty and as a right, as described in Chapter 8. One Hadith, unanimously popular among women, which emphasises sex in married life as a wife's duty and a husband's right, takes precedence over the Qur'anic message on mutual sexual satisfaction between wife and husband. The Qur'anic text suggests that sex in marriage is not the wife's duty but should be mutually shared and mutually fulfilling. Presenting both texts and analysing their validity is important in providing a balanced understanding of sexual guidance in Islam and promoting a positive attitude towards sex in married life by acknowledging women's sexual desires. Giving prominence to both texts avoids hiding one text behind another or favouring certain texts that privilege one gender over another.

In many Muslim societies, including Indonesia, there has been a shift away from giving authority to the texts towards the opinions of individual Muslim scholars. Many individuals rely more heavily on certain religious scholars' opinions than the actual text of the Qur'an as their primary source. Data showed that many women who acquired Islamic knowledge from *pesantren* or *majlis ta'lim* referred heavily to the opinion of its *kyai* or preachers and failed to acknowledge whether those opinions were taken from the Qur'an or Hadith or were simply the scholars' opinions. This reflects the idea that the transmission of Islamic knowledge in Indonesia is an oral tradition. Accordingly, as this book has also revealed, *pesantren* and *majlis ta'lim* contribute significantly to the dissemination of texts relating to marriage and sexual relations for women. Thus, it is important to provide gender sensitivity training to *mubaligh* (male preachers) and *mubalighah* (female preachers) who preach in *majlis ta'lim*, as well as to leaders of *pesantren* (*kyai*). This effort has already been initiated by several NGOs such as P3M, FK3, and Rahima who provide gender sensitivity training among students in *pesantren,* among the *penghulu* (marriage registrars) and among *mubalighah*. These programs should be recognised for their work and they need further support from the government.

The future of marital sexual relationships: breaking the silence

Apart from the repression of sexual desire experienced by women in their marriages, agency was exercised by women in their everyday lives as a survival strategy as explained in Chapter 7. In reality, the women did have various strategies they employed to excuse or exempt themselves from having sex with their husbands and a few women managed to discuss with their husbands their preferences so that sex could be pleasurable for them both. Four women were notably able to exercise agency in this area. Heterosexual relationships are not always based on domination/subordination, but can also offer the recognition and fulfilment of women's desires and pleasures. Some women are able to discuss their sexual preferences and negotiate their experiences of sexual pleasure with their husbands, but reports of this are very rare. The strategies used by the women to avoid sex included falling asleep, caring for the children, sleeping in a child's room, or wrapping themselves tightly around the lower half of their bodies to prevent access to their genital area. However, the belief that sex is a wife's duty was strongly embedded in each woman's mind, so she often felt guilty when avoiding sexual activity.

A few women suggested that while having sex with their husbands, they were aiming to achieve pleasurable sex for themselves. Four women argued that a husband should not care solely for his own satisfaction but also for his wife's. They told me that women also have sexual desires and deserve to experience pleasurable sex. These women's ability to negotiate was a good sign of a road opening up towards mutual recognition and mutual satisfaction in marital sexual relationships. Although only a few women had this opinion, they are significant because they not only resisted common beliefs concerning married women's sexuality but also privately demanded equal recognition in their sexual relationships.

In being able to discuss matters with their husbands, these women negotiated their sexual preferences and had the opportunity to build understanding and respect. By exercising agency, the women had the capacity to resist inequality in sexual relationships. The experiences expressed by four women in the study signals possibilities for changes in marital sexual relationships towards mutual recognition of desire and pleasure in marriage. Nevertheless, changes in sexual relations will not be possible unless men are willing to participate and support the changes. Mutual recognition of desire and pleasure in marriage is a good way to start building marital sexual relationships beyond domination, with two people relinquishing self-interest to form gender-equal sexual relations through 'meaningful consent and mutuality' (Ali 2006, 151). This ideal marital and sexual relationship is supported by Qur'anic verses on marriage where God 'created for you mates from among yourselves, that ye may dwell in tranquility with them, and He has put love and mercy between your [hearts]' (Q. 30: 21), with an equal sexual relationship being described as: 'They [wives] are your garment and ye are their garments' (Q. 2: 187). Thus, 'live with them on a footing of kindness and equity' (Q. 4: 19).

During the interviews, women emphasised that they were more influenced by Islamic prescriptions on marriage and sexual relations than cultural values. Islam in Sunda is quite strong. The people of West Java are identified as being Sundanese as well as being Muslim (Kahmad 2006; Newland 2000). Although in some areas ritual ancestral practices are still performed, their significance has faded away in later generations. With the Islamic revival that has gained great momentum in contemporary Indonesia, Islam is now incorporated into many aspects of social life, for example, the ubiquity of Islamic symbols and increasing public piety (Fealy 2008; Hefner 1997). This revival was evident among my participants, many of whom wanted to be identified as being guided more by Islam in their marital and sexual relationships than as preserving cultural values. The women believed that religious guidance has a higher authoritative affect than cultural norms, as it is considered to be sacred. The divine aspect of religious teaching leaves a deep psychological impact on women's experience of their relationship: their obedience, hope, and faith. Many associate sexual relations with *ibadah* for which they will receive rewards in the afterlife. Thus, although they experience unwanted and unpleasurable sex, they invest in it for their future happiness in the life to come.

In fact, the divinity of Islamic texts applies only to the Qur'an which is believed to be the verbatim revelation of God. Thus, Muslims should regard the Qur'an as the highest authoritative text in Islam. Texts other than the Qur'an, such as the Hadith, should be critically analysed because although they are attributed to the Prophet, they were written three decades after His death. Special attention should be drawn to the possible fabrication of the Prophet's sayings, the authenticity of the report in terms of the credibility of the person (*sanad*) who narrated the Hadith and its content (*matan*). Other 'texts' referred to during the interviews included the opinions of various *ulama* and/or their commentaries, in oral or written form. It is important to examine the personal and political interests behind the production and construction of the texts. In Muslim societies, including Indonesia, religious texts are frequently used to sustain power. It is because of this that the hermeneutical approach to Islamic texts finds its significance.

The hermeneutical approach aims to analyse the text not merely through its grammatical structure, but equally by paying attention to the socio-historical context of the production of the texts. Another important aspect of the hermeneutical approach is the idea of intertextuality, which means that texts in Islam are interconnected. No text is isolated. A comprehensive understanding of texts in Islam requires treating the texts as a whole. The

Islamic feminist hermeneutical approach to Islamic texts critiques patriarchal readings of texts—readings that are used to justify men's superiority over women.

It is important to provide a better understanding of women's sexuality so that women know what happens to their bodies and what they should do when their body changes, for instance, when they begin menstruating. Positive attitudes towards women's bodies are also significant in promoting women's hygiene and health. In writing this book, I have contributed to the body of knowledge surrounding the religious construction of female sexuality in Indonesia, with a particular emphasis on married women's sexuality. The book also contributes new knowledge on women's understanding of their sexuality and their sexual practices.

I am grateful to the women who participated in this study. In my opinion, they are strong and resilient in facing their marital hardships and applying their own strategies for survival in the patriarchal society prevalent in West Java. In the research associated with writing this book, some women demonstrated that in resisting their unjust circumstances they were empowered to create a more stable life. Initially, the research process was hard and uncertain for them; the women needed courage to speak and act, and they needed support for their decision-making. However, in the end, these women felt good about speaking out and breaking the burden of silence they had carried for so long.

Note

1. A bill on Family Resilience has been drafted and lodged in the House of Representatives that will strengthen the division of labour between husband and wife in the family. In fact, the content of the draft seems to overlap with other existing laws and regulations. The reaction to this draft has been submitted by Komnas Perempuan (2020). (National commission on violence against women). See *Pernyataan Sikap Komnas Perempuan Tentang Polemik RUU Ketahanan Keluarga Fokuskan Pembahasan Legislasi Nasional Untuk Kebutuhan Hukum yang Mendesak* (Statement of the National Commission on Violence Against Women regarding the Polemic on the Family Resilience Bill to Focus on the discussion of national legislation for urgent legal needs), 24 February 2020, available from: https://drive.google.com/file/d/19HzRwNfqB4SsJdcRt3xuHWvqBnfgQjqq/view (accessed 3 March 2020).

References

Ali, Kecia. (2006). *Sexual Ethics and Islam: Feminist Reflections on Qur'an, Hadith, and Jurisprudence*. Oxford: One World.

Bennett, Linda Rae. (2005). *Women, Islam and Modernity: Single Women, Sexuality and Reproductive Health in Contemporary Indonesia*. London: Routledge Curzon, DOI: 10.4324/9780203391389.

Blackwood, Evelyn and Saskia E. Wieringa (2007). 'Globalization, sexuality and silence: Women's sexualities and masculinities in an Asian contexts.' In Saskia E.

Wieringa, Evelyn Blackwood, and A Bhaiya (eds.), *Women's Sexualities and Masculinities in Globalizing Asia*, 1–22. New York: Palgrave Macmillan, DOI: 10.1057/9780230604124.

Fealy, Greg. (2008). 'Consuming Islam: Commodified religion and aspirational pietism in contemporary Indonesia.' In Greg Fealy and Sally White (eds.), *Expressing Islam: Religious Life and Politics in Indonesia*, 15–39. Pasir Panjang: Institute of Southeast Asian Studies, DOI: 10.1355/9789812308528-006.

Giddens, Anthony. (1992). *The Transformation of Intimacy: Sexuality, Love and Eroticism in Modern Societies*. Cambridge: Polity Press.

Hefner, Robert W. (1997). 'Islam in an era of nation-states: Politics and religious renewal in Muslim Southeast Asia.' In Robert W. Hefner and Patricia Horvatich (eds.), *Islam in an Era of Nation-States: Politics and Religious Renewal in Muslim Southeast Asia*, 3–40. Honolulu, HI: University of Hawai'i Press, DOI: 10.1515/9780824863029-004.

Jennaway, Megan. (2002). *Sisters and Lovers: Women and Desires in Bali*. Lanham, MD: Rowman & Littlefield.

Jones, Gavin W., Terence H. Hull, and Maznah Mohamad. (2011). 'Marriage trends in Insular Southeast Asia: Their economic and socio-cultural dimension.' In Gavin W. Jones, Terence H. Hull, and Maznah Mohamad (eds), *Changing Marriage Patterns in Southeast Asia: Economic and Socio-Cultural Dimensions*, 1–10. London: Routledge.

Kahmad, Dadang. (2006). 'Agama Islam dan budaya Sunda' (Islamic religion and Sundanese culture). In Ajip Rosidi, H. Edi S. Ekadjati, and A. Chaedar Alwasilah (eds.), *Konferensi International Budaya Sunda* (International conference of Sundanese culture), vol. I. Bandung: Yayasan Kebudayaan Rancage.

Komnas Perempuan (2020). (National commission on violence against women). *Pernyataan Sikap Komnas Perempuan Tentang Polemik RUU Ketahanan Keluarga Fokuskan Pembahasan Legislasi Nasional Untuk Kebutuhan Hukum yang Mendesak* (Statement of the National Commission on Violence Against Women regarding the Polemic on the Family Resilience Bill to Focus on the discussion of national legislation for urgent legal needs), 24 February 2020, available from: https://drive.google.com/file/d/19HzRwNfqB4SsJdcRt3xuHWvqBnfgQjqq/view (accessed 3 March 2020).

Newland, Lynda. (2000). 'Under the banner of Islam: Mobilising religious identities in West Java.' *The Australian Journal of Anthropology*, 11(2), 199–222, DOI: 10.1111/j.1835-9310.2000.tb00056.x.

Parker, Lyn. (2008). 'Theorising adolescent sexualities in Indonesia – Where "something different happens".' *Intersections: Gender and Sexuality in Asia and the Pacific*, 18(October), available from: http://intersections.anu.edu.au/issue18/parker.htm (accessed 27 April 2011).

Utomo, Iwu Dwisetyani. (2003). 'Reproductive health education in Indonesia: School versus parents' roles in providing sexuality information.' *Review of Indonesian and Malaysian Affairs*, 37(1), 107–34.

Legislation

Bill on Family Resilience, 2020 (Rancangan Undang-Undang Ketahanan Keluarga), available from: http://www.dpr.go.id/uu/detail/id/413 (accessed 3 March 2020).

Glossary

Arabic (A.); Indonesian (Ind.); Sundanese (S.); Bugis (B.); Lombok (L.)

'alaqa (A.) a leech-like clot
'arrijalu qawwamuna ala nisa' (A.) man is in charge of woman
'awra (A.) the body parts that should be covered from public sight under Islamic law
'azl (A.) coitus interruptus
'iddah (A.) waiting period after divorce or the death of the spouse
'uyun (A.) eyes
aabat (A.) to refuse
adat (Ind.) custom
agresif (Ind.) sexually active
Agustusan (Ind.) Indonesian Independence Day celebration, 17 August
ahl kitab (A.) Christian and Jews; people of the Book
ajengan (S.) leader of the *pesantren*
akad (Ind.) contract
akad nikah (Ind.) marriage contract
akhlak/adab (Ind.) morality/etiquette
aku berkuasa (Ind.) I have power
Allahumma jannibna syaithan wa jannibi syaithan ma razaqtana … (A.) O God, protect us from Satan and keep Satan away from the children You grant us …
ammaling-maling (B.) intense feelings of love and intimacy
anak mami (Ind.) dependent on his mother
anak shaleh/shalehah (Ind./A.) good child/ren
aneh (Ind.) weird
apél (Ind.) a man visits a woman in her house
aqidah (A.) the belief system
asbab al-nuzul (A.) the specific socio-historical context following the revelation of the Qur'an
aurat (Ind.) the body parts that should be covered from public sight under Islamic law

awewe mah dulang ti nande (S.)   women are like a big rice bowl waiting to be filled
awewe mah pondok lengkah (S.)   women's footsteps are short

babat (S.)   social equivalence
balagan (S.)   group reading
banci (Ind.)   transgender
bandungan (S.)   *majlis ta'lim*, listening
basa kasar (S.)   coarse language
basa lemes (S.)   refined language
bebet (S.)   personal character
beda kepala, beda pemikiran (Ind.)   different head, different opinion
berbadan tegap (Ind.)   good physical appearance
berdoa (Ind.)   to pray
berhubungan (Ind.)   having sex
berhubungan badan (Ind.)   to have a body relationship
berhutang budi (Ind.)   indebted
berjodoh (Ind.)   destined to be matched
bersetubuh (Ind.)   to become one body
biar mamah nu ngageol (S.)   let me do the move
bibit (S.)   family background
Bimas Bimbingan Masyarakat Islam (Ind.)   Islamic Guidance division
bingung (Ind.)   puzzled
bissu (B.)   androgynous shamans
bobogohan (S.)   dating
bobot (S.)   economic capability
bodoh (Ind.)   ignorant
bogoh (S.)   romantic love
buku nikah (Ind.)   marriage book

cabul (Ind.)   lewd
calabai (B.)   transgender males
calalai (B.)   transgender females
cinta (Ind.)   romantic love
cinta monyet (Ind.)   puppy love
cocok (Ind.)   suitability
curhat curahan hati (Ind.)   lit. to overflow one's heart; pour out their feelings

da'a (A.)   to invite someone politely and with good manners
dakwah (A.)   propagation
dalil (A.)   religious argument; proof-texts
demi Allah (Ind.)   I swear to God
didawamkan (A.)   routine; regular
diin (A.)   religion

dilaknat (Ind.) cursed
dilalah al-dilalah (A.) the meaning of meaning
dingin-dingin saja (Ind.) cold
disundut rokok (S./Ind.) to poke with burning cigarettes
dla'if (A.) weak/unreliable
do'a (A.) prayers
do'a-do'a mustajab (A.) the accepted supplications
dosa (Ind.) sin
dua anak cukup (Ind.) two were enough
dzu-mahram (A.) a woman's relatives that are categorised as *muhrim* (someone it is forbidden to marry)
dzurratun nasihin (A.) the compilation of advice

estetika (Ind.) aesthetic
eta (S.) 'that'

faddala (A.) strength; preference
faidah (A.) virtue
fasakh (A.) annulment of the marriage for reasons such as failure to fulfil marriage requirements or other circumstances deemed harmful to the marriage.
fiqh (A.) Islamic jurisprudence
fitnah (A.) gossip associated with illicit intimacy; social disorder
fitrah (A.) human nature

ganteng (Ind.) handsome
gedebog cau (S.) dead banana trunk
gingiapeun (S.) shocking
gusl (A.) obligatory bath

hajatan (S.) wedding or male circumcision celebrations
hal seperti itu (Ind.) 'something like that'
hijab (A.) Islamic veil
hirabah (A.) forcibly taking; highway robbery
hoyong teu? (S.) do you want it?
huap lingkung (S.) feeding each other
hubungan seks (Ind.) sexual relationship
hubungan (Ind.) to have a relationship; bond

ibadah (A.) part of worship; religious duty
idribu (A.) to beat lightly
ijab and qabul (A.) offer and acceptance
ijab kabul (Ind.) marriage contract; offer and acceptance
ikhlas (A.) acceptance
ikrah (A.) duress

inkah (n-k-h) or tazwij (z-w-j) (A.)   sexual intercourse (original meaning); marriage contract
istikharoh (A.)   a prayer for seeking guidance
istri mah dulang ti nande (S.)   woman should always wait for the husband's instruction
istri yang ta'at (Ind.)   an obedient wife
itu (Ind.)   that
iwadh (A.)   financial compensation

jalan-jalan (Ind.)   walking around
jamal (A.)   beauty
jamu (Ind.)   herbal concoctions
janda (Ind.)   divorcee and widow
jender (Ind.)   gender
jenis kelamin (Ind.)   lit. genitalia, sex
jilbab (A.)   Islamic headscarf
jodo, pati, bagja, cilaka kagungan Gusti Allah (S.)   soul-mates, death, happiness, and accidents are in God's command
jodoh ada di tangan Tuhan (Ind.)   *jodoh* is in the hands of God
jodoh (Ind.)   soul-mate
jomlo (Ind.)   without a partner
jorok (Ind.)   dirty; indecent
jumhur ulama (A.)   the majority opinion of *ulama*

kabungbulengan (S.)   lovesick
kafa'ah (A.)   equivalence
kahyangan (Ind.)   celestial world
kaku (Ind.)   stiffness
kaku (Ind.)   uncomfortable
kalau sudah jodoh tidak akan lari ke mana (Ind.)   when it is destined to be united, nothing can prevent them from being united
kamar kost (Ind.)   rented rooms
kantor catatan sipil (Ind.)   civil registration office
Kantor Urusan Agama (Ind.)   Office of Religious Affairs
kasihan (Ind.)   pity
kawin gantung (Ind.)   suspended marriage
kawin liar (Ind.)   wild marriage
kaya (Ind.)   wealthy
kebobolan (Ind.)   broken into; penetrated
kecamatan (Ind.)   sub-district
keluarga sakinah (Ind./A.)   harmonious marriage
kemaslahatan akhirat (Ind.)   heavenly welfare
kemaslahatan dunia (Ind.)   earthly wellbeing
kendang (S.)   drum
kepala rumah tangga (Ind.)   breadwinner and head of the family

keruwetan (Ind.) complexities
ketegangan (Ind.) tensions
keterbukaan (Ind.) level of openness
kewalahan (Ind.) frantic
khalifah (A.) successor/vicegerent on Earth
khifadl (A.) circumcision
khitan (A.) circumcision
khuluʻ (A.) lit. compensation; dissolution of marriage requested by the wife with the husband's consent, by giving the husband certain compensation
kikindeuwan (S.) lover
kitab fiqh (A.) book of Islamic jurisprudence
kitab kuning (Ind.) classical Islamic textbooks
kitab uqud al lujayn (A.) book of *uqud al-lujayn* (two-silver ties)
kitab/bab al-nikah (A.) chapter/section on marriage
kuda renggong (Ind.) a dancing horse; traditional cultural performance
kufuʻ (A.) compatible; equivalence
kyai (Ind.) leader of the *pesantren*, preacher

laʻana (A.) to curse
laku (Ind.) marriageable
lamaran (Ind.) marriage proposal
libas (A.) garment; clothing
lillahi taʻala (A.) all the matter surrendered to God
lunas (Ind.) paid

maal (A.) wealth
madzhab (A.) four schools of law
mafhum mukhalafah (A.) contrary understanding; divergent meaning
mahar (A.) bride price; payment from groom to bride
mahram (A.) persons one is forbidden from marrying
majlis taʻlim (A.) women's religious study gatherings
majmuʻ syarief (A.) the compilation of the respectable
makruma (A.) a noble act; honourable
malam Jumʻat (Ind.) Thursday night
malam minggu (Ind.) Saturday night
malam pertama (Ind.) 'first night'
malam zafaf (Ind./A.) the wedding night
malas (Ind.) lazy
malu (Ind.) shame, shy
mandi wajib (Ind.) taking a bath as a symbol of purification
mas kawin (Ind.) bride price; payment from groom to bride
matan (A.) content of Hadith
mati (Ind.) died
mawaddah (A.) love

Glossary 231

mawaddah wa rahmah (A.) love and mercy
melahirkan anak-anak yang shaleh (Ind.) to have good children
melakukan 'hal itu' (Ind.) to do 'that thing'
melampaui batas (Ind.) out of bounds
memaafkan (Ind.) forgiveness
mendengarkan (Ind.) listening
mengalah (Ind.) to give in
menimpali (Ind.) contribute
menstabilkan syahwat (Ind.) stabilise the sex drive
menyatukan dua kepala itu susah banget (Ind.) it is difficult to unite two heads
midang (L.) customary courtship in a woman's natal home,
midang (S.) exhibit, good performance; active participation; or to go about for pleasure
milk nikah (A.) the husband's exclusive dominion over his wife
milk wath' (A.) a permissible sexual enjoyment
milk (A.) ownership; dominion; control
mimpi basah (Ind.) wet dreams
minder (Ind.) inferior
mitra sejajar (Ind.) equal partner
mu'amalah (A.) social action
mu'minin (A.) believers
mubaligh (A.) male preachers
mubalighah (A.) female preachers
mubtadi' (A.) beginners
mudah tersinggung (Ind.) easily upset
mudgha (A.) a morsel of flesh
muhrim (A.) close relatives of the opposite sex
mula'abah (A.) foreplay
muqaddimah (A.) lit. introduction; foreplay
murinding (S.) creepy
mushala (A.) praying hall
musyrikun (A.) those who worship gods other than the one God
musyrikun (A.) a worshipper of idols
muta'ally (A.) advanced learners
mutawassith (A.) intermediate students

nafkah (Ind.) maintenance
nahwu (A.) syntax studies
nakal (Ind.) naughty
nasb (A.) lineage
nasib (Ind.) fate
neundeun omong (S.) entrusting a message
ngadagel, ngadalil jeung ngadumel (S.) to make jokes, to use appropriate scriptural quotations, and to voice social protest

ngalap barakah (S.) to gain divine good fortune
ngalogat (S.) annotating the text word by word
nganjang (S.) to pay a visit
ngaos (S.) to recite
ngawayuh (S.) polygyny
nifas (A.) bleeding after giving birth
nikah bawah tangan (Ind.) underhand marriage
nikah massal (Ind.) mass wedding
nikah secara agama (Ind.) religiously accepted marriage
nikah siri (Ind.) a marriage conducted secretly; secret marriage; unregistered marriage
nikah syiri secret marriage (different pronounciation of different area)
nikah (A.) marriage; sexual intercourse (*wath', dlom'*); the marriage contract
nisaukum hartsun lakum (A.) 'your wives are as a tilth unto you (to cultivate)' (Q. 2: 223)
nushuz (A.) ill-conduct
nutfa (A.) sperm
nya kitu wae lah, neng (S.) something like that, dear
nyaah (S.) affection
nyai (S.) the *kyai's* wife
nyawer (S.) sprinkling rice, turmeric and coins as blessings for good fortune
nyeureuhan (from seureuh, lit. betel leaf) (S.) symbolic acceptance
nyunah (A./S.) taken from *sunnah*, and is a way of referring to the practice of the Prophet

orang awam (Ind.) non-specialists

pacaran backstreet (Ind.) secret courtship
pacaran modern (Ind.) modern courtship practices
pacaran (Ind.) courtship
pahala (Ind.) reward from God for every good deed
pamali (S.) taboo
pangaosan (Ind pengajian) (S.) religious gathering
pangaosan ibu-ibu (S./Ind.) *majlis ta'lim*
pangaosan rutin (S./Ind.) regular religious gathering
pasar kaget (Ind.) temporary market
pasrah (Ind.) to accept him submissively; compliance; to accept things the way they are
pemaaf (Ind.) forgiving
pemanasan (Ind.) stimulation
pembantu petugas pencatat nikah (Ind.) marriage registrar's assistant
pengajian (Ind.) religious gathering
penghulu (Ind.) person in charge of conducting a marriage contract; marriage celebrant

perawan tua (Ind.) old maid
pesantren (Ind.) Islamic boarding school
pesantren khalaf (Ind./A.) modern Islamic boarding school
pesantren mahasiswa (Ind.) university student *pesantren*
pesantren salaf (Ind./A.) traditional Islamic boarding school
plong (Ind.) free
posisi biasa (Ind.) ordinary position; missionary position
posyandu (Ind.) health service post
puasa (Ind.) fasting
puber kedua (Ind.) a second puberty
pupuh (S.) different stanza forms

qanitat (A.) devoutly obedient
qawwam (A.) protect and support
qawwamun 'ala (A.) protectors and maintainers of
qiro'ah mubadalah (A.) a reciprocal reading

rahmah (A.) mercy
rapalan (S.) marriage contract ceremony
Reformasi era (Ind.) reform era
rumah kontrakan (Ind.) rented houses

sabar (A.) patience
safinatun najah (A.) book of Islamic jurisprudence
sahabat (Ind.) the Prophet's companions
sakinah (A.) tranquillity
sakit hati (Ind.) heartbroken; frustrated
sakit (Ind.) ill
salafiyyah pesantren (A./Ind.) traditional Islamic boarding school
salafiyyah (A.) taken from the word *salaf*: 'the righteous ancestor'; the first three generations after the Prophet; pesantren that continue to studying the classical Islamic textbooks known as *kitab kuning*
sanad (A.) chain of transmissions of Hadith
santri (Ind.) student
santri putri (Ind.) female student
sapu lidi (Ind.) broomstick
Satan (A.) evil
sedekah (Ind.) alms
sederhana (Ind.) simple
segan (Ind.) restraint
seksualitas (Ind.) sexuality
selingkuh, nyeleweng (Ind.) having an affair
sepadan (Ind.) equivalence
serba salah (Ind.) confused
seserahan (S.) assigning

setengah hati (Ind.) half-heartedly
shahih (A.) valid; reliable report
shalat (A.) praying/to pray
shalihaat (A.) righteous women
sharaf (A.) inflection studies
shighat taklik talak (A.) three conditions for the annulment of marriage
sholawatan (Ind.) prayers containing praise for the Prophet Muhammad
sikatutui (B.) mutual respect
sinden (S.) singer
siraman rohani (Ind.) spiritual cleansing
siri (B.) family honour
siri (A.) secret
sirrun-sirri (A.) secret
sorogan (S.) individual reading
subuh (Ind.) morning prayer
sudah terlanjur (Ind.) it was too late
suka (Ind.) liking
sukun (A.) tranquillity; free from worry
Sundanese tembang (S.) sung verse
sungkeman (Ind.) getting the blessing
sunna (A.) recommended
Sunnah (A.) practised by the Prophet Muhammad
surah (A.) chapter of the Qur'an
surga dunia (Ind.) pleasurable sex

ta'at (S.) obedience
tabi'in and tabi'it tabi'in (A.) predecessors; generations after the companion of the Prophet
tafsir (A.) interpretation
Tafsir al-Qur'an (A.) Qur'anic exegesis; interpretation
Takdir (Ind.) destiny; human fate
takut (Ind.) fear
takut berdosa (Ind.) afraid of sin
taqwa (A.) righteousness
tarekat (Ind.) the Sufi order
tata krama (Ind.) manners
taubat (A.) repentance
tawhid (A.) the oneness of God, Islamic monotheism
tegang (Ind.) tense
terpaksa (Ind.) grudging agreement
thahara (A.) perform cleanliness; purification
thalaq (A.) lit. release; divorce
thalaq ba'in (A.) irrevocable divorce
thalaq raj'i (A.) revocable divorce
tidak neko-neko (Ind.) normal or uncomplicated

tidak rela (Ind.) protested
tidak sopan (Ind.) coarse and inappropriate
tidak/belum cinta (Ind.) to have no romantic feelings
tikar (Ind.) carpet or mat
tolong menolong (Ind.) caring

ulama (A.) Islamic scholars
ummah (A.) society
undak-usuk basa (S.) distinguish between speech levels
uqud kitab (A.) book of *uqud al-lujayn*
urang sunda (S.) Sundanese
ushul fiqh (A.) principles of Islamic jurisprudence
ustadz (A.) religious teacher

wahdah mawdlu'iyyah li al-Qur'an (A.) the unity of Qur'anic themes
wali (Ind.) bride's/woman's guardian
wali hakim (Ind.) a judge (acting as a woman's guardian)
wayang golek (S.) wooden puppet
wetu telu (L.) to pray three times in Sasak tribe, Lombok.
wudhu (A.) ablutions

yang penting bucat (Ind.) just let it burst
yasinan (Ind.) reading surah Yasin of the Qur'an

zawaj (A.) marriage
zina bil ikrah (A.) *zina* by force; rape
zina (A.) fornication; adultery.
zulm (A.) doing harm to others by transgressing their rights

Abbreviations and acronyms

BIMAS	Bimbingan Masyarakat Islam (Islamic guidance division).
BP4	Badan Penasihatan, Pembinaan dan Pelestarian Perkawinan (Advisory body for developing and maintaining marriage).
CEDAW	Convention on the Elimination of all forms of Discrimination against Women.
CSIS	Centre for Strategic and International Studies.
FGD	Focus Group Discussions.
FGC	Female genital cutting.
FGM	Female genital mutilation.
FK3	Forum Kajian Kitab Kuning (Forum for the study of kitab kuning).
FPI	Front Pembela Islam (Islamic Defenders Front).
HIV–AIDS	Human immunodeficiency virus – Acquired immunodeficiency syndrome.
HTI	Hizbut Tahrir Indonesia (Hizbut Tahrir of Indonesia).
IAIN	Institut Agama Islam Negeri (State Institute for Islamic studies).
IUD	Intrauterine device.
JKP3	Jaringan Kerja Prolegnas Pro Perempuan (National network of pro-women's national legislation program).
KBCM	Kursus Bimbingan Calon Mempelai (Pre-marital guidance course).
KHI	Kompilasi Hukum Islam (Compilation of Islamic law).
KTP	Kartu Tanda Penduduk (Residential identity card).
KUA	Kantor Urusan Agama (Office of Religious Affairs).

Abbreviations and acronyms 237

LKiS	Lembaga Kajian Islam dan Sosial (Institute for Islamic and Social Studies)
LBH APIK	Lembaga Bantuan Hukum Asosiasi Perempuan Indonesia pro Keadilan (Institution for legal aid of Indonesian women's association for justice).
MBA	Married by accident.
MUI	Majlis Ulama Indonesia (Indonesian Council of Ulama).
NGO	Non-governmental organisation.
NU	Nahdlatul Ulama (Largest religious organisation in Indonesia).
P3M	Perhimpunan Pengembangan Pesantren dan Masyarakat (Society for pesantren and community development).
P3N	Pembantu Pegawai Pencatat Nikah (Marriage registrar assistant).
PKS	Partai Keadilan Sejahtera (Prosperous Justice Party).
PPN	Petugas Pencatat Nikah (Marriage registrar).
RUU-PKS	Rancangan Undang-Undang Penghapusan Kekerasan Sexual (Bill on sexual violence eradication).
SIS	Sisters in Islam.
STI	Sexually transmitted infections.
SUSCATIN	Kursus Calon Pengantin (Pre-marital information session).
UU PKDRT no. 23/2004	Undang-Undang Penghapusan Kekerasan dalam Rumah Tangga (Law against domestic violence no. 23/2004).

Index

abortion 12, 38, 41, 52, 57–8, 149–50, 168n7
abuse 40, 83, 117, 133, 161–8, 206, 213, 221
adat 29, 40–1
adjustment: marital adjustment 17, 89, 121–4, 128, 136
agency ix, 11, 17, 173, 180–4, 197, 222
Al-Bukhari 3, 42, 56, 59n7, 60n12, 203–4, 208
Anthropology 71, 74
Anti-Pornography Law 37, 41
authorities: Muslim 3, 55, 186; religious authorities 87
authority: husband's authority 167, 190, 199, 201–2; male's authority 29, 41, 48, 93, 200, 203; religious authority 5, 8, 188, 195, 207, 212

Badran, M. 10–1
Bandung 7, 8, 18, 35–6, 91, 95, 131–2, 136, 187, 212; Eastern Bandung 95, 118n4, 187, 188, 196, 211
Barlas, A. 13–15, 46, 49, 51, 210, 213n10
Bouhdiba, A. 2

CEDAW (Convention on the Elimination of all forms of Discrimination against Women) 10, 18n2
chastity 36, 40, 42, 108–9, 156, 210, 218–19
circumcision: female circumcision 41, 52, 54–55, 60n11
condoms 147, 148
conflict 17, 81, 98, 121, 123–4, 128–34, 146

context: cultural context 2, 4, 9, 32, 36, 39–40, 72, 74, 139; Indonesian context 12–13, 16, 27, 36–7, 86, 121, 154; Islamic context 10; Socio-historical context 13–14, 187, 202, 223
contraception 41, 52, 56, 145, 147–50, 219
contraceptive 147–8
Cooke, M. 11
Court 166, 168n4; Religious Court 36, 46–7, 50, 113, 131, 133
courtship 32, 84, 103, 105–11, 118, 136, 142, 151, 218
critical: critical examination 16, 73, 212; critical thinking 191–2
criticism 9, 41, 52, 58, 94, 112, 188
cultural: construction 14, 36; norms 2, 39, 155–6, 180–4, 204, 217, 223

divorce 128–37; divorce law 112–16
domestic violence 3, 7, 40, 115, 117, 128–9, 137, 161–2, 166–8, 200, 211, 221
dosa 153, 168, 198, 204
duty: sex as duty 139–69

Eradication of Domestic Violence Law (UU-PKDRT/2004) 3, 37, 161
ethnographic research 16, 27, 29, 76
ethnography: feminist ethnography 7, 73, 76

family background 32, 81, 122, 134
family planning 7, 41, 52, 56–7, 145, 148
Female genital cutting/Mutilation (FGC/FGM) *see* circumcision
feminism 1, 9–14, 50, 76; Indonesian feminism 12
feminist: Muslim feminist 10–1, 13, 206; Western feminist 9

fertility 80, 145–6
fieldwork 71–7, 7–9, 16, 117, 118n4, 119n11, 155, 187, 190
fiqh 2, 15, 43, 53, 58, 81, 115, 189, 193, 208–9
fitnah 41, 52–3, 162
Focus Group Discussion (FGD) 7–9, 117, 155, 196, 203
foreplay 90, 94–5, 144, 157–8, 164, 179, 204–6, 220
Forum Kajian Kitab Kuning, 39, 94, 99n3, 190, 222
Front Pembela Islam (FPI) *see* Islamic Defenders Front

Gagnon, J. 139
gender: gender bias 15, 40, 127, 184; gender equality 2, 11, 12, 27–8, 37, 112, 117, 190, 198, 211; gender ideology 2–4, 6, 18, 28, 30, 37, 80, 121, 125; gender norms 36, 150, 166; gender relations 4–7, 11, 27–8, 30, 121

hermeneutics: hermeneutical approach 13, 15–16, 18, 187, 212–13, 223–4
heteronormativity 37
heterosexual 4, 37, 41, 51, 71, 139, 180, 222
HIV AIDS 148
household: household affairs 85, 125, 127; household income 30, 82, 125, 127, 218; household management 121–37
housework: housework negotiation 85, 126–7; participation in housework 30, 127–8; women's responsibility in housework 125, 127, 218
Hizbut Tahrir Indonesia (HTI) 56
human rights 2, 37, 60n11

ibadah 42, 83, 116, 159–60, 205–6, 218, 220, 223
'iddah 46–8
Indonesian Marriage Law 29–30, 44, 45, 59n1, 60n10, 112–13, 139, 146, 219
inequality 2, 9–10, 40, 52, 124, 127, 150, 154, 207, 222
infidelity 129, 132, 137, 146, 153, 167, 176, 177, 220
intimacy 33, 95, 108, 109, 159, 162, 177, 205, 221; emotional intimacy 178, 220; sexual intimacy 92, 202
Intra Uterine Device (IUD) 147
Islamic Defenders Front 2

Jakarta 5, 32, 35, 72, 117, 149
janda 135–7, 166
Jaringan Kerja Prolegnas Pro Perempuan (JKP3) 112
Java: Javanese 5–7, 27–9, 40, 154, 156
jodoh 17, 103, 105, 107, 118, 218

Kantor Urusan Agama (KUA) 8, 17, 33, 44, 99, 113–17, 118n9, 119n11, 131, 137n1
kekerasan dalam rumah tangga (KDRT)*see* domestic violence
Kesehatan Ibu, Bayi, Bayi baru Lahir dan Anak (KIBBLA) 212
Komnas Perempuan 39, 166–8
Kartu Tanda Penduduk (KTP) 113
kitab kuning 87, 93, 18–19, 195, 213n3
Kursus Calon Pengantin (SUSCATIN) 17, 99, 115, 117
kyai 8, 31, 95, 157, 186–96, 198, 206, 212, 221

mahar 41, 44, 46
majlis ta'lim 9, 18, 95–6, 100n7, 186–7, 191–2, 195–8, 211, 212, 221
Majlis Ulama Indonesia (MUI) 55, 150
malu 76, 143, 156, 173, 179, 199, 206
manual: marriage manual 87–8; sex manual 16, 86–9, 93–4, 143, 152, 157, 217
menopause 144, 150–2, 220
Mernissi, F. 2, 12, 51–3
Middle East/ern 2, 4, 12–13, 16, 50, 59, 142, 187
moderate Islam 56
Muhammadiyah 2, 56
Mulia, M. 15, 50
Musallam, B. 2
Mutuality 51, 73, 95, 98, 181–4, 203, 208, 210, 222

nafaqa 45, 200
Nahdlatul Ulama (NU) 2, 56, 93, 187
New Order 2, 12, 28, 30, 37, 112, 125, 145
Non-governmental organisation (NGO) 18, 117, 187, 190, 211, 212, 221
nikah siri 29, 132, 137n1, 151, 164

obedience 45, 48, 58, 81, 190, 196–201, 209, 212, 219, 223
oppression 2, 10, 52, 58, 206
orgasm 90, 144, 153, 155, 158–9, 173, 178–9, 181

pahala 160, 179, 197, 205
pamali 153, 168, 204, 220
pangaosan 191–5
passive 37, 52, 108, 139, 143, 152, 181, 183, 190, 195, 210, 217
passively 144, 201
passivity 108, 179
patriarchal: patriarchal reading 14–15, 206, 224; patriarchal society 53, 71, 197, 224
patriarchy 14, 182, 197
penghulu 113–17, 119n11, 222
pesantren 186–213
pleasure in sex 56, 141, 144, 149–50, 153, 155–6, 173, 178–84, 205–6; women's sexual pleasure 40, 155, 181, 209, 222
polygyny: polygyny practice 114, 130, 177
positionality 173–84
pregnancy 31, 39, 56–7, 84, 97, 127, 134, 144–9, 154, 176, 203, 211, 220

Qur'an: Qur'anic text 15, 50, 221; Qur'anic verses 13–15, 45, 51, 57, 75, 95, 103, 208, 211
Qurratul 'Uyun 91, 93–4, 189, 190

Rahima 39, 117, 119n13, 190, 222
rape 41, 52, 55–6, 71, 82, 150; marital rape 40, 167–8
reflexivity 71–7
Reform era (*Reformasi*) 2–3, 27, 37, 41, 145
reproduction 17, 29, 37–8, 81, 144, 148, 150

sacred 15, 212, 223
SAPA Institut 211–2, 213n13
Sasak 29, 32
Satan 108–9, 157–8
Script 4, 139, 155, 156, 192
sexuality: married women's sexuality 4, 59, 139, 222, 224; research on women's sexuality 3, 39–41, 156, 219; women's sexuality 1–3, 37, 58–9, 139, 144, 224 16, 27, 36, 51

Sexual Transmitted Diseases/Infections (STDs/STIs) 38, 166
Shafi'i school of law 42–4, 57; Shafi'i jurist 43, 57
Shighat Taklik Talak 47, 114, 119n12
silence 9, 40, 58, 154, 166, 198, 222, 224
sin 39, 153, 159–60, 168, 190, 198, 204–5, 220
sinful 7, 37, 107
Southeast Asia 59
stigma 129, 135–7, 146
submissive sexual act 37, 52, 58, 81, 107, 139, 152, 155–6, 219
Sunda 6, 33, 82, 223
Sundanese society 6, 31–2; Sundanese culture 6, 31, 59n2, 81, 139
Sunnah 42, 83, 93, 95, 184n1, 206
Sunni 42–3

taboo 1, 9, 40, 52, 74, 173, 179, 189, 204, 220
tawhid 14, 189, 193
thalaq 46
transgender 3, 37, 39

Uqud al-Lujayn 90, 93, 99, 182, 190

vaginal dryness 150–52
violence: sexual violence 17, 38, 40, 140, 161, 166–8; *see also* domestic violence
virginity 28, 39, 41, 52–3, 82, 97, 108–9, 140, 156, 219

Wadud, A. 9, 11–14, 45, 49, 51, 201, 209, 213n10
Wahid, A. 94
West Java 30–6; Islam and West Java 31, 223; map of West Java 5
Wetu Telu 29

yasinan 192
Yayasan Rumah Kita Bersama 57, 81

zina 32, 41, 51–6, 97
Zuhaily 43, 44, 45, 55, 208